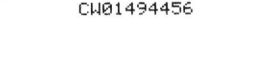

ISBN 978-1-5278-8578-3
PIBN 10896845

# 1 MONTH OF
# FREE
# READING

## at
## www.ForgottenBooks.com

By purchasing this book you are eligible for one month membership to ForgottenBooks.com, giving you unlimited access to our entire collection of over 1,000,000 titles via our web site and mobile apps.

To claim your free month visit:
www.forgottenbooks.com/free896845

NEW BURLINGTON STREET,
JANUARY, 1833.

# MR. BENTLEY

(SUCCESSOR TO MR. COLBURN)

## HAS JUST PUBLISHED THE FOLLOWING

# NEW WORKS.

---

### COLONEL MACKINNON.

DEDICATED BY PERMISSION TO HIS MAJESTY.

In Two Volumes 8vo. with numerous Embellishments,

## THE ORIGIN AND SERVICES OF THE COLDSTREAM GUARDS:

FROM THE FORMATION OF THE REGIMENT UNDER GENERAL MONCK,
TO THE BATTLE OF WATERLOO.

### BY COLONEL MACKINNON.

---

### LADY HARRIET HOSTE.

In Two Volumes 8vo. with fine Portrait,

## MEMOIRS OF SIR WILLIAM HOSTE,

### BART., R.N. K.C.B. K.M.T.

INCLUDING HIS CORRESPONDENCE, &c.

### BY LADY HARRIET HOSTE.

---

In Two Volumes, post 8vo. price 18s.

## TWO YEARS AND A HALF IN THE AMERICAN NAVY.

COMPRISING THE JOURNAL OF A CRUISE TO ENGLAND, AND IN
THE MEDITERRANEAN AND THE LEVANT, ON BOARD THE
UNITED STATES FRIGATE, CONSTELLATION, IN 1829-30-31.

### BY E. C. WINES.

1

3

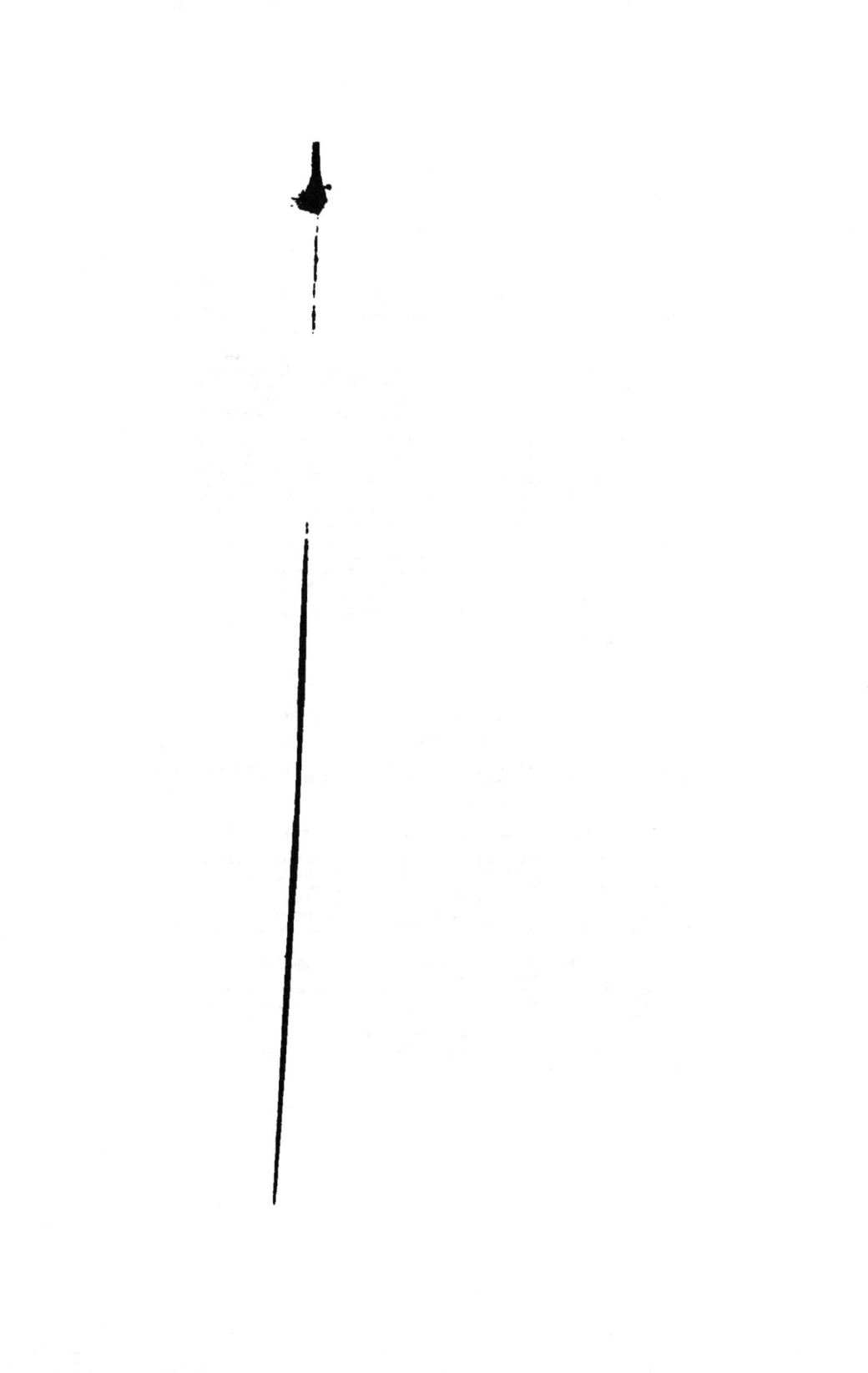

In Three Volumes post 8vo.

# THE LIFE OF A SAILOR.

### BY A CAPTAIN IN THE ROYAL NAVY.

*" Far as the breeze can bear, the billows foam,*
*Survey our empire, and behold our home."—Byron.*

" The actual adventures of a Post Captain in the Royal Navy, in various parts of the world. The career of the sailor is full of strange vicissitudes; and whether we view him in calm or storm, in fire or fight, from the roughest specimen before the mast to the intellectual perfection of the quarter-deck, his story is always replete with the most eventful interest."—*Courier.*

" Three most various and amusing volumes. They will be best characterized as maritime travels, told as our travellers used to tell their adventures, simply and earnestly. Lord Byron, Sir Peter Parker, Bolivar, Paez, are names to attract any reader ; and the scenes are north, south, east, and west. This work embodies the real adventures of a Post Captain in the Navy, and does its author much credit. He has seen a deal of service, and describes what he has seen with great animation."—*Literary Gazette.*

" A British naval officer must necessarily have enjoyed admirable opportunities of seeing both nature and the external foreign world ; and if he has a happy command of language, fearful are the accidents by flood and field that present themselves for description. Captain Chamier has had a full share of adventure, and undoubtedly possesses a facility of style and a playful manner. If ever there was a story to excite sympathy, and interest the feelings, and awake the imagination of the reading world, it is a story of sharks in this autobiography."—*Spectator.*

———————

In Two Volumes 8vo. with Two Portraits, price 24s.

### THE ENGLISH TRANSLATION OF

# MEMOIRS OF GENERAL LAFAYETTE,

### BY B. SARRANS.

#### PRIVATE SECRETARY TO GENERAL LAFAYETTE.

" This Work gives an entire biography of the venerable General who has acted a distinguished part in three Revolutions; but its chief interest hinges on the details which it supplies on the part which he and his friends played in the last. Its disclosures have all the attractions of novelty, and will enable us better to judge of the feelings and views of existing persons and parties than any contemporary work with which we are acquainted."—*Times.*

" The staple of these interesting volumes consists of unpublished letters, private thoughts, communications within closed doors, and memoranda of occurrences which took place behind the scenes, where characters appear in a sort of undress, and circumstances present themselves without exaggeration or distortion. These very lights which history so much requires, and generally wants, are here collected with laudable industry.—*Caledonian Mercury.*

" A most interesting and valuable work—interesting in every point of view."—*Sunday Times.*

# ORIGIN AND SERVICES

OF THE

# COLDSTREAM GUARDS.

BY COLONEL MAC KINNON.

IN TWO VOLUMES.

VOL. I.

LONDON:

RICHARD BENTLEY,

NEW BURLINGTON STREET.

MDCCCXXXIII.

PRINTED BY A. J. VALPY,
RED LION COURT, FLEET STREET, LONDON.

# DEDICATION.

## TO THE KING.

Sire,

With pride, and diffidence, I avail myself of the gracious permission to dedicate to your Majesty, an account of the origin and services of a Corps intrusted with the important charge of guarding the Person of their Sovereign.

In fidelity, and in the zealous fulfilment of every duty, the Coldstream, Sire, will at all times be found true to its motto—" Nulli Secundus."

Next to the honour of commanding so brave a body of men is that conferred on me when allowed to submit to your Royal notice the result of my researches, and to subscribe myself

  Your Majesty's

   Most devoted, obliged, and obedient

    Humble servant,

     DANIEL MAC KINNON,
     Colonel, and Lieutenant-Colonel Commanding
      Coldstream Guards.

10, Hertford Street.

# PREFACE.

A CIRCULAR order from the Horse Guards, sent to the Commanding Officer of every corps, requiring him to give such particulars as could be collected of the regiment under his command, occasioned the following account to be undertaken. As the facts relating to the Coldstream accumulated, they comprehended so many circumstances interwoven with the most important periods of our history, and included so many names connected with the first families in Great Britain, that it was thought they might not prove uninteresting to the public. It can scarcely be expected, that the education of an individual.who entered the regiment before he was fifteen years of age, should entitle him to success in the field of literature; on this ground, therefore, indulgence is claimed for whatever defects may appear in style or arrangement. To support his statements by careful investigation and accurate detail, has been the anxious wish of the writer. The

movements of contending armies during a series of
protracted campaigns, he has endeavoured to place
in a clear and concise form.　This was necessary
to carry the reader through nearly two centuries
without rendering tedious a work that had to em-
brace, and bring under notice, occurrences already
known to all who are conversant with the History
of England.

The object of these pages is to give a faithful
narrative of the proceedings of the Coldstream, from
their first formation, to the present time; and further
to demonstrate, that wherever our troops have been
engaged, steadiness in the field has always signalized
the sons of Britain.　The Guards are as distinguished
for this quality as for their devotion to their King
and country.

It was the Earl of Munster's intention to have
written the History of the Coldstream : his Lordship's literary talents are such, as to make it a subject of regret that the plan was not carried into
effect.　In allowing this duty to devolve on his
friend, Lord Munster has deprived the public of the
benefit of his remarks, and himself of the credit,
that would assuredly have been the fruit of his

# INTRODUCTION.

---

THE infantry[1] of our Army, from an early period, has been celebrated for its discipline and intrepidity. British troops of the line are seldom, if ever, known to waver in presence of an enemy; the Guards have always kept their station. The impetuosity and powerful charge of the French, so rarely withstood by any other European soldiers, make no impression on British infantry. Many brilliant instances might be quoted; but Crécy, Poictiers, Agincourt, Blenheim, and Waterloo, sufficiently prove the fact.

At Crécy[2] the troops of France were far more numerous than those of England.

---

[1] Infantry; a term first applied to foot-soldiers in Spain; and so called from the Infanta, who commanded them. The Spanish infantry were for a length of time the best in Europe, and their final destruction at the battle of St. Quentin, was one of the causes of the decline of that kingdom.

[2] Vilani, an Italian, says the English used cannon at the battle of Crécy. Froissart does not mention it; or any of the historians who have described that battle.

Grose's Military Antiquities, vol. 1. page 339:

" At the battle of Crécy, fifteen thousand archers began to yell in a most frightful manner, to terrify the English."

King Edward formed his army on a gentle ascent; he divided his troops into three lines, and threw up trenches for the protection of his flanks. His preparations were made with perfect order: on the approach of the enemy, the English remained immoveable. The attack was begun by the French with their accustomed energy and daring valour; but by the firmness of their opponents they were repulsed, and entirely routed.

At Poictiers, the English, finding their retreat impracticable, took every precaution that prudence could suggest. They rendered it impossible for the enemy to reach their main body except through a narrow lane, on each side of which the archers, placed behind the hedges, deliberately took their aim, and slaughtered the enemy with impunity.

At Agincourt, from similar causes, similar results again followed. Henry, with an army reduced by sickness and warfare to ten thousand men, was anxious to avoid a battle, the French being in the proportion of four to one. The English army received the first onset with steadiness; the archers, supported by the men at arms, then advanced on the

---

The old English cry was, " St. George!"—*Froissart*.

Edward Davies (1619) says, "this cry was in such estimation the beginning of the last century, that the observance of it was among the ordinance of military laws, to the obedience which he would have all soldiers march."

" All souldiers entering into battaile, assault, skirmishe, or other action of arms, shall have for their common crie and word, 'St. George! St. George!' 'Forward,' or 'Upon them, St. George!' whereby the souldier is much comforted, and the enemie dismaide, by calling to mind the auncient valour of England, which with that name hath been so often victorious: therefore he that shall maliciously omit it, shall be severely punished for his obstenacie."

enemy, who were soon overthrown, and actually hewed in pieces by the battle-axe men, almost without resistance.

The battle of Blenheim was commenced by the British and Hessians, who with difficulty passed a rivulet, and filed off to the left, in face of the enemy: soon after this attack Marlborough was charged three times by the French cavalry with the greatest impetuosity; but each time he defeated them. While Marlborough's troops were engaged, twenty-seven battalions and twelve squadrons of the enemy in the village of Blenheim kept up a continued flank fire. He, however, was enabled by the firmness of the infantry to form his wing, routed Tallard's cavalry, and forced his way between the two bodies of the French army. Prince Eugene, who commanded the right, was repeatedly repulsed, but at length succeeded. Tallard being made prisoner, and Blenheim surrounded, the twenty-seven battalions and twelve squadrons posted in that village, after a gallant defence, laid down their arms. The rout became general; all fled: the confusion in the French army was so great, that officers and soldiers rushed headlong into the Danube.[1]

The victory was complete; the French lost forty thousand men, "together with the honour of their nation, and every hope of recovering the ascendancy."

Next day Marlborough visited Tallard, who complimented him on having vanquished "the best troops in the world."[2]

---

[1] Smollett says thirty squadrons of horse and dragoons.
[2] The victors lost about 5000 men killed, and 800 wounded.
The French army was almost destroyed: out of 60,000, Voltaire says, not more than 20,000 could be collected again.

Perhaps the characteristic difference of the two nations may be adequately illustrated by a parallel between the respective commanders in this battle. " Marshal Tallard," says Voltaire, " had all the impetuous and sprightly courage of a Frenchman, an active and penetrating understanding, and a genius fertile in expedients and resources. He was allied to glory and fortune, by the requisites of genius and courage."

The powerful mind of Marlborough gathered fresh strength from difficulty and peril. During the tremendous conflict at Blenheim, he conducted himself with composure, vigilance, and energy: superintending the manœuvres in every part, his presence alone was sufficient to inspire confidence.[1]

Intrepidity is the distinguishing feature of Englishmen, and fiction has only borrowed and compressed, from the page of general history, the following graphic delineation of a British soldier, at the period of the expulsion of the Moors by Ferdinand and Isabella, in the fifteenth century:

" He brought with him a hundred archers, all dexterous with the long bow and the cloth-yard arrow; also two hundred yeomen, armed cap-a-pie, who fought with pike and battle-axe, men robust of frame and of prodigious strength."

The description is thus continued:

" This Cavalier was from the island of England, and

---

[1] Voltaire in his History of Charles XII. says, Marlborough was equally qualified for the field or cabinet, and that he did as much mischief to France by his mental faculties as by the force of his arms.

Marlborough was called by his soldiers, " Corporal John."

brought with him a train of his vassals; men who had been hardened in certain civil wars which had raged in their country. They were a comely race of men, but too fair and fresh for warriors; not having the sun-burnt martial hue of our old Castilian soldiery: they were huge feeders also, and deep carousers, and could not accommodate themselves to the sober diet of our troops, but must fain eat and drink after the manner of their own country. They were often noisy and unruly also in their wassail, and their quarter of the camp was prone to be a scene of loud revel and sudden brawl. They were withall of great pride, yet it was not like our inflammable Spanish pride; they stood not much upon the *pundonor* and high punctilio, and rarely drew the stiletto in their disputes; but their pride was silent and contumelious. Though from a remote and somewhat barbarous island, they yet believed themselves the most perfect men upon earth, and magnified their chieftain, the Lord Scales, beyond the greatest of our grandees. With all this, it must be said of them, that they were marvellous good men in the field, dexterous archers, and powerful with the battle-axe. In their great pride and self-will, they always sought to press in the advance and take the post of danger, trying to outvie our Spanish chivalry. They did not rush forward fiercely, or make a brilliant onset like the Moorish and Spanish troops, but they went into the fight deliberately, and persisted obstinately, and were slow to find out when they were beaten.[1] Withall, they were much esteemed, yet

---

[1] Napoleon and Marshal Soult are said to have made the same remark.

Complete in One Volume, price 6s. (originally published in 3 Volumes, price 18s.) revised and corrected, with a new Introduction and Notes by the Author, *written expressly for this Edition,* embellished with engravings by Charles Rolls.

# THE PIONEERS;

## Or, the Sources of the Susquehanna.

"Extremes of habits, manners, time, and space,
Brought close together, here stood face to face,
And gave at once a contrast to the view,
That other lands and ages never knew."

" Perhaps the most powerful and interesting of all Cooper's novels. The characters of the old Indian, of Leatherstocking, and of the sailor steward of Mr. Temple, are destined to live as long as the most classical productions of fancy in the English language."—*Bath Herald.*

" Never has Cooper shown himself more happy in describing the grand and imposing scenery of his native country than in this story."—*Globe.*

" Cooper was born at Burlington, upon the Delaware, in 1789; he quitted in boyhood the place of his nativity, and took up his residence in the town of Cooper, connected with which he has given so many interesting details in his ' Pioneers.' "—*Scotsman.*

---

Complete in One Volume, price 6s. (originally published in 3 Volumes, price 1l. 4s.) revised and corrected, with a new Introduction and Notes by the Author, *written expressly for this Edition,* with engravings by Greatbach, from designs by Pickering.

# THE PRAIRIE.

" Mark his condition and the event; then
Tell me if this be a brother."

" We really most cordially praise the progress of ' The Standard Novels, and Romances;' embodying the mass of our lighter literature, neat, portable, prettily ornamented, and singularly cheap, it deserves universal recommendation and encouragement. Cooper's American novels open an entirely new vein of fiction equally interesting and fertile; with a value, too, quite independent of their attraction as narratives, being the most vivid and exact pictures of a country, whose face is now almost wholly changed, and of a race that have almost utterly passed away. The vignette to the ' Prairie,' representing the grave of the old Hunter, is full of poetry; and there is also a very sweet engraving from a design by Pickering."—*Literary Gazette.*

" This work has powerful claims upon our admiration. The author has here given us many vivid and faithful descriptions of trans-atlantic scenery and manners; his Indians are real savages, and speak like men who have the sky for their roof, earth for their carpet, war for their business, and the chase for their food and pastimes."—*Monthly Review.*

" The adventures of the Squatter in the interminable Prairie—the awful and impressive scene on his discovering the mangled body of one of his sons —the summary vengeance inflicted upon the murderer—the grand and sublime spectacle presented by the flaming wilds—and the desperate situation of our fellow-beings amidst the conflagration—cannot easily be effaced from

# CONTENTS

## THE FIRST VOLUME.

---

Monck returns from Ireland—Accepts an appointment in the army
intended for Scotland—Placed in command of five companies drafted
from Hesilrige's regiment, and five companies from Fenwick's—
Monck's regiment put on the establishment of the Commonwealth—
Hesilrige appointed Governor of Newcastle—Berwick and Carlisle
taken—Langdale defeated in Northumberland—Fenwick nominated
Governor of Berwick—Quarters of the army in England—Monck's
regiment enters Scotland with Cromwell    .    .    .    . *page* 3

Sketch of Monck's life—List of the army that accompanies Cromwell from Berwick — Collington House taken—Redhall stormed—
Cromwell destroys the Scots army at Dunbar    .    .    .    . 12

Derlton House, Edinburgh Castle, Tantallon Castle, and Blackness,
surrender—Strength of the Scots army—Monck appointed Lieutenant-General of the Ordnance—Charles II. present with the army in
Stirling Park—Cromwell encamps near Redhall—Number of the
English army — Callender House taken — Monck " beleaguers Stirling Castle "—Charles II. and Scots army surrounded—Battle of
Worcester    .    .    .    .    .    .    .    .    .    . 32

## CHAPTER IV.

Monck remains in Scotland—Stirling Castle capitulates—Records
sent to the Tower—Friends of Charles assemble at Ellit—Capture of
Dundee—Monck's illness—Montrose and Aberdeen taken—Culton,
Annandale, and Mohum Castles surrender—Winter-quarters of the
army—Argyle offers to negociate with Monck—Several influential
persons submit to the Commonwealth—Widows of officers in Monck's
regiment petition Parliament for relief—Commissioners appointed for
the affairs of Scotland—Dumbarton Castle surrenders—Monck leaves
Scotland for London—Dunotter Castle besieged by Monck's own
regiment—Morgan's letter to Cromwell, with the Governor of Dunotter's capitulation    .    .    .    .    .    .    .    .    *page* 40

## CHAPTER V.

Army marches into the Highlands—Colonel Lilburn's account of his
progress—Secretary Clarke's letter to Lenthall—Anecdote of Captain
Powell—Parliament votes Generals Blake, Dean, and Monck to command the fleet—Colonel Lilburn replaces Dean in Scotland — English
and Dutch fleets engage between the Isle of Wight and Portland—
Dutch defeated off Ostend—Monck left in sole command—Van Trump
killed off Camperdown—Middleton lands and plants the Royal Standard between Stirling and Dumbarton — War recommences in the
Highlands—Force of English regiments in Scotland — City of London
entertains Cromwell—Monck arrives at Dalkeith—Enters Stirling—
Loch Tay Island, Ballock, Weemys, and Garth Castles taken—Morgan defeats Middleton near Loch Garry — The Earls of Glencairn and
Athol with other chiefs send in their submission—Monck's head-quarters again at Dalkeith — Proceedings of a Court-Martial—Army in
winter-quarters—Several officers arrested—City of Edinburgh entertains Monck — Cromwell proclaimed Lord Protector in Edinburgh —
Death of Cromwell—Richard proclaimed Lord Protector in Scotland
—Parliament dissolved—Richard resigns his office    .    .    .  53

## CHAPTER VI.

Long Parliament revived—Letter to the Speaker from Monck and
other officers of his own regiment—Charles prepares to invade England—Committee of Safety—Officers called into the House to receive
their commissions from the Speaker; Lieutenant-Colonel William
Gough, of Monck's own regiment, one of them—Names of officers in
Monck's regiments of foot and horse read to the House—Lenthall the
Speaker arrested—Monck musters his own and Morgan's regiments to

acquaint them it was his determination to support Parliament—Monck secures several strongholds in Scotland—Letters, in which are detailed accounts of Monck's proceedings—Parliament dissolved—Monck and his army declare for the Parliament — Lambert begins his march towards Scotland — Commissioners of the Militia of London, and several Members of the Committee of Safety, dread the results of Monck's proceedings — Officers sent by Monck to treat with the Committee of Safety—Names of officers who abandoned Monck—His army assembles at Coldstream    .    .    .    .    . *page* 68

## CHAPTER VII.

Monck commences his march from Coldstream—Gives the command of his own regiment to Captain Morgan—Commissioners meet the army near Leicester—The Coldstreamers enter London—Parliament orders Monck to restore order in the City—Monck and Montague nominated Generals of the Fleet—Lambert escapes from the Tower—Ingoldsby defeats Lambert—Granville delivers a letter from Charles to the Parliament—Charles proclaimed King—Colours captured at Preston, Dunbar, and Worcester, removed from Westminster Hall—Army encamps at Blackheath—Charles's triumphal entry into London—Monck created Duke of Albemarle—Charles reviews his troops—Army disbanded, with the exception of the Lord General's own regiment—Insurrection of Venner—Commissioners disband the Lord General's regiment of foot, and they are immediately after formed as an extraordinary guard to the Royal person—List of the Household troops—Royal regiment of Guards under Lord Wentworth—Charles II.'s procession through the City to be crowned    .    . 86

## CHAPTER VIII.

Adjutants first commissioned to the Guards—A regiment of Guards raised for Dublin duty—Charles II. reviews his Horse and Foot Guards—King and Queen visit Bath, and return by Oxford to London—Captain Holmes, of the Lord General's regiment, sails to North America, reduces the New Netherlands, and changes the name to New York—Fleets fitted out in the Thames and Portsmouth—A detachment from the Lord General's regiment embarks — Declaration of War by the Dutch—Dutch fleet defeated—Prince Rupert and Albemarle command the fleet—Albemarle attacks the Dutch off Dunkirk—Prince Rupert and Albemarle drive the Dutch back on their own coasts—Buckingham's account of Monck's determination not to be taken—Sir Robert Holmes burns one hundred and sixty vessels in the Vlie—Bandaris plundered and destroyed—Precedency of regiments—Dutch fleet attacks Sheerness and enters the Medway—Dutch fleet proceeds to Portsmouth, Torbay, and sails again to the Thames—Spragg beats them back—King reviews his Foot and Life Guards—Cosmo's description of Oxford's Horse, and review of the Guards in Hyde Park—Cosmo's visit to Albemarle—Death of Albemarle, and funeral—Earl Craven succeeds to the Coldstream     .     .  *page* 108

## CHAPTER IX.

A detachment embarks for the Mediterranean—Holmes attacks the Dutch fleet—Monmouth joins the French in Flanders—A draft from the Coldstream sent to complete Monmouth's regiment—A fleet equipped under the Duke of York—Three hundred men of the Coldstream embark—English and Dutch fleets engage—Coldstream disembark and return to their quarters—One company of the Coldstream embarks at Dover, and forms part of a regiment to remain in the service of Lewis XIV.—Detachments from the Coldstream embark, and the fleet again sails—Precedency of regiments—The English and French fleets under Prince Rupert and Count d'Estrees ready for sea—Six companies of the Coldstream distributed in the English ships—Prince Rupert attacks De Ruyter—French, in conjunction with Monmouth, take Maestricht—Dutch abandon the intention to invade England —Spragg engages Trump's squadron—The battalion under Captain Skelton returns to London—Monmouth's letter to Craven, enclosing the King's order concerning the rank of regiments—Review in Hyde Park—Monmouth authorised to issue orders for the removal of quarters—Dalrymple's account of Monmouth's appointment to be Lord General of the Army—Duke of Buckingham's explanation—Original Commission intended for Monmouth—A regiment, formed by drafts from the Guards and other regiments, sent to Virginia—First introduction of Grenadiers—Four companies embark for Ostend—Grenadier companies generally adopted in regiments of Infantry—Four additional companies embark for Ostend—Allies assemble in Flanders—Colonel John Churchill commands the brigade, in which are the First and Coldstream Guards—Treaty of Nimeguen—Captain Mutlow's company returns from Virginia—Somerset House converted into barracks for Foot Guards—A detachment sails for Tangiers—Two companies attend Charles II. to Oxford—King's Mews fitted up as a barrack—

Complete in One Volume, price 6s. (originally published in 3 Volumes, price 1l. 11s. 6d.) revised, corrected, with a new Introduction, Notes, &c. written by the Author, *expressly for this edition,* and with engravings by Greatbach, from designs by Pickering.

## LAWRIE TODD;

### Or, the Settlers in the Woods.

### By the Author of " The Ayrshire Legatees."

## NOVELS BY MRS. BRUNTON.

Complete in One Volume, price 6s. (originally published in 3 Volumes, price 1l. 4s.) with two illustrations by Greatbach.

## SELF-CONTROL.

" Of the complete success of ' Self-Control,' and of the authoress's subsequent work, " Discipline,' we need not speak, as they are sufficiently known to

connoitres the position of the Allies, and retires to his camp—Confederates proceed to Gemblours—French leave Braine le Comte and
march to the Sambre—Confederates arrive on the plain of Gerpynes—
Lieutenants of First and Coldstream Guards get the rank of Captains—
Allies reinforced exceed the enemy in numbers—William's head-
quarters at Cour-sur-Heure—Army advances between Fleurus and
the Sambre; crosses the river below Ath—The King leaves the
camp for Loo—Troops go into winter quarters—William embarks
for England    .    .    .    .    .    .    .    .    .    .    page 205


CHAPTER XII.

William embarks for the Hague—Lewis XIV. concentrates round
Mons—Namur invested—William moves towards the Mehaigne—
Confederates form a junction—Namur surrenders—Attempt to surprise Mons—The King reviews his troops—Reinforcements join the
army—Battle of Steenkirk—Grandval hanged—Troops under Talmash
encamp at Oudenbourg—Duke of Leinster arrives at Ostend with
fifteen regiments—Army goes into winter quarters—William returns
to England    .    .    .    .    .    .    .    .    .    .    215


CHAPTER XIII.

William arrives from England—Head-quarters at Dieghem—Lewis
XIV. detained by illness at Quesnoy—Confederate army at Parck
Camp—William advances on Liege—Battle of Landen—William
moves to Louvain—French unable to follow up their success—
Marshal Luxembourg captures Charleroi—Hostile armies go into
winter quarters    .    .    .    .    .    .    .    .    .    .    226


CHAPTER XIV.

William returns to Holland—Head-quarters at Bethlehem—Lux-
embourg and Villeroy join the French near the Sambre—The hostile
armies concentrate—The Dauphin reviews the French at Gemblours—
Strength of Confederates in Flanders—William returns to England—
Straw huts of the Coldstream destroyed by fire—The two armies go
into winter quarters—Talmash dies of his wounds at Plymouth—
Cutts succeeds in command of the Coldstream—Expedition against
Brest, in which were thirteen companies of the Guards    .    .    237

## CHAPTER XV.

William embarks for Holland—Two armies in the Netherlands, one commanded by the Elector of Bavaria and Duke of Holstein, the other to act in Flanders under William and Prince Vaudemont—French concentrate between the Scheld and Dunkirk—Namur invested—William's head-quarters at the Chateau de la Falise—Lord Cutts reaches Templeux—Dutch break ground near Bouge—The Guards suffer severely in an assault—Siege of Namur—Town capitulates—Boufflers retires to the Castle—Cutts wounded—Citadel surrenders—Allies encamp near Nivelle—William reviews his army previous to his departure—Winter quarters of the Allies—English Guards at Ghent . . . . . . . . . . *page* 245

## CHAPTER XVI.

Lewis XIV. prepares an expedition at Dunkirk—Brigade of Guards recalled from Ghent—Fleet fitted out in the Thames—Coldstream returns to Flanders—Athlone bombards Givet—Enemy advance—Allies unable to make a forward movement—William arrives in Holland—Boufflers encamps at Parck—William reviews the troops—Army encamps at Wavre—Boufflers retires—Villeroy encamps between Oudenarde and the Allies—Prince de Conti, Dukes of Chartres and Bourbon, join Villeroy—Duke du Maine and Count de Toulouse join Boufflers—Amount of the French armies—William moves towards Gembloure—Strength of the Confederates—Allies move to the plain of Fleury—Boufflers advances to oppose the passage of the Sambre—Confederates on the plain of Chambron — Enemy encamp near Condé — William leaves the camp—Both armies separate for the winter . . . . . . . . . . . 261

## CHAPTER XVII.

English Guards leave Ghent for the villages between Brussels and Halle—Army of Flanders takes the field—Infantry encamp between Deynse and Nivelle—Brabant army encamps at Waterloo and Ixelles—French assemble about Tournay, banks of the Sambre and Lys—Brabant army between the Abbey of Bois-Seigneur-Isaac and the rivulet of Leu—Catinat invests Ath—Amount of French armies—Strength of army under William and the Elector of Bavaria—Situation of the French—William retreats to the plain of Bois-Seigneur:

Isaac—Boufflers encamps at Steenkirk—Reinforcements arrive from England—William marches through Brussels, and takes up a position for the defence of the town—Peace of Ryswick—French leave the Netherlands — British quartered in Ghent, Bruges, Nieuport, and Ostend—Guards embark for England    .    .    .    .   *page* 267

## CHAPTER XVIII.

Coldstream disembark at Harwich—William's triumphant entry into London—Chamberlayne's account of the Foot Guards—First notice of the Third Guards on the establishment—Death of Charles II. King of Spain—Duke of Anjou declared King of Spain—Army augmented with great difficulty—James II. dies at St. Germain's—Death of King William—A battalion formed from the First and Coldstream sent to Cadiz—Gallant conduct of Colonel Pierce of the Coldstream —Attack on fort Matagorda—Troops re-embark after blowing up Fort St. Catherine's—Confederates under Sir George Rooke attack Chateaurenard in the harbour of Vigo—Duke of Ormond lands his troops—Rondella carried by assault—Enemy destroy their galleons and twelve ships—Fourteen ships taken—Army embark at Rondella —Gibraltar surrenders—A battalion from the First and Coldstream sail from Portsmouth with Lord Galway—Expedition lands at Lisbon —Re-embark—Sail for the relief of Gibraltar—Prince of Hesse Darmstadt makes a sortie—Enemy retire after seven months' siege— Peterborough sails from England with Sir Cloudesly Shovel—Dutch fleet join in the Tagus—Prince of Hesse and Guards embark—Land near Barcelona — Attack on Montjuich—Barcelona taken — Prince Charles received with great enthusiasm—Guards remain with Prince Charles at Barcelona—Peterborough marches with a small force to Valencia   .   .   .   .   .   .   .   .   .   .   .   273

## CHAPTER XIX.

Detachments from the two regiments of Guards embark and sail from Portsmouth to join the battalion in Spain—Philip attempts to ~~recover~~ ~~Barcelona~~—Misunderstanding between Prince Charles and Peterborough—Large sums advanced by the citizens—Troops die in great numbers—Marshal Tessé threatens Tortosa—Allies march for that town—Guards remain to do duty over Prince Charles—Barcelona invested—Lord Donnegal arrives with four regiments from Gerona— Philip joins the French army—Peterborough returns from Valencia—

Enemy repulsed in a night attack—Conflict at Montjuich—Donnegal killed—Anecdote of an officer's dog—French raise the siege—Troops sail for Valencia—Galway takes Ciudad Rodrigo, masks Badajoz, and arrives at Madrid—Cruelty to a party of the Coldstream—Peterborough leaves Spain for Savoy—Galway crosses the Tagus at Fuentes d'Uenna—Joined at Veles by the troops under Lieut.-General Wyndham, with whom was the battalion of Guards—Allies in quarters along the frontier of Valencia and Murcia during the winter . . . . . . . . . . page 295

## CHAPTER XX.

Death of Cutts—Churchill appointed Colonel of the Coldstream—An account of Cutts—Prince Charles deserts Galway—Allies suffer great privations—Lewis XIV. sends reinforcements to Spain—Battle of Almanza—Guards suffer severely—Lerida surrenders—Allies go into winter-quarters—Galway embarks at Lisbon for England—A battalion of English Guards from the First and Coldstream ordered to Scotland—Countermanded at York—Sent to Colchester—The battalion embarks for Flanders—Battle of Oudenarde—Siege of Lisle—Capitulation—Guards quartered during the winter at Brussels . . 305

## CHAPTER XXI.

Tournay surrenders—Villars and Boufflers oppose the investment of Mons—Strength of hostile armies—Battle of Malplaquet—Cardonnel's letter—Capitulation of Mons—Both armies go into winter quarters—First and Coldstream at the Hague—Strength of the Allies—Eugene and Marlborough move from the vicinity of Tournay—Enemy's line forced at Pont-à-Vendin—Villars reconnoitres the allied position—Aire and St. Venant taken—Marlborough returns to England . . . . . . . . . . . 321

## CHAPTER XXII.

Two additional companies of the Coldstream sent to Harwich—Detachment countermanded, from the difficulty of providing for the Tower duty—Second-Major first appointed to the Coldstream—Allies concentrate—French lines, styled the "Ne plus Ultra of Marlborough," forced—Ormond succeeds Marlborough in command of the

army—British encamp at Besieux—Ormond publishes a suspension of
hostilities—British retire—Winter quarters at Ghent—Ormond returns to England—Lumley left in command—Treaty of Utrecht—
British take possession of Dunkirk—Death of Queen Anne—Elector
of Hanover ascends the throne—Death of Churchill—Cadogan appointed Colonel of the Coldstream—Guards encamp in Hyde Park—
The Chevalier St. George lands in Scotland—Flight of the Pretender
—King George embarks at Gravesend—Hostilities recommence with
Spain—Pretender received as King at Madrid—Ormond sails from
Cadiz—Fleet dispersed—Two frigates only reach Scotland—Spanish
troops lay down their arms—Seven companies of the Coldstream embark for Corunna—Expedition attacks and takes Vigo—Rates paid
for commissions—Duke of Grafton purchases Colonel John Russell's
commission—Scarborough appointed Colonel of the Coldstream—
Services of Cadogan—Coldstream encamp in Hyde Park—Death of
George I.—Coldstream attend the coronation of George II.—Roster
of the brigade of Guards—Duke of Cumberland appointed Colonel of
the Coldstream, removed to the First Guards, and succeeded by the
Duke of Marlborough    .    .    .    .    .    .    .    *page* 330

## CHAPTER·XXIII.

George II. supports the Allies—Earl Stair sent ambassador to
Holland—First battalions of the Foot Guards embark at Deptford and
Woolwich—British winter in Flanders—War declared against France
—George II. and Duke of Cumberland sail for Holland—Confederates assemble in Germany—British quit Flanders, and move, under
Lord Stair, towards the Rhine—Confederates encamp between Ments
and Frankfort—Duke de Noailles remains in the Palatinate, on the
banks of the Rhine—George II. and Duke of Cumberland join the
army—Battle of Dettingen—Allies arrive at Hanau—Reinforced
by twelve thousand Hanoverians and Hessians—Confederates go to
Ments, and separate for the winter—Coldstream in quarters at Brussels—Treaty of Worms—George II. goes to Hanover, and returns to
England—France declares war against Great Britain—Lewis XV.
heads his army—French overrun Flanders—Charles of Lorraine enters
France—Allies posted behind the Scheld—Reinforced by the Dutch
—Duke of Cumberland appointed Commander-in-Chief—Allies in
quarters near Ghent—Allies separate for the winter—Coldstream at
Ghent—Death of Charles Duke of Marlborough    .    .    . 352

### CHAPTER XXIV.

Duke of Cumberland arrives at Brussels—Saxe takes the field—Investment of Tournay—Duke of Cumberland and Konigseck, the Austrian General, reach Halle on their march to Chambron—Lewis XV. and Dauphin arrive at the camp before Tournay—Battle of Fontenoy—Tournay surrenders to the French—Allies retire—Ghent taken by surprise—Bruges, Oudenarde, Ostend, and nearly all Flanders, submit to the French—Charles Edward lands in Great Britain—Arrival of the Guards in England—List of rebel army at Dalkeith—First battalion of the Coldstream march to join the Duke of Cumberland—Duke of Cumberland appointed Commander-in-Chief—Troops assemble at Litchfield—Arrival of the Coldstream at Litchfield—Camp at Finchley—Charles abandons Derby—Battle of Culloden *page* 364

### CHAPTER XXV.

Intended expedition under Lestock and Sinclair—Duke of Cumberland lands at the Hague—Second battalion of the Coldstream embarks for Flushing—Second battalion employed at the siege of Bergen-op-Zoom—In quarters at Bois-le-Duc—Confederates leave Maestricht, encamp at Terheyde—Go into winter quarters—Serjeants of the Foot Guards to leave off ruffles—Duke of Cumberland returns from England—Reinforcements arrive — Army assemble near Ruremonde — Brigade of Guards at Eyndhoven—Treaty of Aix-la-Chapelle—British return to England—Coldstream dispersed in a gale, seven companies land at Harwich, rest reach the Downs—Albemarle dies in Paris—Tyrawley succeeds in command of the Coldstream—Second battalion of the Coldstream occupy " the new buildings at Whitehall"—First battalion of Coldstream joins the expedition for St. Maloes—Marlborough's marches to St. Servan and Solidone—Coldstream marches for Dol—Troops embark and land in the Isle of Wight—Marlborough sent to command the British on the Continent—Marine expedition under Bligh sails—Guards commanded by Drury—Fleet anchor in Cherbourg Roads—Army disembark — Troops enter Cherbourg — Troops re-embark—Land to the westward of St. Maloes—Shepherd's dog—Bligh marches for the interior—Rear-guard defeated at St. Cas . . . . . . . . . . . . . . 387

### CHAPTER XXVI.

War in Germany—French under Broglio—Allies leave their cantonments — Hereditary Prince surprises Zierenberg — Cleves sur-

renders—Hereditary Prince repulsed in an attempt to surprise the
French camp—Allies move by Genderick—Enemy attack their van-
guard—Troops cross the Rhine—Hereditary Prince raises the blockade of Wesel—Broglio reinforced by Prince Xavier—Allies in
cantonments about Warbourg—Troops left to defend the passages
of the Dymel—Allies go into winter quarters—Guards at Pader-
horn . . . . . . . . . . . *page* 404


CHAPTER XXVII.

French enter Duderstadt—Town retaken—Confederates assemble—
Brigade of Guards join the advance—Enemy defeated by Prince Fer-
dinand at Kirchdenkern—Soubise raises the siege of Munster—
Brigade of Guards join the main body—Early in December the hostile
armies go into winter quarters—British infantry in the Bishoprick of
Osnaburg . . . . . . . . . . . 411


CHAPTER XXVIII.

The enemy assemble near Mulhausen—Confederates in camp at
Brakel—French advance—Battle of Gravenstein—French retreat—
Cross the Fulda—Allies about Holtzhausen and Weimar—Guards
near Hoff—French between Cassel and Munden—Castle of Waldec
capitulates to Conway—Death of Lieut.-General Cæsar—Battle of
Brucken Muhl—The armies move into winter quarters—British troops
march through Holland and embark at Williamstadt—General Gansell
rescued by some soldiers—Brigade Order . . . . . . 417


CHAPTER XXIX.

Death of Tyrawley—Waldegrave succeeds in command of the
Coldstream—Preparations to reduce America—France encourages
them to hold out—Government stores seized in Rhode Island—Gage
retaliates—Hostilities commence—Congress of Massachusetts—General Congress at Philadelphia—Howe, Burgoyne, and Clinton arrive at
Boston with reinforcements—Colonies of New York and North Carolina united with the other provinces—Washington appointed Commander-in-Chief—A battalion formed by drafts from the three
regiments of Guards embark for America—Battle of Long Island—
British advance—Reinforced by foreign troops in English pay—
Washington retreats—Fort Washington carried—Enemy abandon Fort
Lee—Washington retreats to the Delaware—Guards in quarters at

Brunswick for the winter—British commence operations  Cornwallis obliges Lord Stirling and General Maxwell to retreat—Howe returns to Amboy—Army embarks—Lands at Elk Ferry—Washington crosses the Delaware — Crowns the heights of Brandywine Creek—Battle of Brandywine—Supineness of Howe—Washington attacks Germantown — Fort of Mud Island abandoned — Washington quits his position at Skippack Creek—Burgoyne takes command of the northern army . . . . . . . . . . *page* 430

----

## CORRIGENDA.

### VOL. I.

Page 70, note 2—' on this day' should follow the end of note.

——— 84, line 5—for ' Kelsal' read ' Kelso.'

——— 108, — 18—for ' Spragge' read ' Spragg.'

——— 139, — 16—ditto.

——— 143, — 3 from the bottom—ditto.

——— 157 and 158—for ' fourth of April' read ' thirtieth of March.'

——— 237, line 8—for ' Portsmouth' read ' Plymouth.'

——— 315, — 2—Lieutenant-Colonels Rivett's and Bethell's companies (from Grenadiers) did not join the four companies in Flanders till the following Spring. They were sent down the river to embark from Harwich for Ostend, and sailed on the 6th of May, 1709, with the yearly reinforcements for the army.

——— 396, marginal note—for ' June 11th' read ' June 12th.'

### VOL. II.

Page 30, line 1—for ' Gascogne' read ' Cyscoigne.'

——— 47, — 3—from the bottom—ditto.

——— 59, — 17—for ' Stewart' read Stuart.'

——— 207,—Actg.-Adjt. Walton from Sept. (1814).

    Asst.-Surgeon George Smith from Nov. (1813).

        ,,    ,,    Sept. Worrell    ,,    (do.).

——— 235,—Appendix, No. 4.—should be headed ' Original letter from Monck to Lord Henry Cromwell. MS. Lansdowne, No. 822. Brit. Mus.'

——— 395,—Pay of light infantry serjeants should be ' 2s. 4¼d.' not ' 2s. 6¼d.'

——— 398 to 404.—The totals of the ' Establishment' should have been placed in the centre.

——— 420.— 6th Sept. 1711, 6 comps. should range with ' Avesne le Sec.''

    18th Oct. '   ,,   the dot should range with ' The detachment,' &c.

# EMBELLISHMENTS.

## MEDALS, &c.

### VOL. I.

MEDAL                                                PAGE

A. On the Victory of Dunbar, Sept. 1650     .   .   .   26

B. Defeat of the Dutch Fleet, July, 1653.—Voted to the Generals and Admirals   .   .   .   .   .   .   58

C. Ditto.—Distributed among the Officers   .   .   .  *ib.*

D. In honour of Monck, 1660   .   .   .   .   .   .   93

E. Defeat of the Dutch Fleet, April, 1665   .   .   .   115

F. 1. } Battle of Landen, or of Neerwinden and Neerhes-<br>F. 2. }      pen, July, 1693 .  .  .  .  .  .} 234

G. Capitulation of Namur, Sept. 1695   .   .   .   . 258

H. Battle of Vigo, Oct. 1702   .   .   .   .   .   . 286

I. 1. Taking of Barcelona, Oct. 1705   .   .   .   . 293

I. 2. } Raising of the siege of Barcelona, May, 1706 .  { 300<br>I. 3. }                                                  301

K. Battle of Oudenarde, July, 1708 .  .   .   .   313

K.* Victory at Taisniere, Sept. 1709 .  .   .   .   . 323

L. Battle of Dettingen, June, 1743 .  .   .   .   . 359

### VOL. II.

M. Gold medal presented to the Officers of the Navy and Army by the Sultan, 1801 .  .   .   .   .   . 85

N. Battle of Waterloo, June, 1815   .   .   .   .   219

Plan of Hugomont   .   .   .   .   .   .   .   213

View of Hugomont   .   .   .   .   .   .   .   226

\*\*\* The whole of the embellishments are executed by MR. BRAGGE.

# ORIGIN AND SERVICES

OF

# THE COLDSTREAM GUARDS.

VOL. I.

# TO THE READER.

SEVERAL periodicals, under the titles of " The Faithful Scout," " Kingdom's Intelligencer," " Mercurius Politicus," " Diurnals of the Army," " Moderate Publisher of every Daies Intelligence," " Perfect Diurnal of some Passages and Proceedings of the Armies," with others, are to be found in the British Museum. These documents, with few exceptions, belong to a collection of pamphlets, the gift of George III. The extracts " relating to the great civil war" in this narrative have been taken from those sources, unless other authorities are distinctly stated. It will be seen that, by a few verbal alterations, the substance of these quotations might easily be embodied in the general narrative; but it was not thought expedient, in an historical account, to sacrifice to mere smoothness of style the authenticity which they derive from being given in the original words.

# ORIGIN AND SERVICES

OF

# THE COLDSTREAM GUARDS.

## CHAPTER I.

Monck returns from Ireland—Accepts an appointment in the army intended for Scotland—Placed in command of five companies drafted from Hesilrige's regiment, and five companies from Fenwick's — Monck's regiment put on the establishment of the Commonwealth — Hesilrige appointed Governor of Newcastle Berwick and Carlisle taken — Langdale defeated in Northumberland — Fenwick nominated Governor of Berwick—Quarters of the army in England — Monck's regiment enters Scotland with Cromwell.

THE Coldstream Regiment owes its origin to General Monck.[1] The military talents of this distinguished officer had been found so useful in the settlement of affairs with the rebels in Ireland, that, on his return to England, Cromwell persuaded him to accept an appointment in the army then preparing to invade Scotland. Monck was

---

[1] So spelt by himself, as may be seen in some original letters.— Brit. Mus.

therefore placed in command of five companies drafted from Hesilrige's regiment quartered at Newcastle, and five from Fenwick's at Berwick.

The Journals of the House of Commons notice the formation of the regiment in the following terms : " Colonel " Jones reports from the Council of State, that the Lord " General hath thought fit, upon his marching into Scot- " land, to draw five companies out of the garrison of " Newcastle and five out of Berwick, and to put them " under the command of Colonel Monk, by reason of " which the strength of these garrisons is very much " lessened : To move the Parliament that Sir Arthur " Hazlerig and Colonel Fenwick may be empowered to " recruit their regiments to their former numbers, and " that the regiment of Colonel Monk may be taken on " the establishment. Resolved, That this House doth " agree with the Council of State therein." [1]

At a meeting of the Council of State sitting at White-hall, twenty-fourth August, 1650, it was " Resolved, That " a lr̃e bee written to Coll Fenwicke to give him thanks " for his care in keeping intelligence with the armie, and " sending it to the Council, and for his car$^e$ of his guar- " rison to gett trustie men for it, in lieu of y$^e$ 5 companies " taken away by order of y$^e$ Lo. Gen$^{ll}$, in w$^h$ y$^e$ Council " can onlie assist him by furnishing such officers as hee " shall send out w$^{th}$ trophies for y$^e$ raising of those " companies." [2]

The history of the regiments of Hesilrige and Fenwick, from which the drafts were made, is imperfect. In a list

---

[1] Journal of the House of Commons, Die Martis, 13 Aug. 1650.

[2] From the original book of the Council of State.—State-Paper

of the Parliamentary army under the Earl of Essex, printed by John Partridge, London, 1642, (shortly after it was formed,) the name of Sir Arthur Hesilrige is found as commander of a body of horse,[1] in which character he is better known than as colonel of the regiment of foot afterwards under his orders. His personal valour is frequently mentioned ; and in Vicar's Parliamentary Chronicle, the conduct of himself and his troop is the subject of commendation at the battles of Edge Hill in October, 1642, at Malmesbury, in Wales, and in the West, during March, April, and June, 1643 ; and more particularly at Tong Hill, near Bath, in July, the same year. It is stated in the account of an action at Lyme, in June, 1644, that " the valiant Blue Coats of Sir Arthur Hazlerig again beat " the enemy." [2]

Clarendon says, that " Sir William Waller received " from London (1643) a fresh regiment of five hundred " horse, under the command of Sir Arthur Haslerig, which " were so completely armed, that they were called on the " other side ' the Regiment of Lobsters,' because of their " bright iron shells with which they were covered, being " perfect cuirassiers ; and were the first seen so armed on " either side, and the first that made any impression upon " the King's horse, who, being unarmed, were not able to " bear a shock with them ; besides, that they were secure " from hurts by the sword, which were almost the only " weapons the others were furnished with." The Lobsters, however, were defeated at Roundaway-Down, near

---

[1] The banner of the troop under the command of Sir Arthur " Haselwrich " in 1642, also his arms emblazoned, may be seen in the MS. Sloan. No. 5247.

[2] Mercurius Politicus.

Devizes, in July, 1643, through the rashness of Sir
Arthur Hesilrige.[1]

On Thursday, thirtieth of December, 1647, a letter was
read, from his Excellency Sir Thomas Fairfax, commander
and captain-general of the army, informing Parliament that
he had given a commission to Sir Arthur Hesilrige to be
governor of Newcastle; " and the House approved thereof, and ordered him forthwith to repair thither."    He
arrived at Newcastle in the beginning of April, 1648, from
which time he had the command of the regiment of foot[2]
in that garrison.

Sir Marmaduke Langdale, a Royalist, was very active
in organising an army in Scotland, and encouraging the
Scots to invade England.    Berwick and Carlisle had already been taken, when offers were made, in May and
June, 1648, by the northern county associations, to raise
a force to oppose Langdale and the threatened irruption.
The Parliament immediately voted money and arms to
enable them to carry their purpose into effect.

On Wednesday the fifth of July, 1648, a letter from Sir
Arthur Hesilrige was read to the House, giving an account
of a victory obtained over Langdale's forces, in Northumberland, on the first of July, by the army under Colonel

---

[1] See " Progress of the Civil War," by Thomas May ; " Be-
hemoth," by Hobbes; as well as Denzil Lord Holles's work,
reprinted in Baron Maseres' Tracts.

[2] Hesilrige died in confinement in the Tower, January eighth,
1660-1, and his estate was confiscated by the Parliament; but afterwards restored to his family.    It appears from the Journals of the
House, that among the charges brought against Hesilrige after his
death, for the purpose of confiscating his estates, one was, " that
" after his late Majesty's death, he received from the pretended
" Speaker a commission to be colonel of a regiment of foot, and
" captain of a troop of horse."—Die Jovis, July 11, 1661.

Robert Lilburn, and stating that " he had sent for the
" Bishoprick regiment of horse, under Colonel Wrenn,
" to come into Northumberland, to join with Colonel
" Fenwick, who commanded the Northumberland new-
" raised regiment and Major Saunderson's two troops ;
" that he also mounted about a hundred of his foot, as
" dragoons, and sent them to them.  They pursued Lang-
" dale, and took three hundred private soldiers, and five
" or six hundred horses, and numerous officers.  The
" enemy was about twelve hundred," and the Parliamentary forces about nine hundred.

On the re-taking of Berwick from the Scots, in October,
1648, Colonel George Fenwick was appointed governor,
and a garrison of twelve hundred men ordered to be raised
for its defence.  Shortly after that event, his regiment of
foot is distinctly spoken of, and appears to have formed
part of the garrison.

On two or three occasions, subsequent to this, Hesilrige
writes to the Speaker, to complain " of the want of payment of assessments[1] due to his regiment ;" and the
House, each time, ordered, " That the committee of the

---

[1] Each county was assessed periodically to raise a certain amount,
by Act of Parliament, for the maintenance of the army and garrisons.

" The assessments were levied on personal estates as well
" as on land, and commissioners were appointed in each county
" for rating the individuals.  The highest assessment amounted to
" £120,000 a month in England ; the lowest was £35,000.  The
" excise during the civil wars was levied on bread, flesh-meat, as
" well as beer, ale, strong waters, and many other commodities.
" Cromwell, in 1657, returned to the old practice of farming.  The
" whole of the taxes during that period might, at a medium,
" amount to two millions a year ; a sum which, though moderate,
" much exceeded the revenue of any former king.  Sequestra-
" tions, compositions, sale of crown and church lands, and of

" army do take care that the assessments of Newcastle
" be duly payed." The following is the first letter
on this subject :—

" Newcastle, 14th December, 1648.

"Sir,

" I entreat an order for assigning of the assessments of
" these adjacent counties, and the town and county of
" Newcastle, towards the maintenance of my regiment.
" I beseech you to think upon Berwick, for the money is
" all gone: if you please to give me leave to charge bills
" for it, I doubt not but to have some supply.

" Sir,

" I am your affectionate servant,

" Art. Hesilrige."

In September, 1649, the subjoined list was published
in London, which shows the stations of Hesilrige's and
Fenwick's corps.

---

" the lands of delinquents, yielded also considerable sums."—*Hume*,
vol. VII.

It appears that the late king's revenue, from 1637 to the meeting
of the Long Parliament, was only £900,000, of which £200,000
may be deemed illegal.

Oh fickle people, rewyn'd londe,
  Thou wylt kenne peace no moe!
While Faction's Sonnes exalt themselves,
  Thy Brookes wythe bloude wylle flowe.

Sale, were ye tyr'd of godlie peace
  And godlie Charles's reigne,
That you dydd choppe your easie daies
  For those of bloude and peyne!

# A LIST OF THE QUARTERS OF THE ARMY IN ENGLAND.

SOMERSET HOUSE TO BE THE HEAD-QUARTERS FOR THE GENERAL AND OFFICERS.

## Regims of Foot. (Lord Fairfax.)

The Lord General's, at Westminster.
Sir Hardress Waller's, in Devonshire.
Col Ingoldsby's, in Old
Col Pride's, at St. James's.
Col. Barkstead's, at Yarmouth.
Sir W.. Constable's, in Glocbe
Sir Arthur Haslerig's at Newcastle, and in the county of Nhml
Col. Overton's, at Hull.
Col. Duckenfield's, in Ches and Salop.
Col. Mackworth's, in Cheshire.
Col. Bright's, in Yorkshire.
Col. Mallivier in Derbyshire.
Col. Fitche's, at Carlisle.
Col. Cox's, in Hertfordshire.
Col. Philip Jones's, in South Wales.
Col. Walton's, at Lynn in Norfolk.
Col. Hean's, at Weymouth.
Col. O Key's Dragoons, for Buckingham, Bedford, and Nor-th
Col. Fenwick's, at Berwick.
Col. Club Fairfax's, in Yorkshire.

## Regiments of Horse. Four Regiments, viz.—

| Regiment | Assignment |
|---|---|
| The Lord -Geal 's. / Col. Whaley's. / Col. Fl.. s. / Col. Rich's. | For the Parliament-guard, and for Kent, Surrey, Sussex, Suffolk, Norfolk, Hertford, and Middlesex. |
| The Lord Lieutenant's (of Ireland), commanded by Col. D.. w, and one troop of Dragoons. | For Cornwall, Devon, Somerset, and Dorsetshire. |
| Col. Tomlinson's. | For Wilts, Hants, Berks, Oxon, and part of Glocces |
| Col. Saunders'. | For Warwick, Salop, Stafford, Cheshire, Derbyshire, and Nhrt Wales. |
| Col. Twisleton's. | For Lincoln, Rutland, Leicest, & Nhr namshire. |
| Major Gen. Lambert's and Col. Lilburn's | For Lancaster, Yorkshire, and the North parts. |
| Col. Harrison's. | For part of Gloucestershire, and South Wales. |
| Col. Hacker's. | Regim t are to go for Ireland. |

In this way, very satisfactory evidence is afforded of the existence of Hesilrige's and Fenwick's regiments of foot up to the period when Cromwell drafted five companies from each to form a fresh corps, for the purpose of giving it to Monck, and the connecting link between these two regiments and the Coldstream Foot-guards is supplied.

Thus formed, the regiment entered Scotland with the army under Cromwell, and did not return until General Monck, on the first of January, 1659-60, quitted his head-quarters at Coldstream, to restore the monarchy, and give peace to his distracted country. From the place whence these brave men set out on their splendid undertaking, and where the plan had been matured, the regiment derives its distinctive appellation ; an event which Gumble, the chaplain of General Monck, has thus recorded : " This town hath given title to a small " company of men, whom God made the instruments " of great things ; and though poor, yet honest as ever " corrupt nature produced into the world, by the no " dishonourable name of Coldstreamers." [1]

Monck was absent from February, 1652, to March, 1654,

---

[1] Life of Monck, by Gumble, London, p. 175.

The MS. Harleian. No. 4178, entitled " The designed Loyalty of General Monck," contains an account of Monck's proceedings after having declared for the Parliament, by Dr. Price, a chaplain of his own regiment, and includes a detailed narrative of the celebrated march of the Coldstreamers to London. The manuscript is beautifully written, bound in blue morocco, stamped with the royal arms, and is believed to have been a presentation copy to King Charles II. His " History of the Restoration" appears to be printed from this MS.

Bishop Burnet says, speaking of the Coldstreamers: " I remem- " ber well of these regiments coming to Aberdeen. There was an " order and discipline, and a face of gravity and piety amongst " them, that amazed all people."

when the breaking out of fresh troubles caused him to return again to Scotland. With the exception of this interval, the services of the regiment are identified with those of its illustrious colonel, in whose triumphs it participated, whether he fought by sea or land. Whilst tracing the history of the Coldstream, it therefore becomes necessary to introduce a sketch of the life of this eminent individual.

## CHAPTER II.

Sketch of Monck's life—List of the army that accompanies Cromwell from Berwick—Collington House taken—Redhall stormed
—Cromwell destroys the Scots army at Dunbar.

GEORGE, second son of Sir Thomas Monck, was born at
Potteridge, in Devonshire, on the sixth of December, 1608.
A pamphlet, dated 1659, which Webster, in his Preface
to Skinner's Life of Monck, thinks was published to make
out a title for that general to the Crown, gives the following account of his descent. It is entitled, " The Pedigree
" and Descent of His Excellency, General George Monk,
" Setting forth how he is descended from King Edward
" the Third by a Branch and Slip of the White Rose, the
" House of York ; and likewise his Extraction from
" Richard, King of the Romans, (brother to Edward the
" Third.) Frances, another daughter, and co-heir of the
" said Arthur Plantagenet, was married ¹ to Sir Thomas
" Monk, of Potteridge, in the aforesaid county of Devon,
" which Sir Thomas was the son of Anthony, the son
" and heir of Humphery Monk, of Potteridge, and of his
" wife Mary, daughter and co-heir of Richard Cham-
" pernoon, in Cornwall, by the daughter and co-heir of

¹ She first married Sir John Basset, in the county of Devon, by

" Sir John Lumley, Knight, and of his wife, the daughter
" and co-heir of Sir Humphrey Talbot, Knight; which
" Richard Champernoon was son to Richard and Joan his
" wife, daughter and heir of Ralph Vautort, and of his
" wife Joan, daughter to Edmund, Earl of Cornwall, son
" to Richard, King of the Romans: Sir Thomas Monk,
" aforesaid, had issue, Anthony Monk, first son, (and
" several other children,) from whom is descended George
" Monk, Lord of Potteridge, and at this time the famous
" and most renowned General."

William Monache, of Potheridge, co. Devon, Esq.

Peter Monache, of Potheridge, Esq.

Hugh le Moigne, of Potheridge, Esq.

William le Moigne, of Potheridge, Esq.

William le Moigne, of Potheridge, Esq.

William Moncke, of Potheridge, Esq.

William Moncke, of Potheridge, Esq.

William Moncke, of Potheridge, Esq.

John Moncke, of Potheridge, Esq.

Humphery Moncke, of Potheridge, Esq.=Mary, da. and cob. of Richard Champernoun, of Insworth, Esq.

Anthony Moncke, of Potheridge, Esq.=Elizabeth, da. and cob. of Edw. Wood, of London

(1st wife) Frances, da. and cob. of Arthur Plantagenet, Visct. Lisle, widow of John Basset, of Womberley.=Sir Thomas Moncke, of Potheridge, Knt.

Anthony Moncke. [1]

Richard Champernoun=Joan, da. and heir of Ralph de Valletort and Joan his wife, da. of Edmund, Earl of Cornwall, son and heir of Richard, King of the Romans, second son of John, King of England.

Thomas

Henry

Richard

John (third son)

Richard

John

Richard Champernoun, of Insworth, co. Cornwall, Esq.=.... da. and heir of Sir John Hameby, of Hameby, knight, and of ..... his wife, da. and heir of Sir Humph. Talbot, knight.

---

[1] "Visitations of the County of Devon."—MSS. Harl. Nos. 1562. 1565. 3185. and 889.

Dr. Thomas Skinner, in his manuscript of the Life of Monck, written when he attended him at New Hall, in Essex, relates, that early in 1626, at the age of seventeen, Monck was placed under the care of Sir Richard Greenville, and went with the expedition to Cadiz, to escape an action for cudgelling the under-sheriff of the county of Devon, at Exeter. That officer had caused Sir Thomas Monck, father of the young assailant, to be publicly arrested on the occasion of Charles the First's visit to Plymouth.

George Monck served as a private soldier in the fleet; which he, however, quitted at the end of the year. He was then appointed ensign under Sir John Burroughs, and accompanied him to the Isle of Rhé and to Rochelle. Subsequently, at the age of twenty, on going into the Low Countries, he was made an ensign in the Earl of Oxford's regiment; afterwards he removed into the Lord Goring's, and became captain of the colonel's company "before he was thirty years of age."[1] In this service he remained ten years, and was present at most of the great actions fought during that period. Through some misunderstanding with the burghers at Dort, Monck gave up his commission, and returned to England. He was lieutenant-colonel to the Earl of Newport's regiment, in the expedition against the Scots. After the conclusion of the peace with Scotland, a fresh rebellion broke out in Ireland; and in 1642 he joined the regiment of his relative, the Earl of Leicester,[2] which was sent to that country. For his services in Ireland, Monck was made governor of Dublin.

The war now broke out between Charles and the Parliament; but " when it was in debate to order his"

---

[1] Skinner's Life of Monk, page 14.
[2] The Earl of Leicester was Lord Lieutenant of Ireland.

(Monck's) " regiment to the support of the King in
" England, he had no mind it should be sent on that
" expedition." His answer to Lord Ormond " was so
" rough and doubtful, that he thought not fit to trust
" him." On the regiment landing at Bristol, Monck was
seized and sent to the King at Oxford, and the command
given to his lieutenant-colonel, Harry Warren.[1]  However, Monck's elder brother (Thomas) was zealous in the
King's cause ; and George Monck's professions were so
frank, that " all men thought him very worthy of all
" trust, and Charles was willing to send him to the west,
" where he was highly esteemed." Clarendon, speaking
of George Monck, says,[2] he desired that he might serve
with his old friends and companions; and so, with the
King's leave, made all haste towards Chester, where he
arrived the very day before the defeat at Nantwich ; and
though his lieutenant-colonel was desirous to resign the
command, and to receive his orders, " he would by no
means at that time take it," but preferred. serving as a
volunteer in the first rank, with a pike in his hand.  The
next day he was made prisoner ;[3] and with most of the

---

[1] Extract of a letter from the Earl of Ormonde, dated " Dublin,
1st of December, 1643," addressed to the Mayor of Chester :

" There is now shipped from hence another part of his Majesty's
" army, under the command of Colonel Robert Byron and Colonel
" Harry Warren, with orders, if practicable, to land at Chester."—
MS. Harleian. No. 2135.

[2] Clarendon, Oxford edition, vol. VII. p. 381.

[3] By Sir Thomas Fairfax.

Webster, Gumble, and many others, state, that he had been
appointed Major-General to the Irish brigade in Cheshire.

Webster, in his Preface, denies Clarendon's account of his being
there as a volunteer, and asserts that he was entrusted with a high
command.

In the periodical pamphlets of that time it is stated, " that two other officers sent to Hull, and shortly after to the Tower [1] of London, where he remained till the Parliament gave him a command in Ireland. This happened in 1646, when " a message was sent by the Lords to the Com-" mons, that Colonel George Monk, who was a " prisoner to the Parliament, had taken the solemn " league and covenant, and was also ready to take the " negative oath ; and conceiving him to be a fit person to " be employed in the service in Ireland, in respect of his " valour and abilities in martial affairs, desired that he " might have a commission for that service ; to which the " House of Commons agreed, and a commission was " granted." [2]

---

" colonels, namely Warren and Monk, were formerly entertained " in the service of the Parliament to go to Ireland, and were since " taken in the North in actual war against the Parliament ; and, " being prisoners in Hull, were sent for by special order from the " Parliament, and were this day (July 8th, 1644) brought to the " House, impeached of high treason, and sent prisoners to the " Tower. Monk is said to have done good service in Ireland till he " received a countermand from the King, whereupon it is reported " he deserted his regiment, and was drawn in to serve in person " against the Parliament here."

[1] Skinner, in his Life of Monk, says, " he spent almost four years" there ; but this is evidently a mistake.

During his confinement, Mouck wrote his " Observations upon Military and Political Affairs ;" edited by John Heath, after his death. The editor states it to have been written " twenty-five " years since, and sent from the author, then prisoner in the " Tower, unto the Lord Viscount Lisle :" a work much commended at the time.

[2] Die Jovis, 12° die Novembris, 1646.

" *Die Mercurii*, 11° Nov. 1646.

" At a Committee of Lords and Commons, at Derby House, " Ordered, That it be reported to both Houses that Colonel Monke

On the twenty-eighth of January, 1646-7, Monck accompanied Lord Lisle (eldest son of the Earl of Leicester)
to Ireland, but returned again shortly after to England.
In July he was appointed Major-General of the Forces
" which were not under Sir Charles Coote," in Down and
Antrim, including the whole province of Ulster, and made
his third voyage to that country.[1]   " When beset by

---

" hath been at this Committee, and hath engaged his honour that
" he will faithfully serve the Parliament in this war in Ireland, if
" he may be employed thither; that he hath taken the negative
" oath and is ready to take the covenant ; and is ready to take his
" journey at a day's warning :  That the opinion of this Committee
" is, That he may be of very good use now at Dublyn, if the Houses
" please to leave it to this Committee to employ him thither as they
" shall think fit.

" That it be reported to the Houses, That power may be granted
" to the Commissioners now employed for Ireland, to grant Com-
" missions of Martial Law to such as they shall think fit, for the
" punishing of offending soldiers.

" Ex'r. GUALTER FROST,
" Secretary to the same Committee."

" Agreed to."

" The question was put, ' Whether Colonel Monk shall now be
" sent into Ireland, or not?'  It was resolved in the affirmative."—
Lords' Journal.

" Die Jovis, 12° Nov. 1646.

On " the Lord Lieutenant of Ireland's Report from the Commit-
" tee of Lords and Commons, at Derby House, for the affairs of
" Ireland,

" Agreed that ' The House doth leave it to the Committee to
" employ him thither as they shall think fit.' "

[1] " An Ordinance was pass'd, giving power to Colonel Monk to
execute Martial Law."—Proceedings in Parliament from November
1st till December 4th, 1647.  Rushworth's Historical Collections, vol.
VII. page 858.

On Colonel Monk beating Major-General Munroe in Ireland, he

1647.    " many difficulties, be thought it advisable to close up
" a hasty pacification with O'Neil, and returned to
" England."

1649.    About this time, his elder brother, Thomas, died[1] of a
fall from his horse.   The family estate devolved on
1650.    Monck; who continued unemployed until Cromwell was
nominated to the chief command in Scotland.  He had
taken particular notice of the abilities displayed by
Monck in Ireland; and " because he would by no means
" want his company, he furnished him with an extempore
" regiment, drawn out of several others; and after-
" wards made him Lieutenant-General of the Ordnance. [2]

---

was made governor of Belfast, besides £500 which was voted him
by the House. On Wednesday, October 4, 1648.—The Lords
concurred with the Commons in the £500 to be given to Colonel
Monk, and making him governor of Carickfergus.—*Rushworth's
Historical Collections*, vol. vii. pages 1277, 1278, 1284.

" From Dublin, by Letters, May 4, (1648,) was certified,

" That Owen Mac-Art, going some days since with a party into
" Ulster to waste that little left the Parliament's Friends, Co-
" lonel Monk, whose valour and fidelity was ever eminent, having
" knowledge of their coming, marched with such a party as he
" could make; and, having laid 300 horse in ambush, fell with the
" rest upon their quarters, which gave them a hot allarm, many
" being suddenly slain: they drawing together to oppose the first,
" were charged by the 300, totally routed, between 500 and 1000
" slain, all their arms and baggage taken, the residue flying several
" ways. Corn is, in all the rebels' quarters, at £8 a quarter, or
" 20s. an English bushel: the people die within, and the cattle
" without; and many thousands of both are like to perish."—
*Rushworth's Collections*, vol. vii. page 1108.

[1] Leaving two daughters; Monk was heir in tail.—*Skinner*,
page 33.

[2] On the twenty-sixth of June, 1650, an Act passed constituting
Oliver Cromwell, Esq. Captain-General of all the Forces raised

"Early in July, Cromwell joined the army, and arrived "at Newcastle on the 9th. He was entertained by the "governor, Sir Arthur Hazlerigg, with much freedom "and gallantry." On the sixteenth of July, Cromwell marched from Newcastle to Morpeth and Alnwick. On the nineteenth he proceeded to the rendezvous of the troops, near Berwick. On the twenty-fourth his head-quarters were at Mordington House.

The following regiments accompanied Cromwell from Berwick, as appears from several publications of the period, preserved in the British Museum :[1]

---

and to be raised by authority of Parliament within the Commonwealth of England, with a power of granting renewry and altering the officers' commissions.

[1] The subjoined account, from the Journals of the House, show to whom these publications were entrusted :—

"Friday, May 13, 1659.

"Resolved, That Mr. Jo: Canne be, and he is hereby autho-"rized to write the Weekly Intelligence.

"Resolved, That Mr. Needham be, and he is hereby prohibited "from henceforth to write the Weekly Intelligence."

"Monday, August 15, 1659.

"Resolved, That Marchmount Needham, Gentleman, be, and "he is hereby restored to be writer of the Public Intelligence, as "formerly.

"Ordered, That Mr. John Canne be referred to the Council of "State to consider him for a pension, or to put him in some other "employment."

## TEN REGIMENTS OF FOOT.

| | Men. |
|---|---|
| The Lord General's (afterwards given to Goffe, his lieutenant-colonel) . . | 1307 |
| Colonel Pride's [1] . . . . . . . . . | 1307 |
| ,, Bright's (the Major-General's) . | 1307 |
| ,, Maliverer's . . . . . . . . | 1307 |
| ,, Charles Fairfax's . . . . . | 1307 |
| ,, Coxe's . . . . . . . . . | 1307 |
| ,, Daniel's . . . . . . . . | 1307 |
| Colonel Monck's regiment { Sir Arth. Hazlerigg's (5 companies) . | 550 |
| George Fenwick's, Governor of Berwick, (5 companies) | 550 |

Total, Officers and Men . . . 10,249

The Train consisted of 690 men, making a total of—

| | |
|---|---|
| Horse . . . . . | 5415 |
| Foot . . . . . | 10;249 |
| Train . . . . . | 690 |
| | 16,354 |

From the two last corps on the list was formed Monck's own regiment of foot, of which Captain Gough, of Berwick, was appointed lieutenant-colonel, and Captain Holmes, of Newcastle, major.

July.

---

[1] This is the same Pride that stationed himself in Palace Yard with his regiment, and arrested the Members, from a list in his hand, as they proceeded to the House previous to Charles's trial: he afterwards became Master of Worcester Park, near Kingston.

were driven from their position, and the memorable victory
of Dunbar was gained.[1]

The following is an extract from Cromwell's Letter to
Lenthall,[2] the Speaker of the House of Commons, dated
fourth September, 1650. "We called for Colonel Monk,
" and showed him the thing. The Major-General, the Lieu-
" tenant-General of the Horse, the Commissary-General,[3]
" and Colonel Monk to command the brigade of Foot,

---

[1] MS. Harleian. 6844, folio 123.   British Museum.

"LIST OF Y[e] SCOTTISH ARMY AT DUNBAR.

| The Horse at Dunbar Battaile. | | The ffoott at Dunbarr Battaile. | |
|---|---|---|---|
| The Earle of Leavens Rgi; | 1 | Leuetenant Gen Lumsdale | 1 |
| Leu: Gen Lashle [*] | 2 | Maior Gen Hobron | 2 |
| Maior Gen Mongonry | 3 | Maior Gen Pettscobbie | 3 |
| Ma: Gen Browne | 4 | Coll Lawnes | 4 |
| Coll Cragg | 5 | Coll Innis | 5 |
| Coll Arnott | 6 | These comanded Brigades | |
| Coll Strathan | 7 | | |
| Master of fforbos | 8 | Coll Glanagis | 6 |
| Coll Scott | 9 | Coll Tallifeild | 7 |
| Sir James Hackert | 10 | Lord Killcowberry | 8 |
| Lord Mackline | 11 | Lord of Egell | 9 |
| Lord Brichen | 12 | M[r]. Loueit | 10 |
| Coll Scotts Cragg | 13 | Lord of Buchannon | 11 |
| Sir Robert Adaerr | 14 | S[r]. Elex Stuard | 12 |
| Coll Steward | 15 | Gen: of the Artillery's Regi: | |
| Earl of Casseats | 16 | Weams | 13 |
| Robert Harkbert | 17 | Coll Hume | 14 |
| Coll Gibby Carr | 18 | Coll ffreeland | 15 |
| Adintant Gen Bickerton | 19 | | |
| Regiments of Horse | 19 | Reg. of ffoot | 15 |

[2] See Appendix, No. 1.

[3] Commissary-General Whalie.

[*] Leslie.

1650.   " should lead on the business.  The Enemy's word was,
" ' the Covenant ; ' ours, ' the Lord of Hosts.'  In less
" than an hour's dispute, their whole army being put in
" confusion, it became a total rout, our men having the
" chase and execution of them near 8 miles.  We believe,
" upon the place, and near about it, were about 3000
" slain.  Prisoners taken, 10,000.  The whole baggage
" and train taken.  Artillery, great and small, thirty
" guns.  Left behind them, not less than 15,000 arms.
" Already brought in, near 200 colours, which I herewith
" send you.  I do not believe we have lost 20 men, and
" not many wounded (300 or 400).  One cornet slain,
" and Major Rocksby, since dead of his wounds."

A long list of officers made prisoners follows ; including,
Lieutenant-General Sir James Lumsden, Colonel Sir
William Douglas, William Lumsden, Gurdon, eleven
lieutenants-colonels, ten majors, forty-seven captains,
seven captains-lieutenants, four quarter-masters, seventy
lieutenants, twelve cornets, seventy-eight ensigns : the
Lord Liberton and Colonel Lumsden were mortally
wounded ; some thousand men were wounded ; twenty-
seven thousand routed.[1]   On receiving the news of

---

[1] The Lord General's Proclamation concerning the wounded men
left in the field :—

" Forasmuch as I understand there are several soldiers of the
" Enemies army yet abiding in the field, who by reason of their
" wounds could not march from thence : These are therefore to
" give notice to the inhabitants of this nation, that they may and
" have free liberty to repair to the field aforesaid, and with their
" carts, or any other peaceable way, to carry the said soldiers to
" such place as they shall think fit ; provided they meddle not or take
" away any of the arms there : and all officers and soldiers are to
" take notice that the same is permitted.  Given under my hand, at
" Dunbar, 4 September, 1650.          O. CROMWEL.
        " To be Proclaimed by Beat of Drum."

this important victory, Parliament voted that the two 1650.
hundred colours captured from the enemy should be hung
up in Westminster Hall,[1] and that the officers and men

---

[1] Saturday, the twenty-first September, 1650, these colours were
placed, with others, in Westminster Hall.

MS. Harleian. 1460. " A Perfect Registry of all the Collours,
" Both Horse and Foot, Taken from the Scotts at Dunbar, 3ᵈ Sep-
" tember, 1650 : by F F: F F: (Fitz Paine Fisher.)"

In number 138.

" Die Martis, 10° September, 1650.

" Ordered, That all the Colours, both Horse and Foot, now
" brought up, which were taken from the Scottish Army, be deli-
" vered to the Clerk of the Parliament, to be inventoried with the
" mottoes, devices, and number, and be by him delivered to Mr.
" Ryley, Norrey King of Arms, to be set up in Westminster Hall,
" as a monument of this great mercy to posterity : It is also
" ordered, That those Colours, which were formerly taken at Pres-
" ton from the Scotts Army that invaded this nation in 1648, now
" in the custody of Mr. Ryley, be likewise inventoried with the
" mottoes and devices upon the same, with their number, by the
" Clerk of the Parliament: And that they be likewise hung up in
" Westminster Hall, and set . . . . . on the one side, and the other
" on the other: And that the Surveyor-General do take care to
" prepare conveniences for that purpose: And the Committee of
" the Revenue are authorised and required to pay the charges
" thereof."

" Wednesday, the 10ᵗʰ September, 1651.

" The House being informed, That Captain Edward Orpyn was at
" the door, he was called in, and brought with him to the bar the
" Colours taken in the Fight at Worcester.

" Ordered, That these several Colours, taken in the Fight at
" Worcester, be hung up in Westminster Hall, by Mr. Riley,
" Norrey King at Arms: And the number, with the mottoes and
" devices, be by him entered in the book with the rest ; and that
" the Surveyor-General do prepare convenience for that purpose :
" And the Committee of Revenue are authorised and required to
" pay the charges thereof."

1650. " which did this excellent service" should be presented with gold and silver medals."[1]

On the sixth of September[2] the towns of Edinburgh and Leith surrendered : and on the fourteenth the regiment formed part of the force under Cromwell, which followed the enemy towards Stirling Bridge; Fairfax's, Daniel's, and another regiment, being left in Edinburgh and Leith. At this time, the army had been re-inforced with one thousand horse and fifteen hundred foot, recruits from England. On the twenty-first of September,[3] Cromwell returned to Edinburgh, having relinquished his intention of storming Stirling Castle. The prisoners taken at Dunbar were removed to Newcastle and Durham.

At a meeting of the Council of State, sitting at Whitehall,—" Die Jovis, 19 September, 1650," it was " Re-" solved, That a letter be written to Sir A. Hesilrige, to " give order for the delivery of two hundred Scots pri-" soners unto Mr. Isac le Guy, to be transported to " Virginia."[4] Afterwards, an order was transmitted for a large proportion to be sent to Ireland.

The annexed letter, from Heslerige to Parliament, will explain the fate of the unfortunate captives :—

" GENTLEMEN,

" I received your letter dated the twenty-sixth of " October; in that you desire me, that two thousand

---

[1] See Appendix, No. 2; also engraved medal A.

[2] It is said, that Cromwell had a superstitious impression that September was always a fortunate month to him.

[3] About this time Lord Liberton, the Scots General, died of his wounds received in the late fight.

[4] From the original book of the Council of State.—State-Paper Office.

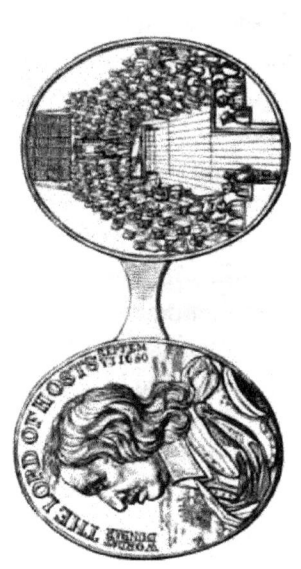

" three hundred of the Scotch prisoners now at Durham,
" or elsewhere, able and fit for foot-service, be selected,
" and marched thence to Chester and Liverpool, to be
" shipped for the South and West of Ireland, and that I
" should take special care not to send any Highlanders.

" I am necessitated, upon the receipt of this, to give
" you a full account concerning the prisoners. After the
" battle of Dunbar, in Scotland, my Lord General wrote
" to me, that there was about nine thousand prisoners ;
" and that, of them, he had set at liberty all those that
" were wounded, and, as he thought, disabled for future
" service ; and their number was, as Mr. Downing wrote,
" five thousand one hundred : the rest the General sent
" towards Newcastle, conducted to Berwick by Major
" Hobson, and from Berwick to Newcastle by some foot
" out of that garrison, and the troop of horse. When
" they came to Morpeth, they eat up the raw cabbages,
" leaves and roots ; and so many, as the very seed and
" the labour, at fourpence a day, was valued by sufficient
" men at nine pounds ; which cabbages, as I conceive,
" (they having fasted, as themselves said, near eight
" days,) poisoned their bodies ; for, as they were coming
" from thence to Newcastle, some died by the wayside :
" and when they came to Newcastle, I put them into the
" greatest church in the town ; and the next morning,
" when I sent them to Durham, about seven score were
" sick and not able to march, and three died that night ;
" and some fell down in their march from Newcastle to
" Durham, and died : and when they came to Durham, I
" having sent my Lieut.-Colonel and my Major with a
" strong guard both of horse and foot, and they being
" then told into the great Cathedral Church, they could
" not count them to be more than 3000, although Colonel
" Fenwick wrote to me that there were about 3500 : but

" I believe they were not told at Berwick, and most of
" those that were lost was in Scotland ; for I heard that
" the officers that marched with them to Berwick were
" necessitated to kill about thirty, fearing the loss of them
" all, for they fell down in great numbers, and said they
" were not able to march ; and they brought them far in
" the night, so that doubtless many ran away. When I
" sent them first to Durham, I wrote to the Major, and
" desired him to take care that they wanted nothing fit
" for prisoners, and what he should disburse I would
" repay it. I also sent them a daily supply of bread from
" Newcastle, and an allowance equal to what had been
" given to former prisoners ; but their bodies being in-
" fected, the flux increased among them. I sent many
" officers to look to them, and appointed that those that
" were sick should be removed out of the Cathedral
" Church into the Bishop's Castle, which belongs to Mr.
" Blakiston, and provided cooks ; and they had pottage
" made with oatmeal and beef and cabbage, a full quart
" at a meal for every prisoner. They had also coals daily
" brought to them, as many as made about one hundred
" fires both day and night ; and straw to lie upon ; and I
" appointed the Marshal to see all these things orderly
" done, and he was allowed eight men to help him to
" divide the coals, and their meat, bread, and pottage,
" equally. They were so unruly, sluttish, and nasty, that
" it is not to be believed ; they acted rather like beasts
" than men, so that the Marshal was allowed forty men
" to cleanse and sweep them every day ; but these men
" were of the lustiest prisoners, and had some small thing
" given to them extraordinary ; and these provisions were
" for those that were in health. And for those that were
" sick and in the Castle, they had very good mutton
" broth, and sometimes veal broth, and beef and mutton

" boiled together; and old women appointed to look to
" them in the several rooms. There was also a physician
" which let them blood, and dressed such as were wound-
" ed, and gave the sick physic; and I dare confidently
" say there was never the like care [1] taken for any such
" number of prisoners that ever were in England. Not-
" withstanding all this, many of them died, and few of
" any other disease but the flux. Some were killed by
" themselves, for they were exceedingly cruel one towards
" another: if a man was perceived to have any money, it
" was two to one but he was killed before morning, and
" robbed; and if any had good clothes, he that wanted,
" if he was able, would strangle him, and put on his
" clothes.

" The disease of the flux still increasing amongst them,
" I was then forced, for their preservation, if possible it
" might be, to send to all the next towns to Durham,
" within four or five miles, to command them to bring in
" their milk; for that was conceived to be the best re-
" medy for stopping of their flux; and I promised them
" what rates they usually sold it for at the markets;
" which was accordingly performed by about sixty towns
" and places, and twenty of the next towns to Durham
" continue still to send daily in their milk, which is boiled,
" some with water, and some with bean-flower, the phy-
" sicians holding it exceeding good for the recovery of
" their health.

" Gentlemen, you cannot but think strange this long

---

[1] Amongst other charges against Hesilrige, after his death,
framed by the Attorney-General, (Sir Jeffery Palmer,) was, " that
" Sir Arthur Haslerig used the Scots prisoners, taken at Dunbar,
" in such a barbarous and horrid manner, that they perished for
" hunger, and were not admitted to have any relief."

1650.    " preamble, and to wonder what the matter will be ;—in
" short, it is this : of the 3000 prisoners that my officers
" told into the Cathedral Church at Durham, 300 from
" thence, and 50 from Newcastle, of the 140 left behind,
" were delivered to Major Clerk by order from the Coun-
" cil; and there are about 500 sick in the Castle, and
" about 600 yet in health in the Cathedral, the most of
" which are in probability Highlanders, they being hardier
" than the rest ; and other means to distinguish them we
" have not : and about 1600 are dead and buried, and
" officers about sixty, that are at the Marshal's in New-
" castle.   My Lord General having released the rest of
" the officers, and the Council having given me power to
" take out what I thought fit, I have granted to several
" well-affected persons that have salt-works at Shields,
" and want servants, 40, and they have engaged to keep
" them to work at their salt-pans; and I have taken
" out more, about 12 weavers, to begin a trade of
" linen cloth, like unto the Scotch cloth, and about 40
" labourers.

" I cannot give you, on this sudden, a more exact
" account of the prisoners; neither can any account hold
" true long, because they still die daily, and, doubtless, so
" they will so long as any remain in prison.   And for
" those that are well, if Major Clerk could have believed
" that they had been able to have marched on foot, he
" would have marched them by land ; for we perceive
" that divers that are seemingly healthy, and have not at
" all been sick, suddenly die ; and we cannot give any
" reason for it, only we apprehend they are all infected,
" and that the strength of some holds out till it seizes
" upon their very hearts.

" Now you fully understand the condition and the
" number of the prisoners : what you please to direct I

" shall observe, and intend not to proceed further upon    1650.
" this letter untill I have your answer upon what I have
" now written.

" I am,

" Gentlemen,

" Your affectionate servant,

" ARTHUR HESILRIGE."

" Newcastle,
  " 31st October, 1650."

## CHAPTER III.

Derlton House, Edinburgh Castle, Tantallon Castle, and Blackness, surrender—Strength of the Scots army—Monck appointed
Lieutenant-General of the Ordnance—Charles II. present with
the army in Stirling Park—Cromwell encamps near Redhall—
Number of the English army—Callender House taken—Monck
" beleaguers Stirling Castle"—Charles II. and Scots army surrounded—Battle of Worcester.

1650.
Nov. 8th.
COLONEL MONCK, with sixteen hundred foot and a detachment of horse, four pieces of ordnance and a mortar,
proceeded to attack Derlton House, near Haddington,
which was occupied by some Moss-troopers. [1]   Fleetwood
and Lilburn's horse surrounded the house to keep in the
enemy.   Lambert and Monck appeared before it with the
artillery and foot on Friday night, " broke open the gates,
" beat down the draw-bridge, and rent and tore the
" house ; the lieutenant of the Moss-troopers was killed,
" and his body smashed, when the remainder called for
" quarter."

No terms were allowed the garrison but unconditional
submission ; ladders were then supplied from within for
Monck's soldiers to enter.   Major John Hamilton the

[1] The Moss-troopers were very troublesome in Cumberland and
Northumberland in 1647.—*Rushworth's Historical Collections*, vol.
VII. pages 824-833, 847.

governor, Captain Waite (commanding the Moss-troopers), <sup>1650.</sup> Nov. 8th. and about sixty of his men, were taken. Waite and the two most notorious were shot on the spot; the remainder were sent to Edinburgh. Monck, with six hundred Nov. 13th. foot, reconnoitred Roswell Castle, [1] " a very strong and considerable place," which surrendered " all upon mercy."

Edinburgh Castle, styled the Maiden from its never Dec. 19th. having been taken, had been besieged immediately after the battle of Dunbar. Walter Dundass, the governor, appointed Major Abernethie and Captain Robert Henderson to frame articles of capitulation with Colonels Monck and White. At a conference, which lasted the whole night, it was agreed that on Tuesday the twenty-fourth of December, the Castle, ordnance, arms, ammunition, and provisions of war, should be given up. The garrison marched out with " one red ensign, and one drum beating." Sixty-seven guns were taken, amongst which was the great " iron murderer " called " Muckle Meg." [2]

---

[1] Or Bashall, near Pencland Hill, seven miles from Edinburgh.

[2] Muckle Meg. A celebrated piece of ancient ordnance familiarly known by the name of Mons Meg. The bed *she* is believed to have occupied during the siege is still shown, upon a battery projecting over the sea, of a size far exceeding that of the other embrasures, and from which *she* still gets the credit of having dismasted an English vessel, steering for the harbour of Stonehaven, at the distance of a mile and a half. In the accounts of the High Treasurer during the reign of James IV. of Scotland, are entries to be found relative chiefly to the expense of her transportation from Edinburgh Castle to the Abbey of Holyrood, apparently on some occasion of national festivity. In the festivities celebrated at Edinburgh by the Queen Dowager, Mary of Guise, on the occasion of her daughter's marriage to the Dauphin of France, in 1558, Mons Meg was of course not allowed to remain silent or inactive. In the Treasurer's accounts there is the following article :

" *Item*, the third day of Julii, (1558,) By the Quenis precept

Colonel George Fenwick, who had arrived, was named, for the present, governor of the castle.

In February, Colonel Monck was before Tantallon [1] Castle, belonging to the Earl of Angus, with three regiments of foot. The garrison, on his approach, fired the town, and burnt all the corn, valued at one thousand pounds. The writer of the account says, that " after battering the " place, and playing with our granadoes, it surrendered " upon mercy. Our mortars had played forty-eight " hours ; but when our six battering-guns began to play, " they beat a parley, but would not be heard. Then " they hung out a little clout: after that, they hung " out a great sheet; our men shot at it: at last, the " governor himself came upon the walls, and entreated he " might be heard ; he desired terms. Mercy was the only

---

" and speciale command, to certane pyonaris for their lauboris in " the mounting of Mons furth of hir lair to be schote, and for the " finding and carrying of hir bullet efter scho waer schot fra " Weirdie Mure to the Castell of Edinburgh, x s. viij d."—Note to Mr. Bell's *Observations on the Regalia of Scotland*, page 35. Printed and presented to the Bannatyne Club, 1829.

" At the celebration of the Restoration in Edinburgh, on the nineteenth June, 1660, " the Major-General, after his remembrance of " His Majesty to the Earl of Seaford, fired the great cannon called " Mounce Megg, (a cannon never fired but on extraordinary " occasions,) after which followed all the guns in Edinborough " Castle, Leith Cittadel, and the ships in the road."—*Mercurius Publicus*, No. 27.

" Edinburgh, April 29th, 1754.—Mons Meg, the famous great " forged cannon, which is above two feet diameter in bore, and " weighs 4000 stone, is put on board a vessel for London."—*Gent. Mag.* for May, 1754.

The garrison during the siege exercised their skill, and were in the habit of firing down the streets, by which they destroyed the ~~inhabitants,~~ their own people.

[1] Spelt also Tom Tallent, in the periodical journals.

" terms offered to him. On the surrender of the Castle,
" there were 91 officers and soldiers in it, besides the
" governor. Since our coming into Scotland, this Castle
" had done more injury to Cromwell's army than all the
" whole Scots army or their other garrisons." Colonel
Monck next undertook, with one thousand men, in concert
with the " sea-force," to reduce Blackness, which surrendered; and " the garrison were permitted to march
" away with their wearing-apparel only. This was a
" strong place, and formerly a prison of the Scots, lying
" near the water-side, between Edinburgh and Stirling."

" Colonel Massey,[1] who had joined the King's party,
" intended to fall on Monk in his quarters at Black-
" ness; but was prevented by Lambert's division, who
" caused them to wheel about and make a dishonourable
" retreat without exchanging a blow or shot."

About this time, Cromwell was dangerously ill, and it
was currently reported that he had died. After a partial
amendment, he again relapsed, and suffered greatly from
the stone and ague-fits. In May, General Lord Fairfax
sent his coach from London, with Doctors Wright and
Bates to attend him. They arrived on the thirty-first at
Edinburgh. Permission was granted by the Parliament for
Cromwell to leave Scotland for change of air; but, his
health improving, in June the Doctors returned to London.

The army, consisting of twelve regiments of foot and
eight of horse, besides eight thousand men, who were to be
landed from boats in rear of the enemy, moved toward Fife
and Stirling. The hostile armies came daily in contact.
Head-quarters had been established in Glasgow; but

---

[1] He was seriously wounded at the battle of Worcester, and
after his flight surrendered to the Countess of Stamford, mother
to Lord Gray.

1651.
May 7.

want of food obliged the troops to return to Leith and Edinburgh, where they received provisions for a week. [1]

The Scots army, composed of about twenty thousand men and fourteen pieces of artillery, occupied Stirling and its neighbourhood.

### SCOTS ARMY.

| HORSE. | | FOOT. | |
|---|---|---|---|
| Col. the Earl of Crauford's horse | | Col. the Earl of Rothe's foot | |
| Col. Edward Massie's | ,, | Lord Erskine | ,, |
| Lord Balcarras's | ,, | Lord Drummond | |
| Lord Buchanan's | ,, | Lord Kellie | |
| Lord Bogie's | ,, | Lord Adie | |
| Lord Carnegie's | ,, | Lord Brown | |
| Lord Ogleby's | ,, | Lord Hume | |
| Lord Couper's | ,, | Lord Sinclair | |
| Lord Acanglass's | ,, | Lord Montgomery | ,, |
| Lord Erroll's | ,, | Lord Douglas | ,, |
| Lord Thornton's | ,, | and about nine Lairds Colonels. | |

Train of artillery 14 pieces.

May 26.

Cromwell appointed General and Admiral Dean Major-General of his foot, and Colonel Monck Lieutenant-General of the Ordnance.

June.

The Scots were in Stirling Park, " with their best " soldiers under David Leasley; the remainder under " Middleton : they consisted of about 16,000 foot, and " 7000 horse and dragoons. The King, who was with " the army, was dressed all in buff, which," says the ~~Writer,~~ " sets off the blue ribbon and George suspended

---

[1] The troops were in the habit of falling back for some days' provisions, after which they again advanced, as appears by the accounts of the proceedings of the army in the periodicals from which these extracts have been taken.

A drummer of Colonel Pride's regiment was tried and shot " against the Cross in Edinburgh," by sentence of a Court-Martial, for having killed a soldier in a duel.

" from his person. On Wednesday, the 4th of June, a 1651. June.
" merchants-man in Colonel Monk's regiment was shot to
" death in the High Street in Edinburgh, for killing a
" soldier of that regiment."

The Scots having determined to enter England, Major- June 25th.
General Harrison was sent with a large force into Cumberland to oppose them. The Lord General, with his
army, marched from Edinburgh, and encamped near Redhall; next day he moved to Pencland Hills, and then to
Linlithgow, within five miles of the Scots army. The July 3rd.
English consisted of fourteen regiments of horse, six troops
of dragoons, and twelve regiments of foot, and the garrisons at Leith and Edinburgh :— [1]

---

[1] The following list is extracted from the MS. Harleian. 6844.
folio 124 :—

" A List of the Regim[ts] of Horse, ffoot, and Dragoons, belonging
to the English fforces in Scotland, in the yeeres 1650 and 1651.

| Horse. | | ffoote. | |
|---|---|---|---|
| 1 His Ex[cie] owne Regin[t] | | His Ex[cie] owne Regim[t] | 15 |
| 2 Major Gen[ll] Lambert's | | Major Gen[ll] Lambert's | 16 |
| 3 Lieut. Gen[ll] ffleetwood's | | Co[ll] Ingoldsbye's | 17 |
| 4 Com[ry] Gen[ll] Whalley's | | Co[ll] Pride's | 18 |
| 5 Major Gen[ll] Harrison's | | Co[ll] ffairfaxe's | 19 |
| 6 Co[ll] Twisleton's | | Co[ll] Malevorye's | 12 |
| 7 S[r] Arthur Haslerigg's | | Co[ll] Moncke's | 21 |
| 8 Co[ll] Tomlingson's | | Co[ll] Phenixe's | 22 |
| 9 Co[ll] Hacker's | | Co[ll] Coxe's | 23 |
| 10 Co[ll] O Key's | | Co[ll] Daniell's | 24 |
| 11 Co[ll] Alured's | | Co[ll] Goffe's | 25 |
| 20 Co[ll] Grosvenor's | | Co[ll] Alured's | 26 |
| 12 | | Co[ll] Seylor's | 27 |
| | | Co[ll] Saxbye's | 28 |
| Dragoones | | Co[ll] West's | 29 |
| Co[ll] Alured's | 13 | Co[ll] Cooper's | 30 |
| Co[ll] Morgan's | 14 | 16 | |
| 2 | | | |

| THE HORSE. | FOOT. | FOOT. |
|---|---|---|
| 1 The Lord General's | 1 The Lord General's | On the Fife side |
| 2 Maj.-Gen. Lambert's | 2 Maj.-Gen. Lambert's | of the Forth, |
| 3 Lt.-Gen. Fleetwood's | 3 Lt.-Gen. Monk's | Col. Overton's |
| 4 Com' Gen. Whaley's | 4 Maj.-Gen. Dean's | (forces). |
| 5 Col. Tomlinson's | 5 Col. Fairfax's | At Leith was |
| 6 Col. C. Twisleton's | 6 Col. Pride's | Col. Fenwick's, |
| 7 Col. Hacker's | 7 Col. Goffe's | Col. Syler's. |
| 8 Col. O Key's | 8 Col. West's | At Edinburgh, |
| 9 Col. Lidcot's | 9 Col. Cooper's | 19 July, |
| 10 Col. Berry's | 10 Col. Ashfield's | Maj.-Gen. Har- |
| 11 Col. Grosvenor's | 11 Col. Daniel's | rison's horse, |
| 12 Major Husband's | 12 Col. Reade's | Maj. Mercer's |
| (6 troops of Dragoons) | | dragoons, and |
| 13 Col. Alured's | | Col. Ingolds- |
| 14 Col. Lilburn's | | by's foote. |

Cromwell, desirous to draw the Scots from their intrenchments at Stirling Park and Torwood, drew off
towards Linlithgow, in the hope they would follow him;
however, they preferred retiring behind their lines. On
the third, a cannonade took place, without much loss on
July 5th. either side. Cromwell then moved from Linlithgow to
July 7th. Pickham,[1] and on to Debath, Glasgow, and Kilsith. " The
" enemy kept pitching, and keeping in boggy ground and
" inaccessible places, so that they were constrained to
" be content not to engage them, but again returned to
July 14th. " Linlithgow for a fresh supply of provisions. A party,
" sent forth by the army, brought in between three and
" four thousand oxen and sheep."

July 16th. Callender House, a strong place, was taken by storm
in sight of the Scots army; those that resisted had no
quarter given them. The governor, Lieutenant Gebath,
and sixty-two men were killed, and thirteen taken prisoners. " Forty horses and some oxen were found in the

---

[1] Or Pickemotte.

" house : our loss was only two men, one captain[1] in   1651.<br>
July 16th.
" Monk's own regiment killed, and a master-gunner."

" Lieutenant-General Monk, with four regiments of Aug. 3rd.
" horse and three regiments of foot, marched towards
" Stirling, with orders to beleaguer that place." Colonel
West's regiment, and about five or six thousand men from
" Brunt " Island, and four battering-pieces, were sent to
him.

The King, with the Scots army, had quitted Stirling,
and proceeded to Glasgow, and thence towards Carlisle.
" Cromwell and Lambert, with all their forces, excepting
" the regiments with Monk left to beleaguer Stirling
" Castle, followed in pursuit of them, and were at Leith
" on this day, 5th of August." General Harrison, with
three hundred horse, also moved from Newcastle to oppose
them.

Charles, with about twelve thousand men, reached Lan- Aug. 10th.
cashire, leaving Cromwell in his rear. Fairfax, Harrison,
Crumpton, and Birch, surrounded him in great force. The
Scots arrived at Warrington on the fifteenth, and two days
after were between Nantwich and Chester. They entered
Worcester with sixteen thousand men ; at which place, on
the third of September, the anniversary of the battle of
Dunbar, Cromwell attacked, defeated, and almost annihilated them ; but Charles escaped.

---

[1] Captain James Rose. See Journal of the House of Commons,
November 20th, 1651.

# CHAPTER IV.

Monck remains in Scotland—Stirling Castle capitulates—Records sent to the Tower—Friends of Charles assemble at Ellit—Capture of Dundee—Monck's illness—Montrose and Aberdeen taken —Culton, Annandale, and Mohum Castles surrender—Winterquarters of the army—Argyle offers to negociate with Monck— Several influential persons submit to the Commonwealth— Widows of officers in Monck's regiment petition Parliament for relief—Commissioners appointed for the affairs of Scotland— Dumbarton Castle surrenders—Monck leaves Scotland for London — Dunotter Castle besieged by Monck's own regiment— Morgan's letter to Cromwell, with the Governor of Dunotter's capitulation.

1651.     MONCK, who remained in Scotland with about five thousand men in addition to his own regiment, commenced
ug. 11th. operations with success.   On the day that his batteries opened against **Stirling** Castle, thirty of the garrison were
ug. 14th. killed ; the loss on his side was one gunner.   Monck wrote to Cromwell that " the guns had been playing on Stirling Castle, and the enemy had craved leave to capitulate."
15th. The governor, the Honourable William Cunningham, and about three hundred men, marched out with drums beating, and permission to go where they pleased.   Mr. William Clarke,[1] in a letter to Lenthall the Speaker, states that

---

[1] Secretary to the Commander of the Forces : he was knighted after Charles's return, and was the first Secretary at War.

" there was in the Castle 40 pieces of ordnance, pro-
" visions to serve 500 men for twelve months, about
" 5000 new musquets and pikes, 26 barrels of powder,
" 20 or 30 vessels of claret wine and strong water, and
" numerous instruments of war; all the Records[1] of Scot-
" land, the chair and cloth of State, the sword and
" other rich furniture of the King; the Earl of Mar's
" coronet and stirrups of gold, with his parliament robes.
" The 32 English prisoners taken at Newark were re-
" leased." He adds, " the Castle is one of the stateliest
" and fairest buildings in Scotland. Over the chapel-
" door is this motto—' J. VI. R. Nobis hæc invicta mi-
" serunt centum sex proavi. 1617.' It seems it had passed
" the one hundred and seventh unconquered, but not the
" one hundred and eighth."

After the capitulation, Monck began his march with
two regiments of horse and two of foot towards Dundee,
leaving Colonel Read's regiment in Stirling; and on Thursday, the twenty-first of August, he quitted the latter place
with nine companies of his own regiment of foot, nine
companies of Colonel Ashfield's, five troops of Colonel
Grosvenor's, Colonel O Key's, and Colonel Berry's regiments of horse, two troops of Colonel Morgan's dragoons,
nine battering-guns, and a mortar. Monck took up his
quarters for the night at Dumblain. On Friday he

---

[1] " Resolved, That all the Records, together with the Regalia "
(not the Crown and Sceptre, " the Honours of Scotland," which
had been sent to Dunotter Castle for safety,) " and Insignia taken
" in the Castle of Stirling, be brought into England and placed in
" the Tower of London."

" Resolved, That it be referred to the Council of State to take
" order for removing the brass guns from the Castle of Stirling,
" and placing some iron guns in their room."—Journals of the
House, Wednesday, 27th Aug. 1651.

1651.    marched to Blackford.  The next day he encamped within
Aug. 24th.  two miles of St. Johnston's.   On the following day, " the
" foot, and a good part of the horse, got over on the
" other side the river; the horse, for want of boats, were
" obliged to swim over, and two or three men and horses
" were drowned."  The rest of Monck's forces, with the
addition of Alured's horse and some dragoons, afterwards
joined him on his route to Dundee.  Monck having received intelligence that a number of Charles's friends had
assembled at Ellit, about seven miles from Dundee, despatched Colonel Alured, with his regiment of horse and
Aug. 28th.  two troops of dragoons, who succeeded in surprising
them.   Colonel Fenwick, in a letter written by him,
enumerates among the prisoners, General Leslie, Earl
Marshall, Earl Crauford, Lord of Leith, Lord Ogleby,
Lord Burgimie, Lord Humbie, Lord Lee, nineteen gentlemen of quality, eight ministers, a captain, a cornet, and
seventy soldiers.   Ludlow, speaking of the affair, says :—
" Lieutenant-General Monck, whom the General had
" raised to that employment, and ordered to command in
" Scotland during his absence, took Stirling Castle, and
" then marched with about 4000 horse and foot before
" Dundee.  But being advised that General Lesley, the
" Earl of Crawford, and others, were met at Elliot to
" consult of means to relieve that town, he sent a party of
" horse and dragoons commanded by Colonel Alured and
" Colonel Morgan to surprise them, which they did ;
" and the principal of them being taken, were sent pri-
" soners to London, where they were committed to the
" Tower." [1]
Monck arrived before the town of Dundee on the twenty-

---

[1] Memoirs of Lieut.-Gen. Edmond Ludlow, 8vo. Vevay, 1698.
vol. i. page 368.

sixth of August, when he immediately summoned the garri-
son to surrender : the result is thus described in his letter, dated September the first :—" We lost in the storm about " six officers and 20 private soldiers [1] killed.  There was " killed of the enemy 500, and about 200 taken pri- " soners.  The governor was killed.  Sixty sail of ships " in the harbour, and about forty iron guns in and about " the place.  The stubbornness of the people forced " the soldiers to plunder the town. [2]  St. Andrews is " come in, whom I ordered to pay £500 for refusing the " first summons.  I believe a town called Montrose will " likewise come in upon summons, which place I intend " to make our winter-quarters." [3]  A further account of the capture is given in a letter from Colonel O Key, dated 1651, September first, who says, " It was resolved " to storm the place : our two regiments of foot were very " weak by reason of sickness, and we ordered that 650 " horse should fall on with sword and pistol ; 250 on " foot, and 400 on horseback, to second them.  All the " seven troops of dragoons, and 150 seamen.  Our guns " began to batter at 5 o'clock in the morning, and " made some breach ; and at 10 o'clock we fell on with " such courage and spirit in our men, that I never saw " more in no place in all my life.  The whole body of " horse, that was to stand as a reserve at some distance, " as soon as ever our forces fell on, gave a shout and

---

[1] O Key's letter states ten men.

[2] Ludlow in his Memoirs, vol. 1. page 368, observes, " After " this he summoned the town of Dundee ; but the place being " well fortified and provided with a numerous garrison, refused to " surrender ; whereupon he stormed it, and being entered put five " or six hundred to the sword, and commanded the governor, with " divers others, to be killed in cold blood."

[3] Went into winter-quarters at Dundee.

" came up to the work, and kept under the cannon's
" mouth, and many of them got over as soon as those
" that were on foot, which was a mighty encourage-
" ment. The enemy stood very stoutly to it for a quarter
" of an hour; and most of them that kept their posts
" were killed in the very place. The enemy (as they tell
" us) were near three thousand: there were killed some
" eight hundred; four hundred were taken prisoners, with
" arms in their hands; the rest of the town got into their
" houses. We had not above ten men killed, besides
" those that were wounded,[1] whereof Captain Hart[2] was
" one. It was the richest town that I ever saw in
" England or Scotland for the size of it. Some of our
" soldiers got £500 a-piece. We are now to march to-
" wards Aberdeen." Captain Hart, alluded to in Colonel
O Key's letter, was the officer that led on the forlorn of
Lieutenant-General Monck's own regiment, as is stated in
other accounts from the army. In this assault, " Sir
" Robert Lumsden, the Governor, was slain; the Lord
" Newton, Captain Fergusson, the Minister of the town,
" with many other officers and gentlemen of quality."
Major Scott, who commanded a regiment in Monck's
army, defeated a small body of the enemy, and took
Sept. 7th. Dumfries on the fourth. Monck was attacked with sick-
ness, during which Colonel Overton, with Alured and
O Key, took Montrose and Aberdeen: afterwards Overton
captured Culton Castle; and Major Butler, of Colonel
Berry's regiment, took possession of Annandale and Mo-

---

[1] Ensign Francis Norris, of Monck's regiment, died of the
wounds he received at Dundee. See Commons' Journal, Nov. 20,
1651.

[2] Of Monck's regiment. See Periodicals. (Diurnals of the Army,

hum Castles: " he reduced all Liddisdale, where the 1651.<br>Sept. 7th.
" country as far as Carlarrok Castle submitted to the
" power of the Commonwealth."

In October, the army went into winter-quarters, and Oct. 5th.
were stationed as follows : the regiments of Colonels
O Key, Alured, and Berry, were on the south of the Tay ;
Colonel Grosvenor's horse, Lieutenant-General Monck's
own regiment, which was usually near his person, and
Colonel Ashfield's regiment, with four companies from
Leith, were " appointed to maintain the garrison at Dundee,"[1] where Monck was still confined by illness. The Oct. 15th.
Marquis of Argyle offered to enter into negociations with
him, but received for answer that he would not treat without the consent of Parliament. Amongst other proclama- Oct. 27th.
tions [2] issued at this time by Monck, was one ordering the
soldiers not to " put away English coin at a higher rate
than it goes for in England." A letter, dated Dundee, Nov. 7th.
states that, " On Friday last, at a Court-Martial here,
" one Ramsey, of the Lieutenant-General's (Monck's)
" regiment, was condemned to be shot to death for
" striking a serjeant, who corrected him for his misde-
" meanours."

Lord Balcarras, Major-General Stirling, the Marquis
of Argyle, Marquis of Huntley, Lord Callender, several
highland chiefs, and many other influential persons, submitted to the English Commonwealth.

The widows of the officers who had fallen in the war,
petitioned Parliament for relief ; among whom were
" Elizabeth, widow of Captain James Rose, of Colonel
" Monck's regiment, who was slain in the service in Scot-

---

[1] In October, Colonel Cobbet was appointed Governor of
Dundee.

[2] All proclamations were published by beat of drum.

" land ; Sarah, widow of Lieutenant Thomas Parker, of
" Major Holmes's company in Colonel Monk's regiment,
" who died in the service in Scotland ; Mary, widow of
" Ensign Francis Norris, of Captain Gardiner's company
" in Colonel Monk's regiment, who died of the wounds he
" received at Dundee ; Fortune, widow of Ralph Walton,
" Lieutenant to Captain Nichols, of Colonel Monk's regi-
" ment, who died in the service in Scotland ; Mary,
" widow of Captain John Robbins, of Colonel Monk's
" regiment, who died in the service in Scotland." [1]

Nov. 12th.     Monck's own regiment was now quartered at Aberdeen,
where Captain Robbins, before mentioned, died.

December.     In the beginning of December, [2] only four Castles held
out, namely, the Basse, Dumbarton, Dunotter, and the
Castle in the Highlands in which the Lord Chancellor
Loudon kept himself shut up.

Dec. 18th.     Oliver St. John (Chief Justice of the Common Pleas),
Sir Henry Vane, jun., George Fenwick, Esq., Richard
Saloway, Esq., John Lambert (Major-General of the
army), Richard Dean (Major-General of the foot), George
Monck (Lieutenant-General of the Ordnance), Robert
Tichborne (Alderman of the City of London), commis-

---

[1] Journals of the House of Commons, Nov. 20, 1651.

[2] " On the 1st of December, a Court-Martial was held at Leith,
" when it was ordered that the divorced wife of Lieutenant Emer-
" son, formerly whipped out of this garrison " (for profligate conduct) " by sentence of the Court, and ordered never to enter the
" town again, being now taken upon suspicion of the same act,
" should be led, with her face uncovered, her back bare, with a
" rope about her in the one hand of the Martial and a whip in the
" other, from Edinburgh Port by the main guard, to Sand Port
" in Leith, and then led back to prison, till a conveniency of ship-
" ping be had to send her for England ; and in case she re-enters
" the garrison again at any one time hereafter, then to be whipped
" forth again."

sioners for the affairs of Scotland, received their instruc- 1651.<br>December.
tions from the hands of the Speaker.

In December Dumbarton Castle surrendered " without
any force being used."

Monck, as one of the commissioners, passed through 1651-2.<br>Jan. 17th.
Leith on his way to Dalkeith, to hold a conference with
the others at that place, and was received with a salute
from the battery. In January, his own regiment of foot
marched from Aberdeen to Dundee, and relieved Colonel
Cooper's, " who were ordered on the Northern design,"
the occupation of the Orkney Islands ; which was effected February.
by Colonel Overton, with eight hundred men in February.

A letter from Berwick, dated eighteenth of February, Feb. 18th.
printed in the periodicals of the day, states that " Major-
" General Lambert came yesterday, about noon, to this
" town, in the commissioner's coach, with Lieutenant-
" General Monk also with him ; Major-General Lambert
" stayed not an hour, but took post presently towards Lon-
" don ; Lient.-General Monk took journey this morning
" after him." General Monck reached Newcastle on the
nineteenth of February, and London on the fourth of March. March.
On his arrival in town, the Commonwealth proposed sending him "suddenly" to France with ten thousand men : but,
it appears, that he shortly afterwards went to Bath for the
"repair of his health." Dean's troops made themselves mas- April 6th.
ters of the Castle of Braddock in the Isle of Arran, lately
the residence of the Duke of Hamilton, and the Castle and April 10th.
Island of Basse. On the sixth of May, the following May.
report was sent from Dundee :—" Lieutenant-General
" Monck's regiment, under Colonel Morgan, with some
" horse and dragoons, will march on Monday next against
" Dunotter Castle, to lay siege to it." Monck's own
regiment was probably selected for this service, that it
might have the credit of the capture of the " Honours of

1652.   Scotland," it being well known that the regalia were de-
May 26th. posited for safety in this Castle. The siege was carried
on under Colonel Thomas Morgan ; and the governor
surrendered on the day before the assault was to have
been given. The following is the official letter announcing this event :—" Meeting of Parliament, Saturday, 5th
" June, 1652. A letter from Colonel Thomas Morgan,
" dated at Dunotter Castle, 26th May, 1652, with a
" copy of a letter from the Governor of the said Castle,
" and also Articles for surrendering the said Castle, were
" this day read."

" FOR HIS EXCELLENCY
" THE LORD GENERAL CROMWEL.

" May it please your Excellency.

" Since my last, I shall give your Lordship this account
" of Dunotter Castle. We had brought our approaches
" very nigh unto them, and were ready for to mount
" another battery. Upon the 23rd inst. our cannons did
" play very sharply, and we sent them in three granado-
" shells, which I perceive did cause them to beat for a
" parley ; which, after some time, I did adhere unto, and
" caused them to furl up their colours and take them off
" their works, or else I would not have admitted of a
" parley ; accordingly they did, and afterwards sent me
" out this enclosed letter. I could not well approve of
" Colonel Barkley's being there, but of the Laird of Mor-
" phie's I did, which when he came, he with other two
" officers of the Castle was commissionated by the Gover-
" nor for to treat with me for the surrender of the said
" Castle. The Articles of our agreement I have sent
" your Excellency here enclosed, being authorized by the
" Major-General so to do, for to prevent the ruining of

" the said Castle.  This morning the enemy did march
" out; and Captain Gardiner, of Colonel Monk's regi-
" ment, with his company, is marched into the said Castle.
" The place is very considerable, and naturally fortified of
" itself.  I have appointed Lieutenant-General Monk's
" Lieutenant-Colonel, Captain Gardiner, Captain Powel,
" and Lieutenant Hellin,[1] to inventory the King's goods
" and the Lord Marshall's, with all other goods therein,
" that so they may be the better preserved for the use of
" the Parliament of the Commonwealth of England.  I
" shall give your Excellency this account that there is in
" the Castle :

" 38 pieces of ordnance, great and small ;

" 16 barrels of powder ;

" Match and bullet proportionable.

" A great quantity of other goods belonging to the late
" King and the Lord Marshall, a true account of which I
" cannot give your Lordship till the inventories be taken
" thereof.

" As concerning that article of the Crown and Sceptre,
" the late Governor can give me no other account for the
" present, but that his wife hath transported it without
" his consent ; which is not satisfactory to me,[2] for I judge

---

[1] Lieutenant-Colonel William Gough, Captains Gardiner and
William Powel, of Monck's own regiment, and Lieutenant Hellin,
of Colonel Morgan's regiment of Dragoons.

[2] The Regalia of Scotland were not forthcoming, and Ogilvie
and his Lady were imprisoned within Dunotter Castle for several
months.

In 1829, William Bell, Esq., printed and presented to the Bannatyne Club, of which he is a member, a collection of papers
relative to the Regalia of Scotland ; in the observations on the
history of which, every particular of their preservation is noticed,
and many original documents are given relative to the defence of
Dunotter, the fortress to which the Regalia were sent for safety by

1652.    " he hath forfeited his articles if he give not better satis-
" faction what is become of it ; to which intent I have writ
" to the Major-General (Dean) to know his pleasure, that
" so the late Governor and his wife may both be laid into
" prison till they shall give a better account thereof ; for
" truly I am of opinion that they are not out of Scotland
" as yet.   I have no more at present to trouble your
" Excellency with, but that I am

" Your Excellencies most humble

" and faithful servant,

" THO. MORGAN."

" THE GOVERNOR OF DUNOTTER'S LETTER.

" For COLONEL MORGAN, these.

" SIR,

" I expected to have seen some friends before this
" time, who should have resolved mee in some things
" anent the up-giving of this house ; and since they are
" not returned, these are to desire you, that you would be
" pleased to permit me to goe for the Laird Morphie and

---

order of the Parliament of Scotland in June, 1651, and which was
the last to surrender to the forces of the Commonwealth. It
appears that the Regalia were transported in safety from Dunotter
to the Manse of Kinneff by the contrivance of Mrs. Ogilvie, unknown to her husband, and there placed under the charge of the
Reverend James Granger, Minister at Kinneff, and husband of the
dauntless Mrs. Granger, who had brought them away at much
personal risk : they were interred in the Church by Granger himself ; and, at the restoration of Charles II., Ogilvie revealed the
secret in a petition to the King, who conferred on him the dignity of
a Knight Baronet and other honours.

A pamphlet, entitled " A True Account of the Preservation of
the Regalia of Scotland, by Sir George Ogilvie, of Barras, K<sup>t</sup>
and Barronet," was published at Edinburgh, 1701, which is reprinted
by Mr. Bell in the work referred to.

" Colonel Barclay, that they may come and speake with
" me, by whom I shall be willing, upon honourable con-
" ditions, to give you satisfaction : not that I am weak-
" ened any thing in men or any thing else, (I thanke
" God,) but only to prevent the effusion of blood, much
" whereof doubtlesse will follow upon a further debate ;
" upon these considerations I hope you will permit some
" countryman, or one from myselfe, to goe for these gen-
" tlemen, untill whose coming I desire a cessation may
" be on both parts from acts of hostility. So expecting
" your answer, I am your servant,

" GEORGE OGLEVY."

" Dunotter,
" 23rd May, 1652."

" Articles of Agreement between Colonel Thomas
" Morgan, in the behalfe of the Parliament of the Com-
" monwealth of England, and Captain George Oglevy,
" Governor of Dunotter Castle, for the surrender thereof.

" 1. That the said Captain Oglevy delivers up unto
" mee the Castle of Dunotter, with all the ordnance,
" armes, ammunition, provisions, and all other utensels of
" warre, for the use of the Parliament of the Common-
" wealth of England, upon Wednesday the 26th instant,
" by nine of the clocke in the morning, without waste or
" embezlement.

" 2. That the late King's goods, with the Lord Mar-
" shal's, and all other goods within the said Castle, shall
" be delivered to mee, or whom I shall appoint, for the
" use of the Parliament of the Commonwealth of Eng-
" land.

" 3. That the Crowne and Scepter of Scotland, together
" with all other ensigns of regality, bee delivered unto
" mee, or good account thereof, for the use of the Parlia-
" ment of the Commonwealth of England.

1652. " 4. That upon the true performance of the above-men-
" tioned Articles, Captain George Oglevy, with the offi-
" cers and souldiers under his command, shall have liberty
" to march forth of the said Castle at the houre appointed,
" with flying colours, drums beating, match lighted,
" compleatly armed, and to have passes to goe to their
" owne homes, and there to live without molestation, pro-
" vided that they act nothing prejudicial to the Com-
" monwealth of England.

" 5. That the said Captain Oglevy shall (free from
" sequestration) enjoy all that personal estate which he
" hath now without the Castle of Dunotter, and all such
" necessary household stuffe of his owne which is now in
" the Castle, as shall be thought fit by mee or by them
" whom I shall authorise to deliver in unto him.

" THO. MORGAN."

" At Blacke hill, at
" the Leager, 24th May, 1652."


" A CERTIFICATE FROM COLONEL MORGAN.

" I am credibly informed, that the said Captain George
" Oglevy his personal estate is not worth above fifty
" pounds per annum.

" THO. MORGAN."

## CHAPTER V.

Army marches into the Highlands—Colonel Lilburn's account of his progress—Secretary's Clarke's letter to Lenthall—Anecdote of Captain Powell—Parliament votes Generals Blake, Dean, and Monck to command the fleet—Colonel Lilburn replaces Dean in Scotland—English and Dutch fleets engage between the Isle of Wight and Portland—Dutch defeated off Ostend—Monck left in sole command—Van Trump killed off Camperdown—Middleton lands and plants the Royal Standard between Stirling and Dumbarton—War recommences in the Highlands—Force of English regiments in Scotland—City of London entertains Cromwell—Monck arrives at Dalkeith—Enters Stirling—Loch Tay Island, Ballock, Weemys, and Garth Castles taken—Morgan defeats Middleton near Loch Garry—The Earls of Glencairn and Athol with other chiefs send in their submission—Monck's head-quarters again at Dalkeith—Proceedings of a Court-Martial—Army in winter-quarters—Several Officers arrested—City of Edinburgh entertains Monck—Cromwell proclaimed Lord Protector in Edinburgh—Death of Cromwell—Richard proclaimed Lord Protector in Scotland—Parliament dissolved—Richard resigns his office.

THE army, divided into three brigades, was ordered to march into the Highlands. Colonel Overton commanded his regiment of foot and Colonel Blackmore's horse; Colonel Lilburn, Hacker's horse and Ashfield's foot; Morgan, the Major-General's regiment of horse and Monck's own regiment of foot: a troop of Dragoons was also attached to each of the three brigades, which were to meet at Loughaber on a certain day. A vessel of fifty tons, mounting four guns, to supply provisions and am-

1652.
June.

" are come in to the Major-General, and markets settled
" in some places for the bringing in of provisions to our
" soldiers, where there never was any market before.
" The people generally speak Irish, and go only with
" plaids about their middle, both men and women : there
" are scarce any houses of stones, but only earth and
" turfs."

On the eighteenth of July, Monck's own regiment was
at Bashenough with Major-General Dean, Hacker's horse,
and Fairfax's regiments of foot.   Dean left the command
to Colonel Morgan, at which time they were assembled at
Lough Tamer.   In the middle of August, Captain Powell,
with a detachment of the regiment, was still at the Bray
of Mar and Ruthven Castle.   The following anecdote is
told of this officer, in a letter dated the first of December,
1652.   " Captain Powell, of Lieutenant-General Monk's
" regiment, deserves special notice, who having some pro-
" visions and clothes brought to him for his garrison in
" the Blair of Athol, some Highlanders waylayd them,
" and, with some opposition from a small party, took their
" provisions and clothes ; but Captain Powell, who had
" gained much love amongst the chief Clans of the High-
" landers, putting on his troses and belted plaid, pursued
" them (himself) without any assistance from his soldiers,
" taking with him only about three score of the chief
" Clans, and recovered all the prize."   His subsequent
murder is thus described in a letter dated Leith, fourteenth
December, 1652.   " We are yet very quiet, and doubt
" not but we shall continue so, notwithstanding all fears
" and jealousies.   I have only one unhappy accident to
" acquaint you with, which is the death of that hopeful
" young gentleman, Captain William Powell, Governor of
" the Bray of Mar, who was killed by the Highlanders as
" he was going from Dunotter Castle to his garrison on

1658.    " Monday sennet last : there was only himself and his
" man, who travelled together ; he being confident of
" the interest he had in the Lairds and heads of Clans
" in the Highlands, which indeed was very great ;—but
" though the Lord Eura (who bath a very large command
" over them) was in his company as his convoy, after an
" affront given to his man by some of them at Talton ;
" yet they followed him, and first shot his man, and after-
" wards, he quitting his horse and pursuing them over
" a bog (with the Lord Eura), was shot in the head
" with three bullets : and the Laird asking them, if they
" durst injure any in his company ? they told him they
" would shoot him too.  And having committed this vile
" murder, the actors fled, leaving his body, which was
" buried in a church near the place he was killed.  He
" was one of the most improved gentlemen that I know,
" and had, during his little stay in the Highlands, gained
" the seeming love of all the chief Clans, Lairds, and
" gentry about him, both in the Highlands and Low-
" lands ; but those villians, upon some discontent taken
" against his lieutenant, who had kept them in the
" guard for buying fire-arms of his soldiers, executed
" their revenge upon this gallant and ingenious gentle-
" man."

Towards the end of the autumn, Monck's regiment left
the Highlands and marched for Edinburgh, at which
place it was quartered.  As the country enjoyed perfect
tranquillity, it was determined at a council of war to make
a partial reduction of the forces, for the purpose of di-
minishing the expense of the army.  Two hundred men
from Monck's own regiment, two hundred from Fenwick's
at Leith, and a company of firelocks out of the train, were
disbanded and sent home to England with " some money
in their pockets."

From February, Monck had remained in England, but he was not unemployed. On Friday, November twenty-sixth, 1652, Parliament resolved, " That there shall be three " Generals for governing the fleet and fleets at sea for the " year ensuing, from the 3rd of Dec'. 1652 to the 3rd of " Dec'. 1653; and it was voted that General Blake, " Major-General Dean, and Lieutenant-General Monk, be " the three Generals of the Fleet for the year ensuing. " Captain Penn was appointed Vice-Admiral." Colonel Robert Lilburn succeeded to the command, on Dean's appointment as one of the Generals of the Fleet for the ensuing year. *1652.*

*November.*

*1652-3.*
*January.*

The three Generals, with the English fleet, sailed from Queenborough for the Downs: General Monck was on board the Vanguard. The Dutch fleet of sixty sail, with an immense convoy, was encountered between the Isle of Wight and Portland. After a severe conflict on the eighteenth, nineteenth, and twentieth of February, seventeen sail of the enemy's ships of war were taken or destroyed, besides the greater part of their valuable convoy. " Blake " was badly wounded in the thigh by an iron bar and " splinter, which also carried away great part of Dean's " breeches. Captain Mildmay, of Monck's ship, was " slain, and many other Captains and Officers killed and " wounded." *Feb. 10.*

The fleet refitted, and stood for the Texel: Generals Dean and Monck were on board the Resolution. On the second of June they discovered the Dutch fleet, under Van Trump, off the North Foreland, when an action commenced, in which Deane was killed. Next day Blake joined Monck with his squadron, and the fleets engaged off Ostend. In this battle the enemy were defeated with great loss. Five Dutch ships were sunk, two blown up, and seven taken. On Friday the third, eleven men-of-war and three small vessels were also *1653.*
*May 5th.*

taken, six sunk, four blown up, which destroyed another
" next to them." Monck, after his victory, landed six
thousand men at Cadsand Island near Flushing, and took
the fort, which was filled with stores, arms, and ammunition.
" This," says the Editor of a Journal of that period, " will
" prove a piece of singular service to the Commonwealth,
" and an eternizing the honor and fame of the thrice noble
" and valiant General Monk throughout all ages." Blake
landed on account of ill health, and went to Ipswich :
Monck remained in command, and led the van off Camperdown, on the twenty-ninth, thirtieth, and thirty-first
of July.   During the action, the Dutch Admiral Van
Trump was killed, his flag was shot away, and his men
were unable again to hoist it.   Thirty-eight ships, three
of them bearing the flags of Vice and Rear-Admirals, were
destroyed.   The Garland frigate, which had been captured from the English, was retaken and burnt.   After the
battle, ten other ships fell into the hands of the victors;
the enemy lost nine hundred men killed.   The two Com-
monwealths fought seven battles within the year.   The
Parliament after these three actions voted gold chains and
medals to the different Generals and Admirals.[1]

Smaller medals were also distributed amongst the
Officers.[2]

August.    Lieutenant-General Middleton landed in Scotland, and
planted the Royal Standard between Stirling and Dumbarton.   Colonel Morgan with a strong force marched
for the Highlands to keep down the clans, who, confi-
ding in the strength of their mountain passes, and the
inaccessible nature of their remote districts, had shown a
disposition to turbulence and hostility.   These inhabitants
of the hills knew no law but the will of their chiefs,
nor any country but their native glens, and neither under-

---

[1] See engraved medal a.          [2] See engraved medal c.

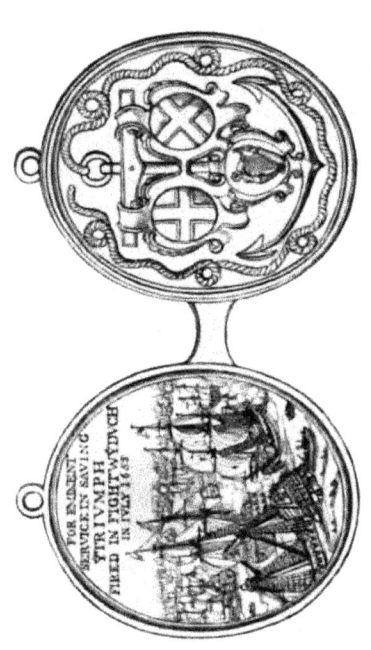

FOR EMINENT
SERVICE IN SAVING
TRIVMPH
FIRED IN FIGHT WITH
IN JULY 1653

stood nor cared for the political and religious differences **1653.** which brought the English army into Scotland : but deeming themselves the rightful owners of the plains, whence their ancestors had been driven by foreign invaders, they gladly availed themselves of any pretext for committing depredations on the Lowlands and spoiling the usurpers of their inheritance.

In September Monck commanded the fleet, and was nearly lost in his ship, the Resolution, during a severe gale off Cromer in Norfolk, in consequence of his determination to keep the sea at all hazards, and watch the movements of the enemy. He landed in the course of this month, and witnessed the launch of the Swiftsure at Woolwich ; soon after which he proceeded with the fleet through the Downs to St. Helens. On the first of October Monck attended the House of Commons, when the Speaker was ordered to give him the thanks of Parliament, for the services he had rendered the Commonwealth at sea, where his natural sagacity supplied the place of practical experience, and his valour matched the sullen desperation of the Dutch Admirals, whose skill and courage were ably seconded by the best sailors of that period.

Colonel Lilburn had been appointed commander of the forces in Scotland in September, and on the tenth of October two companies of Monck's own regiment, with other troops, marched from Dalkeith under that officer, who reduced the Western Isles and the Orkneys to subjection. [1]

---

[1] For a more particular detail of these transactions, see an Account of the Earl of Glencairn's Expedition in the Highlands of Scotland in the years 1653 and 1654, edited by Sir Walter Scott, from the original MS. in possession of Sir Alexander Don, Bart., of Newton, entitled Military Memoirs of the Great Civil War, Edinburgh, 4to, 1822.

The English regiments in Scotland consisted of—

| | |
|---|---|
| General Monck's own regiment | Colonel Morgan's |
| Colonel Read's | ,,     Daniel's |
| ,,     O Key's | ,,     Fitch's |
| ,,     Fenwick's | ,,     Ashfield's |
| Rich's | ,,     Cobbet's |
| ,,     Fairfax's | ,,     Salmon's |
| ,,     Twisleton's | ,,     Tomlinson's |
| " That which was Major | Part of Colonel Sanderson's |
| General Harrison's " | The Company at Dumbarton |
| ,,     Alured's | |

The following regiments arrived in February:

Major-General Lambert's,

Commissary-Gen. Whalie's,

and part of Sir Wm. Constable's.

" In January, a lieutenant of General Monk's regiment,
" and several other officers, were taken near Falkirk, and
" carried to the Hills."

February. On the eighth of February, the Lord Mayor and City of London gave a splendid entertainment to the Lord Protector at Grocers Hall. General Monck and the chief officers of the Commonwealth were there.

March. In March such an inclination to rebellion manifested itself in the Lowlands, that Monck was again directed to assume the command of the troops in Scotland.[1] On reaching Newcastle,[2] he was received " by the Mayor and " Corporation, who showed him great affection, and sent " him every description of wine, sweetmeats, &c. The " shipping hung out their colours on his entry and depar-

---

[1] In February, Morgan marched from Aberdeen, and defeated Glencairn and the Earl of Kenmore near the Lough at the head of Cromar. Colonel Morgan, after this engagement, marched towards Kildrummy.—*Mercurius Politicus*, No. 193.

[2] The middle of April.

"ture, and all the guns in the ships and town saluted 1654.
"him." Monck arrived at Dalkeith, and soon after com- April 22nd.
menced his march for Stirling, which he entered with his
own regiment, part of Colonel O Key's, and Sir William
Constable's. He then proceeded to the Hills, and en- May 22nd.
camped at Kilsith beyond Glasgow, there not being sufficient grass for the horses in the Highlands. Colonel
Pride's regiment re-inforced the troops, who were much
harassed by long marches, "ranging up and down the
Highlands" in pursuit of Middleton's forces, which consisted of several thousand men. During these operations, June 14th.
Monck took the Island of Loch Tay and Balloch,[1] Wee-
mys, and Garth Castles: the last was destroyed. In the
MS. Lansdowne, No. 571. fol. 102., the capture of Loch
Tay is thus noticed, in a letter written by William Clarke.

"Sir,
" This day the Isle of Loughtay was surrendered to the
" Generall uppon granting their bagge, baggage, provi-
" sions, and armes, to march with English prison" they
" had; and likewise this day, the enemy quitted Garth
" Castle upon the approach of a party of horse, which
" were to sumon it; Glenochies howse, Weems and the
" Isle in Loughtay are garrison'd by Capt. Dennis and
" Capt. Beake's two companies; to-morrow we march for
" Loughnes.
" S$^r$, I only desire yo$^r$ care of the inclosed,
" and remaine
" Yo$^r$ Serv$^t$,
" Wm. Clarke."

" From the Camp, near Balloch,
" in Broad Albin,
" 14th June, 1654."

---

[1] Now called Taymouth, and principal seat of the Breadalbane
family.

1654.
June. " On their entrance to the Clan Cameron's bounds,
" they burnt all the houses in their way or near it.
" Glengarry's new house was also burnt."

June 26th. When at Glensinnick, in Kintale, ' " a violent storm
" drove five hundred cattle (cows, goat, and sheep,) into
June 27th. " their quarters."  The army, on their march to Eoghel,
burnt all the houses of the Mac Martins, and those in the
June 30th. Seaford's country.  The last eight miles to Browling
" was so boggy, that 100 baggage-horses were left be-
" hind, and many others bogged ; never was an army,
" till this summer, known to pass that way."

Middleton, anxious to avoid Monck, then on his march
from Strafillan to Glenlyon, was surprised near Loch
July 19th. Garry, and utterly defeated by Morgan, who had been
detached by a different route.

In this action the Royal Standard and nineteen other
colours fell into the hands of the victors.  General Middleton's charger and sumpter-horse, with his private papers,
commission, and correspondence with the King, were also
taken ; the General himself narrowly escaping.[1]

Aug. 2nd. Monck returned to St. Johnstone's and Stirling for
provisions, then marched on Aberfoile in pursuit of the
Earls of Glencairn and Athol ; who, with other Chiefs,
were permitted to send in their submission, on having their
lives and property secured.

A Court-Martial, which was held on the first of August

---

| [1] KILLED. | TAKEN. | |
|---|---|---|
| Major Gen[l]. Dylar | 400 Horse | |
| Colonel Hume | Colonel Crauford | |
|   ,,  Ennis |   ..  Meldrum | 2500 men were totally routed. |
|   ,,  Grimes | Major Forbes | |
| L[t]. Col. Ogleby |     23 other Officers, | |
| Major Brown | and subsequently L[t]. | |
|   9 Captains | Col. Peter Hay and | |
|   50 Men | Capt. Graham | |

at Stirling, affords a specimen of the discipline of the period. " Yesterday we had a Court-Martial for trying " stragglers : eleven came within the compass of the third " article of duties in marching : two did draw lots, which " fell upon the most notorious stragglers, and those who " were worst characterized ; the one to die, which the " General thought fit; who was acquainted with the pro- " ceedings of the Court, and gave order touching those " two, that they should cast lots again, and he upon " whom of the two the lot fell should suffer. This day " the execution is to be done." The same occurrence is thus reported, with some embellishment, in other periodi- cals of that time. " From Scotland our Scout[1] bringeth " intelligence that some soldiers being tryed by a Court of " War for certain misdemeanours by them committed, " were adjudged to cast dice for their lives; but one " amongst the rest, being a man of some new coyned " estate, lamented his most unhappy fortune pitifully, " which a soldier perceiving, came to him, saying—' If " thou wilt give me £5, I'le throw' for thee, for I have " obtained leave ;' and being assented to, he took the " dice, and throwing sink cater, escaped the halter. His " captain, standing by, said—' Oh, suppose you had " thrown alms ace, and so have lost your life ?'—' Oh, " Sir, I have hazarded my life many a time for 8d. a " day, and might I not as well adventure to do 't for " £5 a minute ?—'tis  a a   pay, Captain; nothing " venture nothing have.' "g ll nt

1654.<br>Aug. 2nd.

At the end of the month, Monck's head-quarters were again at Dalkeith House. Several Officers in Scotland were ; arrested by him for devising a scheme to seduce

1654-5.<br>January.

---

[1] A periodical paper called " The Scout."

the army,[1] and drive them from their allegiance to the Commonwealth; for which purpose the assassination of Monck was in contemplation. The principal officers seized were, Major-General Overton; Major Bramston, of Colonel Morgan's regiment; Major Holmes, of the General's own regiment; Captain Hedsworth, of Sir William Constable's regiment; Mr. Oates,[2] chaplain of Colonel Pride's regiment, with several other officers. Major-General Overton[3] was sent on board the Basing frigate, and on his arrival in London committed to the Tower. A Court-Martial assembled in February for the trial of the conspirators, at which Major Bramston,[4] Lieutenants Braymer, Rawson, Cornet Coombs, and three Quarter-Masters of Colonel Lord Charles Howard's regiment were cashiered, and Chaplain Oates was dismissed the service.

Two companies of Monck's regiment, and two of Colonel Salmon's, marched from Edinburgh to Berwick to strengthen that garrison. In August, the regiments in

---

[1] On Monday, December 18, 1654, Parliament resolved, the present establishment of the army should be 20,000 foot and 10,000 horse and dragoons, and the assessment £60,000 per month for their maintenance.

[2] Father of the infamous Titus Oates.

Major Holmes seems to have been acquitted, as he signed the address to the Lord Fleetwood and the General Council of Officers, as Major of Monck's regiment. See Appendix, No. 5.

[3] Overton was afterwards, in 1659, restored to his rank and pension: a new regiment was given him, and he was made governor of Hull.

[4] This officer was soon after appointed lieutenant-colonel of a regiment drawn out of the forces in Scotland for service in Jamaica, under the command of Lieutenant-General Brayne, then Governor of Lochaber: they embarked September, 1656.

Scotland were reduced twenty men per company, leaving 1655.<br>August. each regiment eight hundred strong.[1]

A writer, in one of the diurnals before mentioned, says, " The forces are peaceably settled in their winter-quarters, " and not any visible enemy at all stirring, although this " year there was not any Captain of the Watch as for- " merly, yet I hear not so much as the stealing of a cow " or horse from the Lowlanders, even so that thro' Pro- " vidence Scotland is wholly brought into the most " peaceable condition that ever it was since the memory " of this age." The following extracts from letters in- serted in the Mercurius Politicus confirm this represen- tation.

" Edinburgh, 25th of December, 1655. — Since the December. " late Lord Chancellor, Lord Loudoun, his bringing in " and surrendering the old great Seal of Scotland, as he " was required by an order of the Council here, I can " tell you little from this barren country which is of " public concernment, save that General Munk having " secured the Earl of Glencarn for holding correspondence " with Charles Stuart and his party, and endeavouring to " raise new broils here, he the said Earl is clapped up " close prisoner in the Castle of Edinburgh."

" Edinburgh, 22nd January, 1655-6.—There is a very 1655-6.<br>January.

---

[1] " Leith, 17th August.

" The businesse of disbanding twenty souldiers in each company " of the several regiments in Scotland, or rather reducing the regi- " ments to 800, goes on apace, and divers are daily disbanded, " many of which would be ready to go for the West Indies, if " there were shipping here provided for them."—*Perfect Proceed- ings of State Affairs*, Aug. 16 to 23, 1655.

" Dalkeith, 11th Sept. 1655.

" The work of reducement is now quite over here."—*Mercurius Politicus*, from 13th to 20th Sept. 1655.

1655-6.
January.

" peaceable spirit in the generality of the people, so that
" much news cannot be looked for hence while things are
" so.   General Monk is considering of sending some of
" the forces that have had their time of more warm and
" convenient quarters in the Lowlands, to relieve their
" brethren, who have taken their turns in the remote Isles
" and cold Highlands, and to send a convenient recruit of
" provisions and necessaries of all kinds with them."

1656.
March.

" Leith, 31st March, 1656.—Since the taking of Bruce
" by a party from St. Johnstone's, we hear not of any
" offering to stir about the Hills.   I believe no story can
" tell us of the like universal composure and calmness in
" this nation."

August.

The public tranquillity continued undisturbed ; and in
the month of August the City of Edinburgh " made a
" gallant entertainment for my Lord Broghill (one of their
" burgesses), the Lord General Monk, and the rest of
" the Council, the Judges, Commissioners at Leith, and
" divers officers of the army.   The place of reception was
" in the Parliament House, it being the first entertainment
" of that nature since the late King was entertained there."

1657.
July 7th.

A letter [1] from Edinburgh thus describes the state of
affairs :—" Military action or news, you can expect none
from hence, for all is in peace and quiet here."   On the
fifteenth of the same month, Cromwell [2] was proclaimed, in
the capital of Scotland, Lord Protector, having been this
year " inaugurated anew in Westminster Hall, after the

---

[1] See Appendix, Letter from Monck, No. 4.
[2] Sir John Freswick, Bart. in his " Respublica," in the list of
persons who walked in the procession at the installation of Oliver
Cromwell in Westminster Hall on June twenty-sixth, 1657, has
inserted the name of George Lord Monch, Commander in Chief of
the Forces in Scotland ; whence it would appear that Monck had
gone to London for the occasion.

" most solemn and most pompous manner. The two re-
" giments quartered in town (Edinburgh) were drawn up
" with their colours flying. They made a guard all the
" length of the High Street ; the great guns from the
" Castle and the Abbey were discharged. After all, a
" banquet was prepared. A great many officers of the
" army attended the procession, and the Marshall General
" before them."

At this period, addresses were sent by every regiment in
the army to the Lord Protector; among them was one
from " the Lord General Monk's regiment of foot, and
Colonel Talbot's," both of which were quartered in Edinburgh. Monck, from his services, had become so great a
favourite [1] with the people, and the troops under his command, that it occasioned much uneasiness to Cromwell.
In one of his letters to Monck he writes, "there be that
" tell me that there is a certain cunning fellow in Scotland,
" called George Monk, who is said to be in wait there to
" introduce Charles Stuart : I pray you use your diligence
" to apprehend him, and send him up to me."

Cromwell died on the third of September, the anniversary of the battles of Dunbar and Worcester. On the
ninth, Richard, the son of Cromwell, was proclaimed in
Scotland Lord Protector by order of Monck and the
Council; but, in the early part of the subsequent year,
the new Protector was compelled to dissolve the Parliament he had so recently called together, and in April
resigned his office.

---

[1] Monk was soon noticed for his talents and calm deliberative
valour : without ostentation, expense, or caresses, merely by his
humane and equal temper, he gained the good-will of his soldiers,
who, with a mixture of familiarity, good-nature, and affection,
called him honest George Monk.—*Hume*, vol. vii. page 307.

# CHAPTER VI.

Long Parliament revived—Letter to the Speaker from Monck and other officers of his own regiment—Charles prepares to invade England—Committee of Safety—Officers called into the House to receive their commissions from the Speaker; Lieutenant-Colonel William Gough, of Monck's own regiment, one of them—Names of officers in Monck's regiments of foot and horse read to the House—Lenthall the Speaker arrested—Monck musters his own and Morgan's regiments to acquaint them it was his determination to support Parliament—Monck secures several strongholds in Scotland—Letters, in which are detailed accounts of Monck's proceedings—Parliament dissolved—Monck and his army declare for the Parliament—Lambert begins his march towards Scotland—Commissioners of the Militia of London, and several Members of the Committee of Safety, dread the results of Monck's proceedings—Officers sent by Monck to treat with the Committee of Safety—Names of officers who abandoned Monck—His army assembles at Coldstream.

1659.
May 9th.

THE Long Parliament being revived, a letter[1] was read from Monck and the army in Scotland, directed to the Speaker, expressive of their entire concurrence with the army in England, and great anxiety that the same Parliament should continue its labours. This address was

---

[1] Another letter was afterwards addressed by Monck and the Council of Officers in Scotland to Lord Fleetwood and the General Council of Officers in England. See Appendix, No. 5.

signed by Monck and twenty-five officers. The following 1659.<br>May 9th.
names appear from Monck's own regiment :—

George Monck.
Abraham Holmes, (Major.)
Ethelbert Morgan, (Captain.)
Robert Winter, (Capt.-Lieut.)

Also of his regiment of horse :—

Thomas Johnson, (Captain.)
Jeremiah Smith, (Capt. and Adjt.)
Anthony Nowers, (Lieut.)

Early in May, Parliament received authentic information that Charles meditated the invasion of England with
a considerable force, which had been collected in Flanders,[1] and measures were promptly taken to oppose him.
A Committee of Safety was appointed, who recommended[2]
" that Commissioners be authorised to nominate the Com-
" mission Officers of the Forces, and present the same
" to the Parliament for their approbation, after which the
" Commander-in-Chief do issue their commissions." Returns were made to the House, of all the officers then serving in the army; the name of every officer in each regiment
was read over, and either approved or disapproved. The
officers present in London were ordered to be in attend-
ance to receive their commissions from the Speaker, who
had previously signed them.[3] " The House being in-
" formed that divers Officers of the Army and of the
" Militia were at the door, they were called in ; and being
" come up at the clerk's table, Mr. Speaker acquainted
" them with the great trust reposed in them, and that the

---

[1] See Life of James II. from original Stuart MSS. by the Rev.
T. S. Clarke, LL.B. 4to. London, 1816. vol. i. pages 369—380.

[2] Journals of the House of Commons.

[3] A copy of the commission is printed in the Journals of the
House of Commons.

1659.
May.
" Parliament and Commonwealth expected faithfulness
" from them to the Parliament and Commonwealth : and
" thereupon Mr. Speaker delivered them their commis-
" sions." Amongst those who attended and were called in
on the thirtieth of July, was Lieutenant-Colonel William
Gough, lieutenant-colonel to Monck's regiment.

July.
    It was " ordered, that such Commission Officers of the
" Army as are already passed, or hereafter shall pass, the
" Parliament's approbation, who are absent in Scotland,
" whose commissions are not, nor cannot conveniently be
" delivered to them in the usual way in the House, their
" commissions shall be delivered by such commissioners
" as shall be appointed for the government of Scotland,
" the said officers declaring or signing the engagement
" appointed by the Act of Indemnity, which these said
" Commissioners are to certify to the Parliament or Coun-
" cil of State." [1]

At a meeting of the Parliament on Saturday the thirtieth
of July, " Sir Arthur Haslerig reports from the Commis-
" sioners for nominating commissioned officers, a list of
" persons for commission officers " for the regiment of
foot under Monck.

| Colonel and Captain. | Lieutenants. | Ensigns. |
|---|---|---|
| George Monk | Capt. Lt. Rob. Winter | Wm. Brangman |
| Lt.-Colonel and Captain. | | |
| Wm. Gough | Joseph Pellow | John Rooke |
| Major and Captain. | | |
| [2] • • • • • | Robert Carter | John Saunders |
| Captains. | | |
| Thadbert Morgan | John Painter | James Hubbard |

---

[1] Journal of the House of Commons.

[2] Abraham Holmes, the Major on this day, was appointed Lieutenant-Colonel and Captain to Colonel Roger Sawrey's regiment of

| | | | |
|---|---|---|---|
| Francis Nicholls | Thomas Mansfield | Thomas Goodwin | 1659. July. |
| George Parker | John Wells | John Clarke | |
| Benjamin Groome | Nicholas Parker | Robert Burrowes | |
| Geo. Walton | James Wilson | Roger Lawrence | |
| Roger Hachman | Augustine Richards | John Harrison | |
| Wm. Downes | Christopher Browne | Wm. Underhill | |

Chaplain, Mr. Price.[1]

Surgeon, Nicho. Priddy.

Quarter-Master and Marshall, Henry Dennis.

" Which persons' names were read, and every one of them
" being put to the question, were approved of." [2]

" Monday, September the 19th; at the meeting of Par- September.
" liament, Sir Arthur Haslerig reports from the Committee
" appointed to nominate commission officers, a list of
" names of officers for Colonel George Monk's regiment
" of horse, which was read, and upon the question ap-
" proved of, viz.

| Colonel. | Lieutenants. | Cornets. | Quarter Masters. |
|---|---|---|---|
| George Monck | Captain-Lieut. John Coventry | Phil. Wilkinson | Thos. Gallant |
| Major. | | | |
| Ralph Knight | George Parke | Edward Austin | Richard Hooker |
| Captains. | | | |
| Robert Glynne | Anth. Nowers | Jas. Horingold | Edward Crispe |
| Thomas Johnson | John Smith | Rd. Shepheard | John Smith |
| [3]Jeremiah Smith | Peter Wilmot | Henry Smales | Daniel Dalton |
| Thos. Symmell | Christ. Keymer | Thos. Roper | Wm. Grant |

Surgeon, Thos. Reves."

On the thirteenth of October the Speaker (Lenthall) was October.

---

[1] Author of " The Restoration."

[2] General Ludlow, in his Memoirs, states that no officer in Monck's regiment was removed, " all of whom were old officers."

[3] This officer was Adjutant " of Horse" to Monck, as is stated by Gumble, Price, May, and Hobbes.

arrested by order of the Military Council, consisting of Lambert and the other officers, whose troops had been dismissed by Parliament for presenting an address which was not approved by the House.   Monck took advantage of this transaction to disclose his intentions; and wrote a letter to the officers who styled themselves a Committee of Safety, " importing somewhat of dissatisfaction in himself " and some of the officers of the army in Scotland, in re- " ference to the things newly done in England."   They sent some " persons to give him an account of the reason " of their late actings, some part of Monk's letter seeming " to intimate as if he wanted information touching the " state of affairs."   On the nineteenth of October he mus- tered his own regiment and Colonel Morgan's in the High Street of Edinburgh; from thence he marched to the Grey Friars' Church, where he told his officers he was resolved to make the military power subordinate to the civil, and that since they had protection and entertainment from the Parliament, it was their duty to serve and obey them against all opposition.   The officers and soldiers unani- mously declared they would live and die with him. [1] Shortly after, intelligence came from Scotland of Monck's " having secured divers of the strong holds of that nation, " and several officers of his own in Tantallon Castle, who " could not concur with him."   The writer adds, " He " hath possessed himself of Berwick, in which Colonel " Cobbet was awhile detained by Lieutenant-Colonel " Mayr, the governor; but afterwards coming to know " that the Colonel was going with letters to General " Monk from the officers of the army in England, he per- " mitted him to proceed on his journey."

The following " letter from a person of quality in

[1] History of Illustrious Persons, vol. II. page 161.

1659.
October.

Edinburgh to an Officer of the Army," gives a further account of General Monck's proceedings, dated twenty-fifth of October, 1659.[1] " Though I have not been want-" ing (by using various wayes and means) to impart to " you the state of affairs here, yet lest there should be a " miscarriage in all or any of them, I thought it a duty " incumbent upon me, in this our day, to dispatch a sure " messenger to Newcastle, where I trust he may meet " with you, to give you a full account of things as they " stand here; who is able to make you an ample relation, " and to whom I desire you would give credit in what he " shall impart to you; and lest he should omit any thing " of moment, I shall, as briefly as I can, hint it to you in " these following lines.    Upon Tuesday last, the 18th " instant, the General had notice that the Parliament was " dissolved.    Whereupon he called Colonel Wilkes, and " Captains Miller, Morgan, Hubblethorn, Jeremiah Smith, " Gumble, and Lieut.-Colonel Cloberry, (who had been " with him two or three days before,) to consult what to do; " and it was resolved that he, with the army under his " command, should declare for the Parliament against the " proceedings of the army in England, and for the better " effecting thereof, agreed to turn out all that should " oppose the design.    The next day he came to Edin-" burgh, where he had appointed his own regiment and " Colonel Talbot's to be in armes.[2]    The latter had orders " to have lighted matches, powder, and bullets; but his " own had not.    When he came to them, he declared to

[1] Printed by Sarah Griffin for Thomas Hewer, London, 1659.

[2] " He came to Edinburgh, where were usually quartered two " regiments of foot, excepting some few companies, who were sent " out upon particular service, ready to be remanded and ex-" changed.  The regiments was his owne and Colonel Talbott's." —MS. Harl. 4178.

" them that a factious party of the army in England had
" interrupted the Parliament, and that he resolved with
" the army under his command to stand to the Parliament
" in opposition to them, and expected that they would
" stand by him accordingly ; declaring that he would
" satisfie them all their arrears ; at which they were made
" to shout, and gave him three volleys of shot : which
" being done, he caused Captain Parker, Hatchman,
" Stone, Lieutenant Carter, Wells, Wilson, Lindon, and
" all the rest of the Anabaptists officers, (except Groome
" and Walton,) to be secured.  Then coming to Leith,
" (the regiment of Colonel Wilkes being drawn up,) he
" declared the same things to them, and past from them
" with the like ceremonies ; and Colonel Wilkes, for a
" farewell, gave him 15 or 17 great guns from the citadel.
" Of whose regiment, the General caused to be secured,
" Major Knoles, Lieutenant Burrel, Lieutenant Hughes,
" Ensign Wilkes, and Ensign Wood.   Having thus
" secured these three regiments, and placed other officers
" in the roomes of those whom he turned out, he dis-
" patched letters to Lieutenant-Colonel Young, of Colonel
" Cobbet's regiment, and Lieutenant-Colonel Keyn and
" Major Kelke, of Pearson's [1] regiment, to come over and
" consult with him about some weighty affairs ; and when
" they came, he clapt up Lieut.-Colonel Young and
" Major Kelke ; and at the same time received adver-
" tisement from Colonel Read that he and his regiment
" was at his service, as likewise the same from Colonel
" Fairfax.
      " Upon the 21st instant, he marched with some troops
" of horse and some companies of foot to Lithgowe, in
" order (as it was thought) to have gone to Ayre ; but

---

[1] See a letter from this officer, page 77.

" receiving intelligence there that Lieutenant-Colonel
" Holmes was got thither, he did not proceed for fear he
" should meet with a repulse, which in the beginning of
" this enterprize would have been of ill consequence to
" his affairs. So that upon the 22nd he retreated to
" Edinburgh again with his forces, where he created new
" officers by commission, under his own hand and seal;
" viz. Colonel Cloberry he made Colonel of Cobbet's
" regiment, Hatt Lieutenant-Colonel, and Dennis Major.
" To his own regiment he hath made Morgan Lieutenant-
" Colonel, Nichols Major, and Winter Captain of Holmes
" his company.

" Collins, of Wilkes' regiment, hath Hatchman's com-
" pany. Bishop, the farrier, is a Lieutenant; Sherman (one
" of our cashiered waiters) is made an Ensign, and all the
" rest of the vacant places supplied by some such men.
" Hublethorn is made Lieutenant-Colonel, and Emerson
" Major of Talbot's regiment. All the forces hereabouts
" being by this means at his devotion; he being assured
" of the rest in all other parts but Ayre. He resolves to
" draw all to a rendezvous in and about Edinburgh against
" the last of this month at furthest, except such as must
" be left in the garrisons, (which he intends shall be but
" few,) and expects to make 5000 foot and 800 horse,
" with which he intends (as it is said) immediately to
" march for England. Witter commands in the Citadel
" of St. Johnston's, and Keyn is this day gone over to
" fetch hither the rest of that regiment; Fairfax's, Cob-
" bet's, and Read's are already on their march hither-
" wards. This day, Captain Groome told me that both
" he and Walton would throw up their commissions, as
" many that are inferior officers and private soldiers (who
" had the face of honesty) have already done. The General
" hath wrote three letters, one to the Speaker, another to
" the Lord Fleetwood, and a third to the Lord Lambert,

" which he hath put in print, and are herewith sent.[1] He
" hath also put forth a declaration, which you shall re-
" ceive from the bearer, signed by Clark in behalf of the
" rest ; when none was at the contriving of it, but him-
" self, Wilks, Morgan, Emerson, Smith, and Gumble.
" There is likewise a letter he hath written to the
" Churches, drawn by Mr. Collins, stufft with much of
" Booth's language ; but I doubt I shall not get it for
" you before the bearer goes away. All these printed
" papers he is dispatching away in whole bundles to Hull
" by the Pearl frigate, whereof Captain Nixon is com-
" mander, who sailes to-morrow if wind and weather
" serve. Holmes came very safe to Ayre, though a party
" of horse was at his heeles. That place, he and Colonel
" Sawry with all the officers resolve to keep till they
" receive orders from the Council of Officers, as I was
" assured by letters from themselves to me the last
" night. The General threatens that he will quarter some
" horse about that garrison, and will not let them have a
" penny of money. Major Kelke desires that some of
" them will acquaint his wife he is in health, and that his
" son is this day arrived safe from London, which I
" entreat you will signifie to her accordingly.

" I had almost forgot to tell you that the General hath
" secured Barwick, Lieut.-Colonel Mears having received
" in there two of his foot companies and one of horse.
" And as Colonel Cobbet and Mr. Brown passed by there,
" they were detained prisoners till the General sent a
" party of horse[2] for them. This night they are both
" come with a guard to Edinburgh, where (I heard from

---

[1] The letters are printed in the journals of the day.

[2] Commanded by Capt. Johnson, (of Monck's regiment of horse,)
who brought Cobbet prisoner to the General, and by him committed
to the Castle of Edinburgh.—MS. Harleian. 4178.

" Colonel Goffe, Mr. Caryl, and Mr. Barker (ministers of
" the Scotch Church), began a journey to Scotland to
" make application to General Monk, and demonstrate
" to him the state of affairs in England, and thereupon to
" mediate with him for avoiding the effusion of blood, and
" for preventing the manifold mischiefs that must ensue
" by a new civil war.

" The Officers here have written a new letter to General
" Monk and the officers under his command in Scotland,
" to expostulate with them touching the necessity of
" brotherly union."

The Commissioners of the Militia of London sent a
letter of expostulation to General Monck. Besides which,
several members of the Committee of Safety, viz. "the
" Lord Fleetwood, Lord Whitelock, General Disbrowe,
" and Alderman Titchbourne, gave a meeting to the Lord
" Mayor and Court of Aldermen," to represent the nature
of General Monck's proceedings, and the necessity of
securing the peace of the City: on which the Court of
Aldermen declared their readiness to concur in all expedient measures.

It was announced from Scotland, that the officers
secured by General Monck in Tantallon Castle were by
his order removed from thence to the Bass Island, and
that Colonel Cobbet was still imprisoned in Edinburgh
Castle: it was further stated, that four troops of horse
under Major Knight, and six companies of foot under
Captain Miller of General Monck's regiment, had marched
from Berwick to Newcastle,[1] which place they were prevented entering by Colonel Lilburn: they then retreated
to Alnwick, till remanded to their former station.

" Whitehall, November 3rd.—This day the Lord Lam-

---

[1] MS. Harleian. No. 4178.

" Of General Monk's own Regiment of Foot :—

| | | | |
|---|---|---|---|
| Lt.-Col. Gough,[1] | Lieut. Carter, | Ens$^a$ Lawrence, | Serj$^t$ Jennings, |
| Major Holmes, | ,, Wells, | Q$^r$-M$^r$ Dennis, | ,, Bradford, |
| Capt. Parker, | ,, Wilson, | Serj$^t$ Grange, | Corp$^l$ Cox, |
| ,, Hackman, | ,, Brown, | ,, Lawes, | ,, Nichols, |
| ,, Walton, | ,, Richards | ,, Peck, | ,, Hidge, |
| | | | Gunsmith, John Nichols. |

" Of General Monck's Regiment of Horse :—

Lieutenant Smith,[1]
,, Keymer,[1]
Cornet Smalles.[1]

| [2] Of Col. Wilks's Reg$^t$., 5 Officers, 2 Serj$^s$. | [2] Of Col. Fairfax's, 12 Officers, 5 Serj$^t$., 5 Corp$^ls$., 1 Drum$^r$., 1 Chaplain. | [2] Of Col. Smith's, 5 Officers. |
|---|---|---|
| [2] Of Col. Morgan's Reg$^t$., 1 Captain with his whole Troop. | [2] Of Col. Talbot's Reg$^t$., 10 Officers, 1 Surgeon, 1 Serj$^t$., 3 Corp$^ls$. | [2] Of Col. Saunders's Reg$^t$., 2 Officers, 4 Quarter - Masters, 2 Corp$^ls$. |
| [2] Of Col. Read's Reg$^t$., 2 Officers, 1 Corp$^l$. | [2] Of Col. Saurey's Reg$^t$., 2 Officers, 1 Chaplain. | [2] Of Col. Pierson's Reg$^t$., 16 Officers, 4 Serj$^s$., 1 Chaplain. |
| [2] Of Col. Cobbet's Reg$^t$., 18 Officers. | [2] Of Col. Twisleton's Reg$^t$., 5 Officers, 56 Troopers. | [2] Berwick Officers, 8 Officers, 1 Serj$^t$., 1 Drum$^r$." |

General Monck, in his letter to Lord Fleetwood, from Edinburgh, dated November the twenty-fourth, acqui-

---

[1] Absent in London.

[2] The names of all these officers are stated in the " Intelligencer " and other Journals.

1659.
November. esces in what his Commissioners had done, and proposes that two more may be added; and further, that they should meet at Newcastle to conclude whatever was left unfinished. Alnwick was afterwards fixed on as the place of meeting, and five from each party accordingly met

Dec. 5th. there. " In December, General Monck was at Berwick, which place he intended making his head-quarters," and on the eighth his army assembled at Coldstream, where they remained till the end of the month.

Dec. 15th. At Newcastle, great discontent prevailed : the report sent up says, " many have declared that they will never " engage against the Parliament; and the soldiers gene- " rally say they will never fight against General Monck, " but leave their officers to dispute their own quarrel."

The writer of a letter from Berwick, at this period, thus expresses himself: " His Excellency the Most Re- " nowned and ever to be Honored General Monk, the " restorer of the liberties of this nation, is here, and all " his army quartering upon the borders: he is very " resolute and firm to his declaration. Colonel Fairfax " and Colonel Lydcot are added to the three Commis- " sioners formerly appointed by his Excellency and the " Officers of Scotland; but the first instruction before " any other is treated on, as a preliminary point, is the " restoring the Parliament."

Dec. 23rd. The troops in London declared for the Parliament, and assembled before the Speaker's house in Chancery Lane.

Dec. 29th. The following account from General Monck's quarters at Coldstream arrived in London. " His Exc' hath two " designs in agitation, and if either of them succeed, " we will break my Lord Lambert's forces : one of them " will be put in practice this week, and the other the " next; and then we shall leave him no place to nestle " in but Newcastle, and in a while we shall ferret him

" from thence. We are here sixty foot companies, and
" four and twenty troops of horse : and a regiment of foot
" and two troops of horse are raising for us in Northum-
" berland.' We may perceive by this express from this

---

¹ Gumble, page 187, gives the following account of some of the
troops who accompanied Monck to London.

" Of the horse there was his own regiment, commanded by Major
" Johnston, an honest stout man.

" Major-General Morgan's: this had been sinful dragoons, but
" now converted into troops ; yet some turned apostates.

" Colonel Sir Ralph Knight, this was Colonel Sanders his
" regiment.

" Colonel Sir John Clobery; his was Colonel Twisleton's regi-
" ment, and had formerly been Colonel Bossiter's; with him, and
" under him, accounted brave, but now degenerated, till it was
" headed and recruited by a gallant new colonel.

" Of the foot there was the General's own regiment, which was
" almost totally purged of its old officers.

" Major-General Morgan's regiment of foot, which had been
" Daniel's, now given him for his service at this time.

" Colonel Charles Fairfax his regiment.

" Colonel Read his regiment.

" Colonel Lidcot's regiment.

" Colonel Hubblethorn's, the brave Black colours, who were
" worthy of the best titles that can be given; yet all did like men
" of honour, especially Colonel Mayer, Major Miller, Lieut.-
" Colonel Witter, Lieut.-Colonel Bannister, Major Dennis, Lieut.-
" Colonel Read, Lieut.-Colonel Mutlow, Major John Clark,
" Captain Mansfield, Captain Winter, Captain Mutlow, Captain
" Peters, Captain Hewson, Lieut.-Colonel Hatt, Colonel Hughs,
" Colonel Man, Colonel Robson, Lieut.-Colonel Morgan, Lieut.-
" Colonel Rogers, Lieut.-Colonel Emerson, Lieut.-Colonel Hill,
" Major Farmer, Major Durdo, Major Nichols, Major Baylie,
" Captain Cliston, Captain Newman, Captain Cooper, Captain
" Seymour, Captain Francis, Captain Kellie, Captain Collins,
" Captain Thompson, Captain Saunders, Captain Paddon, Captain
" Nours, Captain Simnell, Captain Barnadiston, Captain Hacker,
" Captain Downs, Major Friar, Captain Man, Captain Lovel,

" faithful army, that all the divisions in Lambert's army
" have been probably the effects of the Lord General
" Monck's diligence and wisdom."

Early in January a messenger arrived in town with letters from General Monck, who was at Kelsal in Scotland,
" wherein is signified the continued resolution and good
" condition of his army for the Parliament; but the same
" messenger giveth an account of this great news. That
" as he came on the road by North Allerton, he found
" Major-General Lambert was there with only about fifty
" horse, the rest of the forces having, upon such notice of
" what passed here, submitted to the authority of Parlia-
" ment and declared for the Parliament, as himself also
" hath done; and the forces are all dispersed into several
" quarters, expecting orders for the service of the Com-
" monwealth.    The same messenger coming also by
" York saith, that the Lord Fairfax with about two or
" three hundred horse, and Colonel Lilburn with some
" troops, had both of them declared for the Parliament,
" together with the city of York itself."—" This is cer-
" tain ; for late this night also, letters are come from the
" Lord Fairfax himself, dated Poppleton, Jan. 1st, to the
" Speaker, signifying the same, which letters are this
" Thursday to be communicated to the Parliament, toge-
" ther with another letter from the Lord Lambert, dated
" North Allerton, 31st of December.    These letters con-
" firm the messenger's account."

---

" Captain Wilkinson, and many others whom I have forgotten; but
" all deserve to have their names remembered at Coldstream in a
" table, as well as William the Conqueror's assistants in the Abbey
" of Battel."

# CHAPTER VII.

Monck commences his march from Coldstream—Gives the command of his own regiment to Captain Morgan—Commissioners meet the army near Leicester—The Coldstreamers enter London —Parliament orders Monck to restore order in the City—Monck and Montague nominated Generals of the Fleet—Lambert escapes from the Tower—Ingoldsby defeats Lambert—Granville delivers a letter from Charles to the Parliament—Charles proclaimed King—Colours captured at Preston, Dunbar, and Worcester, removed from Westminster Hall—Army encamps at Blackheath —Charles's triumphal entry into London—Monck created Duke of Albemarle—Charles reviews his troops—Army disbanded, with the exception of the Lord General's own regiment—Insurrection of Venner—Commissioners disband the Lord General's regiment of foot, and they are immediately after formed as an extraordinary guard to the Royal person—List of the household troops — Royal regiment of guards under Lord Wentworth — Charles II.'s procession through the City to be crowned.

ALL arrangements being completed, on Sunday, the first of January, Monck commenced his celebrated march from Coldstream, by ordering his infantry to cross the Tweed. He had previously given the command of his own regiment to Captain Morgan, his Lieutenant-Colonel being absent ; the majority was bestowed by Monck on Captain Nichols, the officer who had held that commission not being in his confidence. On the second, he was at Wooler; next day he reached a small village on his way to Morpeth. Thence he marched to Newcastle, and remained there

"the foulness of the ways [1] may chance to hinder them
"from being so soon there as most men imagine." On the
twenty-third the Coldstreamers marched to Leicester.
Before they had entered the town, Mr. Scott and Mr.
Luke Robinson, Commissioners from the Parliament, "who
"had awaited his arrival in that city, went forth six miles
"from thence to meet General Monck. He marched with
"his own regiment, and a great train of his officers and
"gentlemen of the county attending him; the bells ring-
"ing in every town through which he passed : the rest of
"the army marched in such a manner as might least bur-
"then the country. As he passed to the place where he
"met the Parliament's Commissioners, the Irish brigade
"being drawn up gave a volley; and when the Commis-
"sioners drew near, as they alighted out of their coach,
"he, riding on horseback, at the same instant dismounted,
"and having saluted each other with all demonstrations of
"respect and courtesy, they all three went together into
"the coach. All the bells rang at their entrance, and
"the people flocked to behold them. He went with the
"Commissioners to their quarter, and supped with them
"there."—"To manifest the respects of this city to this
"honorable person," says the writer of the account, "the
"mayor, with all his brethren, in their gowns and forma-
"lities, went and presented him with a banquet, and a
"solemn profession of the high esteem they have of his
"great services performed for the Parliament and Com-
"monwealth." [2]

---

[1] During the march of the Coldstreamers to London, the ground
was the whole time covered with snow; " so that all their way they
had scarce yet seen the plain earth of their native country."—
*Skinner.*

[2] Monck was received in all the large towns through which he
passed on his line of march with similar marks of distinction.

" The most famous addresses of the countryes to Monck were at
Northampton and St. Albans."—MS. Harl. 4178.

Next day, Monck and the Commissioners arrived at Harborough : on the twenty-fifth they reached Northampton, on the twenty-sixth Stony Stratford, on the twenty-seventh Dunstable,[1] and St. Albans on the twenty-eighth ; whence Monck wrote to the Parliament, desiring that all the troops then in London might be removed to more distant quarters. The House was greatly perplexed at so unexpected a message. A meeting took place among the soldiers ; and one regiment, stationed in Somerset House, positively refused to give place to the Northern army. They afterwards deemed it more prudent to comply with
Monck's wishes. At Barnet he was informed of the tumultuous behaviour of the troops in Somerset House, and determined to hasten his march. This intelligence gave him but little concern, and on Friday the third of February he triumphantly entered the city. The regiments that had been obliged to quit London, as well as the Coldstreamers who accompanied Monck, were distributed in quarters according to the annexed list :—

" Regiments marched out of London, and distributed as " followeth :—

FOOT.

| | |
|---|---|
| Col. Eyre's Regiment. | Sandwich, Dover, Canterbury, Rye. |
| Col. Markham's Reg<sup>t</sup>. | Ipswich, Colchester, Sudbury. |
| Col. Streater's Reg<sup>t</sup>. | Buckingham, Northampton, Newark. |
| Col. Lord Fleetwood's late Reg<sup>t</sup>. | Hereford, Oxford, Worcester. |
| Col. Moss's Reg<sup>t</sup>. | Cambridge, Ely. |
| Col. Fitch's Reg<sup>t</sup>. | Exeter. |

---

[1] This day, General Monck's lady and his son arrived in apartments, which had been prepared for them at Whitehall, where she was received and congratulated by several people of distinction.— *Mercurius Politicus.*

HORSE.

Col. O Key's Reg<sup>t</sup>. { Bedford, Buckingham, Aylesbury, Northampton, Peterborough.

Col. Sir Arthur Haslerig's Reg<sup>t</sup>. } Reading, Oxford, Gloucester, Worcester, and Hereford.

Col. Sir Anthony Ashley Cooper's (late Lord Fleetwood's, Reg<sup>t</sup>.) } Basingstoke, Bath, Bristol, Salisbury.

Col. Riche's Reg<sup>t</sup>. { Ipswich, Colchester, Norwich, Bury, Yarmouth.

" The Horse and Foot that marched into London with " Gen<sup>l</sup> Monk, and distributed as followeth :—

FOOT.[1]

The Lord General's Regiment of Foot. } In St. James's and parts adjacent.

Col. Read's Reg<sup>t</sup>. { In Somerset House, the Strand, Long Acre, Covent Garden, and Martin's Lane.

Col. Lydcot's Reg<sup>t</sup>. { Thanet House, Peter House, and parts adjacent.

Col. Hubblethorn's Reg<sup>t</sup>. (late Col. Talbot's Reg<sup>t</sup>.)[2] } Holborn, Smithfield, and the parts adjacent.

HORSE.[3]

The Lord General's Reg<sup>t</sup>. of Horse. } In the Mews, and in the Strand.

Col. Knight's Reg<sup>t</sup>. (late Col. Saunders's Reg<sup>t</sup>.) { 4 Troops in King Street, and Tothill Street, Westminster; 2 Troops in Holborn.

Col. Cloberry's Reg<sup>t</sup>. (late Col. Twisleton's Reg<sup>t</sup>.) { 2 Troops in Southwark, 1 Troop in Bishopsgate St., 3 Troops in Smithfield and the parts adjacent.

Col. Farley's Reg<sup>t</sup>. in Southwark.
Col. Morley's  ,,  in the Tower. { Lately arrived from the Isle of Wight and Portsmouth.

---

[1] Total, forty companies—four thousand five hundred men.

[2] Gumble was chaplain to this regiment.—*Journal of the House of Commons.*

[3] Eighteen troops of one hundred men per troop, one thousand eight hundred men.

The Londoners were not so favourably inclined to the Royal cause as Monck anticipated; but he took precautionary measures to guard against the disaffected. For this purpose, the ordnance was requested to furnish a fresh supply of arms, in order that his regiment might be placed on the most efficient footing.[1]

Soon after the arrival of the Coldstreamers in London, General Monck received orders from Parliament to reduce the citizens to obedience, some of the principal of whom had shown a disposition to coalesce with the usurping Committee of Safety: accordingly, he led his army into the City, destroyed the gates, portcullises, and other means of defence,[2] which, as there was no danger of foreign invasion, could only have been made subservient to factious purposes. The troops then returned to their quarters.

The first act, therefore, of the regiment whose services are now recorded, on their arrival in the Metropolis, was to repress anarchy, to enforce due obedience to the laws, and secure that respect for the civil government, with which the welfare and happiness of a country are at all times so closely interwoven. Having deprived the military usurpers of their strong hold, Monck, two days after, justified himself to the Londoners, and gained their confidence, by explaining to them that his object was the security and settlement of the Commonwealth.

" These Coldstreamers,"[3] says Gumble, " were like " the nobles of Israel with whom Deborah was so much " in love, and of whom she sings in the Book of Judges, " because they offered themselves willingly among the

---

[1] See Appendix, No. 6.          [2] Clarendon, Rapin, Hume.
[3] Gumble, page 189.

" people, and jeoparded their lives unto death in the high
" places of the field.  Danger was these men's election;
" and though there was such a presence of God accom-
" panied them, that no blood was shed, yet they were
" ready to have spent to the last drop for the public
" safety."  The following orders and resolutions of Parliament show that Monck acted throughout with the entire concurrence of the House; for, whatever doubts the
old Republican members might entertain respecting Monck,
the usurpations of Lambert and his military council left
them no alternative.

" Thursday, the 29th of December, 1659.

" Resolved, That this House doth approve of what
" General Monk hath done in placing and displacing of
" officers."

" And it is
" Ordered, That the said respective officers placed by
" General Monk be, and are hereby confirmed, in their
" respective offices and places."

" Ordered, That the hearty thanks of this House be
" given unto General Monk for his fidelity and faithful
" service."

" Ordered, That a letter of thanks be sent to General
" Monk, and that the same be signed and sealed by
" Mr. Speaker with the seal of the Parliament; and that
" Mr. Scott and Mr. Martyn do draw the same."

" Friday, January 6th, 16$\frac{59}{60}$.

" A letter from General Monk, from Coldstream, of
" the 29th of December, 1659, was read."

" Ordered, That letters of thanks from the Parliament

" be written to General Monk, acknowledging his faithful
" service and high deservings, and that he, taking care for
" the safety and preservation of Scotland in his absence,
" be desired as speedily as he can to come up to Lon-
" don."

" Thursday, January 12th, 16$\frac{59}{60}$.
" A letter[1] from General Monk, from Newcastle, of the
" 6th of January, 16$\frac{59}{60}$, was read."
" Resolved, That the Parliament doth justify and ap-
" prove of what General Monk hath done, in taking up
" horses, and in his marching into England, and all other
" things by him acted and done in order to the service of
" the Parliament and Commonwealth."

" Wednesday, February the 22nd, 16$\frac{59}{60}$.[2]
" Ordered, That Sir William Wheeler do bring in a
" commission to constitute General George Monk, Cap-
" tain-General under the Parliament of all the land forces
" in England, Scotland, and Ireland."
The bill was read twice on Friday, the twenty-fourth of
February, and again on the following day, when it passed :
two members were then directed to present the act to
Monck.

" Friday, March the 2nd, 16$\frac{59}{60}$.
" Resolved, That commissions be granted under the

---

[1] This letter was brought by Mr. Gumble.
[2] Twenty-first of February, " the secluded members " having
signed the articles dictated by Monck, which may be seen in MS.
Harl. 4178. by Dr. Price, " were conducted by Adjutant Miller "
(of his own regiment) " to take their former places in the House of
Commons."

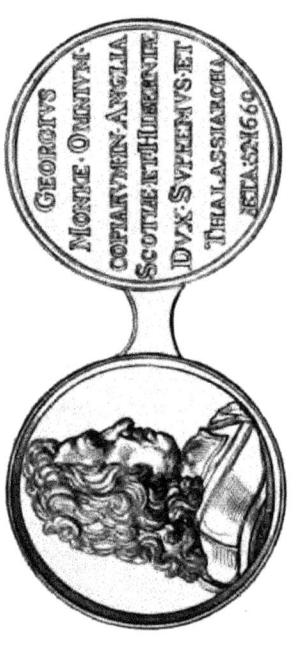

D

" Great Seal unto General George Monk and General
' Edward Montague, to be Generals and General, jointly
" and severally, of the Fleet, for the next summer's
" expedition : and that the Commissioners for the Great
" Seal do pass commissions to them under the great seal
" of England." [1]

After the dissolution of the Long Parliament by
Monck's intervention, Lambert, who had been confined
in the Tower, escaped.[2] His popularity with the Republican troops was such, that fresh disturbances might have
arisen. On the circumstance being made known to Monck,
he ordered Major Nichols, with four companies of his own
regiment, to the Tower.[3] This officer is spoken of as a
person in whose " fidelity, courage, and prudence, he
hath had long experience." Monck lost no time in detaching the remainder of his own regiment, under Ingoldsby,[4] with authority to take with him any troops that
might lie on his line of march. Lambert drew together
some horse and foot at Daventry; but Ingoldsby over-
took, defeated, and sent him back to the Tower, thirteen
days after his escape.[5]

Parliament assembled on the twenty-fifth of April, when
the members indulged in the bitterest invectives against
the murderers of their late Sovereign. Monck, intimately
acquainted with the feelings of the House, without giving

---

[1] See engraved medal D. This medal, by Simon, was struck
in honour of Monck at this time, and is said to be a good like-
ness.

[2] Phillips, page 698.; Rapin, 1660. vol. II. page 616.

[3] See Appendix, No. 7.

[4] Rapin, 1660. vol. II. page 616.; Clarendon, vol. III. part 2.
page 1100.

[5] Rapin, vol. II. page 616.

previous notice, sent Sir John Granville, a servant of
Charles, to the Commons, with a letter from the King,
when it was resolved, " That he have leave of this House
to return to his Majesty an answer thereunto." Granville
was called in, amidst the most enthusiastic acclamations,
and with one voice a committee was appointed, and the
letter immediately answered and published. " Monk, in
" the afternoon, convened his officers together, and caused
" the letter and declaration of his Majesty to be read unto
" them. His officers with great joy received it, and agreed
" unanimously upon a certain number to draw up an
" address to his Excellency, to be signed by them the
" morrow morning, to shew their full concurrence there-
" in." Both Houses of Parliament declared, " that ac-
" cording to the ancient and fundamental laws of this
" kingdom, the government is, and ought to be, by King,
" Lords, and Commons." No longer in a state of sus-
pense, the delight and exultation of the people were beyond all bounds. Oughtred,[1] the mathematician, is said
to have expired from joy on hearing the news: many
other instances are related of the enthusiasm felt by individuals.

Charles was proclaimed King in London, on the eighth
of May. On the tenth, the Commons resolved that the
colours captured at Preston, Dunbar, and Worcester,
hanging up in Westminster Hall, should be forthwith
taken down.

May 28th.    Monck's regiment encamped at Blackheath with the
rest of the army, in readiness to receive the King.[2]

---

[1] Oughtred, Rector of Albury.—*Evelyn's Memoirs*, vol. 1. page
295.

[2] At Blackheath the whole army was drawn up; when his Ma-

When Charles the Second landed, he was met by General Monck. " Never subject received such honours, " even to a kind of idolatry ; which he wisely declined, " knowing he was but a morning star to usher in a rising " sun." [1]   His cautious, firm, and judicious conduct, [2] during the short interval which had occurred since he left Coldstream, made him the instrument of restoring tranquillity to Great Britain, long distracted by violent convulsions, and by civil war, the greatest of all national calamities.

The regiment attended Charles's triumphal entry into London,[3] which event took place on the day he attained his thirtieth year.   A grant was made to Monck of seven thousand pounds per annum for himself and his heirs : he was created Baron Monck, Earl of Torrington, and Duke of Albemarle ; Knight of the Garter,[4] a Privy Counsellor, and Captain-General.[5]

---

jesty received them, giving out many expressions of his gracious favour to the army, which was received with loud shoutings and rejoycings.—*Triumphs of Charles*, by Heath, page 132.

[1] Gumble's Life of Monk, page 386.

[2] " 20th of February, 16⅗. The Republicans endeavoured to per-" suade Monk to take the government upon himself, which he " rejected : Sir Arthur Haslerig, to preclude the King's Restora-" tion, offered him 100,000 hands that should subscribe his title." —*British Chronologist*, 8vo. London, 1775.

[3] Hume, vol. VII. page 330. ; Rapin, vol. II. page 617.; Clarendon, vol. III. part 2. page 1170.

[4] He was made a Knight of the Garter at Canterbury.
The Dukes of York and Gloucester put on the Garter and George out of respect.—*Hist. Dict.* 1694.
His Majesty was pleased to invest the renowned General with the most honorable order of the Garter, putting it with his own hands round his neck.—*Triumphs of Charles*, by Heath, page 122.

[5] See Appendix, No. 9. for commission.

When Charles reviewed the troops, he was struck with their " beauty, discipline, and martial appearance," and felt inclined to retain them in his service : on reflection, however, it was thought that men who had fought under the Usurper, ought not to have that confidence placed in them to which they might otherwise be entitled : and an Act of Parliament was passed [2] for the " speedy disband-" ing of the army and garrisons of this kingdom." " The " regiments of the Duke of York and Gloucester, the " Lord General's of horse and foot, were to be the last " disbanded."

Previous to this, the army had been re-organized by the appointment of men of influence and loyalty to command the regiments ; the actual field-officers consenting to serve one step lower in their respective corps. The Lord General's regiment was an exception, as will be seen by the following statement in the " Mercurius Publicus :"—

From Thursday, 16th August, to Thursday, 23rd August, 1660.

" Saturday,.18th August, 1660.

" After so many changes of officers in several regiments, " you may now take a list of all the officers in his Excel-" lencies own regiment, both horse and foot, wherein " there is no mutation, his Grace having chosen such " approved officers as require no alteration."

---

[2] Received the Royal Assent in person, the 13th of September, 1660.

1660

| George Monk, Duke of Albemarle, &c. Capt. Gen. of all his Majesties Forces in England, Scotland, and Ireland ; Colonel of the regiment. | Capt. Lieut. John Paynter | Ensign Ralph Butcher |
|---|---|---|
| Lieut. Col. and Capt. Ethelbert Morgan | Lieut. Tho. Goodwin | ,, Rd. Rowcastle |
| Major and Captain Francis Nichols | ,, John Saunders | ,, John Cobb |
| Captain John Miller (Adjutant General) | ,, Robert Cooper | ,, Edw. Basenet |
| Capt. Wm. Downs | ,, Wm. Underhill | ,, Mich. Adderses |
| ,, Robt. Winter | ,, James Hubbard | ,, John Clerk |
| ,, Tho. Mansfield | ,, John Rook | ,, Daniel Court |
| ,, John Collins | ,, John Harrison | ,, Tho. Figg |
| ,, John Peters | ,, Wm. Brangman | ,, Wm Mackerith |
| ,, John Mutlow | ,, Tho. Feiges | ,, John Balder (Waller) |

Chaplain, John Price.
Chyrurgeon, Nich. Priddy.
Quarter Master and Marshall, Rich. Collins.

" His Excellencies Regiment of Horse :—

| | Capt. Lieut. | Cornets | Quarter-masters |
|---|---|---|---|
| • • • • • | Phil. Wilkinson | John Maynard | Nich. Hudson |
| Major | Lieutenants | | |
| Tho. Johnson | John Cogan | John Smith | Tho. Aldy |
| Captains | | | |
| Tho. Symnell | Tho. Roper | Tho. Gallant | Hugh Whittle |
| Anv Nowers | Walt. Partridge | Dan. Smith | Benj. Serjeant |
| Peter Wilmot | William Grant | Daniel Dalton | Jos. Hurandel |
| John Paddon | Tho. Buller | John Britain | Obadiah Boole |

Chyrurgeon, Tho. Reeves.

Duke of Albemarle's troop appointed to be disbanded at Lewes, } January, 1660-1.

| Major Johnson's | do. | at Reading | .. |
|---|---|---|---|
| Capt. Symnell's | do. | at Ipswich | |
| ,, Paddon's | do. | do. | |
| ,, Wilmot's | do. | at Maidstone | |
| ,, Nowers' | do. | do. | |

At this period an Anabaptist of the name of Venner, with a few enthusiasts, fancied they were inspired, and, pretending to set up the kingdom of Christ with the sword, caused great alarm in the city.   Some soldiers sent against them were quickly routed.   These infatuated men imagined themselves invincible : they marched through the city, and eventually retired to Caen Wood.

The Duke of Albemarle ordered out two hundred of his own regiment, and a troop of horse under Colonel Sandys, who made several prisoners; the rest returned to the city, and on the ninth engaged in a furious contest with the newly-raised Trained City Bands.[1]   Twenty of his Majesty's Life Guard,[2] despatched by Albemarle under Colonel John Corbet, found the rebels in Wood Street, when nine of the Guard charged and dispersed them.   The gentlemen who charged were, Sir Horatio Carew, Lieutenant-Colonel Luntley, Major Bennet Henshaw, Captains Henry Cleaver, John Madan, Henry Chapman, Timothy Doughty, Mr. Adderly, and Ralph Skipwith : Captains Doughty and Madan were wounded.

The army was disbanded by act of Parliament, with the exception of the Lord General's own regiment, which, at the request of the Chancellor,[3] was not broken up.   His fears of insurrection, added to his dislike of all sectaries, induced him to conjure the King to retain Monck's regiment.[4]   The King resolved to constitute them his house-

---

[1] Rapin (vol. ii. page 623) says newly-raised Guards.

[2] Secret History of Great Britain, from the Restoration to the Accession of the House of Hanover ; by James Mac Pherson, Esq. Vol. i. page 18.

[3] Who was raised to the peerage in the month of November, by the title of Lord Hindon.

[4] General Monk's regiment, called the Coldstream, and one other of horse, were accordingly retained by the King in his service ; another was formed out of troops brought from Dunkirk : and thus

hold troops, for the security of his person and government.

---

began, under the name of Guards, the present regular army of
Great Britain.—*Ralph*, 35. *Life of James*, 447. *Grose's Military
Antiquities*, t. 61.

For this reason it was that the Duke proposed to the Councill,
which was called in the time of the Insurrection, that they should
write to his Majesty,* and desire him to stop the disbanding of the
Generall's troop of Horse Guards and the regiment of Foot, which
were to have been payd off that day, and that he would rather
think of raising more men for the security of his person and government; which advice his Majesty follow'd, and immediately
gave orders for the raising a new regiment of Guards, of twelve
companies, to be commanded by Collonel John Russell, and a regiment of Horse of eight troops, of which the Earle of Oxford was to
be Collonel, and also a troop of Horse Guards to be commanded
by the Lord Gerard: he likewise sent for the Duke's troop of
Guards, which were then at Dunkirk. Moreover, he gave out
commissions to the Earle of ......, and the Earle of ......,
for regiments of horse, and that they should name their under
officers, who likewise had commissions, and should list men in their
severall counties, who were not to be in present pay, but in readiness in case there should be any occasion for their service.—*Memoirs of James II., by Clarke.* Vol. I. page 390.

" Commissions also for the Earls of Cleveland, Northampton,
" and two other Earls, for regiments of horse, and to name their
" own officers, who had commissions to enlist men in their several
" counties, not to be in present pay, but to be ready in case of
" need."

" Lord Hawley told the King he now looked on him as one of
" the most considerable men in England, since he had raised these
" troops; as his enemies would fear him, and his friends love him
" the better. The nation saw the sectaries would not be quiet."—
*Secret History of Great Britain; by James Mac Pherson, Esq.* 4to.
London, 1775. Vol. I. pages 18, 19, 20.

* Then at Portsmouth.

" On Friday, the 11th of January, his Majesty was
" pleased to establish the Lord General's, the Duke of
" Albemarle's, regiment of foot; and on Saturday, the
" 19th instant, Lieutenant-Colonel Morgan drew forth
" eight companies into Tuthill Fields, (the other two com-
" panies being upon the guard,) where he acquainted
" them how much they were obliged to his Majesty, who
" not only had made good all his gracious promises for-
" merly made to them and the rest of that army, but had
" particularly chosen them, both officers and soldiers, to
" be still continued."

The following account appears in the " Mercurius Pub-
licns," and the " Kingdom's Intelligencer," of February,
1660-1 ; both published by authority :—


" Westminster, February 20th.

" On Thursday, the 14th of February, the Commis-
" sioners disbanded the Lord General's regiment of Foot,
" and Life Guard of Horse, on Tower Hill, (being the
" only remaining land-forces of the army,) with more
" than ordinary solemnity.   Sir William Doyley, William
" Prynne,[1] Esq., Colonel Edward King, and Colonel John
" Birch, (four of the Commissioners,) sent from West-
" minster in a coach to Tower Hill, about ten of the clock
" on Thursday, the 14th of this instant, (being Valentine's
" day,) when the Lord General's regiment of Foot and
" Life Guard appearing with their arms before them, they
" ordered five companies of the Foot to draw up in a ring
" about Mr. Prynne, and the other five about Colonel
" Birch, who made two short speeches to them to this

---

[1] The celebrated antiquary and Keeper of the Records in the
Tower.

" effect : ' That God had highly honoured them in the
" eyes and hearts of the King and kingdom ; yea, and
" made them renowned throughout the world and to all
" posterity, in stirring them up to be eminently instru-
" mental in the happy restoration of his Majesty to
" his royal throne, the Parliament to their privileges,
" and our whole three kingdoms to their antient laws,
" liberties, and government, without any battle or blood-
" shed : for which signal services his Majesty and the
" whole kingdom returned them not only their verbal but
" real thanks ; the King having freely given them one
" week's pay by way of gratuity over and above their
" wages, and the Parliament and kingdom provided mo-
" neys for their just arrears stated in their respective
" accounts, which, upon their disbanding, should be forth-
" with paid for their use into their officers' hands.   That
" this regiment, as it was the first of all the army who
" promoted his Majesty's glorious restoration to his
" crown, so it hath this signal badge of honour now put
" upon them, to be the last regiment disbanded ; and al-
" though they were ordered and declared to be disbanded
" in relation to the kingdom's pay, yet they were imme-
" diately to be advanced to his Majesty's service, as an
" extraordinary Guard to his Royal Person, whom God
" long preserve in health and happiness.'

   " Which speeches being ended, they all cryed out with
" reiterated shouts and acclamations, ' God save King
" Charles the Second ! '   Waving and throwing up their
" hats, displaying their ensigns, beating their drums,
" and discharging their musquets over and over, till com-
" manded to draw off to their respective colours, when
" they were all called over and disbanded by Mr. Prynne,
" Colonel King, and Colonel Birch ; Mr. Prynne caus-
" ing all those four companies he disbanded to lay down

" their arms [1] at his feet, in testimony of their disbanding,
" and then to take them up again as entertained by his
" Majesty in service."

" In the mean time, Sir William Doyley made a speech
" to the Life Guard of Horse," (Monck's) " whom he
" called over, and disbanded. Most of them are since
" entertained by his Majesty for his Horse Guards." [2]

After this ceremony, and the Lord General's own regiment had been formed into an extraordinary guard to the
King, " the regiment marched back in regimental order
" to their quarters, by the Lord Mayor's house, who, hav-
" ing notice thereof, came forth to the door, on whom the
" soldiers bestowed several volleys of shot as they passed
" by him : most of the officers dined with him ; desiring
" him further to provide moneys for payment of their
" arrears out of the City's three months' present assess-
" ment, designed to them by the Commissioners' order.
" Their stated arrears amounted to £13,038 16s. 3d.,

---

[1] Accordingly, on the fourteenth of February, General Monk,
who had been created Duke of Albemarle, reviewed his regiment,
commanded them to lay down their arms, and to consider themselves as disbanded : they were afterwards ordered to take them up
again, and were formed into a regiment of guards for the King's
person.—*Mac Pherson's Secret History of Great Britain.*

The retention of the King's Guards excited some jealousy, though
no complaints seem to have been made of it.—*Hallam,* vol. ii. page
513.

The year 1660 may be considered as the era of the formation of
the Foot Guards ; and of the regiments in point of date, Monk's, or
the Coldstream, has undoubtedly the priority. But other regiments
were added.—*Grose's Military Antiquities,* vol. ii. page 207.

[2] This was the present regiment of Oxford Blues, who were then
raised, and their first muster took place, February the sixteenth,
1660-1, in Tutbill Fields.

" beside £3,800 advanced to them to defray their 1660-1.<br>February.
" quarters; in all £16,838 16s. 3d."[1]

Orders were also issued for raising twelve companies to form an additional regiment of Guards,[2] under Colonel Russel; and a regiment of horse of eight troops, commanded by the Earl of Oxford. [3]

The Mercurius Publicus, from the fourteenth to the March. twenty-first March, 1660-1, gives the names of the officers belonging to the three troops of Life Guard as 'follows.

" His Majesty's Life Guard of Horse being lately mus-
" tered and fully completed, we here give you a list of
" the officers, viz.

---

[1] An idea may be formed of the surplus of the pay of a soldier (ninepence per diem) previous to this date, from such arrears due after defraying all expenses.

From January the pay of the Guards was tenpence per diem, whilst attending the King's person or doing London duty.—See Appendix, No. 261. January 1660-1.

[2] Mercurius Publicus from January thirty-first to February seventh, 1660-1, states, "The new-raised regiment for His Ma-
" jesty's Life Guard of Foot are armed and mustered, whose
" Officers are commissionated by His Majesty and the Lord Gene-
" ral the Duke of Albemarle."

[3] A Dutch regiment of horse, commanded by the Earl of Portland, came with William III. to England; they then served in Flanders, and returned again to England after the Peace of Ryswick; and were always styled the *Blue* Horse Guards: they returned to Holland on the twentieth of March, 1698-9. It was after this the present regiment of Oxford Blues got that appellation.

### HIS MAJESTY'S OWN LIFE GUARD.

Charles Lord Gerard of Brandon . . Captain.

Major General Randolph Egerton .  
Sir Thomas Sandys, Baronet . .  
Sir Gilbert Gerard, Baronet . .  } Lieutenants.  
Colonel Thomas Panton . . .  

Mr. Edward Stanley, brother to the  
Earl of Derby . . . .  } Cornet.

Colonel James Prodgiers . . . Quarter-Master.

Col. Francis Lovelace . . .  
Col. Charles Scrimshaw . . .  
Col. Francis Berkeley ' . .  } Corporals.  
Col. Edward Roscarrick . . .  

Dr. Matthew Smallwood . . . Chaplain.  
Mr. Thomas Woodall . . . . Chirurgion.

### HIS HIGHNESS ROYAL THE DUKE OF YORK'S LIFE GUARD.

Sir Charles Barkeley, (Deputy Gover-  
nor of Portsmouth) . . . .  } Captain.

Robert Dongan . . . . . Lieutenant.  
John Godolphin . . . . Cornet.  
Edward Barkeley . . . . . Quarter-Master.

Francis Bedlow . . . .  
James Somervill . . . .  
Thomas Davenport . . . .  } Corporals.  
Thomas Stourton . . . .  

John Robinson . . . . . Chirurgeon.

### HIS MAJESTY'S LIFE GUARD UNDER THE COMMAND OF HIS GRACE GEORGE DUKE OF ALBEMARLE.

Sir Philip Howard . . . . Captain.  
Henry Monck . . . . . Lieutenant.  
Daniell Collinwood . . . . Cornet.  
Francis Watson . . . . . Quarter-Master.  

Sir Edward Fish . . . .  
Mark Robinson . . . .  
Christopher Bacon . . . .  } Corporals.  
William Upcot . . . .  

Thomas Gumball . . . . Chaplain.  
John Troughtback . . . . Chirurgion."

The Royal Regiment of Horse Guards.[1]
His Majesty's Regiment of Foot Guards.[1]
The Lord General's Regiment of Foot Guards.[1]

The " Royal Regiment of Guards," under Lord Wentworth, was at this time at Dunkirk.

The authorities for the following account of it are the " Military Memoirs of Captain Gwynne, of the Royal Regiment of Guards," " Life of James II. from the original Stuart MSS.," " Mercurius Publicus," " The Kingdom's Intelligencer," MS. Harleian. No. 1223, British Museum, State-Paper Office, and records in the War-Office.

When peace was concluded between France and the Commonwealth in November, 1655, Charles and the Duke of York quitted the French court, repaired to Brussels, and joined the Spaniards against Cromwell and the King of France. The Loyalists assembled round the Duke of York enabled him to raise six regiments early in the year 1657, in the pay and for the service of Spain ; one of which was denominated " The Royal Regiment of Guards." It consisted of about four hundred men, chiefly English. This corps took the field with the Spaniards, in the Netherlands, and was at the siege of Ardes and Mardyke, and before Dunkirk on the fourteenth of June, 1658, in which action the royal regiment particularly distinguished itself, but shared the fate of the Spanish forces, who were defeated and dispersed. Those not killed or wounded, surrendered as prisoners. The few who remained of " the royal guards" after the action, with the officers on parole, were stationed at Ipres, Ghent, Nivelles, or Namur, without pay or scarcely sub-

---

[1] The names of the officers of both Horse and Foot Guards are in the State-Paper Office.

sistence; " the soldiers were given passes to go up and down the countrey a-begging." A short time after the restoration, the regiment was quartered in Dunkirk, " the officers being on half-pay."

On the twenty-sixth of August, 1660, the King appointed Thomas Lord Wentworth Colonel of the regiment, who proceeded to Dunkirk, and re-organized the corps. Colonel Wise, " the eldest Captain," was promoted to the Lieutenant-Colonelcy, and in June following the Royal " Regiment of Guards was almost fully completed to " its new establishment of twelve hundred men, composed " of twelve companies of one hundred men each, besides " officers." When the sale of Dunkirk was afterwards effected on the twenty-seventh of October, 1662, the English garrison was withdrawn, and Lord Wentworth's regiment of guards arrived in London. Fresh disturbances broke out among the sectaries and the disaffected, which was the cause assigned for increasing the King's Guards by putting Lord Wentworth's regiment on the home establishment. Several companies were detached to do duty in the garrisons of Portsmouth, Hull, Berwick, Tinmonth, and York. On the death of Lord Wentworth, on the twenty-eighth of February, 1664-5,[1] this Royal Regiment of Guards was added to the establishment of " the King's Regiment, under Colonel Russel," which had been raised in January, 1660-1. Thus united, the two regiments became the present Grenadier Guards, making together twenty-four companies, " amounting to two thousand four hundred men, " besides officers." Ten or twelve of these[2] companies were usually in the garrisons before mentioned, and at Rochester and Dover.

[1] See MS. Birch.  No. 4182.  fo. 53.  Brit. Mus.
[2] See Appendix, No. 20.

In the "Kingdom's Intelligencer" the following account is given of the reception of Charles II. on his passing through the City from the Tower to Whitehall, the day previous to his coronation. " Nor was the City and " Liberty of Westminster wanting in their duty at this " royal solemnity, having also gravelled and railed in " their streets from Temple Bar to Westminster, which " were guarded on both sides by the Train Bands " of the City and Liberty, and His Majesty's two re- " giments of foot, under the command of His Grace the " Duke of Albemarle and Colonel John Russell, brother " to the Earl of Bedford; the houses were also richly " adorned with the best carpets and tapestry, and musick " in several places, all along His Majesty's passage."

1661.
April 22nd.

# CHAPTER VIII.

Adjutants first commissioned to the Guards—A regiment of
Guards raised for Dublin duty—Charles II. reviews his Horse
and Foot Guards—King and Queen visit Bath, and return by
Oxford to London—Captain Holmes, of the Lord General's regiment, sails to North America, reduces the New Netherlands, and
changes the name to New York—Fleets fitted out in the Thames
and Portsmouth—A detachment from the Lord General's regiment embarks—Declaration of war by the Dutch—Dutch fleet
defeated—Prince Rupert and Albemarle command the fleet—
Albemarle attacks the Dutch off Dunkirk—Prince Rupert and
Albemarle drive the Dutch back on their own coasts—Bucking-
ham's account of Monck's determination not to be taken—Sir
Robert Holmes burns one hundred and sixty vessels in the Vlie—
Bandaris plundered and destroyed—Precedency of regiments—
Dutch fleet attacks Sheerness and enters the Medway—Dutch
fleet proceeds to Portsmouth, Torbay, and sails again to the
Thames—Spragge beats them back—King reviews his Foot and
Life Guards—Cosmo's description of Oxford's Horse, and review
of the Guards in Hyde Park—Cosmo's visit to Albemarle—
Death of Albemarle, and funeral—Earl Craven succeeds to the
Coldstream.

TRANQUILLITY being restored, the King crowned, and
the army disbanded, the Duke of Albemarle for some
years lived in comparative privacy; however, he generally
attended the Privy Council, constantly went to the House
of Lords, and on all occasions was consulted by Charles.

1661.
June.

Adjutants were now first commissioned to the Guards; [1]

---

[1] See Appendix, No. 10.
Grose states, vol. I. page 253:—The appointment of adjutants

no regiment was formed from this period till the Dutch war in 1664, when an adjutant was included in the establishment as part of the regimental staff of the " Admiral's Regiment" and the " Holland Regiment,"[1] and to all other regiments of infantry as they were afterwards raised. 1661. June.

The next notice of the Coldstream in the periodicals of the day is as follows :—" That loyal gentleman, Sir James " Smith, a Member of this Parliament (Exeter[2]), is, by " commission from his Majesty, made Major of his Ma- " jesty's regiment of Guards under his Grace the Duke of " Albemarle, the former Major (Major Nichols[3]) having " for his good services acquired a preferment in the Tower " of London."— " On Tuesday last, Sir James received " his charge in the Artillery Yard, when that gallant " regiment with many volleys and shouts testified their " joy at the reception of so deserving a gentleman."[4] 1661-2. Mar. 11th.

A regiment of Guards was raised for duty in Dublin, under the command of the Earl of Arran : they marched from London in May, to embark for Ireland.[5]

---

is uncertain : according to father Daniel, they were not introduced into the French service before 1666 : they were first found in a list of the English army reviewed on Putney Heath, 1684.

[1] Present 3rd Foot or Buffs. The Tangier regiment (present 2nd Foot) was raised in October, 1661, to form part of that garrison.

[2] See list of members in " Mercurius Publicus," No. 16.

[3] June, 1660.

" The grant of Surveyor of the Ordnance within the Tower " of London, and of all his Majesty's stores within the Kingdoms " of England and Ireland, during his good behaviour, with the fee " of 2 shillings per diem, unto Francis Nicholas, Esq."—MS. Harl. 1684. Entitled " Grants passed the Sygnet from June to November, 1660."

It appears Major Nichols did not vacate his majority in the Lord General's regiment until Sir James Smith's appointment.

[4] Mercurius Publicus, from 6th to 13th March, 1661-2.

[5] " Chester, May 9th, 1662.—On the 9th instant, Sir William " Flower, who had the conduct of his Majesty's regiment of Guards

The subjoined paragraph is inserted, as evincing the sentiment entertained towards an officer of the Coldstream in those days:—" Hampton Court, 3d July, 1662.  That " worthy and loyal gentleman, Sir James Smith,[1] having " received a commission from his Majesty under the " great seal of England, for the regulation of the Cor- " poration of the City of Exeter, is gone down thither to " put the said commission in execution, and to settle " the militia of that town, which he is to do in a short " time, and then to return to his command of Major to " his Grace the Duke of Albemarle's regiment."[2]—The following interesting account of a review in which the Coldstream was present, is given in the same publication : —" Westminster, Saturday, 27th September.  This day " his Majesty's regiments of Guards, both Horse and " Foot, were drawn up in Hide Parke.  It was a very " noble sight at all capacities, and (with reverence be it " spoken) worthy those royal spectators, who purposely " came to behold it : for his sacred Majesty, the Queen, " the Queen-Mother, the Duke and Dutchess of York, " with many of the nobility, were all present.  The Horse

---

" for Ireland under the command of the Earl of Arran, arrived " here with that regiment, in order to their transportation for " Ireland.  Sir William commenced (14th May) to ship twelve com- " panies in eleven ships at Weston."——" During the march from " London with this regiment, Sir William himself constantly marched " with the men.  Sir William Flower, my Lord Callen, and other " chief officers of the regiment, were entertained by the Mayor."

" Dublin, May 28th.—The King's regiment of foot, under the " command of the Earl·of Arran, consisting of 12 companies, that " came this week from England, marched this day completely " armed and clothed through this City, and are all quartered in and " about it, for the Guards."—*Mercurius Publicus*, Nos. 21 and 22.

[1] Sir James Smith commanded " the Militia of the City of Exon."—*Mercurius Publicus*, No. 18.

[2] Mercurius Publicus, from 3rd to 10th July, 1662.

" and Foot were in such exquisite order, that 'tis not easie
" to imagine any thing so exact ; which is the more cre-
" dible if you consider that there were but few of that
" great body who had not formerly. been commanders,
" and so more fit to be Guard to the person of the most
" excellent King in the world." [1]

In December several men were executed for high treason, having conspired to assassinate the King, the Duke
of York, " and among the rest, more especially, the Duke
" of Albemarle, Lord General of all his Majesty's forces,
" and Sir Richard Brown,[2] Major-General of the city of
" London, by seizing the Tower, firing the city, the court,
" and places adjacent, and massacring all the better sort
" of citizens." [3]   At the place of execution the prisoners
are stated to have confessed their guilt.

Evelyn, in his Memoirs, says :—" I saw his Ma[ty]'s
" Guards, being of horse and foote 4000,[4] led by the Ge-

---

[1] Mercurius Publicus, from Sept. 25th to Oct. 2d, 1662.

[2] Father-in-law to Evelyn.

[3] " This was made a pretence " for the increase of the foot
guards, by retaining the King's regiment under Lord Wentworth,
which had arrived from Dunkirk, on the home establishment.

[4]     THE HOUSEHOLD TROOPS AT THIS TIME WERE:

|  | Private Men. |
|---|---|
| The King's troop of Horse Guards   .   .   . | 200 |
| The Duke of York's do. .   .   .   .   . | 150 |
| The Duke of Albemarle's do.   .   .   . | 150 |
| The Royal Regiment of Horse Guards   .   . | 500 |
| The King's Regiment of Foot Guards under Lord } Russell   .   .   .   .   .   . | 1200 |
| The Lord General's Regiment of Foot Guards   . | 1000 |
| The King's Regiment of Foot Guards under Lord } Wentworth   .   .   .   .   .   . | 1200 |
| Total   .   .   .   . | 4400 |

Besides Officers and Non-Commissioned Officers.

From Official Establishments.—State-Paper Office.

" neral the Duke of Albemarle, in extraordinary equipage
" and gallantry, consisting of gentlemen of quality and
" veteran souldiers, excellently clad, mounted, and or-
" dered, drawn up in battalia before their Ma^{ties} in Hide
" Park, where the old Earle of Cleveland trail'd a pike
" and led the right-hand file in a foote company com-
" manded by y^e Lord Wentworth his son; a worthy
" spectacle and example, being both of them old and va-
" liant souldiers. This was to shew y^e French Ambass',
" Mons' Comminges; there being a greate assembly of
" coaches, &c. in y^e Park.[1]

" His Majesty's Guards of Horse (commanded by Lord
" Gerard of Brandon), and four companies of the King's
" Guards of Foot, are ordered to attend his Majesty and
" his Royal Consort in their progress to the city of Bath.
" The first day's progress begins from Whitehall, on
" Wednesday, August the 26th, to Maidenhead. Thurs-
" day, August 27th, to Newbury. Friday, August 28th,
" to Marlborough. Saturday, August 29th, to Bath."[2]
The " Intelligencer " of Monday, seventh of September,
contains the particulars of their Majesties' journey, and
arrival at Bath on Saturday the twenty-ninth of August.
It states also that his Majesty proposed to return by
Oxford, and that their Royal Highnesses the Duke and
Duchess of York had determined to go to Portsmouth,
and the Duke's Guards were to accompany them. The
week after their Royal Highnesses set out for Portsmouth,
purposing to join their Majesties on the Tuesday se'nnight
at Oxford. This publication further announces that " his
" Majesty's resolution for Cirencester, Cornbury, Oxford,
" and so for London, holds where it was, and that their

---

[1] Evelyn's Memoirs, 1663, vol. i. page 358.
[2] Kingdom's Intelligencer, from 17th to 24th August, 1663.

" Majesties left Bath on Tuesday the 22nd, and arrived at
" Oxford on Wednesday, 23rd of September, 1663." The
Court removed from Oxford, and arrived at Whitehall the
first of October.

" Some time after this, the King gave the Duke a
" patent for Long Island in the West Indies, and the
" tract of land between New England and Mary Land,
" which always belong'd to the Crown of England since
" it was first discover'd; upon which the Dutch had also
" incroached during the rebellion, and built a town, and
" some forts, to secure the Bever trade to themselves:
" wherefore the Duke borrow'd two men of war of the
" King, in which he sent Collonel Richard Nicholas, (an
" old officer, and one of the Grooms of his Bed-chamber,)
" with three hundred men to take possession of that
" Country; which the Dutch gave up upon composition
" without striking a stroke, most of the Dutch inhabitants
" remaining there, together with the old English inhabit-
" ants, and some other Nations, who had first planted there
" with the English; so that Collonel Nicholas remain'd in
" peaceable possession of that Country, which was then
" called New York, and the fort up the river nam'd Albany.
" And as the Duke did all on his side to advance trade,
" the Parliament, press'd on to it by the King, were no
" less active to make it flourish, which they chiefly did
" by the Act of Navigation, and other Bills for the
" encouraging of Trade, and building of Ships." [1]

A few years previous to the breaking out of the Dutch    1664.
war, complaints had been repeatedly urged by the English
and Dutch, reciprocally, of the frequent interruption they
experienced in their foreign trade. These complaints

---

[1] Life of James, from the Stuart MSS., vol 1. page 400.

1664.   related more especially to the hostile proceedings of the Dutch West-India Company, and of the English chartered African Company, unauthorised by their respective governments, which became more serious in 1664. Captain, afterwards Sir Robert Holmes, [1] in February that year, with a squadron and some land-forces, made a descent on the Dutch settlements on the coast of Guinea: he captured several vessels, and took some of their principal forts.

May.   Fifty men of the Lord General's regiment were drafted for the expedition to Guinea,[2] whence Captain Holmes sailed to North America, and reduced in August the Dutch settlement called New Netherlands, which he changed to that of "New York," in honour of the Lord

October.  High Admiral. Captain Holmes sailed from England in October, 1663, with four frigates, and returned to Plymouth in December, 1664. He was committed to the Tower in January, until his conduct to the Hollanders should be investigated; but in March was honorably acquitted, and after his release the King showed him decided marks of favour.

The English made great preparations, and in October and November large fleets were fitted out in the Thames and Portsmouth under the Duke of York, Prince Rupert, and the Earl of Sandwich. A detachment of the Lord General's regiment embarked for this service, and each corps of the army furnished a proportion of men to serve in the fleet; a practice that continued till the time of Queen Anne.

A new corps, called the Admiral's, was on this occasion

---

[1] Holmes was knighted by the King on the 28th of March, 1666. —*London Gazette*, No. 39.

[2] See Appendix, No. 13.

ordered to be raised, intended for sea-service, which probably laid the foundation of the institution of Marine
Regiments in the reign of Anne.    Before any declaration
of war, Rear-Admiral Sir Thomas Allen attacked the
Dutch convoy and Smyrna fleet off Cadiz: he took eight
merchant ships, and the remainder escaped much shat-
tered.

In January 1664-5, war was declared by the Dutch, and
by the English in the ensuing month.    Five hundred men
were added to the Lord General's regiment for sea-service,
and distributed on board the fleet.[1]    The Duke of York
with one hundred and fourteen sail stood for the coast of
Holland.    On the third of June the two fleets engaged
about three A. M. off Harwich.    Admiral Opdam's ship,
which opposed the Duke of York, was blown up.    Several
officers of rank were killed.    The action terminated in the
total defeat of the Dutch.    Eighteen ships were taken,
fourteen sunk, and several blown up.    To commemorate
the victory a medal was struck :—[2]

The enemy's loss exceeded six thousand men killed and
wounded, including two thousand three hundred prisoners.[3]    The English lost one ship, two hundred and fifty
men killed, and three hundred and forty wounded.

When the plague had driven Charles to Oxford, he
entrusted the Duke of Albemarle with the care of the
metropolis.

This year, Sir James Smith, Major of the Coldstream,

---

[1] See Appendix, No. 14.

[2] See engraved medal E.

[3] Evelyn, in his Memoirs, states that he went to London to
speak with his Majesty and the Lord General for more guards for
the prisoners of war committed to his charge.

became Lieutenant-Colonel, and was succeeded by Captain Miller.[1]　A company was given to Major John Hinton, who had distinguished himself in Lockart's regiment at Dunkirk, in the action against the Spaniards, when Charles II. and his brother were present.[2]

---

[1]　" Docquet of a Grant of Arms and Crest to Serjeant-
　　　" Major John Miller, of his Majesties Coldstreamer
　　　" regiment of Foot Guards, dated 27th May, 1672."
" Whereas Serjeant-Major John Miller, born at Balicusson, in
" y[e] parish and county of Ardmagh in Ireland, sonne of Robert
" Miller of y[e] county of Huntington, did from his youth apply
" himself to military actions, and by his merit and courage came
" to be eldest Captaine of y[e] late illustrious and heroick Generall
" George Moncke his regiment of Coldstreamers, who was also
" Adjutant-Generall unto y[e] said Generall Moncke when he en-
" tered into England in order to his Maj[ties] happy Restitucōn, and
" shortly after was made Serjeant-Major of y[e] said regiment,
" being made a regiment of his Ma[tties] Foote Guards under y[e]
" com̄and of y[e] said illustrious Generall, deservedly created
" Duke of Albemarle, soe as he justly meritts, &c.　Know ye,
" therefore, &c., Viz[t]. Argent, a treshure flory, counter flory,
" and over it a fess imbattelled gules :　Crest, a lyons pawe erased,
" gules, holdinge y[e] hilt, or on y[e] blade proper.　A chaplet alsoe
" gules.　May 27[th], 1672, in 24[th] yeare of Charles y[e] 2d."—MS.
Harleian. 1172, folio 76.
[2]　" 1658.　Boniface, as I have already said, was posted on the
" highest sand-hill, which was somewhat advanced before any of
" the others, so that the battell began there.　It was Lockarts own
" regiment which charged those Spaniards, and was commanded
" by Lieut.-Coll. Fenwick ; who, so soon as he came to the
" bottom of the hill, seeing that it was exceeding steep, and dif-
" ficult to ascend, commanded his men to halt and take breath for
" two or three minutes, that they might be more able to climb and
" do their duty.
" While they were thus preparing themselves, their commanded
" men opening to the right and left, to give way to their main

The fleet was commanded by Prince Rupert and the Duke of Albemarle, when a large portion of the Duke's regiment again embarked. They sailed early in May, but were separated by a gale of wind, which obliged Albemarle to fight the Dutch off Dunkirk with an inferior force, on the first of June. Sir John Harman, who commanded the Henry, in his relation of the action blames the Duke for his eagerness to engage. The battle continued on the second, and was renewed during the two following days. De Witt was on board the Dutch fleet; he is said to be the inventor of chain-shot, which was used for the first time, and did much damage to the English rigging.

---

" body, which was to mount the hight, were continually firing at
" Boniface ; and as soon as the body were in a condition to climb,
" they began their ascent with a great shout, which was generall
" from all their foot. But while they were scrambling up in the
" best manner they were able, the Lieutᵗ.-Coll. fell in the middle
" way, being shott through the body ; which yet hinder'd not the
" Major, who was called Hinton, (since a Captain in the Duke of
" Albemarle's regiment,) from leading on his men, together with
" the rest of their officers, who stopt not till they came to push of
" pyke ; where, notwithstanding the great resistance which was
" made by the Spaniards, and the advantage they had of the higher
" ground, as well as that of being well in breath, when their
" enemies were almost spent with climbing, the English gain'd
" the bill, and drove them from off it. The Spaniards leaving
" dead upon the spott, seven of eleven Captains which commanded
" the regiment, together with Slaughter and Farrell, two Captains
" whom I had joyn'd to that regiment just before ; besides many of
" their reform'd officers, (their stands of pykes being for the most
" part made of such,) yet this ground had been so well disputed,
" that the English, besides their Lieutᵗ.-Coll., lost several officers
" and soldiers."— *Life of James IId., from the Original Stuart
MSS. in Carlton House*, by the Rev. T. S. Clarke, L.L.D. &c.
4°, London, 1816, vol. I. page 348.

1666.

Campbell, in his " Lives of the Admirals," says it was
" the most terrible battle fought in this war : it was by
" no means easy to say who were victors upon the whole,
" or what was the loss of the vanquished." That of the
English was computed at sixteen men of war, of which ten
were sunk and six taken. The Dutch lost fifteen ships of
war. " The Duke of Albemarle [1] was much blamed for
" his rashness and great contempt of the Dutch ; but he
" thought that fighting was, almost on any terms, pre-
" ferable to running away, in a nation who pretend to the
" dominion of the sea." [2]

On the twenty-fifth of July, and two subsequent days,
the English and Dutch once more engaged, when Prince
Rupert [3] and Albemarle gained the most decisive victory
that had been achieved during the war. The battle commenced off the North Foreland, and the Dutch were
driven back on their own coasts. The enemy lost four
admirals, twenty men of war, four thousand killed, and
three thousand wounded. Of the English, three captains
and three hundred men were killed. The Duke of Buckingham, then serving as a volunteer on board, gives the
following curious account of Monck's determination not to
be taken :—" 'Hearing everywhere the Earl of Ossory
" commended for being a volontier that summer in a hot

---

[1] In the London Gazette from the 4th to the 7th of June, 1666,
is an account, dated Harwich, 4th of June, stating " That the
" Duke had all his tackle taken off by chain-shot, and his breeches
" to his skin were shot off."

[2] Campbell's Naval History.

[3] Prince Rupert and Albemarle were on board the same ship.

[4] Memoirs of John Duke of Buckingham, written by himself.
4º, London, 1723, vol. ii. page 4.

" engagement at sea, I went thither directly, on board
" that ship in which Prince Rupert and the Duke of Al-
" bemarle jointly commanded the fleet against the Dutch.
" While I was in that ship with Prince Rupert and the
" Duke of Albemarle, I observed the latter to leave all
" things to the conduct and skill of the other ; declaring
" modestly upon all occasions himself to be no seaman.
" And yet there happened once a hot dispute between
" them, which will show some part of the Duke's cha-
" racter. When we first espied the Dutch fleet sailing
" towards us, our whole blue squadron was astern, much
" farther from us ; so that Prince Rupert thought it abso-
" lutely necessary to slacken sail, that they might have
" time to join us. But the Duke of Albemarle opposed it
" eagerly, undertaking that the ship in which they were,
" with about twenty ships more, would prove sufficient to
" beat all the enemies fleet; at least, hold them in play
" till the rest of ours came up. The Prince, astonished
" at such unaccountable intrepidity, made a smile to see
" him take on himself the timerous, cautions, and pruden-
" tial part, which did not use to be his custom ; he de-
" clared he would never consent to such a rashness as
" might very probably cost us the loss of our Admiral's
" ship, and consequently of our whole fleet afterwards ;
" which obliged the good old man to yield at last, but
" with a great deal of reluctance. As soon as the bloody
" flag was set up, before the storm arose which parted us,
" Mr. Savill and myself being on the quarter-deck, 'spied
" him charging a very little pistol and putting it in his
" pocket, which was so odd a sort of a weapon on such
" an occasion, that we two could imagine no reason for it,
" except his having taken a resolution of going down into
" the powder-room to blow up the ship, in case at any

1666.  " time it should be in danger of being taken ; for he had
" often said he would answer for nothing but that we
" should never be carried into Holland: and therefore
" Mr. Savill and I, in a laughing way, most mutinously
" resolved to throw him overboard, in case we should ever
" catch him going down to the powder-room."

Aug. 9th.    In August, one hundred and sixty vessels within the
Vlie were attacked and burnt under the direction of Sir
Aug. 10th. Robert Holmes.  As it was deemed more expedient to
land on the Island of Schelling than upon Vlie, Sir Robert Holmes, with eleven companies, disembarked with
but little opposition, leaving one company for the security of his boats, and with the remainder marched to
September. Bandaris, which town he destroyed by fire, after it had
been plundered by the soldiers; the inhabitants having
quitted on his approach.

Sept. 2nd.    Monck was not present at the great fire that raged
in the city : on which occasion the people declared, that
if their hero had been in London, they would have
escaped the calamity.  The King sent for the Duke,
who was on board the fleet at Portsmouth: he arrived
on the seventh.

At this time, the following order [1] was issued under the
sign manual.

" CHARLES REX.
" For the preventing of all questions and disputes that
" might arise for or concerning the ranks of the severall
" regiments, troops, and companies, which now are or at
" any tyme hereafter shall be employed in our service,

---

[1] State-Paper Office.

" and of the several officers and commanders of the same,
" as well upon service and in the field, as in all Councills
" of Warr and other military occasions—Where they
" shall be called to appear in their respective quallities,
" We have thought good to issue out these following
" rules and directions.

" First, as to the Foote. That the regiment of Guards
" take place of all other regiments, and the Colonell be
" always reckoned, and take place as the first Foote
" Colonell; the Generall's Regim$^t$ to take place next,
" the Admirall's immediately after, and all other Regi-
" ments and Colonells to take place according to the date
" of their commissions."

" 2ndly. As to the Horse, That the three troopes of
" Guards take place before all others, that the Captaines
" take their ranke as eldest Colonells of Horse, the Lieu-
" tenants as eldest Majors, and the Cornetts as eldest
" Captains of Horse. That the King's regiment of Horse
" take. place immediately after the Guards, and the
" Colonell of it to have precedency immediately after the
" Captaines of the Guards, and before all other Colonells
" of Horse; all other Colonells of Horse to take their
" ranke according to the date of their commissions."

" 3dly. That the eldest Colonell doe in all occasions
" command; and when there shall be noe Colonell upon
" the place, then the Lieutenant-Colonell of the eldest
" regiment, and in like manner where noe Lieutenant-
" Colonell, the Major, and so downe to the Captaines and
" other inferior Officers."

" 4thly. That all Officers under the condition of a
" Generall Officer, when they shall happen to be put
" into any guarrison, shall, dureing their being there,
" obey the Governour of the same or his deputies."

1666. "Given at our Court at Whitehall, the 12th day of "September, 1666."

"By his Ma^{ties} command,

"ARLINGTON."

Nov. and Dec.

While the negotiations for peace were in progress, and all the arrangements for it far advanced, De Witt resolved to carry into execution his plan for entering the river Thames. It received the sanction of the French Minister in Holland, and also of the Deputies of the States. On the supposition that peace would shortly be concluded, no 1667. June. preparations for defence had been made in England. The Dutch fleet under De Ruyter, consisting of seventy men of war, exclusive of fire-ships, attacked Sheerness on the seventh of June. The Duke of Albemarle, with a considerable force, was ordered to protect the Medway,[1] which he did by sinking ships and fastening a chain from one side of the river to the other. On the twelfth the chain was

---

[1] " London, 18 June.——alarm'd by the Dutch, who were fallen " on our fleete at Chatham by a most audacious enterprise, enter- " ing the very river with part of their fleete, doing us not only " disgrace, but incredible mischiefe in burning severall of our " best men-of-war lying at anker and moor'd there, and all this " thro' our unaccountable negligence in not setting out our fleete " in due time. This alarme caus'd me, fearing y^e enemie might " venture up the Thames even to London, (which they might have " don with ease, and fir'd all y^e vessells in y^e river too,) to send " away my best goods, plate, &c. from my house to another place. " The alarme was so greate, that it put both country and citty into " a paniq feare, and consternation, such as I hope as I shall never " see more; every body was flying, none knew why or whither. " Now there were land forces dispatch'd with the Duke of Albe- " marle, Lord Middleton, Prince Rupert, and the Duke, to hinder " y^e Dutch coming to Chatham, fortifying Upnor Castle, and

broken, and several of the English vessels burnt. Next day 1667.<br>June. the Dutch advanced as far as Upnor Castle, but returned, capturing some vessels. Two of the enemy's ships ran on shore and were destroyed. They afterwards proceeded to Portsmouth and Torbay; then sailed back to the Thames, and reached the Hope. Being there opposed by a small squadron under Sir Edward Spragge and beaten off, they landed and attacked Languard Fort,[1] but suffered severely. On the twenty-fourth they were again encountered by Sir Edward Spragge, who with the assistance of another small squadron obliged them to fly before him. The Dutch fleet August. continued to cruise on the coast although peace was actually proclaimed.[2] The following is extracted from the 1668. London Gazette :—

" Whitehall, September 16th, 1668.—This morning His
" Majesty, accompanied by His Royal Highness, was
" pleased to take a view of his regiments of Foot Guards,
" and his Life Guard of Horse, at their rendezvous in Hide
" Park ; where he placed His Grace the Duke of Mon-
" mouth in the command as Captain of his Life Guards of
" Horse, vacated by the resignation of Charles, Lord
" Gerard, Baron of Brandon."

Cosmo the Third, Grand Duke of Tuscany, after travel- 1669. ling through Spain, embarked about this period at Co-

---

" laying chaines and booms ; but y° resolute enemy brake thro'
" all, and set fire on our ships, and retreated in spight, stopping up
" the Thames, the rest of their fleet lying before the mouth of it."
—*Evelyn's Memoirs,* 1667, vol. 1. page 384.

[1] Darrel was Governor.

[2] The Duke of Albemarle and Prince Rupert drew up separate narratives of these occurrences from the time of the entrance of the Dutch in the Thames, which were laid before Parliament, and are preserved in the MSS. Harleian. 7170, British Museum.

runna, and arrived in England.  He was met near Basingstoke by a troop of the Earl of Oxford's Horse Guards,
ordered to attend him as a guard of honour, which he
politely declined.    In alluding to this corps, he states that
the regiment consisted of eight troops of seventy men, and
that in each troop the Colonel had the privilege of keeping
two places vacant, and of appropriating the emoluments to
himself, which amounted to more than fourteen pounds
sterling every week.    " [1] The officers," he says, " wear a
" red sash with gold tassells, and they receive as pay half
" a ducat a day."    From another part of the same work
it appears that during his stay in London, [2] " The King
" commanded a review of his Guards, both Foot and
" Horse, in Hyde Park, for the entertainment of His High-
" ness.   On the 21st [3] of May, 1669, the review took
" place."

" His Highness with his suite pushed forward to meet
" His Majesty, who with a numerous retinue was riding
" round the field.   The Duke of York, on seeing his
" Highness, saluted him first.   His Highness perceiving
" his politeness, returned the compliment, and Joining him,
" rode after his Majesty, who having taken a view of the
" soldiery that were arranged in the places assigned them
" on either side, commanded them to march by in files,
" retiring in the mean time with all his retinue to the
" shade of the trees to protect himself from the sun, and to
" observe the march without interruption.   The whole
" corps consisted of two regiments of infantry and one of

[1] Travels of Cosmo the 3d through England, &c. (1669) trans-
lated from the Italian MS. in the Laurentian Library at Florence,
4°, London, 1821, page 157.

[2] Page 304.

[3] The review took place on the eleventh (O.S.).  See London
Gazette, No. 364.

1669.
May.

" cavalry, and of three companies of the Body Guard
" which was granted to the King by Parliament since his
" return, and formed of six hundred horsemen, each armed
" with carabines and pistols, all well mounted, and dressed
" in jackets which are uniform in every thing but colour;
" they are now, however, reduced to three hundred, the
" King having the power of re-establishing them at plea-
" sure."

" The first or King's own [1] regiment of Infantry,
" having a white flag with a red cross in the middle, com-
" manded by Colonel Russel, was composed of twelve
" companies of eighty men each, who are increased to
" three hundred in time of war, all dressed in red coats
" turned up w th light blue, (which is the colour of the
" Royal livery,[2]) except the pikemen, who are distin-

---

[1] London Gazette, No. 364. " London, May 12th, 1669. Yes-
" terday, being the 11th inst., the three troops of his Majesty's
" Horse Guards, seven of the regiment of Guards commanded by
" the Earl of Oxford, with fourteen companies of the ffoot Guards
" of his Majesty's regiment, and the General's regiment of Guards,
" were drawn up in Hyde Park in an excellent order and equi-
" page, where his Majesty, accompanied by his Royal Highness,
" and his Highness Prince Rupert, was pleased to take a view of
" them, where were also present his Highness the Prince of Tus-
" cany, with several of the Ambassadors and Foreign Ministers,
" residing in this Court."

[2] Probably the red liveries were brought to this country by
King William, as appears from the annexed Order by the Earl
Marshal. An ORDER by HENRY Duke of NORFOLK, Earl Mar-
shall of England, &c.

WHEREAS His Majesty hath Signified to me His Royal Will
and Pleasure, That no Person whatsoever presume to Use, (or
suffer to be Worn,) for their Liveries, any sort of Scarlet or Red
Cloth, or Stuff. Except such as are, or shall be Worn by His
Majesties Servants, and Guards, and those belonging to the Royal

" guished from the others by wearing a coat of a silver
" colour turned up with a light blue."

" The second regiment, that of General George Monk,
" Duke of Albemarle, whose standard was green with
" six white balls and a red cross, commanded by Colonel
" Miller, was composed of fourteen companies also of
" eighty men, who wore red jackets with green facings,
" the pikemen being in green, faced with red."

" The third regiment, (of Cavalry,) that of the Earl of
" Oxford, was formed of seven companies of sixty men
" each.

" The first of the three companies of the Body Guards,
" called the King's company, composed of gentlemen and
" half-pay officers, dressed in red jackets faced with blue,
" and richly ornamented with gold lace, and wearing
" white feathers in their hats, was commanded by the
" Duke of Monmouth."

---

Family, or Foreign Ministers: THESE are therefore to require
all His Majesties Subjects to take Notice of, and conform to His
Majesty's Royal Will and Pleasure hereby Signified. Neverthe-
less, His Majesty is pleased to permit the Wearing out such
Scarlet or Red Liveries that have been made, and in Use before
the Signification of this His Majesties Pleasure. Dated the Twen-
tieth day of December, One Thousand Six Hundred Ninety and
Eight, in the Tenth Year of the Reign of Our Sovereign Lord
WILLIAM the III., by the Grace of God of England, Scotland,
France, and Ireland, King, Defender of the Faith, &c.

NORFOLKE, E.M.

London, Printed by H. Hills in Black-fryers, 1698.

" See London Gazette, March 27, 1699, No. 3482, where the
" notice signed by the Earl Marshall is dated March 10th, 1698-9,
" and to limit the time allowed for wearing what might be made
" when the order came out, untill Septr. 29th, but no longer."

" The second, called the Duke's, commanded by the
" Marquis of Blandford, nephew of Marshal Turenne,
" wore red jackets with blue facings without gold, and
" white feathers in their hats.

" The third, that of the General (Monck), whose place
" was supplied by Sir Phillip Howard, of the family of
" the Earl of Carlisle, wore a dress similar to that of the
" Duke's, and instead of feathers, a ribbon of a crimson
" colour.

" Each of these companies has its lieutenant, who are
" Sir Thomas Sandys, Sir Gilbert Gerard, Major-Gene-
" ral Egerton, and Sir George Hamilton.

" They marched by in files in sight of his Majesty and
" their Highnesses. The van-guard consisted of the
" company of the Duke of Monmouth, who marched at
" its head in full dress. This was followed by the Gene-
" ral's company, and a troop of cavalry of the Earl of
" Oxford's regiment. The infantry regiment of the King
" came next with six pieces of cannon, that of General
" Monck following; which was succeeded by the regiment
" of cavalry of Oxford, the Duke of York's company form-
" ing the rear-guard.

" When they had marched by without firing either a
" volley or a salvo, his Majesty dismounted from his horse,
" and entering his carriage with the Duke and Prince
" Robert (Rupert), returned to White Hall, his Highness
" going home, and the soldiers being dismissed to their
" quarters."

Cosmo left London for Chelmsford, and, on the morning of the twelfth of June, the son of the Duke of Albemarle went there and invited him to the Duke's house.
After viewing Chelmsford, his Highness set out for New-
hall, to dine with the Duke, who was at this time confined

to the house by " confirmed dropsy." The Grand Duke,
in describing his distinguished host, says, " General
" George Monk, Duke of Albemarle, in point of personal
" appearance, is of the middle size, of a stout and square-
" built make, of a complexion partly sanguine and partly
" phlegmatic, as indeed is generally the case with the
" English ; his face is fair, but somewhat wrinkled from
" age, he being upwards of sixty years old ; his hair is
" grey, and his features not particularly fine or noble.
" As to the qualities of his mind, he is a man of
" talents, of courage, and of sound judgment ; and to
" him belongs the glory of having re-established the
" King in England, an achievement to which he was
" manifestly incited, not by the fear of being deposed
" from the command of the army, as was anticipated by
" some on account of the disunion of the rebels after
" Cromwell's death and the confused state of Parlia-
" ment, which had already appointed four commissioners to
" supersede him, but by his love for the tranquillity of the
" kingdom, and the uprightness of his loyalty ; so that,
" besides the peaceable enjoyment of the highest rank in
" the kingdom, he receives from the King that considera-
" tion which is due to a person of his distinction, whose
" name deserves to be handed down to posterity as one of
" the greatest commanders that the present age has
" produced.

" Monk is married to a lady of low origin, she having
" been formerly employed in one of the mercers' shops in
" the Exchange in London. Falling in love with this
" lady, he overlooked every other advantageous connexion
" that might have been more suitable to his rank, and
" made her his wife. Her former station shows itself in
" her manners and her dress, she being no way remark-

"able for elegance or gentility. Her son, however, 1669.
"which she has borne to the General, makes up for his June.
"mother's deficiency."

Monck died of dropsy, at the Cock-pit, near Whitehall, 1669-70.
in the sixty-second year of his age. His remains, after Jan. 3rd.
lying in state at Somerset House, were deposited in Henry
the Seventh's Chapel, Westminster. He married Ann
Clarges,[1] a milliner, the daughter of John Clarges, a

---

[1] Ann Clarges, Duchess of Albemarle, was the daughter of a
blacksmith, who gave her an education suitable to the employment she was bred to, which was that of a milliner: and as the
manners are generally formed early in life, she retained something
of the smith's daughter even at her highest elevation. She was
first the mistress, and afterwards the wife of General Monck. The
General was afraid to offend her, as she presently took fire, and
her anger knew no bounds. She was a great mistress of all the
low eloquence of abusive rage, and seldom failed to discharge a
volley of curses against such as thoroughly provoked her. The
following quotation is from a Manuscript of Mr. Aubrey, in the
Ashmolean Museum:—

"When he" (Monck) "was prisoner in the Tower, his semp-
"stress, Nan Clarges, a blacksmith's daughter, was kind to him in
"a double capacity. It must be remembered that he was then in
"want, and that she assisted him. Here she was got with child.
"She was not at all handsome nor cleanly: her mother was one
"of the five women barbers, and a woman of ill fame. A ballad
"was made on her and the other four; the burden of it was—

'Did you ever hear the like,
'Or ever hear the same,
'Of five women barbers
'That lived in Drury-lane?'"

—*Biographical History of England*, by the Rev. James Granger,
8º, London, 1824, vol. v. page 356.

The following singular circumstance occurred during the trial of
an action of trespass, between William Sherwin, plaintiff, and Sir
Walter Clarges, Bart., and others, defendants, at the bar of the

D.
7.
blacksmith. She was a woman of the lowest description, and of a violent temper, but had secured Monck's gratitude while his mistress, by her constant and affectionate attention to him during his imprisonment in the Tower. She died on the twenty-third of January, and was buried on Monday evening, the twenty-eighth of February, in Henry the Seventh's Chapel, Westminster Abbey. Monck left an only son, Christopher, in whom the family be-

---

King's Bench at Westminster, 15th November, 1700. "The Plaintiff, as heir and representative of Thomas Monk, Esq., elder brother of George, Duke of Albemarle, claimed the Manor of Sutton, in the county of York, and other lands, as heir at law to the late Duke, against the Defendant, devisee under the will of Duke Christopher his only child, who died in 1688, s. p. Upon this trial it appeared that Anne, the wife of George, Duke of Albemarle, was daughter of John Clarges, a farrier, in the Savoy, and farrier to Colonel Monk. In July 1632, she was married, at the church of St. Lawrence Pountney, to Thomas Ratford, son of Thomas Ratford, late a farrier, servant to Prince Charles, and resident in the Mews. She had a daughter born in 1634, who died in 1638; her husband and she lived at the Three Spanish Gipsies, in the Exchange, and sold washballs, powder, gloves, and such things, and she taught girls plainwork. About 1647, she being sempstress to Monk, used to carry him linen. In 1648 her father and mother died; in 1649 she and her husband fell out, and parted, but no certificate from any parish register appears, reciting his burial. In 1652 she was married in the church of St. George, Southwark, to General George Monk, and in the following year was delivered of a son, Christopher, who was suckled by Honour Mills, who sold apples, herbs, oysters, &c." which son, Christopher, succeeded his father as stated in the text.

Note to *Burke's Extinct Peerage.* London, 1831.

See also History of St. Lawrence Pountney, by the Rev. H. B. Wilson, D.D. 4°. London, 1831. p. 134, in which a copy of her first marriage certificate is given, and shows that it took place on the 28th of February, 1632-3, and not July, as stated. The "Gentleman's Magazine" for 1793, page 886, confirms this anecdote, as well as Brayley in his "Londiniana," vol. III. p. 361.

came extinct.[1]    On the death of Monck, the King    1669-70.
directed his funeral to be conducted with all possible
splendour, and that every thing should be suitable to
the melancholy occasion.    An order to that effect was    1670. April.

---

[1] In the " Ellis Correspondence," edited by the Hon^ble George Agar
Ellis, from the original letters preserved in the British Museum
among the Birch collection of manuscripts, the following account is
given.  " London, May 14th, 1687," v. i. p. 294.  " There was a
" Spanish galleon lost in 43, which the Duke of Albemarle, Lord
" Falkland, &c. had a patent last September to search for, and they
" sent out one Pips " (Sir William Phipps), " who a few days ago re-
" turned with twenty-six tons of silver, and eighteen pounds weight
" of gold, and reported he left another vessel to take in the rest of
" the riches, which he could not bring away, which likewise arrived
" yesterday.  Mountains are made of the matter, but it is certainly
" a very considerable thing : the Duke of Albemarle hath a fourth
" part, which will be 35 or £40,000."
Mr. Ellis gives the subjoined note to the preceding.
" Christopher Duke of Albemarle, who was entirely ruined in
" fortune, had been persuaded by certain speculators to join in
" partnership with them for the purpose of weighing up a Spanish
" galleon, sunk near the island of Jamaica.  In order to faci-
" litate their proceedings, he procured himself to be made Governor
" of that island, where he died in 1688.*  Tradition goes that the
" Dutchess, his widow, cheated the other partners of their share of
" the money recovered, and sailed with the whole in her possession
" to England. There she became mad, and determined to marry no
" one but the Grand Turk.  Ralph, Duke of Montague, attracted
" by her riches, wooed and married her, disguised in a Turkish
" dress.  He then shut her up, and built Montague House, now the
" British Museum, with her money."

* Christopher Duke of Albemarle's death is variously stated in
several works : he is said to have died in 1687, 1688, and 1689; but
in the MS. Sloan. No. 1599, British Museum, containing official
accounts of the Council of the Island of Jamaica, it is shown that he
died the begining of October, 1688, as the Council assembled on the
sixth of October, to report on his death, which took place on that
day.

issued for the troops :—" 28th April, 1670.   It being
" his Majesty's pleasure that his three troops of Horse
" Guards ; that part[1] of his Majesty's own regiment
" of Foot Guards under Colonel John Russell's com-
" mand, who are quartered about London and West-
" minster ; and the regiment of Foot Guards under the
" command of the Right Hon^ble William Earl of Cra-
" ven, (whereof his Grace, George Duke of Albemarle,
" Lord General of his Majesty's forces, deceased, was
" lately Colonel,) shall attend and proceed in the funeral
" solemnities of his Grace the said late Lord General, de-
" ceased, from Somerset House to the Cathedral or Col-
" legiate Church in Westminster, on Saturday next, being
" the 30th of this instant April : His Majesty hath ap-
" pointed and given orders for the same as followeth ; that
" is to say, that the said three troops of Horse Guards
" rendezvous in the street before St. Dunstan's Church in
" the West, (facing westward,) on the said 30th of April,
" by nine of the clock in the forenoon, in the order fol-
" lowing, that is to say :—His Royal Highness the Duke of
" York's troop of Horse Guards, under the command of
" the Marquis Blancqfort, to be in the van ; his Majesty's
" own troop of Horse Guards, under the command of his
" Grace the Duke of Monmouth, to come next after
" them :—in which order they are to march to the street
" before Somerset House, and to march before the said
" funeral solemnities.   And her Majesty's the Queen's
" troop of Horse Guards, which was the late Lord Gene-
" ral's troop, are (when the said other troops of Guards
" march before the said funeral solemnities) to expect in
" the Strand, eastward of Somerset House, to take pro-
" ceeding of all the said funeral solemnities westward, on
" the way to the said Abbey Church ; and then they are

---

[1] 14 Companies.

" to march in the rear of the whole train of the said fune-
" ral solemnities, to the west end of the said Abbey
" Church. That the fourteen companies of his Majesty's
" said regiment of Foot Guards about town, shall rendez-
" vous in Covent Garden ; and the said Earl of Craven's
" regiment of his Majesty's Foot Guards shall rendezvous
" in Lincoln's Inn Fields, on the said 30th of April, by
" nine of the clock in the forenoon; from which places of
" their rendezvous, the said Foot Guards are to march
" into the Strand before Exeter House, to expect till two
" of the said troops of Guards pass by, and then the said
" Foot Guards are to march in the rear of the said two
" troops of Horse Guards ; in this order, to wit, the said
" fourteen companies next to his Majesty's said troop of
" Horse Guards aforesaid ; and the said late Lord Gene-
" ral's, and now the Earl of Craven's, regiment of his
" Majesty's Foot Guards to come next after the said
" fourteen companies, so to be nearest (of the said Guards)
" before the chariot and effigies ; and so march on to the
" west end of the said Abbey Church, and attend till the
" said funeral solemnities are entered into the Church.
" And the said whole train is to be closed by her Majesty's
" said troop of Guards (which was the said late Lord
" General's troop) as aforesaid."

The " London Gazette " gives the following account of
the funeral :—" London, April 30, 1670. This day, about
" two in the afternoon, the solemn funerals of George
" late Duke of Albemarle set forward from Somerset
" House towards the Abbey of Westminster, in this fol-
" lowing order.
" First marched his Roy[l] Highnesses troop of Guards,
" next his Majesties troop, then his Majesties regiment of
" Foot Guards, and next them the regiment of Cold-

" streames, as having been the General's own regiment,
" all of them in excellent funeral order.

" Then followed the conductor, and a train of poor men
" in mourning gowns; after them, a large trayn of the
" servants of the gentry.

" Then six classes or companies, each of them led by
" three trumpets, an officer of armes, an ensign of the
" several atchievements of the deceased, and a mourning
" horse.

" The first and second classes, before which were borne
" a standard and a guidon, consisted of the servants of
" the nobility.

" The third, before which was borne a banner of the
" barony of Teyes, consisted of servants to the deceased
" Duke.

" The fourth was a banner of the barony of Beauchamp,
" followed by forty officers which attended the body lying
" in state, the most principal servants of the highest nobi-
" lity, clerks of the Council, Parliament, and Crown,
" masters of Chancery, knights, and knights of the Bath.

" The fifth was a banner of the barony of Monk, fol-
" lowed by several eminent officers of his Majesties Court,
" baronets, sonnes of the nobility, the four principal of-
" ficers of the deceased's house, bearing white staves;
" Barons, Bishops, and Earls.

" The sixth classe was led by the great banner, the
" horse caparison'd with black velvet, as the other horses
" were with cloth and plume; after which followed seve-
" ral of the heralds, bearing the trophies; then came an
" open chariot, covered with black velvet, and a canopy
" of the same, in which lay the effigies of the Duke in
" azure armour, a golden truncheon in his hand, having
" on his ducal robe and coronet, a collar of the order
" about his neck, and a Garter on his left leg; drawn by

" six horses, caparison'd with velvet as the former, with
" escutcheons, chafferons, and plumes; in the chariot, at
" the head and foot of the effigies, sate two gentlemen in
" close mourning; the *poêle* was supported by three Ba-
" rons and the Treasurer of his Maj$^{ties}$ Household; and
" on each side of the chariot were carried five banner-rolls
" of arms of the Duke's paternal descent.   Next after the
" chariot came Garter principal King of Arms, with a
" gentleman usher preceding his Grace the present Duke
" of Albemarle, the chief mourner, his train born up, him-
" self supported by two Dukes, assisted by nine Earls
" and a Baron, all in close mourning, those of them that
" were of the order wearing their collars.   After them
" came the horse of state, richly caparison'd with crimson
" velvet, embroidered and embossed with gold and silver,
" adorned with plumes of the Duke's colours, led with
" long reins by the master of his horse; the whole train
" closed by the troop of her Majesties Guards.

" At the west door of the Abbey of Westminster the
" effigies were taken out of the chariot, and under a
" canopy received by the dean, prebends, and the whole
" quire in their copes and formalities, and conducted into
" the quire, betwixt which and the altar was erected a
" magnificent hearse, whereon the effigies being placed,
" and the service of the church read, an excellent sermon
" was preached on the occasion by the Lord Bishop of
" Salisbury; which ended, they proceeded to offer the
" several trophies; and to conclude the ceremony, the four
" officers of the deceased Duke broke their white staves
" at the head of the hearse, and Garter proclaimed the
" stile of his Grace according to custom; then the trum-
" pets sounding, the regiments and troops which were
" drawn up near the Abbey gave their several vollies.

" This is, in short, an account of this great solemnity,

" which was carried on with extraordinary order, pomp,
" and magnificency, and is by command to be published
" at large, and the whole represented in sculpture, to per-
" petuate this last honour done by his Majesties command
" and at his expence, to the eternal memory of this glo-
" rious person." [1]

In the " Life of James the Second," edited by the Reverend J. Clarke, from the Stuart MSS., an interesting
passage occurs connected with this subject.[2]

" On the 3rd of January, of the year 1670, dyd the old
" General, the Duke of Albemarle, who was the chief
" instrument of the King's wonderfull Restoration; and
" had received from his Majesty, honours and estate pro-
" portionable to his merite.  Some days before his death,
" his R. H. being inform'd that he could not recover,
" speaking of it to the King, he took that occasion to
" advise his Ma$^{ty}$ not to make any body General in his room,
" for that it was too great a power and trust, as matters
" stood, to be put in any one body's hand, not excepting
" even himself: tho' if his Majesty would have a General,
" he hoped he would not think of any other body for that
" place but himself; which, however, he did not desire for
" the reason above given, and that in time of peace there
" was no need of one; and in case of a war, his Ma$^{ty}$
" might make such General Officers as should be fitt and
" proper for the occasion; and since the number of his
" troops at present was so small, it would look oddly, as
" an unusual thing, to have a General over them.

" For these and other reasons, his Ma$^{ty}$ at that time
" resolved to have no new General in the place of the
" Duke of Albemarle.

---

[1] London Gazette, No. 466.        [2] Vol. i. page 446.

"At the same time, the Duke desired the King, that
"upon this occasion of the Duke of Albemarle's death,
"his own troop of Guards might not lose their rank of
"being the second troop of Guards, which would be a
"hardship both to himself, and to all the officers of
"his troop, who were very good men, to be so postpon'd;
"that when his own regiment of foot was rais'd, call'd the
"Duke's Regiment, he did not then desire or expect they
"should have their rank before the Coldstream Regiment,
"they being first rais'd; and therefore, since his Majesty
"saw he did not desire to do wrong to others, he hoped
"that he should not have wrong done to him, nor to his
"troop of Guards; and his Ma'y was then so well satisfied
"with these reasons and the justice of the Duke's desire,
"that he assur'd his R. H. that his troop should not lose
"their rank of being the second troop of Guards.

"But so it was, that upon the General's death, his regi-
"ment of foot, called the Coldstream, was given to Lord
"Craven, and made a second regiment of Guards, and his
"troop of Guards was the Queen's troop; and thereupon
"the Queen, who was not of herself over-kind to the Duke,
"was put upon it by some, who were glad of any occasion
"under hand to put any mortification upon his R. H., to
"ask it of the King, that her troop of Guards might have
"the next rank to that of the King's; which she press'd
"so hard by herself and others, that his Ma'y was very
"much embarrass'd what to do in it, remembering what
"he had said to the Duke upon that subject: of which
"his Royall Highness being inform'd, he went to the
"King, and said, that he saw his Ma'y was teas'd by the
"women and others upon that account; that for his own
"part, he would be more reasonable than they, and was
"content his Ma'y should not stick to his first resolution
"and promise, (tho', at the same time, he could not (*but*)

" think it a hardship upon him); but would quietly ac-
" quiesce to what (*was*) easiest to his Ma^ty, for what ever
" others did, it was his resolution never to make him
" uneasy for any concern of his own ; and so the Queen's
" troop had the rank given it of the second troop of
" Guards."

The inscription[1] on Monck's coffin was in these words :—

Depositum
Illustrissimi Principis,
Georgii Ducis Albemarliæ, Comitis Torringtoniæ,
Baronis Monke de Potheridge, Beauchamp & Teyes,
Carolo II^do. Regi Augustissimo à sanctioribus Consiliis,
nec non ab intimis Cubiculis, omnium Regis Exercituum
Ducis supremi,
incliti Ordinis Aureæ Periscelidis Equitis, &c^a.
Obiit Westmonasterii, Anno Ætatis LXII°. die III°. Januarii,
Anno reparatæ salutis humanæ MDCLXIX.

After the Duke of Albemarle's death the Coldstream
was given to William, Earl of Craven. Hitherto it had retained the appellation of "The Lord General's Regiment;" but from this period it was better known under the
present designation of the Coldstream Guards.

---

[1] MS. Harl. 1045. (f. 80).
In another MS. in the Harleian collection, No. 6815, is a detailed
account of "The manner to be observed at the Funeral of His Grace
" the Duke of Albemarle." Also " Arms in the Banners, &c. at
" the Funeral of the Duke of Albemarle." MS. Harl. 1045. " Bill
" of Arms, Paynters' work at the funeral of the Duke of Albe-
" marle." MS. Harl. 1099.

# CHAPTER IX.

A detachment embarks for the Mediterranean—Holmes attacks the
Dutch fleet—Monmouth joins the French in Flanders—A draft
from the Coldstream sent to complete Monmouth's regiment—A
fleet equipped under the Duke of York—Three hundred men
of the Coldstream embark—English and Dutch fleets engage—
Coldstream disembark and return to their quarters—One company of the Coldstream embarks at Dover, and forms part of a
regiment to remain in the service of Lewis XIV.—Detachments
from the Coldstream embark, and the fleet again sails—Precedency of regiments—The English and French fleets under Prince
Rupert and Count d'Estrees ready for sea—Six companies of the
Coldstream distributed in the English ships—Prince Rupert attacks De Ruyter—French, in conjunction with Monmouth, take
Maestricht — Dutch abandon the intention to invade England —
Spragge engages Trump's squadron—The battalion under Captain
Skelton returns to London—Monmouth's letter to Craven, enclosing the King's order concerning the rank of regiments—
Review in Hyde Park—Monmouth authorised to issue orders
for the removal of quarters—Dalrymple's account of Monmouth's
appointment to be Lord General of the Army—Duke of Buckingham's explanation—Original Commission intended for Monmouth—A regiment, formed by drafts from the Guards and other
regiments, sent to Virginia—First introduction of Grenadiers—
Four companies embark for Ostend—Grenadier companies generally adopted in regiments of Infantry—Four additional companies embark for Ostend—Allies assemble in Flanders—Colonel
John Churchill commands the brigade in which are the First,
and Coldstream Guards—Treaty of Nimeguen—Captain Mutlow's company returns from Virginia—Somerset House con-

verted into barracks for Foot Guards—A detachment sails for
Tangiers—Two companies attend Charles II. to Oxford—King's
Mews fitted up as a barrack—Captain Wakelin, of the Coldstream, walks round St. James's Park five times in two hours
—Arms of the Coldstream exchanged for Snaphance muskets
and pikes—Matchlocks discontinued by the Guards—Return of
the troops from Tangiers—Another Grenadier company added
to the regiment—Change in the appointments of Infantry Officers
—The two regiments of Guards on the same footing—King
reviews his troops at Putney Heath.

1669-70.
February.

A DETACHMENT from the regiment, of one officer, one
serjeant, one corporal, and fifty men,[1] embarked to reinforce the ships sent under Sir Thomas Allen's orders in the
Mediterranean to check the depredations committed by
the Algerine pirates. The squadron returned in November.

1671.

This year the Coldstream continued in their quarters,
doing duty in and about London.[2]

1671-2.

On the thirteenth of January, Sir Robert Holmes, whilst
cruising off the Isle of Wight, fell in with fifty of the Dutch
Smyrna fleet under convoy of six men of war, and on the
Dutch refusing to strike to the British flag and lower their
topsails, he engaged them, captured five of their richest
merchantmen, and boarded their Rear-Admiral's ship,
which was afterwards sunk. This occurrence and other
causes of complaint occasioned a declaration of hostilities
on the twenty-eighth of March. The French co-operated
with the English, and sent an army into Flanders.

February.

At this period a regiment was formed, and the command
of it given to James, Duke of Monmouth, who with a considerable force joined the French in Flanders.[3]  Ten men

---

[1] See Appendix, No. 17.
[2] See Appendix, Nos. 27 and 29.
[3] ": The force amounted to 6000 men.  The French army, though
" nominally under the command of Louis the 14th, was directed by

out of each of the twelve companies of the Coldstream 1672.<br>February. were drafted to assist in completing Monmouth's regiment.[1] A fleet was also equipped of sixty-five ships of war under the Duke of York and the Earl of Sandwich, having on board three hundred of the Coldstream, under Captains Bertie, Huitson, and Coke. Surgeon Joseph Troutbeck of the Coldstream was appointed to act as surgeon of the York frigate. They were followed by another detachment of four officers and two hundred men, under Lieutenants Francis and Lascelles, and Ensigns Meade and Cotton. The English anchored in Solebay; and on the Dutch fleet May 28th. appearing in sight, several captains in the British navy cut their cables to enable them to take their stations in the line. The battle commenced by De Ruyter's attack on the centre, his own ship engaged the Admiral, on board of which was the Duke of York. In this action Lord Sandwich perished, having refused to quit his ship although it was in flames. One of the enemy's vessels was captured and three sunk. " The English lost the Royal James, several officers of " note, and between seven and eight hundred men killed " and the same number wounded."[2] The Dutch did not

---

" the two greatest Generals of the age, Marshal Turenne and the " Prince of Condé. With a boldness and rapidity till then almost " unknown, they reduced in the space of a few months the fortresses " on the Rhine to its separation from the Meuse, overran the Pro- " vince of Utrecht, and advanced to the vicinity of Amsterdam. " Charles the 2ᵈ permitted the 6000 English troops to continue in " the French service after the accommodation with Holland."— Coxe's " Marlborough," p. 4, and Mr. Hare's (afterwards Bishop of Chichester) Journal.

[1] See Appendix, No. 31.

[2] Mr. Saville, in a letter to the Earl of Arlington, dated "Prince," 6th of June, 1672.

Campbell in his " Naval History" states 2500 men were killed, and as many wounded.

publish their casualties ; but the Admiral in his letter to
the States says, " it was the hardest fought battle that he
ever saw."

On De Ruyter's return to Holland the fleet was " laid
" up, and forced to remain so from the want of gun-
" powder."[1]   Three hundred men of the Coldstream
Guards landed from the ships, and were sent in ketches to
Gravesend, from whence they returned to their quarters in
London.   Thirty men were also put on shore at Portsmouth, and proceeded to London under Ensign Peryn, who
had previously marched the detachment from Gravesend.[2]

In November eight companies of one hundred men
each, formed into a regiment, were sent to France with
orders to remain in the service of Lewis XIV.   One company of the Coldstream, under Captain Huitson, made,
*pro tempore*, part of this regiment, which was commanded
by Captain Belville Skelton of the First Foot Guards, as
senior captain.[3]   These companies were employed by the
French against the Dutch until after the capitulation of
Maestricht.

November.   The hostile fleets were refitted, and the British having
taken on board a strong body of land-forces, again sailed.
On this occasion eighteen men from each of the twelve
companies of the Coldstream were embarked ; but no
other action was fought during the year.

The precedency of the several regiments of foot was
regulated as follows :—


       " CHARLES R.

1672-3.        " For the preventing of all questions and disputes for
March 1st. " or concerning the ranks of our several regiments of foot,

---

[1] Campbell's " Naval History."        [2] See Appendix, No. 37.
[3] See Appendix, No. 40, from additional MSS. British Museum,
5752. folio 204.

" Wee have thought fitt to issue these following rules and
" directions :—

" First. The Captains of our own regiments of Foot
" Guards take place of all other Captains of Foot, and
" command accordingly ; and in the town, or other quar-
" ters where they come to do duty, they are to have the
" main guard without dispute as being their fixt post;
" and upon all drawings-up they are to have the right,
" and upon all marches to be in the vann.

" Secondly. That the Captains of the Coldstream
" Regiment of our Foot Guards be ranked and command
" next to the Captains of our own regiment of Foot
" Guards, and to have preference of other regiments in
" having the main guards ; the right-hand in drawing up,
" and the vann in marches accordingly.

" Thirdly. That Captains of other regiments of Foot
" shall be ranked and command according to the seniori-
" ties of the regiments they are of, and not otherwise.

" Fourthly. That when the eight companies, which Wee
" sent out of several regiments into France, shall be in
" the field, that then they make a battalion apart, and
" draw up on the right hand of our dear and intirely
" beloved son James Duke of Monmouth's regiment.
" Given at our Court at Whitehall, the first day of
" March, 167$\frac{2}{3}$.

" By His Ma<sup>ts</sup> command,

" ARLINGTON."[1]

In May, the English fleet under Prince Rupert and Sir
Edward Spragge, and the French under the Count
d'Estrees, were ready for sea. Six companies of the
Coldstream, distributed on board the English ships;

---

[1] War-Office Records.

besides strong detachments from other regiments, were, if
practicable, to make a descent on the Dutch coast. His
Majesty and the Duke of York visited the fleet on the
nineteenth ; and, in a council of war, held in their presence, it was resolved to attack the enemy on their own
shores. In pursuance of this determination, Prince Rupert
sailed for Holland, and found De Ruyter with the enemy's fleet between the Rand and the Stony Bank. On
the twenty-eighth a battle was fought. The English and
French fleets amounted to eighty-four men of war, the
Dutch to seventy, under De Ruyter, Tromp, and Baukert.
The contest lasted till night, and both parties claimed the
victory. The English lost four captains, and Colonel
Hamilton, who had both his legs shot off. Two Dutch
admirals and six captains were killed, and one of their
ships was captured in the retreat. Two French men of
war and some fire ships were destroyed. In case the
confederate fleet had succeeded, it was intended that
Count Schomberg, with six thousand men, then encamped
at Yarmouth, should be conveyed to the Dutch shores and
landed.[1]

June 4th.    The Dutch fleet being refitted, and equal in strength to
that of the confederates, unexpectedly put to sea. The
French betrayed as little inclination to fight as they had

----

[1] " The Court was inclined before not to be over-partial to Prince
" Rupert, who seemed as jealous as any body of its growing ar-
" bitrary by any great success over Holland, tho' himself was Gene-
" ralissimo against it ; and I was obliged to write an account of it
" to the King so plainly and impartially, that all the Prince's com-
" plaints on his side were insignificant ; which, added to his jealousy
" of the Court, incited him to command away all the land forces to
" Yarmouth, where they lay encamped all summer by the sea side,
" without being ever re-embarked or able to do the least service."
— *Memoirs of John Duke of Buckingham*, written by himself.
4°, London, 1723. vol. ii. p. 10.

previously evinced in the action on the twenty-eighth of
May. About five in the evening Sir Edward Spragg's
and Trump's divisions engaged ; a furious contest ensued,
which continued till near midnight, when the Dutch made
their way back, each party claiming the victory, as
before.[1] The loss was inconsiderable, and nearly equal
on both sides. The English ships were so indifferently
manned, that, had it not been for the troops on board,
they could not have risked a battle. Both fleets went
into port for the purpose of refitting. In the mean time
the French, in conjunction with the Duke of Monmouth,
took Maestricht.[2]

The Dutch had long planned to invade England,
but now relinquished the intention, being obliged to
defend their own shores, and protect their commerce.
Prince Rupert again proceeded with troops for a descent
on Holland. The Dutch fleet however bore down on
him, and another engagement took place. The French
on this, as on the two former occasions, were not on the
alert, and their tardiness gave the Dutch a decided advantage. Prince Rupert ordered the French to the van,
placing himself in the centre, and Sir Edward Spragg in
the rear. The English force consisted of about sixty men
of war, the French of thirty, the Dutch of not more
than seventy. The battle lasted from eight o'clock A.M.
till dark. Prince Rupert behaved with great intrepidity,
and " encouraged all his officers so effectually by his own
" example, that by degrees he cleared himself of his ene-

---

[1] See Prince Rupert's official account of this action, to the Earl
of Arlington, dated " Sovereign," off Lowestoff, fifth of June,
1673.

[2] Surrendered on the third July, 1673.

" mies.  Sir Edward Spragg and Trump fought ship to
" ship; both their ships were so disabled, that they quitted
" them and hoisted their flags in other vessels, and
" renewed the battle with incredible fury.  Sir Edward
" Spragg's ship being terribly torn, he designed to go on
" board a third ship, but before he got ten boats' length, a
" shot struck his boat, and Sir Edward was drowned."[1]
The French squadron not supporting Prince Rupert, and
his ships being much damaged, he leisurely made sail for
England.  The conflict, as on many occasions, was indecisive.  No ships were taken, nor did either party sus-
1673-4.  tain great loss.[2]  This was the last battle fought: soon
after the English and French sailed for their respective
ports.  Peace was concluded and signed in London,
February the ninth, 167$\frac{3}{4}$.  " The extent of the British
" seas were particularly mentioned, and the States un-
" dertook that not only separate ships, but whole fleets,
" should strike their sails to any fleet or single ship car-
" rying the King's flag, as the custom was in the days of
" his ancestors."[3]

March.  The regiment was stationed in and about London, attending King Charles.  Two companies were quartered
at Rochester.

1674.  The battalion under the command of Captain Belville
Skelton, including Captain Huitson's company of the
Coldstream, which had been lent to Lewis XIV. in No-
vember, 1672, embarked at Rotterdam, and returned to

---

[1] Campbell's Naval History.
[2] See Captain Sir John Narborough's account of this action,
preserved in the MS. Harleian, 6845, which gives the details at
great length.
[3] Bishop Parker's History of his own Times.  London, 8°,
1727, page 159.

London.[1] Captain Huitson's company, which had been reduced to forty-eight men by a transfer of fifty men to Colonel John [2] Churchill's regiment, was recruited to sixty.[3] *1674.*

To prevent disputes concerning rank among the different regiments in the service, the following letter and order were issued :— *1675. December.*

" MY LORD,

" His Majesty having made and passed under his Royal " signature and privy signet, certain late orders, bearing

---

[1]     Sr,

I send you here inclosed a certificate of Capt<sup>ne</sup> Bevill Skelton, concerning one hundred and twenty pounds, disbursed by the Officers of three companies of the Guards that were in the ffrench service, and are lately by his Majesties order return'd back hither ; to wit, fourty pounds for transporting the horses of the officers of those and of Capt<sup>n</sup> Churchill's companies when they went for France, and forescore pounds for transporting the said three companies of the Guards from Rotterdam back hither. And I desire you would putt that businesse in the right course for their obtaining satisfaction of those disbursements for shipping and otherwise for the said transportations.

I am,

30<sup>th</sup> of April, 1674.         Your friend to serve you,

MONMOUTH.

To Matthew Lock, Esq.,
  (Secretary at War.)

London, Aprill 20<sup>th</sup>, 1674.

The three companies of Guards as lately came over out of the ffrench service, hired two vessells at Rotterdam to transport them, paying forescore pounds for them: They also at their going for ffrance paid £40 for a vessell to transport the horses of those three companies and of Capt<sup>n</sup> Churchill's. In all being disburst by them £120, which is desired may be repaid.

BE. SKELTON.

Official Records, War-Office.

[2] Afterwards Duke of Marlborough.
[3] See Appendix, Nos. 45 and 46.

" date the first day of this instant December, concerning
" the precedencies of the troops of his Majesty's Horse
" Guards, of the respective regiments of Guards, and
" other the regiments established in his Majesty's pay and
" entertainment; and also concerning precedencies of of-
" ficers : which said order his Majesty hath been pleased
" to direct and send to me to be communicated unto them
" respectively in such manner as is declared in the said
" orders. Therefore, in obedience to his Majesty's said
" commands, I send your Lordship, here inclosed, a copy
" of the said orders attested with my hand, and remain,

" My Lord,

" Your Lordship's most affectionate

" and most humble servant,

" MONMOUTH."

" Cockpit,
" 3d December, 1675."

　" To the Right Hon. William, Earl of Craven,
" Colonel of his Majesty's Colds" Reg^t of Foot Guards."


" CHARLES R."

" For the preventing of all questions and disputes that
" might arise for or concerning the ranks of the several
" regiments, troops, and companies, which now are or at
" any time hereafter shall be employed in our service, and
" of the several officers and commanders of the same, as
" well upon service and in the field, as in all councils of
" war and other military occasions, when they shall be
" called to appear in their respective qualities, We have
" thought good to issue out these following rules and
" directions : viz.

　" First as to the Foot. The regiment of Guards take
" place of all other regiments, and the Colonel to be
" always reckoned and take place as the first Foot Colonel.

"The Coldstream regiment of Guards to take place next. 1675.
"Our most dear and most entirely beloved brother James
"Duke of York's regiment[1] immediately after; and all
"other colonels to take place according to the dates of
"their commissions.

"2nd. That the several regiments that are not of our
"Guards take place according to their respective senio-
"rities from the time they were raised, so as that no regi-
"ment is to lose its precedency by the death of their
"colonel.

"3rd. As to the Horse. That the three troops of
"Guards[2] take place before all others. That the captains Dec. 3rd.
"take their ranks as eldest colonels of Horse, the lieute-
"nants as eldest majors, the cornets as eldest captains
"of Horse, and the guydons as youngest captains of
"Horse. That when the troops march with their colours,
"the officers of the same degree do command according
"to the seniority of the troops respectively; but when
"they are commanded out in parties, the officers of the
"same degree are to command according to the dates of
"their commissions.

"That our own regiment of Horse take place imme-
"diately after the Guards, and the colonel of it is to have
"precedency immediately after the captains of the Guards,
"and before all other colonels of Horse, whatever change
"may be of the colonel: and all the officers thereof, of
"like or the same degree, do take place according to the
"dates of their commissions.

"4th. That the eldest colonels do on all occasions
"command, and when there shall be no colonel upon the
"place, then the lieutenant-colonel of the eldest regiment,

---

[1] Since disbanded.          [2] Disbanded.

" and in like manner, when no lieutenant-colonel, the
" major, and so down to the captains and other inferior
" officers.

" 5th.   That all officers under the condition of a gene-
" ral officer, when they shall happen to be put into any
" garrison, shall, during their being there, obey the gover-
" nor of the same or his deputies.

" And it is our further will and pleasure, that our most
" dear and most entirely beloved son, James Duke of
" Monmouth, do communicate these our orders, by send-
" ing copies of them, attested with his hand, to the colo-
" nels and captains of the three troops of our Horse
" Guards, and to the colonels of our several regiments of
" Horse and Foot, and governors of our garrisons, to be
" by them communicated to the respective officers under
" their command.

" Given at our Court at Whitehall, the first day of De-
" cember, 1675.

" By his Majesty's command,

"J. WILLIAMSON."

" To our most dear and most
    " entirely beloved son, James
    " Duke of Monmouth."

On the twenty-third of May,[1] a review of the household

---

[1]    " SIR,

[1] " His Majesty having appointed a rendezvous of severall of
" his Majesties Horse and Foot Guards in Hyde Park on Tues-
" day next, being the 23rd of this instant, I desire you to cause
" eight field pieces, viz'. foure demi culverings, and foure
" saker brasse ordnance, and two mortar pieces, with all their
" carriages and furniture thereunto belonging, together with two
" waggons, two tumbrells, and foure tents, attended with a com-
" petent number of gunners, fifty pioneeres, with their respective

troops took place in Hyde Park.  In September following, 1676.
the Duke of Monmouth, who, in March 1674, had received the King's commands to perform the duties of
Captain-General without a commission,[1] was authorised to

"officers, in their best equipage, to attend the exercise of the
"said forces on the day above mention'd, and that they faile not
"to be there by eight of the clock in the morning at farthest.
"                    "I am, your most humble Servant,
"Cockpit, yᵉ                              "MONMOUTH.
"  "19ᵗʰ of May, 1676.
"To the Right Honoᵇˡᵉ Sʳ Thomas
"  "Chicheley, Kⁿᵗ, Master Gene-
"  "rall of his Maᵗⁱᵉˢ Ordnance;
"  "or, in his absence, to the Lieu-
"  "tenant Generall, and the prin-
"  "cipall officers of the same."

[1]   "CHARLES R.
"Trusty and welbeloved, Wee greet you well.  In order to our
"future service of our Guards and established regiments of Horse
"and Foote, as well of our Guards as other in this our kingdome,
"Wee have thought fitt that the respective Colonells, or other
"officers in chiefe commanding them, shall from henceforth ob-
"serve such orders as they shall receive from our most deare and
"intirely beloved sonn James, Duke of Monmouth; and therefore
"Wee doe hereby signify unto you our will and pleasure in that
"behalfe: and that, in what concernes our dearest consort the
"Queen her troope of our Horse Guards, under your command,
"you obey such orders as you shall from time to time receive
"from our said deare sonn accordingly; for which this shall be
"sufficient warrant.  Given at our Court at Whitehall, the 30th
"day of March, 1674.
"                    "By his Maᵗⁱᵉ command,
"                              "ARLINGTON."

"To our trusty and welbeloved
"  "Colonel Sʳ Phillip Howard,
"  "commander of our dearest con-
"  "sort the Queen her troope of
"  "our Horse Guards; or, in his
"  "absence, to the officer in chiefe
"  "commanding the said troope."

1676.  issue orders for the " removal of quarters ;" but he was
not to sign " some kindes of warrants and military orders," which had been formerly done by the Duke of Albemarle *ex officio* as Captain-General.[1]   In the annual

---

" The like Order to observe such orders as his Orace the Duke
" of Monmouth shall give, addressed to

" The Lord Duras (commanding the Duke of York's troop of
" Horse Guards).

" The Earle of Oxford (Royal Horse Guards).

" Colonel John Russell (King's reg[t] of Foot Guards).

" The Earle of Craven (Coldstream).

" Colonel S[r] Charles Lyttleton (the Admiral's regiment).

" The Earl of Mulgrave (the Holland regiment)."—Official Records, War-Office.

[1] " By Order of the 11[th] of August, 1675, his Majesty appointed
" his Grace the Duke of Monmouth to assigne quarters for such
" troopes and companies as hee should thinke fitt."

    " CHARLES R.

" Most deare and most intirely beloved sonn, Wee greet you
" well.  As Wee have formerly given orders to the troopes of our
" Horse Guards, and to our established regiments of Horse and
" Foot, to observe such orders as they should from time to time
" receive from you, soe Wee have now thought fitt to comitt, and
" doe hereby comitt, unto you, the cognisance and care of appoint-
" ing removealls of quarters, the releifes of any of our established
" troopes or companies, and the sending of all convoyes needful
" for our service.  In pursuance whereof, it is our will and plea-
" sure that you give such orders for those respective purposes as
" you shall judge most expedient for our service ; and Wee hereby
" authorize you (in those your orders) to require the officers to
" quarter the respective troopes, companies, and parties, upon
" their march, and at their quarters, in innes, victualling houses,
" tavernes, brandy houses, and ale houses, and to require all our
" justices of peace, and other officers and constables whom it
" may concerne, to be assisting therein ; And considering that Wee
" continue to issue from ourselfe some kindes of warrants and
" military orders, which did belong to the office of our late
" Generall, and which hee was wont to dispatch and signe, Wee,
" being desirous to distinguish such warrants and orders from

army-lists published by the War-Office, the Duke of 1676.
Monmouth's name is included in the list of Captains-
General of the army. No commission as Captain-General
is to be found entered in the Rolls Chapel Office, Chancery Lane. In Sir John Dalrymple's " Memoirs of Great
Britain," the following explanation is to be found, vol. i.
page 47 :—" Upon the death of the Duke of Albemarle,
" the King had abolished the office of Lord General of
" the Army, deeming it too great for a subject. In 1674,
" the Duke of Monmouth prevailed on the King to revive
" the office and bestow it upon him. Monmouth gave
" directions that in the form of his commission he should
" be called the King's son, but that the usual addition to
" his name of the word *natural* should be omitted. The
" Duke of York (who had opposed the appointment) sent
" orders to the officer who was to draw the commission
" to do it in the usual form : the officer obeyed, and deli-
" vered the commission to Vernon, the Duke of Mon-
" mouth's secretary. But Vernon, by his master's orders,
" erased the word *natural*. The Duke of York com-
" plained to the King of the alteration. The King, with-
" out making any answer, clipped with a pair of scissors
" the commission through the middle." The Duke of

---

" other affaires of our crowne passing our signett and signe
" manuall, have thought fitt, and it is our will and pleasure, that
" all such kindes of warrants and orders as formerly issued from
" George Duke of Albemarle, our late Generall, deceased, in re-
" gard of that office, and which Wee continue to issue from our-
" selfe, shall passe our sign manuall onely, and shall be counter-
" signed by the Secretary to our Forces as by our command. And
" soe Wee bid you most heartily farewell. Given at our Court at
" Whitehall, the 7ᵗʰ day of September, 1676."
        " By his Maᵗⁱᵉˢ command,
                " J. WILLIAMSON."
" To our most dear and most
    " entirely beloved sonn, James,
    " Duke of Monmouth."

1676. Buckingham, in his " Memoirs," gives additional information on this subject in vol. II. page 13 :—" The first " step of the Duke of Monmouth's rising to authority in " the army, was his being entrusted with the care, though " not the command, of it ; which the Lord Arlington con- " sented to, (notwithstanding in France 'tis a part of his " province as chief Secretary of State,) both in friendship " to him, and for his own ease, since it saved him the " trouble of such affairs, without diminution either to his " power or profit ; since all commissions still pass through " the Secretary's hands, and only orders now through the " Duke's. The second advance he made, was the King's " sending his commands to every Colonel that they should " obey all directions which came from the Duke of Mon- " mouth. This wanted but the formality of a commission " to make him an absolute General ; and yet even thus " far the Duke of York assisted him, so blinded he was by " his fondness of either husband or wife, or rather, I think, " of both together." On the writer's referring to the State-Paper Office, the instructions to draw up Monmouth's commission, omitting the word *natural*, and the *original commission* in which this word was inserted and cut out, were found, and the parchment cut in the manner described by Sir John Dalrymple. The incision was made through the name of *Charles*, whose sign manual was affixed, and the letters *ar* " clipped " out in the royal signature.[1] The power intended to be granted by this commission appears to be much more confined than that possessed by Monck. An office copy of Monck's commission was also with these papers, as well as a letter from the Duke of Monmouth to Mr. Secretary Williamson, dated from " Bruxelles, 17th August, 1678," requesting that his commission might bear date from the time of his

[1] A detailed account of this affair may be seen in the Memoirs of James II., edited by Clarke, vol. I. page 494.

arrival in Flanders.  Sir John Dalrymple's account is 1676.
therefore correct, except that the occurrence relative to
the commission took place in the year 1678, and not in
1674, as stated by him.  Notwithstanding Monmouth
held no commission, he filled the situation of Captain-
General till September, 1679.  Party spirit ran high, and
on " the 11th of September the Duke of Monmouth,
" coming from Windsor to his house at the Cock-pit, was
" pleased to declare, that it had pleased his Majesty to
" take his commission of Lord General from him."[1]

In October, a regiment[2] was formed for service in Vir-

---

[1] Domestic Intelligencer, or News both from City and Country,
No. 21.

[2]

| | Captains. | Lieut[s]. | Ensigns. | Serjeants. | Drum[rs]. | Men. |
|---|---|---|---|---|---|---|
| Out of the 24 Comp[s] of the King's Reg[t] of Foot Guards, with their arms  . . | 2 | 2 | 2 | 4 | ,, | 168 |
| ,,  ,,  12 Comp[s] of the Cold-stream, with their arms . . . . . | 1 | 1 | 1 | 2 | ,, | 84 |
| ,,  ,,  Admiral's Reg[t] do. do. . | 1 | 1 | 1 | 2 | ,, | 59 |
| ,,  ,,  Holland do. do. do. . | 1 | 1 | 1 | 2 | ,, | 49 |
| ,,  ,,  Garrison Comp[s] at Portsmouth, Plymouth, Hull, Gravesend, Tower of London, and Windsor Castle  do. do. | ,, | ,, | ,, | ,, | ,, | 140 |
| Drummers impressed by Drum Major General John Mawgridge for the occasion . . . . . . . . . . | ,, | ,, | ,, | ,, | 15 | ,, |
| Recruits raised by beat of Drum under a Warrant signed by the King . . . | ,, | ,, | ,, | ,, | ,, | 500 |
| Total . . . . . . . . | 5 | 5 | 5 | 10 | 15 | 1000 |

To be formed into 5 Companies of 200 each.

Also, a detachment from the Ordnance Department.
A Commissary of Provisions.
A Commissary of Musters.
A Deputy Paymaster.
A Chirurgeon and Mates.
Extracted from Various Records at the War-Office.

ginia, by drafts from the Guards, the Admiral's, the
Holland regiment, the "Non Regimented companies in
the Garrisons," and five hundred newly-raised men, under
Captain Herbert Jefferey of the First Guards. The proportion furnished by the Coldstream was two serjeants
and eighty-four rank and file, under Captain John Mutlow
with the senior lieutenant and ensign of the regiment.[1]
They embarked at the Tower Wharf in boats, and were
conveyed to vessels ready to receive them " below
Gravesend."

1677.    King Charles first entertained the idea of introducing
grenadiers into the British army. Two men from each
company of the King's and Coldstream regiments of
Guards were trained and exercised by Captain Lloyd of
the First Guards for the duty of grenadiers.[2]

Charles the Second and the Duke of York, who were
at variance with Lewis the Fourteenth, for not increasing
their pensions, by which he had purchased their conni-
vance at his ambitious designs, felt inclined to renew the
triple alliance. Charles therefore appealed to his Parliament, made his preparations, and entered into a communication with the Prince of Orange, who had recently
married the Princess Mary. Colonel John Churchill,
afterwards Duke of Marlborough, who possessed the entire
confidence of Charles and his brother,[3] was employed on
this occasion.[4]    This mission preceded the embassy of

---

[1] See Appendix, No. 55.

[2] See Appendix, No. 56.

[3] Dalrymple's Memoirs, vol. 1. page 208.

[4] " The arrangement was ultimately of no avail. But it was an
" important transaction in the life of Colonel Churchill, because
" it enabled him to appreciate the character and principles of the
" great Prince by whom Europe was afterwards rescued from
" slavery, and England from Papal bondage."—*Coxe's Memoirs of
John Duke of Marlborough*, 4°, vol. 1. page 13.

Sir William Temple, for the conclusion of an offensive and defensive alliance with the United Provinces.

In January, the regiment was increased[1] by four hundred and eighty men, which completed it to twelve companies of one hundred rank and file: three hundred and twenty were armed with musquets, and one hundred and twenty with pikes. Another augmentation of eight companies took place, each consisting of one hundred men. Among them were distributed eight " partizans, twenty-four hal-" berts, sixteen drums with sticks, five hundred and " fifty musquets with collars of bandeleers, and two " hundred and seventy-four pikes." These companies with a proportionate number of officers were ordered to assemble at Rochester. The names of the captains were Francis Newport, Humphrey O Keover, Thomas Sulyards, Thomas Talmash, James Eastland, Robert Brett, Simon Parry, and Robert Sinklair.[2]

After Parliament had voted the supplies, an army of twenty thousand men was raised, and three thousand sent to secure Ostend. The naval service was not forgotten, and a fleet was fitted out.

Four companies, under Captains John Clarke, Robert Wythe, John Miller, and Herbert Price, embarked at the Tower for Ostend.

It was in this year that grenadier companies were generally adopted in regiments of foot.[3] On the fourth of

1677-8. January.

February.

---

[1] See Appendix, No. 58.
[2] See Appendix, No. 59.
[3] Grenadiers, at their first institution, were not confined to the infantry; for, to each of the three troops of Horse Guards, a corps of sixty-four grenadiers, with two drums, four hautbois, two corporals, two serjeants, and two lieutenants, were attached. These corps were armed with harquebuses and bayonets, and distinguished by caps and looped clothes. They were afterwards formed

1678.
April.

April, a warrant was issued for raising one hundred men, to be added as a company of grenadiers to the Coldstream.[1] Evelyn in his Memoirs, vol. I. page 497, gives the following description of the Grenadiers. "Returned with my Lord (Lord Chamberlaine) by Hounslow Heath, "where we saw the new-rais'd army encamp'd, design'd "against France, in pretence at least, but which gave "umbrage to the Parliament. His Ma[y] and a world of "company were in the field, and the whole army in battalia, "a very glorious sight. Now were brought into service a "new sort of soldiers call'd Grenadiers, who were dex- "trons in flinging hand granados, every one having a "pouch full; they had furr'd caps with coped crownes "like Janizaries, which made them looke very fierce,[2] and "some had long hoods hanging down behind, as we pic- "ture fools. Their clothing being likewise pybald, yellow "and red."

May 1st.

In May, four additional companies of the Coldstream were ordered to embark for Ostend,[3] under Captains Robert Sinclair, Robert Brett, Francis Newport, and Thomas Sulyards.

Considerable expense was incurred for the clothing of

---

into two troops; the first, Oct. 4th, 1693, the second, May 27th, 1702.—*Grose's Military Antiquities,* vol. I. page 161.

See also Appendix, No. 65.

Grenadiers first instituted in France, in 1667, by having four or five men a company.

Charles James, in his "Military Dictionary," says they were first known in England in 1685.

[1] See Appendix, Nos. 62 and 63.

[2] See Warrant, No. 80.

[3] Captains Newport's and Sulyards's companies embarked at the Tower, Sinclair's at Dover, and Brett's at Rochester.—Official Records, War-Office.

"trumpeters, kettle drummers, banners, colours, and en- 1678.
"signs, &c. &c." for the household troops, the King's
Royal regiment of Dragoons, and the Queen's regiment
of Horse, which were furnished and paid for by the
Master of the King's wardrobe.[1]

The company of the Coldstream, previously mentioned
as having sailed for Virginia under Captain Mutlow,
forming part of the battalion commanded by Captain
Jeffery of the First Foot Guards, returned to England
by detachments in the months of March, May, and
June.[2]

The allied armies, being assembled in Flanders,[3] com- July.

---

[1] See Appendix, No. 73.

[2] Captain Mutlow, one lieutenant, three serjeants, three corporals, one drummer, and sixty-nine privates landed on the twenty-
third of March. Ensign Thomas Seymour, one serjeant, and eleven
privates landed the end of May. Lieutenant John Tonge, two
serjeants, two corporals, two drummers, twenty-four privates, and
surgeon's-mate Thomas Buchan, landed on the tenth of June. See
Appendix, Nos. 61 and 70.

[3] Extracts from several letters of the Duke of York to the Prince
of Orange:—

"London, July 5, 1678.—This day a battalion of 8 companies
"embarked at Blackwall for Newport and Bruges; so that, when
"they are landed, we shall have 96 companies of foot in Flanders,
"which will make upwards of 9000 men."

"London, July 26, 1678.—The Duke of Monmouth is to go
"from hence, on Sunday, for Bruges."—"We have now ready in
"Flanders 14 battalions of foot; besides which we have 2 batta-
"lions of foot more, and 3000 horse and dragoons, to be embarked
"from hence by the end of next week."—"Each battalion of foot
"to be about 700."

"Windsor, August 20th. The troops designed for Flanders to
"embark on Monday next;—27 troops of Horse, 60 in each troop,
"12 troops of Dragoons of 60 a piece, and 2 battalions of Foot of
"9 companies each."—"The Earl of Feversham goes over to
"command them."—"The troops to land near Antwerp.—Me-

1678.　menced operations.　The Duke of Monmouth, who commanded the British contingent, united his forces to those of the Prince of Orange.　Several regiments also were detached under the Earl of Ossory to act in conjunction with the Spanish forces.　The battle of St. Dennis was fought near Mons on the fourteenth of September ; the English, headed by the Earl of Ossory,[1] greatly distinguished themselves.　Colonel John Churchill embarked with the last division, and was appointed to command a brigade composed of two battalions of the First and Coldstream Guards, one Dutch regiment, and the regiments of the Prince of Orange and Colonel Legge.[2]

The Duke of Monmouth, in a letter to the Earl of Feversham, dated Whitehall, second of September, 1678, says, " It is thought necessary to send over Coll. Church-" ill and S[r] John Fenwick to act as brigadiers, who begin " their voyage on Wednesday next ; Coll. Churchill com-" mands the first brigade, which is to consist of the two " battalions of Guards, and the Holland, Dutchesses, and " L[d] Allington's regiments, one battalion each.

" Coll. Legge desires his reg[t] may bee in Coll. Church-" ill's brigade, therefore I . . . . have the exchange with " L[d] Allington's battalion." [3]

Soon after Colonel Churchill reached the Continent the

---

*moirs of Great Britain and Ireland,* by Sir John Dalrymple, Bart. 4°, London, 1773, vol. ii. pages from 184 to 192.

[1] Life of King William the Third ; London, 8vo. 1703. page 94. The London Gazette, No. 1329, contains a list of the killed and wounded.

[2] Colonel Churchill's appointment was dated September the third, 1678.　Cox, in his " Memoirs of Marlborough," states the original to be amongst the Marlborough Papers.

[3] Original " Book of Entryes of the Duke of Monmouth's, when Gen[l] of the Army."　State-Paper Office.

Also see Appendix, No. 76.

Prince of Orange signed a treaty with the French, which    1678.
was the prelude to a general peace, and an alliance was
projected between England, Germany, Spain, and Holland.   Charles, contrary to the interest of England, acted
on this occasion in subservience to France.   His assistance was implored by those powers in vain ; unfortunately for the country, his extravagant and dissolute habits
induced him to receive pecuniary donations from Louis
XIV., and the treaty of Nimeguen was the consequence.

As there were in the nation many Papists and converts
to the Romish religion, the King issued a proclamation offering a reward of twenty pounds for the discovery
of any officer or soldier who, having taken the oaths,
had since been perverted to that faith.   An order also
appeared for " displacing and turning out all such officers
" and soldiers as are Popish recusants."[1]

The battalion of the Coldstream, sent to Flanders in
two divisions, returned to their quarters in London.[2]

At the conclusion of the war with France the Cold-    1679.
stream was reduced to twelve companies of sixty men    March.
each.

Somerset House, since the Restoration, had been the    1680.
residence of the Queen Mother, who quitted it to furnish
quarters for the Foot Guards.[3]   A journal of the period
says, " The Queen has already retired, according to his
" Majesties order, to St. James's ; his Majesty intending
" to quarter two regiments in Somerset House, and that

---

[1] See Appendix, Nos. 81, 82.

[2] See Appendix, No. 85.

[3] In 1682, alterations and repairs were made in the palace at
Whitehall, during the time Charles and his Queen resided in
Somerset House.

VOL. I.

" place in the Savoy,[1] where one regiment is now quar-
" tered, is to be turned into an hospital for lame and sick
" soldiers, and his Majesties house at Greenwich is to
" be converted to the same use."[2]

Tangiers being besieged by an army from Morocco,
Charles recommended the House of Commons to take
measures for its preservation ; but Parliament, more in
dread of a Popish successor than anxious to protect a
distant possession, was unwilling to grant further supplies.  The occupation of Tangiers was said by the Court
party to be of importance to the Levant trade, and it was
asserted that the two millions embarked in that commerce
would be lost.  At the end of July a detachment of the
Coldstream, consisting of one captain, one ensign, four
serjeants, six corporals, and one hundred and twenty privates,[3] sailed from Portsmouth with double the number

---

[1] " His Majesty, in pursuance of the late Act of Parliament,
" whereby the subjects of this kingdom are not to be charged with
" the quartering of souldiers, has lately ordered the fitting up the
" Savoy in the Strand for a regiment of Foot souldiers ; And it is
" designed that stables shall be built for the Horse in Leicester
" Fields and Hyde Park upon that account."—*Domestic Intelligence, or News both from City and Country.*  No. 13, Tuesday,
August 19th, 1679.

Part of the Savoy was fitted up as a military prison in 1696.

[2] Protestant (Domestick) Intelligence.  Friday, January 2d,
1679-80. No. 52.

[3] See Appendix, No. 89.

The annexed bill was for making a colour ordered for the company of the Coldstream forming part of the battalion :—

THE EARL OF CRAVEN'S REGIMENT.

|  | £. | s. | d. |
|---|---|---|---|
| 4 ells of blue taffatta at 11s.    .    .    .    . | 2 | 4 | 0 |
| 2 ells of white  do.   at 11s.    .    .    . | 1 | 2 | 0 |
| 2 ells ½ crimson taffatta at 13s.  .    .    . | 1 | 12 | 6 |
|  | 4 | 18 | 6 |

from the First Foot Guards, and detachments from other 1680.
corps, which completed them to five companies, or six
hundred men. The command was given to the Earl of
Mulgrave,[1] and, on their arrival at the garrison of Tangiers, they were styled the King's battalion.

Two companies of the Coldstream went to Oxford to 1680-1.
attend the King.[2]  " The Earl of Craven, Colonel of the March.

| | £. s. d. |
|---|---|
| For making one ensign . . . . . | 1 0 0 |
| For painting in oyle 2 figures of distinctions, at 1s. 3d. p. piece . . . . . } | 0 2 6 |
| For one tassell . . . . . . | 0 2 6 |
| For guilding in oyle the head of the ensign staff . . . . . . } | 0 1 0 |
| | 1 6 0 |

These particulars before mentioned, viz⁴ the painting and making,
were performed by me.  Witness my hand,
ROBERT FISHER.
These particulars aforesaid, were delivered by Nicholas Fownes
to the use of the regiment.  Witness our hands,
ROBERT SHARP,
NICHOLAS FFOWNES.
MS. Additional, No. 5752, British Museum.
[1] See Appendix, Nos. 90, 91, and 92.
[2] " On Friday last," (4ᵗʰ March) " nine score of his Majesty's
" Horse Guards were ordered to be ready to attend his Majesty
" to Windsor, and the Foot Guards to go on Wednesday for
" Oxford, and the rest of the Horse Guards on Thursday."
" April 1ˢᵗ.  This day the Foot which attended his Majesty in
" and about Oxford came to Town, except two companies, which
" are expected this day."—The Protestant Intelligencer, No. 103
and No. 111.
" April 1ˢᵗ, 1681.  His Majesties Guards are returned from
" Oxford, and the forces that were quartered about that city du-
" ring his Majesties abode there, will suddenly return to their
" former quarters which they had before."—The Loyal Protestant

" regiment, remained in the Palace at Whitehall during " the King's absence."

Many members of Parliament,[1] and, in particular, those of the City of London, went there also, accompanied by numerous bodies of well-armed horse, wearing ribbons in their hats, on which were inscribed the words " No Popery!"

The King's absence from Whitehall led to the fitting up of the Mews as quarters for the troops; three companics of the Coldstream occupied them for the first time on the eighteenth of March, and permanently possessed these barracks till the Revolution, after which event the

---

*and True Domestick Intelligencer*, No. 8. Saturday, April 2d, 1681.

" The time now drawing near for the Parliament's meeting at " Oxford, the preparations which were made on all sides, looked " as if the debates were to be managed rather by force, than " argument; for which reason, the King took care, not only to be " accompanied with a good number of his Guards, but had order'd " the greatest part of my Lord of Oxford's regiment to be quarter'd " on the road, to secure his return, and left a good body of men to " be an awe upon the citie in his absence: His Majesty was only " perplexed about Coll. Russel, whose fidelitie he doubted, and " therefore had proposed to my Lord Thanet to buy his regiment, " which he at first agreed too, but after declin'd, on pretence that " the King's not going on with the reforme at Court, as had been " projected, was a discouragement for honest men to venture: the " Duke would have recommended the Earle of Mulgrave, but the " King was prepossess'd against him, so was forced to respite that " matter for the present; but leaveing the chief command with my " Lord Craven, he hoped there could be no great danger in his " absence, he writ to all the Lords not to fail being there, in whose " loyalty he had more confidence than in the Commons, after " which he went to Windsor, and on the 14ᵗʰ of March arrived " together with the Queen at Oxford."—*Life of James IId.*, by Clarke, vol. 1. page 667.

[1] " The Members evidently shewed fears of some violence."—*Ekhard*, vol. iii. page 616.

Dutch Guards, conjointly with the Coldstream, furnished the Tilt Yard, St. James's, Arlington Gate, and Kensington guards.

The following extracts, relating to the changes that took place, are from the Protestant (Domestick) Intelligence:—" Captain Norton (one of the surveyors of the King's " Meuse, and one of the brigadiers of his Majesties " Horse Guards) attended his Majesty on Saturday " morning (26th of February, 168$\frac{0}{1}$) for orders for three " hundred horse and as many foot, which are to be in " the Meuse as a garrison during the time of his Majes-" ty's absence from Whitehall, part whereof are to be of " the Lord Craven's regiment that are quartered about " Spittle-Fields."

" On Monday last (24th of March, 168$\frac{0}{1}$) three com-" panies of my Lord Craven's regiment had orders for to " march into the Meuse, there to keep garrison during " his Majesties absence, and several troops of horse are " speedily to follow them ; the inhabitants there having " made great provision for the quartering of them."

" Tuesday, April the 5th, 1681. We have an account " that ninety horse are ordered forthwith to be kept in " the Mews, as in a garrison, where there will be beds " and all other necessaries provided for them, and also " accommodations for some of the gentlemen of his Ma-" jesties Guards, and that their horses shall be kept " there at 4s. 6d. a week. Two companies of the Right " Honorable the Earl of Craven's regiment went thither " this day, and more will follow as soon as conveniences " are fitted for them."

" November 22d, Tuesday, Whitehall. This day was a " great wrestling match performed in St. James's Park " before his Majesty, by a gentleman of her Majesties

" Guards and one of the Right Honorable the Lord Cra-
" ven's Foot Guards. They both being very dexterous and
" active, it was a long while before they could decide it ;
" but, in fine, the Life-Guardsman had the victory, and
" had several guineys given him by the worthy spectators,
" it being performed to their great satisfaction." [1]

1681-2.
In January Colonel Edward[2] Sackville, formerly of the
First Foot Guards, and who, on the death of Sir Palmes
Fairborne, succeeded to the government of Tangiers, became lieutenant-colonel of the Coldstream, in the place
of Sir James Smith, who had been appointed colonel of
" the Orange Regiment of Trained Bands," and was subsequently elected vice-president of the Artillery Company
in the City. [3]

---

[1] The Loyal Protestant and True Domestick Intelligencer, No.
81. Thursday, November 24th, 1681.

[2] " Tangier, May 14, 1681. Colonel Sackvile, our Commander-
" in-chief since the death of Sir Palmes Fairborne, has gained the
" love of all the soldiers."—*The Domestick Intelligence*, No. 6, from
the 9th to the 13th of June.

" Collonel Sackvile, who upon the death of Sir Palmes Fair-
" borne received the command of Governour of Tangier, being
" now in Town, has obtained that command for the future, a
" patent being under the Seale for that purpose, with as large an
" authority as any Governour heretofore."—*The Impartial Protestant Mercury*, No. 32, from August 9th to 12th, 1681.

" London, January 24th, 1681-2. His Majesty has been pleased
" to make Colonel Sackvile Lieutenant-Colonel of the Queen's
" regiment of Foot Guards, under the Right Honorable the Earl
" of Craven ; the said Collonel's Government of Tangier being
" conferred on Collonel Kirk."—*The True Protestant Mercury*,
No. 110, from January 21st to 25th, 1681-2.

[3] " On Friday last," (May 20[th],) " Sir James Smith, who is
" made Colonel of the Orange regiment in the room of Sir Robert
" Clayton, mounted the guard on the Royal Exchange with his
" company ; several principal officers of the other regiments

" Friday, March 2ᵈ. This day Captain Wakelin, one
" of the captains of his Majesty's Guards (Coldstream),
" was to walk round St. James's Park five times in two
" hours for a considerable sum of money, which accord-
" ingly he began about nine o'clock ; he walked the first
" round in eighteen minutes and a half, the second in
" twenty-one minutes, the third in twenty-three minutes
" and a half, the fourth in twenty-six minutes, and the
" fifth in little more than fourteen minutes. His Majesty
" being present with his Royal Highness and a nume-
" rous company of spectators, many great wagers were
" laid on both sides." ¹

The arms of the Coldstream were ordered to be exchanged and snaphance musquets and pikes only supplied ; matchlocks were discontinued by the Guards, although nsed in regiments of infantry to a later period.²

---

" attending him as volunteers, whom he afterwards treated at a
" splendid collation."—*The Currant Intelligence*, No. 9, from 21st
to 24th of May, 1681.

" London, October 6ᵗʰ, 1681. Sir Thomas Pritchard, before
" Vice-President, was elected President, and Sir James Smith,
" Vice-President of the Artillery Company of the City."—*The
Impartial Protestant Mercury*, No. 48, from 4th to 7th of October,
1681.

¹ The Loyal Protestant and True Domestick Intelligence, No·
240. Saturday, March 3d, 1682-3.

² See Appendix, No. 96.

" His Grace the Duke of Grafton hath ordered, against May
" next, that every officer under his command, from the collonel to
" the corporal, shall have new coats, all laced, and all new arms :
" He hath also ordered, that every common soldier shall have new
" clothes, musquets and pikes, against the aforesaid time ; and
" that two companies only in a regiment shall have firelocks, and
" those always to go before ; the rest to be all matchlocks."—
*The True Protestant Mercury*, No. 130, April 1st to 5th, 1682.

The change is thus noticed in the Loyal Protestant and True.

1684.     The Guards sent to Tangiers in 1680 returned home in April, 1684.  The King's battalion, now consisting of five companies of two hundred and thirty-five effective men only, marched to London and joined their regiments.[1]

Nothing particular occurred till April 1684, when a grenadier company, similar to the one established in 1678, was added to the Coldstream.[2]  A change was introduced in the appointments of infantry officers this year, as directed in the following warrant.


          " CHARLES R.                                    ,

September.     " For the better distinction of our several officers serving " us in our companies of foot, Our will and pleasure is, that " all captains of foot wear no other corselet than of the " colour of gold : all lieutenants, black corselets studded " with gold, and the ensigns corselets of silver.  And we " do likewise think fit that all lieutenants of foot carry " pikes and not partizans, which we do hereby order to be

---

Domestick Intelligence, No. 137, Tuesday, 4th April, 1682.
" His Grace the Duke of Grafton hath been pleased to order, that " every officer under him shall be very richly accoutred against " May next, and every souldier to have new clothes and new arms, " and likewise that only two files in a company shall have fire-" locks to their musquets, and the rest matchlocks."

[1] The following regiments returned to England from Tangiers at the same time :—

|  | Comp[s]. | Effective Men. |  |
|---|---|---|---|
| E[rl] of Dumbarton's regi[ment] | 16 | 628 | Quartered at Rochester. |
| Col. Kirke's . . . . . | 16 | 559 | { 8 comp[s]. Pendennis. 8   ,,      Plymouth. |
| Col Trelawny's . . . . | 16 | 470 | Portsmouth. |
| Troops of Horse . . . . | 4 | 178 | London. |
| Company of Miners . . . | 1 | 48 | London. |
| Independent Comp[s]. . . | 4 | 185 | Ireland. |

[2] See Appendix, No. 98.

" re-delivered into the Office of our Ordnance. And we 1684.<br>September.
" do further direct that authentic copies hereof be sent to
" our several Colonels of Foot, and transmitted to the
" Governors of our forts and garrisons, to the end that the
" respective officers of our forces may govern themselves
" accordingly. Given at our Court at Winchester, the
" first day of September, 1684.

" By his Majesty's command,

" SUNDERLAND."

The Exclusion Bill at this moment occupied the attention of Parliament,[1] and a strong petition was presented to the King, not so much to acquaint him with the danger arising from Popery, as with a view to persuade the people at large of the necessity of the measure.

The two regiments of Guards were precisely on the same footing, as appears by Nathan Brooks' Army List, 1684, which states, that " this regiment of Foot Guards " (Coldstream), established as the former, (viz. as the " first Guards,) consisting of twelve companies, distin- " guished by red coats lined with green, red stockings, " and red breeches, and white sashes fringed green, " attended by a company of grenadiers, as the Duke of " Grafton's, their caps lined green, with green tassels for " their distinction. Flies St. George's cross, bordered " with white in a blue field."

On the first of October[2] the King reviewed his troops at October.

---

[1] The Exclusion Bill was thrown out in the Lords: it passed on the first reading by a majority of two, but was thrown out on the second reading by a majority of sixty-three against thirty.

[2] On the first of October King Charles mustered his Guards, which now consisted of four thousand men, completely trained and effective.—*Rapin*, vol. 11. page 734.

Putney Heath.[1]  One of the battalions of the Coldstream Guards was encamped in the neighbourhood ; the line of horse and foot (amounting to four thousand one hundred and eight men) " extended from the Red House, near the " Bowling-green, 'cross the Heath, and pointing to the

---

[1] Nathan Brooks.  Echard, vol. III. page 716, 1698.

Voltaire says, the first assemblage of troops in time of peace for the purpose of drill and reviews was at Compiegne, where Louis XIV. assembled seventy thousand men, and all the operations of a campaign were gone through, for the instruction of his grandsons.

Review of his Majesty's Forces on Putney Heath, the 1st of October, 1684 :—

|  | Men. |
|---|---|
| Three troops of Grenadiers, commanded by 6 lieutenants . . . . . . . . . | 180 |
| His Majesty's First troop of Guards, commanded by the Duke of Albemarle . . . . . | 200 |
| Queen's troop of Guards, commanded by Sir Philip Howard . . . . . . . . . | 200 |
| Duke's troop of Guards, commanded by the Earl of Feversham . . . . . . . . . | 200 |
| First battⁿ of the First reg. of Foot Guards, commanded by Major Eyton . . . . . | 536 |
| Second battⁿ of the First reg. of Guards, commanded by Captain Sackville Tufton . . . . | 480 |
| Battalion of his Royal Highness's, commanded by Sᵣ Ch. Littleton . . . . . . . | 530 |
| Battalion of the Royal reg. of Foot, commanded by Lᵗ-Col. Sir Jaˢ Halket . . . . . . | 555 |
| Battalion of the Coldstream Guards, commanded by Lᵗ-Col. Eᵈ Sackville . . . . . . | 530 |
| Royal reg. of Horse, commanded by Col. Earl of Oxford . . . . . . . . . | 400 |
| Royal reg. of Dragoons, commanded by John Lord Churchill, Col. . . . . . . . | 300 |
|  | 4108 |

"River. The troops were commanded by the Earl of 1684.<br>October.
"Craven.[1] The Coldstream, my Lord Dumbarton's, and
"the Admiral's battalions, successively exercised, all
"three by beat of drum, the military postures of pike,
"sword, and musquet, every man dexterously discharging
"his duties with an exact general readiness, to the great
"delight and satisfaction of their Majesties and Royal
"Highnesses, vouchsafing all the time of exercise to grace
"their arms with the honor of their presence. The day
"proving wet and showery was a general impediment
"from proceeding at that time to any other motions cus-
"tomary upon like reviews; all decampt sooner than they
"otherwise would have done."

---

[1] Colonel of the Coldstream Guards.

# CHAPTER X.

Death of Charles II.— Coronation of James II.—Extract from
Sandford's " History of the Coronation"—Dress and other details
connected with the " Coldstreamers"—Monmouth lands in Dor-
setshire—First battalion of the Coldstream Guards leave town for
Marlborough — Monmouth defeated, taken, and beheaded —
Bayonets provided for the First and Coldstream Guards; the
Grenadiers only had been previously provided with them —
Allowance granted to the wounded at Sedgmore — Review at
Hounslow—Bank of Lieutenant-Colonel granted to Captains of
companies in the two regiments of Foot Guards—Second Gre-
nadier companies placed on the establishment—Prince of Orange
lands at Torbay—James quits London—Troops ordered out of
London, with the exception of the Coldstream—On the arrival of
William in London, the Coldstream ordered into Kent—Declaration of war against France—Revolt of the Royals—First Mutiny
Bill—Coldstream taken from Craven and given to Talmash—
Some account of Lord Craven—William projects an alliance
against France—Coldstream disembark at Helvoet Sluys—Join
the allies under Prince Waldeck—Failure of the French in
their attack on Walcourt—English regiments go into quarters
for the winter — Coldstream at Ghent — French, Spanish, and
Dutch also move into quarters.                           .

1685.  CHARLES II. having expired of a fit of apoplexy on
the sixth of February, James II., at his accession,

granted fresh commissions to every officer in the army.[1]

The coronation of James took place on St. George's day, the twenty-third of April. The following is extracted from Sandford's " History of the Coronation," and gives an account of the dress of the Guards, and other details connected with that day.[2]

" The First Regiment of His Majesties Foot Guards.

" The officers of this First Regiment of Foot Guards
" (consisting of 24 companies, and two companies of gra-
" nadiers) were exceedingly richly habited ; some in coats
" of cloth of gold, others in crimson velvet, imbroidered
" or laced with gold or silver; but most of them in fine
" scarlet cloth buttoned down the breast, and on the
" facings of the sleeves with silver plate.

" Their scarffs (which they wore about their wastes)
" were either net-work of gold or silver, or crimson taf-
" fata richly fringed with gold or silver. And their hats
" were adorned with tours of white feathers.

---

[1] See Appendix, No. 278, for list of names and dates of confirmation for the officers of the Coldstream.

[2] From " The History of the Coronation of the Most High,
" Most Mighty, and Most Excellent Monarch, James II., by the
" Grace of God, King of England, Scotland, France, and Ireland,
" Defender of the Faith, &c. ; and of his Royal Consort, Queen
" Mary ; solemnized in the Collegiate Church of S[t] Peter, in the
" City of Westminster, on Thursday the 23rd of April, being the
" Festival of S[t] George, in the year of our Lord 1685.
          " By his Majesties especial command.
    " By PRANCIS SANDFORD, ESQ. Lancaster Herald of Arms.
" In the Savoy. Printed by Thomas Newcomb, one of his Ma-
     jesties Printers. 1687."

" The captains were distinguished by corslets or gorgets
" of silver plate doubly gilt; the lieutenants by corslets
" of steel, polished and sanguined, and studded with
" nails of gold ; and the ensigns had their corslets of
" silver plate.

" The private soldiers were all new clothed in coats of
" red broad cloth, lined and faced with blew ; their hats
" were black, laced about with silver, turned up and gar-
" nished with blew ribbands.  Their breeches were of
" blew broad cloth, and the stockings of blew worsted.

" The musquetiers were armed with snaphance mus-
" quets with sanguin'd barrels, three foot eight inches in
" length; good swords in waste belts, and collars of
" bandiliers ; and the pike-men with pikes sixteen foot
" long, each headed with a three-square point of steel,
" and good swords in broad shoulder-belts, wearing also
" about their wastes sashes or scarffs of white worsted
" fringed with blew.

" The granadiers (viz. two companies) were clothed as
" the musquetiers, but distinguished by caps of red cloth
" lined with blew shaloon, and laced with silver galoon
" about the edges ; and on the frontlets of the said caps
" (which were very large and high) was imbroidered the
" King's cipher and crown.　Each of these granadiers was
" armed with a long carabine strapt, the barrel thereof
" three foot two inches in length ; a cartouch-box, bionet,
" Granada-pouch, and a hammer-hatchet."

1685.
April.

"THE Second Regiment of His Majesties Foot Guards, called the Coldstreamers, commanded by the RIGHT HONOURABLE WILLIAM EARL OF CRAVEN, Colonel and Captain.

| 1. | Earl of Craven, Col. and Capt. | Capt. Lieut. Hen. Cope. | Ens. George Wythe. |
| 2. | Lieut.-Col. Edward Sackvile. | Lieut. Edmond Stukeley. | Ens. William Wakefield. |
| 3. | Major John Huison. | Lieut. Hen. Wharton. | Ens. Henry Wynde. |
| 4. | Cpt John Miller. | Lieut. Jon Drake. | Ens. Adrian Moore. |
| 5. | Capt. Anthony Markham. | Lieut. Robert Wilkins. | Ens. Francis Marshall. |
| 6. | Cpt James Kendall. | Lieut. William Gibbons. | Ens. William Matthews. |
| 7. | Capt. William Wakelin. | Lieut. Edward Bradock. | Ens. Gam' Chetwynd. |
| 8. | Capt. William Cholmley. | Lieut. John Clarke. | Ens. John Shepard. |
| 9. | Cpt Charles Cotton. | Lieut. William Hewett. | Ens. Charles Wakelin. |
| 10. | Capt. Richard Pope. | Lieut. William Rigge. | Ens. Bozoon Symons. |
| 11. | Cpt Heneage Finch. | Lieut. Edward Jones. | Ens. John Wybert. |
| | | Lieut. Edward Shenton. | |
| 12. | Capt. James Bridgman. | Lieut. James Warde. | Granadiers. |
| 13. | Capt. Dudley Rupert. | Lieut. John Hope. | Ens. Charles Stanley." |

" The officers of this Second Regiment of Foot Guards
" (consisting of twelve companies and one of granadiers)
" were exceeding richly habited, but differing in their
" imbroideries, laces, and fringes, which were of gold,
" and their buttons of gold thread, from the officers of the
" First Regiment of Foot Guards, which had them of
" silver.

" The captains, lieutenants, and ensigns, were distin-
" guished by corselets or gorgets, as those officers of the
" First Regiment, and their hats were also adorned with
" tours of white feathers.

" The private soldiers, viz. musquetiers, pikemen, and
" granadiers, were in all points armed and accoutred as
" the First Regiment, and agreeable to them in their
" clothing, except their breeches, which were of red broad
" cloth, and their stockings of red worsted.  Their hats
" were black, turned up, and laced about with gold galoon,
" in which they wore red ribbands, and the sashes or
" waste scarffs of the pikemen being of white worsted,
" were fringed on the sides and at the ends with red
" worsted.

" The granadiers had their caps lined and faced with
" blew chaloon, and laced with gold galoon, and imbroi-
" dered on the frontlets with the King's cipher.

" The colours or ensigns of this regiment had been of
" blew taffata : the colonels without distinction ; the
" lieutenant-colonels with a white plain cross throughout,
" surmounted by a cross of crimson taffata, or cross of St.
" George ; as were the ten other ensigns. Only the majors
" ensign was distinguished by a white pile wavy is-
" suing out of the canton of the first quarter, and the
" several captains by numeral letters, viz. The eldest by
" I, the second by II, the third by III, and so to the
" youngest or ninth captain, who had IX, all painted in

" white on the dexter cantons of the first quarters.
" These ensigns were devised by Mr. Francis Sandford,
" for his Grace George late Duke of Albemarle, when he
" commanded this regiment, and approved of by His late
" Majesty King Charles the Second, and by His present
" Majesty when Duke of York.

" But the distinctions in the ensigns of the First Regi-
" ment of Foot Guards being altered by the present King,
" (as is said before,) His Majesty did then also direct
" that the alterations following should be made in the
" ensigns of this His Second Regiment of Foot Guards,
" that they might be more agreeable to the colours of the
" First Regiment;[1] for, excepting the colonel's ensign,
" which was purely of white taffata, the other eleven were
" charged with crosses of crimson taffata throughout.
" The lieutenant-colonel's without distinction; the major's
" had a pile wavy; the cross of the eldest captain was
" charged on the centre with the letter I, in white, en-
" signed with an imperial crown of gold painted thereon;
" the second with II, the third with III, the fourth with
" IV, and so forward to the ninth captain, who was dis-
" tinguished by IX, each of them under an imperial
" crown of gold. And thus did these ensigns fly at the
" coronation.

" This Second Regiment of Foot Guards, repairing to

---

[1] See Appendix, No. 108. Thomas Holford, Port Cullis, Pur-
suivant at Arms, in a petition dated 2nd July, 1685, for payment
of the alteration in the colours, sets forth that a contract was
formerly made with him to furnish thirty-six colours for the two
regiments of Foot Guards, at six pounds each colour, and, by reason of their alterations, they are of much more work and charge
than formerly; now valued at nine pounds a-piece.—Report on
his petition, dated Dec. 3rd, 1686. War-Office Report Book,
1712.

" their parade in Lincoln's-Inn-Fields, were formed in a
" battalion consisting only of eleven companies, inclu-
" ding the company of granadiers ; the two other compa-
" nies of Captain Anthony Markham and Captain James
" Kendal, being upon duty at the Tilt-Yard, near White-
" hal, and at St. James's, (where their Majesties then lay,)
" commanded by the said Captain Markham, with Lieu-
" tenant William Gibbons.

" From Lincoln's-Inn-Fields they marched through
" Covent Garden, the Strand, (and passing by Whitehal,)
" through King Street, Westminster, and thence into
" the Great Sanctuary, where the battalion was drawn
" up, and posted from St. Margaret's church gate, west-
" ward, along the wall of the church-yard, and on the
" south side of the rail, in a single rank, reaching to the
" great west door of the Abbey, ranging likewise with-
" out the north rail to the same great door in opposition;
" Colonel Edward Sackville, Lieutenant-Colonel, stand-
" ing on that side before the centre of the colours, who
" commanded the regiment in chief this day, by reason
" of the Right Honourable William, Earl of Craven, Co-
" lonel, being a peer of the realm, was obliged to attend
" His Majesty at the coronation, among the other earls.

" Major John Huitson was posted at the west end of
" the church, with Adjutant Robert Wilkins, the officers
" having their posts according to the forming of the bat-
" talion.

" There were likewise musquetiers on each side within
" the church reaching to the quire-door, commanded by
" Captain John Miller and Lieutenant William Rigge.

" The company of the granadiers, commanded by Cap-
" tain James Bridgman, with Lieutenant Edward Shen-
" ton, and Lieutenant James Ward, being posted at the
" north door of St. Margaret's church-yard, in a single

" rank, having on their right Sir William Booth's com-
" pany of granadiers of the First Regiment of Foot
" Guards."

Soon after the coronation, and during the sitting of Parliament, Monmouth landed at Lyme in Dorsetshire. A
bill of attainder was immediately passed against this rash
and unfortunate man; the sum of four hundred thousand
pounds was also voted for suppressing the rebellion: an
adjournment then took place. Monmouth's excuse for his
invasion was, that James had occasioned the Fire of London, the death of Charles the Second, and also the mur-
ders of Godfrey and Essex. The King was styled a
" Popish Usurper" in the proclamation issued by his enemies. Monmouth, on his landing, had only about one
hundred followers, of the lowest description, but they
increased so fast, that he was compelled to send numbers
away for want of arms. At Taunton, Bridgewater, and
other places in his line of march, he was proclaimed
King.

As James had no great confidence in his militia, he sent
a battalion of the Coldstream,[1] under Colonel Sackville,
with two battalions of the First Guards, five companies of
Dumbarton's regiment, five companies of Trelawny's, and
a small battalion under Colonel Kirke, who marched on
the twentieth of June for Marlborough, on their way to
Weston. These, with other troops, amounted to two
thousand eight hundred foot, and seven hundred horse[2]

---

[1] See Appendix, No. 107.

[2] The King's account of the battle at Sedgemore states, that the
horse was composed of " 150, commanded out of the three
troops of Horse Guards, and 60 grenadiers on horseback, under
—— Villars," seven troops of the Horse Guards under Sir

1685.
June 11th. and dragoons; the train of artillery consisted of sixteen field-pieces; under the command of the Earl of Feversham.[1]

Monmouth, on learning that his confederate, Argyle, was routed and taken prisoner, fell into a state of despondency.

July 6th. The injudicious arrangements of Lord Feversham in the disposal of his troops induced the rebels to attempt to surprise him at Sedgemore, near Bridgewater. At first the attack made by Monmouth obtained partial success, but his gross misconduct, and the cowardice of Lord Grey, enabled the King's forces to gain an easy victory. After a short combat, the insurgents were defeated with great slaughter.[2] " 8 July. Came news of Monmouth's utter " defeate, and the next day of his being taken by Sᵣ Wᵐ " Portman and Lord Lumley, with the militia of their " counties. It seems the horse, commanded by Lord

---

Francis Compton, and four troops of Lord Cornbury's regiment of dragoons. Douglas's (Dumbarton's regiment) was the only battalion of the King's Foot that had matchlocks; by seeing the light of which, Monmouth was enabled to approach the King's troops the night of the action. The brunt of the rebels' fire fell on the First Foot Guards and Royals.—MS. Harl. No. 6845.

[1] Hume says, six regiments were called from Holland; the army was considerably augmented, and regular forces to the number of 3000 were despatched under the command of Feversham and Churchill, in order to check the progress of the rebels.—*Hume,* vol. vii.

Monmouth was proclaimed King on entering Taunton, 20th of June, by the name of James the Second.—*Rapin,* vol. ii. page 749.

When Monmouth invaded the West of England, James II. sent down the Guards to oppose him, and they conducted themselves with great valour.—*Grose's Military Antiquities,* vol. ii. page 207.

[2] Thirteen hundred men killed, and the same number taken prisoners.—*Rapin,* vol. ii. page 749, and MS. *Lansdowne,* 1152.

" Grey, being newly rais'd and undisciplin'd, were not to
" be brought in so short a time to endure the fire, which
" expos'd the foote to the King's, so as when Monmouth
" had led the foote in greate silence and order, thinking
" to surprize Lieut' Gen' Lord Feversham newly encamp'd,
" and given him a smart charge, interchanging both
" greate and small shot, the horse, breaking their owne
" ranks, Monmouth gave it over, and fled with Grey,
" leaving their party to be cut in pieces to the number of
" 2000.   The whole number reported to be above 8000,
" the King's but 2700.   The slaine were most of them
" Mendip miners, who did greate execution with their
" tooles, and sold their lives very dearely, whilst their
" leaders were pursu'd and taken the next morning, not
" far from one another." [1]

Monmouth fled from the field, and changed his clothes
with a peasant to avoid discovery, but was at length found,
and made prisoner by some men of the Dorset militia.[2]
Several of his officers were taken and carried to Salisbury
Gaol, and afterwards sent to London.[3]   Thus ended Monmouth's enterprise.   He was beheaded on Tower Hill the
fifteenth of July, 1685.

This rebellion being suppressed, and the country in a
state of profound peace, it was thought expedient to reduce the army.   The Coldstream had been augmented
from sixty to one hundred men each company, in June,
and was twice reduced in the next month, first to eighty,
and again to sixty men a company.

---

[1] Evelyn's Diary, vol. i. page 601.

[2] See Appendix, No. 103.

[3] MS. Harl. 6845, contains the examination of Wade and others
of his officers, and also gives a curious and detailed account of
Monmouth's proceedings from the time of his landing.

225. The following allowances were granted to the officers and men wounded at the battle of Sedgemore. Thirty-six gentlemen of the troops of Horse and Grenadier Guards, four hundred and seventeen pounds, ten shillings; and sixteen pounds to one admitted into Chelsea Hospital. The royal regiment of Horse: to one trumpeter and fourteen privates, two hundred and twenty pounds, five shillings. Two battalions of the First Foot Guards;[1] to one captain and lieutenant-colonel, one hundred pounds; to two lieutenants and captains, thirty pounds each; one lieutenant, forty pounds; one lieutenant, eighty pounds; one ensign, fifty pounds; one ensign, thirty pounds; one volunteer, thirty pounds; one serjeant, three corporals, two drummers, and forty-six privates, two hundred and eight pounds five shillings; and sixteen pounds to twelve men admitted into Chelsea Hospital. Seven companies of the Coldstream: to two serjeants, three privates, twenty-seven pounds; and six pounds thirteen shillings and fourpence each, to three men sent to Chelsea Hospital. The royal regiment of Foot:[2] to one captain, forty pounds; three

---

[1] FIRST FOOT GUARDS.

Lt.-Col<sup>l</sup> Ferdinando Hastings.

Captain Edward Rouse.

,,  Edwin Sandys.

Lieutenant Sir W. Querimson.

,,  Thomas Davidson.

Ensign Stephen Bellew.

,,  Henry Hodson.

Volunteer Griffin May.

[2] THE ROYAL REGT OF FOOT.

Captain James Moncreif.

Lieut<sup>t</sup> John Sterling.

,,  Robert Dury.

,,  Thomas Bruce.

,,  John Livingston.

,,  John Mac Kullock.

,,  James Law.

Serjeant Weems, of the Royal Regiment of Foot, particularly distinguished himself, and a warrant, dated twenty-sixth of February, 1685-6, directs that he should be paid " forty pounds for " good service in the action of Sedgemore, in firing the great " guns against the rebells."—War-Office Records.

lieutenants, twenty pounds each; one lieutenant, thirty-five pounds; one lieutenant, twenty-five pounds; one lieutenant, fifteen pounds; three serjeants, two corporals, one drummer, and fifty-seven privates, two hundred and twenty-two pounds; and six pounds thirteen shillings and four-pence each, to twelve men more, admitted into Chelsea Hospital. The Queen Dowager's regiment of Foot: six pounds thirteen shillings and four-pence each, to four men admitted into Chelsea Hospital.

"JAMES R.

"Whereas, by the establishment of our forces, We have
"been graciously pleased to direct an allowance to be
"made to such non-commission officers and soldiers as
"should be wounded or hurt in our service, Our will and
"pleasure is, that out of such monies as are or shall come
"to your hands for the contingent uses of our Guards, &c.
"you cause the summes following to be paid to the non-
"commission officers and soldiers of our Coldstream regi-
"ment of Foot Guards, hereunder mentioned, viz.

|  | £. | s. | d. |
|---|---|---|---|
| To ——— Friend, sargeant | 5 | 0 | 0 |
| To William Robinson | 2 | 0 | 0 |
| To William Baugh | 7 | 0 | 0 |
| To Robert Lindsey | 3 | 0 | 0 |
| To Benjamin Sumner, sargeant | 10 | 0 | 0 |
|  | 27 | 0 | 0 |

"Which summes, amounting to twenty-seaven pounds,
"are to be paid to the said persons in satisfaction for their
"wounds received in our service during the late rebellion.
"Provided none of them be already admitted to the al-
"lowance appointed for our Royall Hospitall, near Chel-
"sea. And for so doing, this, together with the acquit-

" tances of the said persons or their assigns, shall be your
" discharge.  Given at our Court, &c. the 26th day of
" March, 1686, &c.

" By his Ma[s] command,

" WILL[m] BLATHWAYT."

" To Charles Fox, Esq[rs]."

Early in this year new arms were generally supplied  to
the troops, and particular orders issued for their " proper
care and preservation."

A warrant, dated the twenty-second of February, directs
bayonets to be provided for the " two regiments of
Guards ;" and on the twenty-first of May the Coldstream
were supplied with bayonets for the first time.[1]   Only the

---

[1] See Appendix, Nos. 110 and 113.

Le Père Daniel, in his *Histoire de la Milice Françoise*, Paris,
1721, gives the following as the first regular introduction of the
bayonet into the French army.

" On a cru pouvoir suppléer au défaut des piques par la bayon-
" nette au bout du fusil.  Cette arme est très moderne dans les
" troupes.  Je crois que le premier corps qui en ait été armé, est
" le regiment de Fusiliers créé en 1671, et appellé depuis Regiment
" Royal d'Artillerie.  Les soldats de ce regiment portoient la bay-
" onnette dans un petit fourreau à côté de l'épée.  On en a donné
" depuis aux autres regimens pour le même usage ; c'est à dire,
" pour la mettre au bout du fusil dans les occasions.  Quoique
" l'usage ordinaire de la bayonnette au bout du fusil soit aussi
" recent que je viens de le dire, l'idée en étoit venue long tems
" auparavant à quelques officiers d'armée qui l'avoient mise en
" pratique.  Ainsi avoit fait autrefois Monsieur de Puisegur dans
" le département où il commandoit en Flandre.  Pour moy, dit-il
" dans ses memoires, quand je commandois dans Bergues, dans
" Ypres, Dixmunde, et la Quenoque, touts les partis que j'envoyois
" passoient les cannaux de cette façon.  Il est vrai que les soldats

grenadier companies had been previously furnished with
them.

---

" ne portoient point d'épée : mais ils avoient des bayonnettes qui
" avoient des manches d'un pied de long, et les lames des bayon-
" nettes étoient aussi longues que les manches, dont les bouts
" étoient propres à mettre dans les cannons des fusils pour se
" défendre quand quelqu'un vouloit venir à. eux après qu'ils
" avoient tiré."

" Baïonnette. Sorte de Poignard ; ainsi appelé de la ville de
" Baïonne." — *L'Abbé Chastellain, Dictionnaire Etymologique*. A
Paris, M.DC.XCIV.

" The use of bayonets were first introduced by Louis XIV. The
" first regiment that used them was a regiment of French Fusiliers
" established in 1671."—*Voltaire.*

The following warrant contains the first notice of bayonets being
introduced into the English army :—

" CHARLES R.

" Our will and pleasure is, that a regiment of dragoones which
" wee have established and ordered to be raised in twelve troopes of
" fourscore in each besides officers, who are to be under the com-
" mand of our most deare and most intirely beloved Cousin, Prince
" Rupert, shall be armed out of our stoares remaining within our
" office of the Ordinance, as followeth, that is to say ; three corpo-
" ralls, two serjeants, the gentleman of armes, and twelve soldiers
" of each of the said twelve troopes are to have and carry each of
" them one holbard and one case of pistols with holsters, and the
" rest of the soldiers of the severall troopes aforesaid are to have
" and to carry each of them one matchlocke musket, with a
" collar of bandileeres, and also to have and carry a BAYONET or
" great knife, that each lieutenant have and carry one partizan,
" and that two drums be delivered out for each troope of the said
" regiment : And it is our will and pleasure that you cause ye
" armes and other particulars aforesaid to be delivered unto the
" captaines of the said regiment for their troops respectively, that
" is to say, to Capt. Lieuten' Arnold Cooper for our said most
" deare Cousin's owne troope, to Lieuten' Col. Sr John Talbot
" for his troope, to Major Edmond Andros, Captm James Cotter,

1686.   This year the uniform of the Coldstream was red lined with blue, blue breeches, and white stockings.

At the end of May, one battalion of the Coldstream was ordered to march to the camp at Hounslow, previous to a grand review which was to take place on the thirtieth of June.[1]   Among the various orders then given out, was one

---

" Capt⁰⁰ Edward Talbot, Capt⁰⁰ James Barrett, Capt⁰⁰ Ralph
" Heburne, Capt⁰⁰ Francis Newport, Cornifice Count Vlfeldt,
" Capt⁰⁰ S⁰ William Throckmorton, Capt⁰⁰ —— Clifford, and
" Capt⁰⁰ James Walter, for their troopes, respectively ; taking
" care that the armes you delivered out of our stoares unto the four
" Barbados companies, to wit, to the said Major Andros, Capt⁰⁰
" Cotter, Capt⁰⁰ Talbot, and Capt⁰⁰ Barrett's companies (which are
" to be mounted and advanced to be troopes of dragoons in the
" said regim⁰), be then delivered backe into our stoares for our use,
" which they are hereby required to deliver in accordingly : And
" for your soe doeing, this our warrant, together with the respec-
" tive indentures, or receipts of the said captaines respectively, or
" their assignees, for the armes of their severall companies, to be
" delivered as aforesaid, shall be your warrant and discharge.
" Given at our Court at Whitehall, the second day of Aprill,
" (1672), in the 24ᵗʰ year of our reigne.
            " By his Ma⁰⁰ command,
                    " ARLINGTON."
" To our trusty and well-beloved
" Councellour, S⁰ Thomas Chiche-
" ley, Kn⁰, our Master Generall
" of our Ordinance."
                    Official Records, War-Office.

24 September, 1693.  The French, commanded by Catinat, defeated the Confederates, under the Duke of Savoy and Prince
Eugene, at Marsiglia, near Turin.  The Duke of Schomberg, who
commanded the troops of England, was mortally wounded and taken
prisoner.  This was the first time the foot charged with bayonets
on their loaded muskets, to which the success of the French in
this battle was attributed.

[1] " All the army is now at Hounslow, in a line of 2930 paces,

directing that " the Colonel, and other officers upon duty, 1686. shall wear their GORGETTS."

In these encampments, which occurred regularly every year, the troops were exercised in sham fights, and other military manœuvres; forts were erected, besieged, and taken, for the sake of practice.[1] In August, the three Aug. 10th. battalions of the two regiments of Guards returned to their quarters in London.

---

" about 16,000 strong : on Wednesday the great review is."— *The Ellis Correspondence*, Letter dated June 26th, 1686, vol. 1. page 125.

[1] The Ellis Correspondence, vol. 1. page 331.

" I sojourn'd out two peaceable campaigns on Hounslow Heath, " where I was an eye-witness of one mock siege of Buda ; after " which our regiment was ordered to Berwick, where I remained " till the revolution."—*Carleton's Memoirs*, page 39.

### REVIEW OF HIS MAJESTY'S FORCES ON HOUNSLOW HEATH IN 1685.

| | |
|---|---:|
| Two squadrons of the reg.t of Horse . . . | 300 |
| Two do. do. Queen's do. . . . | 240 |
| Batt.n of the Royal regiment of Foot . . . | 550 |
| Col. M'Kay's Scotch regiment from Holland . . | 528 |
| Col. Balfour's Scotch regiment from Holland . | 528 |
| Col. Wachup's Scotch regiment from Holland . | 528 |
| Grenadiers to the 3 troops of Horse Guards . | 192 |
| Three troops of Horse Guards . . . . | 600 |
| Two batt.ns of the First reg.t of Foot Guards . . | 1040 |
| Batt.n of the Coldstream reg.t of Guards . . . | 560 |
| Royal reg.t of Fusiliers . . . . . | 590 |
| | 5656 |

### REVIEW OF HIS MAJESTY'S FORCES ON HOUNSLOW HEATH, AUG. 22, 1685.

| Left wing of Horse 10 sq. | 10 Batt.ns Foot | R.t W. of Horse 9 sq. |
|---|---|---|
| . . . . . | 16 comp.s of the 1st reg.t 1280 | . . . . |
| . . . . . | 8 comp.s of the Colds.m 640 | . . . . |
| Total Horse 1460 | Total Foot 5460 | Total Horse 1512 |

1686-7.    The following is an extract from a regulation for musters, dated Whitehall, twenty-first of February, 1686-7 :—

FIRST ENCAMPMENT ON HOUNSLOW HEATH, 1686.
FIRST BRIGADE.

| | |
|---|---|
| Two batt<sup>ns</sup> of First reg<sup>t</sup> of Guards . . . . | 1120 |
| One batt<sup>n</sup> of the Coldstream reg<sup>t</sup> . . . . | 560 |
| One do.  Scotch Guards . . . . | 560 |
| Prince George's reg<sup>t</sup> of Foot . . . | 650 |
| Col. Cornwall's reg<sup>t</sup> of Foot, with Sir Thomas Haggerston's Grenadiers . . . . . . | 550 |
| | 3440 |

SECOND BRIGADE.

| | |
|---|---|
| Queen Dowager's reg<sup>t</sup> of Foot . . . . | 550 |
| Holland reg<sup>t</sup> of Foot . . . . . | 650 |
| Earl of Bath's reg<sup>t</sup> of Foot . . . . | 560 |
| Mq<sup>s</sup> of Worcester's reg<sup>t</sup> of Foot, with Capt<sup>n</sup> Check's Grenadiers . . . . . . . . | 550 |
| D. of Norfolk's reg<sup>t</sup> of Foot, with Capt<sup>n</sup> Carter's Grenadiers . . . . . . . | 550 |
| E. of Huntingdon's reg<sup>t</sup> of Foot, with the E. of Plymouth's Grenadiers . . . . . | 550 |
| | 3400 |

SECOND ENCAMPMENT OF HIS MAJESTY'S FORCES ON HOUNSLOW
HEATH, 1686.

There appears by the return to have been

| | |
|---|---|
| 2 batt<sup>ns</sup> of the First reg<sup>t</sup> of Guards . . . | 1040 |
| 1  do.          Coldstream . . . . | 560 |
| 1  do.          Scotch G<sup>ds</sup> . . . . . | 560 |

IN A REVIEW, ALSO DATED 30TH JUNE, 1686,

| | |
|---|---|
| appear 2 batt<sup>ns</sup>  First Guards . . . . | |
| 1  do.  Coldstream . . . . | |
| 1  do.  Scotch Guards . . . . | |

IN ANOTHER REVIEW AT HOUNSLOW, DATED 22ND JULY, 1686,

| | |
|---|---|
| are 2 batt<sup>ns</sup> First Guards . . . . . | 1120 |
| 1  do.  Coldstream . . . . . | 560 |
| 1  do.  Scotch . . . . . | 560 |

" The musquetiers of our regiment of Foot Guards ·to
" have Snaphance musquets, with bright barrels, of 3
" ffoot 8 inches long in the barrell, with good swords,
" bandiliers, and bionetts ; and the pikemen (as also the
" pikemen of all other regiments) to have pikes sixteen
" ffoot long, with good swords.

" Musquetiers of all other regiments of Foot (except-
" ing our regiment of Fuziliers, the Granadiers, and the
" company of Miners,) to have matchlock and Snaphance
" musquetts ; the barrells whereof to be 3 ffoot 6 inches
" long, good swords, and bandiliers.

" Our royal regiment of Fuziliers to have Snaphance
" musquets, strapt, with bright barrells of 3 ffoot 8 inches
" long, with good swords, cartouch boxes, and bionetts.

" All the ffoot Granadiers of our army, both regimented
" and non-regimented, to have long carbines, strapt ; the
" barrells whereof to be 3 ffoot 2 inches long, car-
" touch boxes, bionetts, granado ponches, and hammer
" hatchets.

" The companies of Miners to have long carabines,
" strapt ; the barrels to be 3 ffoot 2 inches in length,
" cartouch boxes, bionetts, and extraordinary hammer
" hatchets.

---

IN THE FIRST ENCAMPMENT, 1687, AT HOUNSLOW HEATH,
are 1ᵈ battⁿ First regᵗ . . . . . . 560
    1ⁿ do.  Coldstream   . . . . . 560

IN THE SECOND ENCAMPMENT IN 1687, AT HOUNSLOW,
are 1ᵈ battⁿ do. . . . . . . . do.
    1ᵈ do. Coldstream . . . . . . do.

IN THE ENCAMPMENT OF HIS MAJESTY'S FORCES ON HOUNSLOW
HEATH, ANNO 1688,
appear 2 battˢ of the First regᵗ of Foot Guards . 1040
    1 do.     Coldstream . . . . 520
    1 do.     Scotch Guards . . . 640

" The Dragoons to have Snaphance musquets, strapt,
" with bright barrells of 3 ffoot 8 inches long, cartouch
" boxes, bionetts, granado pouches, bucketts, and hammer
" hatchetts."                                    •

1687.     The rank of Lieutenant-Colonel was this year granted
to Captains of companies in the two regiments of Foot
Guards.[1]

---

[1]     " Whitehall, 30th of July, 1687."

Extract.   " His Majesty hath been pleased to grant new commis-
" sions to the Captains of his Royal Regiment of Guards com-
" manded by the Duke of Grafton, by which every captain. of
" the said regiment is made lieutenant-colonel and captain."—MS.
Add[l]. No. 4194. Brit. Mus.

From various records in the War-Office, particularly the Court-
martial and Commission books, it appears that the captains of
companies in the Coldstream obtained the rank at the same time.

   " Rank of the Captain-lieutenant in the 1st Regiment of Guards.
      " JAMES R.

   " For the better ascertaining the rank and command of the
" Captain-lieutenant in our First regiment of Foot Guards ; wee
" do hereby declare our will and pleasure, that the Captain-lieu-
" tenant of our First regiment of Foot Guards shall att all times
" have the rank and command as youngest lieutenant-colonel and
" captain in the said regiment, according to the date of his com-
" mission of captain-lieutenant in the said regiment.  Given att
" our Court att Whitehall, this 14th day of January 1687-8, in the
" third year of our reign.

                              " By His Mat[s] command,
                                   " WM. BLATHWAYT."

In August, 1688, Lieutenant-Colonel James Bridgeman, John
Burgess and Robert Wilkins, captains of the Coldstream, were appointed to take rank as youngest lieutenant-colonels of foot.

   Military Papers, State-Paper Office.

At Perk, in Flanders, on the 1st of June 1693, several captains
of companies in the First and Coldstream Guards received a re-
newal of their commissions, and " to take rank as lieutenant-
colonels."—War-Office Commission Books.

On Monday evening, the thirtieth of July, Lieutenant- 1688. Colonel Miller was killed by a fall, when riding from the July. camp at Hounslow Heath. He is presumed to be a son of the old Coldstreamer, noticed as Monck's Adjutant-General of infantry in the celebrated march from Scotland, and appointed to introduce the excluded Members into the House of Commons whose votes so materially assisted in the Restoration. [1]

Four additional companies were placed on the esta- September. blishment of the Coldstream from the first of September, 1688, including a second grenadier company. [2]

The Prince of Orange landed at Torbay, and marched Nov. 5th. with the Dutch to Exeter: for some days few persons joined the Prince; Major Burrington was the first, of any consideration, who did so; and shortly after, the respect-

---

[1] "London, August 2, 1688."

Extract. "Colonel John Miller, eldest captain of the Lord "Craven's regiment, riding from the camp on Monday evening, "is said by a fall from his horse to have lost his life."

"London, August 4th, 1688."

Extract. "Captain Miller, in the Earl of Craven's regiment, "mentioned in our last to fall from his horse coming from the "camp, and it being dark, and his servant much in drink, he never "recovered, but died the next day."—MS. Add[l]. No. 4194. Brit. Mus.

"London, Saturday, 4th August, 1688."

Extract. "Col. Miller Commander, of the first company in the "Lord Craven's regiment, coming from the camp on Wednesday "morning last, had the ill fortune, near Hammersmith, to fall off "his horse and break his skull, of which hurt he soon after died, "being a gentleman much lamented." — Add. MS. No. 3929, British Museum.

[2] King William afterwards reduced the regiment to fourteen companies. See Appendix, No. 120. The new establishment took effect May 1st, 1689.

able inhabitants of Devonshire and Somersetshire flocked to his standard. Lord Colchester, son of Lord Rivers, and Lord Churchill, who owed his rise in life, and every thing he possessed, to James's favour, with a degree of ingratitude scarcely paralleled, deserted his unfortunate Sovereign; the example was followed by the Duke of December. Grafton, one of Charles's natural children. The King, thus forsaken, had no one in whom he could confide ; yielding, therefore, to circumstances, he quitted London,[1] having previously directed the army to be disbanded.[2]

---

[1] As the desertion of James's friends one after another was announced, it caused his son-in-law, the Prince of Denmark, to exclaim, " *Est-il possible ?* "

" They had supped with the King the same evening. Prince George " left a letter for James, (which may be seen in Kennet's History " of England,) excusing his own conduct and blaming the unhappy " monarch. This prince had been accustomed, when he heard of " the defection of any of those who had been obliged to the King, " to say, *Est-il possible ?* The only remark James made upon the " Prince's flight was, 'Is *Est-il possible* gone too?'"—See Note in *Diary of Earl of Clarendon*, Singer's Edition, vol. II. page 208. London, 1828.

[2] " The King, (James 2nd), is said to have left a paper behind " him, directed to the Earl of Feversham, for him to disband the " army, which his Lordship read at the head of most regiments, and " accordingly disbanded them, some with, others without their " arms."—Extract of a letter, dated London, Dec. 13th, 1688, to John Ellis, Esq., Secretary to the Commissioners for the Revenue of Ireland, at Dublin. MS. Donat. British Museum, 4194. fol. 397.

" His Majesty sending the Earl of Feversham with a letter to the " Prince of Orange, his Highness detained the said Earl for high " treason, declaring he did it for his disbanding the army without " orders, &c., at which his Majesty was somewhat concerned."— Extract of a letter, dated London, Dec. 18th, 1688, to ditto. Ibid. 4182. f. 72.

The conduct of James had been that of a man rushing headlong to his own destruction. Among the many acts of folly he committed, not the least was his going publicly to the Papistical ceremonials, by which he created universal alarm among his Protestant subjects, and, in the language of Count de Grammont, 'sold three kingdoms for a mass.'[1]

Prior to the entry of the Prince of Orange into London, he sent orders for all the King's forces in and about the capital to march out, with the exception of the Coldstream.[2] The following letter from the Prince of Orange to the Earl of Craven, contains his directions to see the order executed.

" Windsor, 15th December, 1688.

" MY LORD,

" I am very well satisfied with your Lordship's care in
" preserving the publick peace, and cannot doubt of your
" continuance of it in every thing that may be requisite
" for my service. At present I think fitt to acquaint you
" with my resolution to come to London on Tuesday
" next, so that it will be' necessary that the fforces now
" there be removed the day before to such quarters as
" are appointed them;[3] and as I have in their stead

---

[1] King James frequently goeth to the ffrench Kings Chappel, where the Count Grammont seeing him very devout at mass, sayd he did not thinke the King had been such a foole as to loose three Kingdoms for Religion, which complaint being made to His most Xtian Majesty, the Count was committed to the Bastile.—MS. Add¹. No. 3929. f. 138. Brit. Mus.

[2] "London, December 19ᵗʰ, 1688."—Extract. "The Prince of " Orange sent orders to all the King's forces in and about London, " to march out to certain quarters, except only the Lord Craven's " regiment."—MS. Add¹. No. 4194. Brit. Mus.

[3] " Quarters appointed for the English, Scots, and Irish Forces,

" ordered 3000 of my Guards of ffoot to march thither,
" so as to be there on Monday, together with eight

---

" to which all officers and soldiers thereto belonging are forthwith
" to repair, viz. :—

### HORSE.

" First troop of Guards, Maidstone, Kent.
" Second troop of Guards, Chelmsford, Essex.
" Third troop  ,,  St. Albans, Hertfordshire.
" Royal regiment, Northampton.
" Queen's regiment, Cambridge.
" Regiment late of the Earl of Peterborough, Bedford.
" Sir John Fenwick's regiment, Dorking and Ryegate, Surrey.
" Lieut.-Gen. Werden's regiment, Newbury, Berks.
" Earl of Selkirk's regiment, Stamford, Lincolnshire.
" Regiment late of Major-Gen. Hamilton, Fenny Stratford, Bucks.
" Princess of Denmark's regiment, Reading, Berks.
" Queen Dowager's regiment, Guilford and Godalming, Surrey.
" Marquis de Miremont's, Aylesbury and Wendover, Bucks.
" Lord Brandon's, Bishops-Stortford, Hertfordshire.
" Col. Henry Slingsby's, Buckingham and Winslow.
" Regiment late of Col. Holman, Sevenoke, Kent.
"  ,,  late of E. of Salisbury,  ,,  ,,

### DRAGOONS.

" Royal regiment, Farnham and Alton, Surrey.
" Queen's regiment, Dunstable &c., Bedfordshire.
" Princess's regiment, Burford, Oxfordshire.

### FOOT.

" First regiment of Guards, Portsmouth, Hampsh.; Tilbury, Essex.
" Coldstream regiment, Rochester, Dover, and Maidstone, Kent.
" Royal regiment, Oxford.
" Queen Dowager's regiment, Wallingford, Berks.
" Prince George's regiment, Huntington.
" Holland regiment, Chesham and Amersham, Bucks.
" Queen's regiment, Ware and Hertford.
" Royal regiment of Fuziliers, Barnet, Hertfordshire.
" Princess of Denmark's, Southampton.
" Regiment late of Colonel Nicholas, Worcester.
" Earl of Bath's regiment, Canterbury, Kent.
" Regiment late of the Earl of Litchfield, Banbury, Oxfordshire.

" hundred of my Guards of Horse, you are to give such
" orders, that they may be placed before my arrivall in
" the quarters formerly taken up by the English Guards.
" I intend likewise to send on the same day the English
" brigade, consisting of three thousand men, to South-
" wark, the Tower, Tower Hamletts, and places adjacent,
" for the quartering of which it will be requisite that you
" direct the necessary preparations to be made in such
" manner as may be most convenient for my service
" and ease of the inhabitants ; for the better effecting

---

" Earl of Huntington's, Plymouth, Devonshire.
" Regiment late of Sir Edw. Hales, Waltham, &c., Hampshire.
" Col. Tufton's regiment, Berwick.
" Col. John Hales's regiment, Milton and Sittingburn, Kent.
" Col. Mac Elligot's regiment, Chichester.
" Col. Richards's regiment, Sudbury, Suffolk.
" Regiment late of Col. Gage, Chester.
" Duke of Newcastle's regiment, Hull and Berwick.
" Col. Skelton's regiment, Newportpagnel, Bucks.
" Col. Archibald Douglas's, Stony Stratford, Bucks.

#### SCOTS FORCES.

" Troop of Horse Guards, Bicester, Oxon.
" Regiment of Horse, Abingdon, Berks.
" Regiment of Foot Guards, Tame, Oxon.
" Regiment late of Col. Wachop, Woodstock, Oxon.
" Regiment late of Colonel Bochan, Witney, Oxon.
" Earl of Dunmore's regiment of Dragoons, Islip &c., Oxon.

#### IRISH FORCES.

" Lord Forbes's regiment, Hatfield, Hertfordshire.
" Col. Hamilton's regiment, Lewes, Sussex.
" Col. Butler's regiment of Dragoons, East Grinsted &c., Sussex."

London Gazette, No. 2411, from December 17 to
December 20, 1688.

" Quarters for the Fourth troop of Guards is Epsom, and Ewell,
in Surrey.
" For the Irish (Foot) Guards, is Lewes, in Sussex."

London Gazette, No. 2413, from December 24 to
December 27, 1688.

" whereof, I have informed the Lord Churchill more par-
" ticularly of my instructions, to whom I do therefore
" referr you for his assistance as there shall be occasion.
" And so I bid you farewell.

" Your most affectionate ffriend,

" W. H. PRINCE D'ORANGE." [1]

" To the Earl of Craven."

Craven, although eighty years of age, when ordered to
give up his post to Solmes and the Dutch Guards, stated
to James, that he was willing to keep his station, and be
cut to pieces, rather than yield to them. The King persuaded him to comply without bloodshed, as the Dutch
Guards were about to make use of force.[2]  " The last of

---

[1] Official Records, War Office.

[2] " . . . The Prince of Orange dreaded nothing now so much
" as what he gave out to be the only motive of his expedition ; for
" this pretended reconciliation was indeed the first in his pretences,
" but the last in his intentions : so being terrifyd with the King's
" welcome back, and seeing the people's affection so ready to run
" into their antient channel, he resolved to outface all his former
" protestation, and therefore would not vouchsafe his Majesty the
" honour of seeing him, nor so much as an answer to his letter ;
" but sent the Count de Solmes that very night, with his Guards, to
" take the postes about Whitehall.   When the King was ad-
" vertised of this, he could not believe it, because he had heard
" nothing of it, he sayd, from the Prince himself, and therefore
" supposed they were only comeing to take the postes about St.
" James's, to be ready to receive him there next day ; but at eleaven
" o'clock my Lord Craven came to acquaint his Majesty, just as he
" was going to bed, that the Count de Solmes was in the Parke
" with three battallions of the Prince's foot guards and some bors,
" and sayd he had orders to take the postes in and about White-
" hall ; upon which the King sent for the Count de Solmes, and
" tould him, he believ'd he was mistaken, and that his orders were
" only for St. James's : but he was positive they were for White-
" hall, which, he sayd, was first named, and shew'd his Majesty
" the orders themselves ; upon which the King argued the matter

" them that marched ont of the towne was the Lord
" Craven's Reg¹, who being drawn up on Wednesday,
" (19th Dec.) in Moor-fields, and receiving their orders
" to march for Rochester, were very mutinous; a great
" many of them resolutely threw down their arms, and the
" rest went away discontentedly." ¹

The Coldstream were sent to Rochester, Maidstone, and
Dover. At Rochester, the officers waited on James, and
expressed to him their attachment. Major-General Sackville the Lieutenant-Colonel, John Huitson ² the Major,
and his Ensign Gabriel Thorne, who was also his son-in-
law, gave up their commissions³ to the King; but no
other officer followed their example.

Sir John Reresby, in his Memoirs, thus alludes to the
removal of the Guards. " January 22nd, 168⅔. And now,
" being at liberty to go where I pleased, I repaired to
" London, where being arrived, I was presently sensible
" of a great alteration; the Guards and other parts of the
" army, which both for their persons and gallantry were
" an ornament to the place, were sent to quarter at a dis-
" tance, while the streets swarmed with ill-favoured and ill-
" accoutred Dutchmen, and other strangers of the Prince's
" army; and yet the City seemed to be mightily pleased
" with their deliverers, nor perceived their deformity, or
" the oppression they laboured under, by far more unsup-
" portable than ever they had suffered from the English." ⁴

---

" with him for some time, but at last directed my Lord Craven to
" draw out his men, and let Count de Solmes take the postes,
" which they immediately did." — *Life of James II.* by Clarke,
vol. ii. p. 264.

¹ Add¹ MS. 3929. Brit. Mus.

² Colonel Huitson died in April 1689; his will was proved in the
Prerogative Court on the 19th of April.

³ Clarke's Life of James II. vol. ii. p. 268.

⁴ Memoirs of the Honᵇˡᵉ Sir John Reresby, Bart., 8vo., London,
1735. p. 304.

They did not preserve so strict a watch over the King as at Gravesend, " which confirmed him in the belief he " was of before, that the Prince of Orange would " be well enough contented he should get away; and " that the person who brought the pass, had orders like- " wise to the officer that commanded his Guards, not to " look so strictly after the King, for sentinels were only " set at the fore door towards the street, and none at the " back door, which went towards the river; by this the " King was still further convinced the Prince of Orange " had a mind he should be gone."[1]

On the arrival of William[2] in Town, the following order was issued for the recovery of the arms of the regiments disbanded :—

" Whereas upon the late irregular disbanding of the " forces, divers soldiers carried away the arms belonging " to their respective regiments, and have since lost or im- " hezled the same; we hereby direct and require all persons, " to whose hands the said arms or any of them are come, " or with whom they now remain, forthwith to deliver " them to the said soldiers or their officers upon demand, " and, in default thereof, forthwith to bring them to the " officers of the Ordnance now attending at Uxbridge, " Hounslow, or the Tower of London, in order to the re- " turning the said arms into the stores of the Ordnance. " Given at St. James's, this 21 day of December, 1688.

" W. H. PRINCE OF ORANGE.
" By his Highness's command,
" C. HUYGENS."

Dec. 23rd.    James ultimately escaped to France, and was received

---

[1] Clarke, vol. II. p. 267.

[2] The monarchy lay as it were in abeyance from the twenty-third of December to the thirteenth of February.—*Hallam*, vol. III. page 1:96.

with great hospitality by Lewis XIV., who assigned the 1688.
December.
Castle of St. Germain for his residence.

Towards the end of the reign of King James II., the inhabitants of towns were occasionally obliged, wherever soldiers were quartered, not only to furnish them with food and lodging, but also to advance them their daily pay.[1] The Prince of Orange issued an order[2] prohibiting this 1688-9.
Jan. 8th.
practice.

William was now securely seated on the English throne; and, in pursuance of the treaty with the States General, both battalions of the Coldstream[3] embarked for Mar. 19th. Helvoet Sluys, and were reduced in May from seventeen to fourteen companies by transfer; two of them were incorporated into the First Foot Guards, and the remaining company was otherwise disposed of. A battalion of seven companies was raised at the end of the year for home duty, and one battalion only remained on the establishment in Flanders. Several regiments were sent to replace the Dutch corps retained by King William in in England.

War was declared with France, and these troops were reinforced and constituted an auxiliary army to co-operate with the Dutch under the command of the Earl of Marlborough. The present First Foot, or Royals, was also

---

[1] The Journals of the House of Commons furnish many instances where this is complained of.—*Grose's Military Antiquities*, vol. 1. page 342.

See petition to the House of Commons, complaining of the officers of Colonel Hastings's regiment.—*Smollett*, vol. 1. page 240.

[2] See London Gazette, No. 2418. Order dated 8th January, 1688-9.

[3] See Appendix, Nos. 115, 116, 117, 120.

ordered on this service, but mutinied, refused to embark, and marched off with their arms and four guns from Ipswich to the Isle of Ely and county of Lincoln, intending to make their way to Scotland. King William being informed of the revolt, ordered General Ginkel [1] to follow with three Dutch regiments of cavalry; these were joined near Seaford. by the regiments of Horse under Sir John Lanier and Colonel Langston, who forced the mutinous regiment to surrender at discretion.[2]     Lieutenant Alexander Gawen, their ringleader, and the misguided soldiers, amounting to five hundred men and twenty officers, were escorted to London; the rest returned to their colours. The regiment subsequently was sent to its destination.[3] The Royals were not punished as rebels, the new government being yet unacknowledged in Scotland.     Other troops, supposed to be disaffected, were also sent to the Continent, and their place at home supplied from the Dutch forces.     Although the attempts to shake the throne of William proved abortive, yet some apprehension was entertained by his ministers.     The revolt of the Royals is said to have been the origin of the celebrated Bill for the due regulation of the army, now well known by the name of the Mutiny Bill.[4]

On the accession of King William, the Coldstream was

---

[1] Afterwards created Earl of Athlone.

[2] London Gazette, No. 2438, from 21st to 25th March, 1689. Also see Appendix, Nos. 118, 119.

[3] In October, 1689, another battalion of the Royals was ordered from Scotland to join the battalion in Holland.—War-Office Records.

[4] The first regular Mutiny Bill passed on the 3d of April, 1689, and was annually renewed, with the exception of three years during the reign of King William.

taken from Lord Craven, and bestowed on Thomas Talmash, formerly Colonel of the fifth regiment of foot.[1] Lord Craven,[2] first Baron and Earl Craven, was eldest son of Sir William Craven, merchant-tailor, and Lord Mayor of London. He entered the army in early life, and signalized himself in Germany and the Netherlands, under Henry, Prince of Orange. On his return to England he was knighted at Newmarket, and afterwards raised to the dignity of Baron.[3] In 1631 he was sent to the assistance of Gustavus, King of Sweden, who had taken up arms in Germany to support the Protestant cause. In the assault and capture of the Castle of Curtzenack, he was wounded, and afterwards taken prisoner by the Emperor's troops.[4] On obtaining his liberty, he entered the service of the Prince of Orange, and resided with him until the Restoration. By Charles he was created Viscount and Earl of Craven, and his confiscated property restored. He continued in the confidence of Charles during the whole of his reign; attended at the coronation of James the Second; and was much grieved at being obliged to resign his commission as Colonel of the Coldstream; he said, " They had as good take away his life, since he had nothing else to divert himself with." He was allowed to retain his regiment, till finally deprived of it by King William. Lord Craven, one of the most accomplished gentlemen of his day, was much beloved and equally respected.

---

[1] Commission dated May 1st, 1689.

[2] Lord Craven attended King James's Court to congratulate him on the birth of the Prince of Wales, which took place on the tenth of June, 1688, " and told his Majesty it was also his birth-day."— MS. Add[l]. No. 3929. Brit. Mus.

[3] March 4th, 1626.          [4] 1637.

1689.

He died April the ninth, 1697, upwards of eighty-eight years of age.

May 12th.

William, who retained his influence in Holland, projected an alliance of the leading Powers against France. The Princes of Germany prevailed on the Emperor to resort to arms. The States-General and the Elector of Brandenburg also declared against Lewis the Fourteenth.

The Coldstream Guards, commanded by Colonel Bridgeman, and some other regiments from England, assembled on the Sambre, under Marlborough. The allied army was commanded by the Prince of Waldeck.[1] The Prussians and northern contingents of Germany, headed by the Elector of Brandenburg, were to attack Bonn. The Duke of Lorraine, at the head of the Imperialists, was to manœuvre on the Upper Rhine. The Spaniards, who acted separately, advanced to Courtrai, and levelled the lines constructed by the French; they also raised contributions in different parts of their country.

June ⅙

In May, the Elector of Brandenburg laid siege to Key-

---

[1] Marlborough landed at Rotterdam on the ⅙ of May: when the English regiments were ordered to be in readiness to take the field, they joined Prince Waldeck at the camp between Judoigne and Tirlemont, $\frac{May}{June}$ $\frac{11}{10}$, which they left on the 3 of June, for the camp at Fleurus. On the ⅙ of July, the troops, then 36,000 strong, encamped at Tongrenelle, between Namur and Charleroi. They quitted the latter camp on the ⅙ of July for Timeon. From thence they marched on $\frac{July}{Aug.}$ $\frac{30}{ }$ to Nivelle. On the ⅙ of August they moved towards Fontaine l'Eveque, passed the Sambre on the ⅙ and encamped at Ham-sur-Heure. On the ⅙ they approached Philipville. After the action, the ⅙ the allies took up a position near Walcourt, where they remained till the ⅙ of August, when they encamped at Gerpines, recrossed the Sambre on the 7 of $\frac{August,}{September,}$ when head-quarters were fixed at Montigny. On the ⅙ of September they marched to Genappe, and the ⅙ encamped between Tubise and Lembeck, near Halle.

serswaert ; the garrison, divided amongst themselves, surrendered.

The corps of Prince Waldeck was opposed by the troops
under Marshal d'Humieres, who unexpectedly attacked
fifteen hundred of his foragers.  The contending armies
were only separated by the small walled town of Walcourt, in possession of the allies, and about a mile in front
of their camp.  The French Marshal ordered Walcourt to
be carried by assault.  Prince Waldeck succeeded in
planting some guns on a bill that commanded the place,
and brought up a body of cavalry and infantry to oppose
the enemy, posted under cover of a battery they had raised
against Walcourt.  At two o'clock P. M. the Coldstream
Guards and a German regiment were ordered to force
their way to the relief of the town, which was effected in
the most gallant manner.  The attack continued till six in
the evening, when the French retired in great disorder,
leaving upwards of two thousand[1] killed and wounded.
The French Guards were almost destroyed : the loss in
the corps of Prince Waldeck did not exceed forty men and
two officers.[2]  Prince Waldeck and the Governor of Flanders passed through Halle to Enghien, in pursuit of the
enemy.  Next day he left Enghien for Chievre, with the
intention of following them towards Tournay.  The Duke
of Brandenburg also laid siege to Bonn, and, after a
tedious blockade of fifty-five days, carried the counterscarp by storm, when the fortress surrendered.  The fall
of Bonn may be attributed partly to the Duke of Lorraine,
who made himself master of Mentz $\frac{30 \text{ Aug.}}{9 \text{ Sept.}}$ and joined the
Duke of Brandenburg.

---

[1] London Gazette, August 29th to September 2nd, 1689.  No.
2484.

[2] London Gazette, from Thursday August 22nd, to Monday
August 26th, 1689.  No. 2482.

The English regiments now went into quarters. The Coldstream was billeted at Ghent.

The army under Marshal d'Humieres broke up and distributed itself in various garrisons. The Spanish and Dutch troops also moved into quarters for the winter.

## CHAPTER XI.

Battle of Fleurus—Prince Waldeck retires—Reinforced by the Coldstream, four English regiments, and several thousand Hanoverians—The Coldstream and other British troops quartered in Brussels—Both armies go into winter quarters in October – King William embarks for Holland—British troops reinforced in Flanders—William addresses the Congress at the Hague—Reviews his army—Embarks for England—Army go to their former quarters—William returns to the Hague—Confederates assemble at Anderlecht—Luxembourg reconnoitres the position of the Allies, and retires to his camp — Confederates proceed to Gemblours—French leave Braine le Comte and march to the Sambre—Confederates arrive on the plain of Gerpynes—Lieutenants of First and Coldstream Guards get the rank of Captains — Allies reinforced exceed the enemy in numbers—William's head-quarters at Cour-sur-Heure — Army advances between Fleurus and the Sambre; crosses the river below Ath—The King leaves the camp for Loo—Troops go into winter quarters—William embarks for England.

It was determined by the States-General, in their Congress at the Hague, that the Prince of Waldeck, with the Confederate army, should oppose the French, now under the Duke of Luxembourg, in place of Marshal d'Humieres. The Elector of Brandenburg was to observe the corps commanded by Boufflers on the Moselle.

The enemy began operations earlier than was anticipated, which obliged the Dutch to draw a sufficient force

1690.

1690.

from their garrisons to face them, till the Brandenburg troops destined for that service reached their station : the delay gave Boufflers an opportunity of occupying a position between the Sambre and the Mense, which enabled him to keep up his communication with the army under Marshal Luxembourg.

June 18

The Prince of Waldeck was encamped, about the end of June, on the river Pieton, when he had intelligence that the Duke of Luxembourg was crossing the Sambre at Fromont. Aware of the importance of preventing the enemy from passing, the Prince left Pieton, and detached Count Berlo next day to watch their movements ; Count Flodrop was sent to support him with another body of horse. These troops charged, but were repulsed. The Allied army was drawn up in order of battle, and remained under arms all night.

The French, who had received considerable reinforcements, amounted to upwards of forty thousand men ; the Confederate army did not much exceed half that number.

June 21
July 1

Prince Waldeck's position was between Heppignies and St. Amand, with the village of Fleurus in front. The battle commenced about ten o'clock A. M. The Allies neglecting to occupy Fleurus, it was immediately taken possession of by the enemy, who formed line and advanced to the attack. After a severe contest, the cavalry on the left were the first to give way. The Dutch infantry fought " for six hours together, with the greatest bravery ima- " ginable, several battalions firing three ranks deep, on " three sides at once; for the French took them in the " flank and rear, after the horse had left them."[1] Upwards of four thousand five hundred were left dead on the field by the Allies; a large part of their artillery was

---

[1] The London Gazette, from Thursday June 26th, to Monday June 30th. No. 2570. " Hague."

taken, with nearly four thousand prisoners. The enemy **1690.** suffered so severely, that they could not improve their success.[1] Prince Waldeck retired to Nivelle, the Dutch infantry covering the retreat. After the action the Confederates were reinforced by the first battalion of the Coldstream Guards from Ghent, and four other English regiments, besides several thousand Hanoverians, which increased the allied army to about fifty-five thousand men. The Governor-General, with a strong force, was at Dendermond. In July, the Coldstream Guards and other British regiments were in Brussels, and the Prince of Waldeck's army encamped near the town. The hostile troops remained in camp till the end of October, when they went into quarters for the winter.

William proceeded to Holland early in January, to take **1691.** the command in Flanders, and confer with the Princes engaged in the grand alliance assembled at the Hague. At their first[2] meeting he reminded them of the danger they were exposed to from the ambition of France: he

---

[1] The London Gazette, from June 26th to June 30th, 1690. No. 2570. "Brussels."

[2] The Princes who resorted in person to the Congress, were the "Electors of Bavaria and Brandenburg, the Dukes of Zell and "Wolfembuttle, the Duke Administrator of Wirtemburg, the Land- "grave of Hesse Cassel, the Marquis of Guastanaga, Governor- "General of the Spanish Netherlands: the Plenipotentiary Am- "bassadors were, for the Emperor, the Count de Windisgratz, and "the Duke of Savoy, the Count De Prela, and the President De la "Tour.

"*History of the Campagne in Flanders for the year* 1691, by "Edward d'Auvergne, Chaplain to the Third Regiment of "Guards. London, 1735." Page 15. [An account of these campaigns, from 1692 inclusive, was published at the termination of each; that for 1691 was not compiled for many years after, which explains why the Scots Guards are styled "the Third Regiment."]

1691. told them the enemy were already possessed of nearly all the strong places, and might quickly gain the remainder: he added, if divisions arose, or considerations of private interest became prevalent, the enemy would carry every thing before them. He said the time for deliberation was past, that union among the Allies was necessary, and that it was soldiers and powerful armies " that must do the work." With regard to himself, he declared he would spare neither his credit, troops, nor person, to co-operate with them in so just and necessary an undertaking; and that he would return in the spring to head his forces and redeem the pledge he had so solemnly given.

March 6th. The King, on arriving at Loo with the Elector of Bavaria and the Duke of Zell, heard that Mons had been invested on the preceding day, and that Lewis the Fourteenth was hourly expected to carry on the siege in per-

Mar. 18th. son. William placed himself at the head of the army, between Brussels and Vilvorde; he then advanced and

Mar. 30th. encamped in front of Halle. Mons surrendered after a

Mar. 31st. siege of three weeks. William then reviewed his army, which had received reinforcements during the winter, and amongst them a second battalion of the Scots Guards[1] from Scotland, and a battalion of Dutch Guards from England: it amounted to forty-five thousand five hundred and forty men.[2] The English Guards, composed of the second battalion of the First, commanded by Colonel Warcup, and the first battalion of the Coldstream, commanded by Colonel Bridgeman, were on the right of

---

[1] The present Scots Fusilier Guards.

[2] 103 Squadrons of Horse, at 130 per squadron  -  13,390
30 Squadrons of Dragoons, at 100 per squadron  -  3,000
53 Battalions, at 550 per battalion  -  -  -  29,150

45,540

*D'Auvergne's Campaign in Flanders*, page 45.

the line of infantry; the Dutch Guards, one of the battalions of the Scots Guards, and Prince Waldeck's regiments, followed in succession. The Confederates out-
numbered the French, but the vigilance of Marshal Luxembourg was such that William was unable to bring on a
general action; the contending armies were twice drawn
up in order of battle, although neither side would commence the attack. King William quitted Halle, and April 5th.
sailed for England. The troops were directed to occupy
their former quarters.

The King returned from England to the Hague, where May 3rd.
he conferred with the deputies of the States-General
and Council of State, and gave audience to the foreign
ministers.

Orders were issued for the troops to move on the frontier and assemble at Duffel; the Prince of Waldeck
being absent at Aix for the benefit of the waters, the Prince
of Nassau Sarbruck took the command. He marched to
the camp at Anderlecht, and was reinforced by the garrisons of Brussels and Louvain. The troops in Ghent,
Bruges, Ostend, and some other fortified towns remained
stationary till the intentions of the French, who were
assembling in force at Courtrai, could be ascertained. On
the arrival of the Allies at their camp at Anderlecht, the
Prince of Waldeck resumed the command.

Luxembourg with forty-seven thousand six hundred May 15th.
men afterwards crossed the Scheld, and encamped along
the Dender.

The rest of the Allies at Ghent, Bruges, and Os- May 16th.
tend, left their cantonments and assembled at Anderlecht,
with the exception of the Earl of Bath's [1] regiment, which
remained at Bruges a short time longer.

---

[1] D'Auvergne was chaplain to the Earl of Bath's regiment (present Tenth Foot) at this period.

1691.    The French marched for Halle with a view to cut off the communication of that garrison with the Allies. The governor, perceiving their intention, left the town during the night, and early in the morning entered the camp at Anderlecht, which the enemy on the twentieth determined to attack.

After he had made his preparations, and drawn up his troops, Luxembourg discovered that any attempt to force the position of the Allies would be attended with considerable risk; he therefore retired to his former camp.

The Marquis de Gastanaga, governor of the Spanish Netherlands, Prince Vaudemont, and Prince Waldeck, reached Anderlecht, and were soon followed by King William.

May 22nd.    The Marquis de Boufflers approached within two leagues of Liege; this movement was made in concert with the Duke of Luxembourg, who had demolished the fortifications at Halle constructed by the Allies on the capture of Mons.

June 17th to July 10th.    The Confederates moved to the Abbey of Parck on the tenth of June, and afterwards took up a position at Gemblours. Their united force amounted to fifty-six thousand two hundred and seventy.[1]

Luxembourg on the twenty-seventh of June marched to Soignies. Early in July he encamped at Mierbe Potterie, close to the Sambre, where three bridges were laid over the river to enable his army to check the motions of the combined troops.

July 10th.    The Confederates, having passed the Sambre, arrived on

---

[1] " The Landgrave of Hesse joined the Confederate Army with " his forces in this camp, attended with a proportionable train of " artillery, all drawn with white oxen, which made a fine show " upon a march."—*History of the Campaign in Flanders*, 1691, by Edward d'Auvergne, page 87.

the plain of Gerpynes, where they formed in order of   
battle, and remained in that position till all the army
reached the camp.[1]  Their front was covered by the wood
of Florennes, which alone separated them from the French.
A strong guard was left at Fleurus to protect the artillery
and baggage against parties from Mons and Maubeuge.

It was at this camp, in sight of the enemy, and on the
eve of an expected battle, that the lieutenants of the First
and Coldstream Guards were given the rank of captains.[c]
D'Auvergne says, " the captains of the Foot Guards were
" ordered to take rank as lieutenant-colonels in the army
" in this camp, and had commissions given them accord-
" ingly ; whereas, before they only took place of all other
" captains, and in the English and Dutch Guards had their
" pay increased in proportion ; and the lieutenants of the
" Foot Guards had commissions of captains in the army,
" and their pay also increased accordingly."[3]  By the
War-Office commission books, it appears that the rank
of lieutenant-colonel to the captains of the Scots Guards
was now first granted by King William, which accounts
for D'Auvergne's mistake, the captains of the First and
Coldstream having retained the rank from the time it was
bestowed by King James.   Nothing of importance oc-   
curred whilst the armies were respectively encamped at  
Gerpynes and Florennes.   The Confederates received considerable reinforcements, and now consisted of sixty-six
thousand three hundred and ten men ; exceeding the

---

[1] " In the camp of Gerpynes, Lieutenant-General Douglas, who
" had been ordered to leave Ireland to serve under King William
" in Flanders, was attacked by fever and carried to Namur, where
" he died ; the Scots Guards, of which he was colonel, was given
" to Colonel Ramsay." — *D'Auvergne's Campaigns*, 1691, page
102.

[a] See Appendix, No. 122.        [3] D'Auvergne, page 103

1691.
July 28th.

French by eight thousand seven hundred men.  William wished to repass the Sambre before the enemy, and place his army between them and Mons ; he therefore crossed the river Heure in four columns, each over a bridge of boats, and proceeded to the plain.  The artillery with the King's baggage and that of the general officers passed at the stone bridge of Bersé.  The troops encamped, having Chastillon in front and Clairmont in rear of the right ; the left was behind Cour sur Heure, where his Majesty took up his quarters next day.

The Duke of Luxembourg closely observed the Confederates, to obstruct their passing the Sambre at Bussiere ; his object was to prevent any attempt against Mons.

July 31st. From Cour, William moved in the direction of the Sambre ; the rivulet of Beaumont, which ran along the valley, separated the two armies.  When advancing to this position, the King was much disappointed to find that Luxembourg's army had been encamped since the morning on the ground he intended to occupy.

Aug. 1st.   The enemy being strongly posted, it was not deemed prudent to attack him.  A slight cannonade took place, and the Allies returned on the subsequent day to Cour, leaving a garrison in Beaumont to cover their retreat.

Aug. 11th. The army again advanced towards Beaumont, when the garrison quitted the place and set fire to the mines, blowing up the towers and destroying the gates.  The Confederates then withdrew, and the passage of the Sambre was

Aug. 13th. given up for the present.  The army crossed the Heure

Aug. 25th. and afterwards proceeded to the plain of Fleury.  Luxembourg passed his artillery over the Sambre, that he might be enabled to arrive at the Scheld before the Allies, and cover Mons.

Aug. 28th.   King Wilham seeing no chance of any successful enterprise for the remainder of the campaign, crossed the Dyle

between Gemappe and Lambagne, and directed his course   1691.
to Lembeck, on the opposite side of the Senne. The
Brandenburg and Landgrave corps under Marshal Fleming moved towards Namur, to meet the forces from Liege,
in order to watch Boufflers.

. Marshal Luxembourg encamped between Ninove and
Gramont.

The Allied forces encamped near Ath. King William  Sept. 3rd.
left the camp for Loo, and appointed the Prince of Wal-  Sept. 7th.
deck to command in his absence. During the march of  Sept. 9th.
the Allied forces from Leuze to the plain of Cambron,
Luxembourg fell on the rear-guard of the cavalry,[1] and
gained some advantage.[2]

Luxembourg encamped between Avelghem and Auchin,  Sept. 14th.
and ordered Lieutenant-General Rozen to proceed towards
Mons with a body of horse to protect the city and surrounding country, which by his passage of the Scheld
was left exposed to the Allies occupying the plain of

---

[1] In the Paris Gazette and Vaultier's Journal, the loss of the
Dutch amounted to fourteen hundred killed, fifteen hundred wounded, and fourteen hundred prisoners.

[2] " The fortresses of Lessines, Gramont, and Ninove, had been
" dismantled towards the latter end of the former campaign, and
" the towers and gates blown up by the Marshal de Luxembourg's
" order about the latter end of that campaign, a fruit of his victory
" obtained at Fleurus : and as the Abbey of Cambron was encom-
" passed with very strong walls, and the gates towards Ath and
" Brussells of no small strength, they were not forgot in this de-
" molishing work.

" The Dender being cleared by this means of any forts or garri-
" sons from Ath to Dendermond, the French had thereby very near
" the same liberty with the Confederates of marching and encamp-
" ing along this river, without which they could not so easily have
" put the project now mentioned in execution."—*D'Auvergne's*
*Campaigns*, 1691, page 150.

Cambron.   Waldeck, on ascertaining that the intention of
the French was to cross the river, not feeling himself sufficiently strong to make any effectual opposition, marched
the same day to Ninove to cover Ghent, and secure the
country along the canals.   The British troops went into
winter-quarters, and the rest of the forces soon followed.
Prince Waldeck proceeded to the Hague, waited on his
Majesty, and gave an account of the proceedings since his
departure.   King William embarked on the eighteenth of
October, and landed at Margate next day.

## CHAPTER XII.

William embarks for the Hague—Lewis XIV. concentrates round
Mons—Namur invested—William moves towards the Mehaigne
—Confederates form a junction—Namur surrenders—Attempt to
surprise Mons—The King reviews his troops—Reinforcements
join the army—Battle of Steenkirk—Grandval hanged—Troops
under Talmash encamp at Oudenbourg—Duke of Leinster arrives
at Ostend with fifteen regiments—Army goes into winter-quarters—William returns to England.

KING WILLIAM proceeded to the Hague in April. Lewis   1692.
the Fourteenth, with that activity to which in a great
measure may be attributed the first successes of his arms,
moved his troops early in the spring towards Flanders,
and also threatened England with an invasion for the
restoration of James. To carry these plans into effect, the
French Monarch withdrew his forces from the Rhine,
Savoy, and Piedmont; by so doing he left General Catinat too weak to oppose the Duke of Savoy, who entered
Dauphiné with some troops, and laid waste that province.
Lewis the Fourteenth concentrated his army, amounting   April.
to one hundred and twenty thousand men, round Mons,
and took the command in person.

At Duffel, King William received Maximilian Emanuel,
Elector of Bavaria, newly appointed Governor-General of
the Spanish Netherlands, and he afterwards went to   May 4
Brussels to quicken the operations of the Confederates,
who were assembling between Anderlecht and Dilbeck.

1692.    The Coldstream was commanded by Colonel James Bridgeman, who had been lately promoted to the rank of lieutenant-colonel.  Colonel Henry Withers,[1] the Major of the regiment, was "Adjutant-General of the Foot." and Lieutenant-Colonel John Skelton,[2] captain of a company, major of brigade to the Foot Guards.  The Allied army moved towards Louvain.  Lieutenant-General Mackay, with sixteen thousand English and Dutch troops which had concentrated between Dendermond and Ghent, joined on the march.

May 22
June 1    Marshal Boufflers invested Namur; the trenches were opened on the first of June (N. S.), and Lewis the Fourteenth personally superintended the siege.

May 23
June 3    The Allies moved to Parck, and on the road leading to Namur were joined by one thousand four hundred Bavarian Cuirassiers, who took post on the right of the English

May 26
June 5    Foot Guards.  William, anxious to raise the siege of Namur, proceeded towards the Mehaigne, that he might unite with the Elector of Brandenburg and the forces of the Bishop of Liege under Baron Fleming.  The army advanced next day to Lissam, where the reserve was formed, consisting of twelve squadrons of horse, and six

May 28
June 7    battalions, under Count de Lippe.  The Brandenburg and Liege troops, about fourteen thousand strong, and the Spaniards, under the Elector of Bavaria, joined on the twenty-eighth of May (O. S.)  Marshal Luxemburg was also on his route to the Mehaigne.

---

[1] Colonel Withers held his appointment as " Adjutant-General of the Foot" till, and subsequent to, the peace of Ryswick.

[2] Lieutenant-Colonel J. Skelton retained his situation of Brigade-major every campaign till 1695 inclusive.

See Operations before Namur, $\frac{\text{July}}{\text{August}}$ $\frac{23}{2}$, 1695.  See Appendix, Nos. 124. 125. 127.

Before William could reach Namur, the town had surrendered, and the Allies marched to Perweys; but being
followed by the French, they went on to Mellé. The
Castle of Namur capitulated after a siege of twenty days,
during which the French lost about three thousand men
killed and wounded.

An attempt was made to surprise Mons; the inhabitants
of which town " being still Spaniards in their hearts,
" long'd to be deliver'd from the French yoke, and who,
" inform'd that the Garrison was weak, and most of them
" Swissers, who would be as willing as they to joyn in the
" business." [1]   Scaling ladders, and a strong detachment,
with all necessary materials, were forwarded to reinforce
the Prince of Wirtemburg, who directed the enterprise.
A serjeant of Fagel's regiment having been in Mons when
it was besieged, undertook to show the way: a breach
that had not been repaired since the capture of the town
was to afford means of entrance.   The Prince of Wirtemburg arrived at one o'clock A. M. within a short distance
of Mons, where he halted and sent for Sir Robert Douglas
and Colonel O'Farrel, who commanded the English.
These officers, on going back, lost their way, and were
taken prisoners by a party of the garrison of Mons ordered
out by the governor, Count de Vortillac, who was apprised of the design.   The Prince of Wirtemburg finding
the enemy prepared, returned.

The army marched on Genappe; at the same time the
Brandenburg and Liege forces repassed the Meuse.   On
the twenty-ninth (O. S.) the King, accompanied by the
Elector of Bavaria, reviewed the fifteen English batta-
lions.   Among them were two battalions of the First
Guards, and one of the Coldstream, besides two of the

---

[1] D'Auvergne's Campaigns, 1602, page 30.

Dutch Guards. The Danish and other troops, part of the British auxiliaries, were also reviewed; and afterwards the Scotch Infantry, which consisted of ten battalions.

The Allies left Genappe for Halle, and were reinforced by eight thousand Hanoverians and two regiments of En-

glish horse. In the evening preparations were made for attacking the enemy, whose right flank was at Steenkirk, their left at Enghien, and their head-quarters at Hove.

Early in the morning the Allies began to move; they reached the enemy's advance-posts about ten o'clock. The French were fully prepared and drawn up in two lines. Between ten and eleven the column led by the Prince of Wirtemburg gained a wood in front of the enemy's right; the Danes and the second battalion of First Guards were on the left; a narrow valley divided the two armies, which the enemy resolved to defend. Several guns were placed on a rising ground to the left of the wood by the Prince of Wirtemburg; this battery, and another from the right, opened at eleven o'clock; under cover of their fire the army passed the defile, where it deployed in a plain on the right of the Allied position. At this point there was a farm-honse, which the enemy set on fire to cover their advance on Fagel's brigade, posted between the farm and wood. The Allies halted for two hours till the enemy had got in position, during which the cannonade was incessant. The Prince of Wirtemburg commenced the attack with the Danes, who were immediately followed by four English regiments, supported by those of Cutts, Mackay, Angus, Graham, Lawder, the Prince of Hesse, and Leven: the Allied army behaved admirably, and repulsed the repeated charges of several French battalions. The First Guards gallantly dislodged the enemy from one of their batteries, and all the troops engaged acquitted themselves with great heroism: in the

" hedge-fighting their fire was generally muzzle to muzzle, the hedge only separating the combatants." [1]   When the Allies first engaged, the main body was a mile in the rear; William, however, exerted himself to bring them up to deploy, but from the anxiety of his soldiers, confusion ensued; they were unable to form soon enough to support the van-guard, and the left wing, overpowered by numbers, retreated in disorder.   William, as the troops arrived, formed line on the open ground, opposite to which the enemy planted ten pieces in battery.   Several guns were then brought forward by the Confederates, and a heavy cannonade was kept up for a considerable time, during which the Coldstream lost several men.   The advance was deranged by the narrowness of the ground, and the support being too late, only part of the Allies engaged.   They were therefore unable to maintain the post in the wood; and on Luxembourg being reinforced by Boufflers, who arrived at the critical moment with fresh troops, including a large body of cavalry, William was induced to order a retreat, which was conducted with such skill, that, notwithstanding the enemy followed at a short distance, the Allies retired unmolested to their own camp.   This operation was covered by the British Grenadiers, who, when pressed by the enemy's advance, faced about and compelled the French to halt; the Grenadiers then resumed their march: in this manner the Allies reached their ground at Halle, about three o'clock A. M.

---

[1] D'Auvergne's Campaigns, 1692, page 42.

English Officers Killed and Wounded at the Battle of Steenkirk.—
*MS. Harleian.* No. 7018.

### KILLED.

Lord Mountjoy, a volunteer.
Earl of Angus.
Lieutenant-General Mackay.
         Sir Robert Douglas.
     Colonel Hodges.
     Colonel Lowder.[1]
Brigadeer Wells, of Horse Guards.[2]

Colonel Hawley, <br> Captain Jackson,  } of Fitzharding's Dragoons.

Colonel Warcopp,
Colonel Bristow,
Colonel Calthorpe,[3]
Colonel Hamilton,
Captain Warcopp,       } of the First Regiment of Foot
Lieut. Penny,            Guards.
Lieut. Herlackington
Ensign Pickering,
Ensign Gunter,
Ensign Ironside,

Lieut.-Colonel Saville, of Trelawny's Regiment.
Colonel Foxon, of Prince of Hesse's Regiment.

Captain d'Anvers,
Captain Hamilton,
Captain Harbin,
Captain Lowther,        } of Fitzpatrick's Regiment.
Lieut. Grove,
Lieut. Rooke,
Lieut. Beaufort,
Lieut. Pruthser,

---

[1] Not killed, but taken prisoner.—*D'Auvergne,* page 46.

[2] Not the present Blues, but the " Troops of Horse Guards forming the King's Life Guards."

[3] Calthorpe, or Courthorp, wounded and taken prisoner.—*D'Auvergne,* page 46.

Major Keith, &#125;
Captain Cygoe,
Captain Mackenzie,
Captain Sharp, &#125; of O'Ffarrell's Regiment.
Lieut. Charles King,
Lieut. Edward Griffith,

WOUNDED.

Lieutenant-General Tettau.

Sir John Lanier.[1]

Lord Cutts.

Prince of Hanault.

Colonel Cholmley, of First Foot Guards.

Captain Eden,[2] of First Foot Guards.

Lieutenant-Colonel Mackay.

Sir Charles Grahame.

Colonel Stanley.

Colonel Staples, &#125;
Captain Pearcey,
Captain Bennfield, &#125; of the Horse Guards.
Captain Jordan,

Captain Bedford, of Fitzharding's Dragoons.

Major Fox, of Fitzpatrick's Regiment.

Captain Elliot, &#125;
Lieut. Tho. Greenvill, &#125; of the Earl of Bath's Regiment.
Lieut. Jo. Greenvill,

Lieutenant Newton, of O'Ffarrell's Regiment.

Captain Sterling.[3]

Captain Musgrave.[3]

Captain Wildborne.[3]

Captain Hower.[3]

Ensign Harris.[3]

Ensign Deterne.[3]

---

[1] Sir John Lanier died a few days afterwards at Brussels.—
*D'Auvergne*, page 46.

[2] Taken prisoner.—*D'Auvergne*, page 46.

[3] Regiments not specified.

Also :—

Lieut.-Colonel Fullerton, of Angus's Regiment, killed.

Major Carre, of Angus's Regiment, mortally wounded and died.

Lieut.-Colonel Bristol, taken prisoner.

—*D'Auvergne,* page 46.

Captain Mackraken, or Maclachlin, of the Royal Regiment of Foot, killed.

Lieut. Mc Donnell, of the Royal Regiment of Fusiliers, killed.

,,    Mac Donald, of Fitzpatrick's Regt, afterwards Collingwood's, killed.

,,    Babington, of Prince of Hesse's Regt of Foot, killed.

Captain Wm White, of D'O Farrell's Regiment of Foot, killed.

,,    Levingston, of the Royal Regiment of Foot, killed.

Lieut.-Colonel Balfour, of Colonel Lawder's Regiment of Foot, wounded.

—*War Office.*

Several guns were left in possession of the enemy; the army had two thousand men killed, and three thousand wounded. Two English colours were taken.

The French, who also suffered severely, lost three thousand men, the Prince of Turenne and many other officers of high rank included.

It has been asserted that after the battle of Steenkirk, pikes were laid aside and bayonets used in their room, all over Europe ; but this was not the case, as pikes were in use till the commencement of the reign of Queen Anne.[1]

---

[1] " Sir,                    " Whitehall, 20th June, 1702.

    " It is Her Majesty's pleasure, 'that all the pikes already
" delivered to the regiment of Foot under your command, be re-

On the $\frac{3}{13}$ of August, 1692, " the Chevalier de
" Grandval, Knight of Malta, Bartholemew Laniere
" by name, born at Liniere in Piccardy, was hang'd,
" drawn, and quarter'd, (according to the English pu-
" nishment for traytors,) in the midst of our camp, for

1692.
Aug. 3
Sept. 1

---

" turned into the stores of the ordnance, in lieu of a sufficient
" number of muskets, which you are first to receive out of the said
" stores.

" I am,

" P.S. This is not to hinder     " Sir,
" your carrying your pikes       " Yours, &c.
" to Ireland in case muskets      " WILL. BLATHWAYTE."
" be not time enough de-
" livered to you."
" To Colonel Farrington."

Like letter of the same date to
. Lord Mohun,
   Sir Richard Temple,
   Colonel Gibson,
   Colonel Stringer.

The following is an extract of a letter from Mr. St. John, Secretary at War, to the Officers of the Ordnance, dated Whitehall, 13th
of June, 1706, on the occasion of supplying the newly raised regiments, about to embark for Spain, under Lord Rivers, with arms :

" And as to what you write about bayonets, I know it has been
" usual, as you observe, for grenadiers only to have them, and it
" has been usual to furnish pikes to a regiment, which being now
" thought useless, and fire-arms more proper to be given in lieu
" thereof for the good of the service, it seems requisite that as
" many bayonets should be given as muskets, and it is the more
" necessary on this occasion, though the regiments should be
" charged with them, in regard that they have not time to provide
" them themselves."

" In consequence, Lord Mark Keer's and six French regiments
" (raised for Lord Rivers's expedition) were furnished with
" bayonets."—War-Office Records.

See also Appendix for warrant, dated 30th of December, 1695,
providing fourteen pikemen to each company.

1692.    " having conspir'd to assassinate the King, with Du Mont
         " and Lavendael." [1]

Aug. 28     At this time three regiments of horse came from Eng-
Aug. 29
Sept. 1  land.   Lieutenant-General Talmash, who had been de-
         tached " with five battalions, chiefly English and Scotch,
         " viz. his own of" (Coldstream) " Guards, second batta-
         " lion of Scots Guards, Colonel Trelawney's, English
         " Fuziliers, commanded by Colonel Fitz Patrick, and the
         " regiment that was Col. Hodge's, now Col. Stanley's," [2]
         arrived at Bruges, and joined another detachment sent
         under Brigadier Ramsey.   The troops under Lieutenant-
Aug. 30  General Talmash encamped at Oudenbourg; they were to
Sept. 9
         unite with the Duke of Leinster, who arrived at Ostend
         on the first of September with fifteen British regiments.
         Thirty squadrons also joined under Brigadier Boncourt,
         when the force with Talmash amounted to sixteen thou-
         sand men, besides the garrison of Furnes.

Sept. 4     The Coldstream, Selwyn's, and the Fusiliers, with other
         regiments, were sent to occupy Dixmuyde, which was
         placed under the command of Brigadier Ramsey.   At
         Dixmuyde the troops entrenched themselves; their left
         and rear being covered by the river and town.   The
         Dutch were employed in repairing the fortifications: to
Sept. 11 carry on the works with greater celerity, one hundred men
         of every battalion, except the Coldstream, were ordered
         to assist, under a proportionate number of officers.   Tal-
Sept. 29 mash moved towards Bruges; part of the grand army,
Oct. 9
         including the first battalion of Scots Guards, was directed
         to join him: the other regiments, intended to occupy
         Ghent and Mechlin, passed through Bruges, and were
         stationed some days along the canal; these consisted of

--------------------------------------------------------------

[1] D'Auvergne's Campaign in Flanders, 1692, p. 51.
[2] D'Auvergne's Campaign in Flanders, 1692, p. 57.

the Coldstream Guards, Colonel Trelawney's, and the
Fusiliers.

The enemy again made an attempt on Charleroi, which
was abandoned after bombarding the lower town.  Both
armies then went into winter-quarters.

King William departed for Breda on the sixteenth of
September; the command of the army during his absence
devolved on the Elector of Bavaria.  The King then went
to the Hague, whence he embarked for England, and
landed at Yarmouth.  No decisive results arose from this
campaign, but the advantage was in favour of the Allies,
who kept the French in check.

Oct. 11

## CHAPTER XIII.

William arrives from England—Head-quarters at Dieghem—Lewis XIV. detained by illness at Quesnoy—Confederate army at Parck Camp—William advances on Liege—Battle of Landen—William moves to Louvain—French unable to follow up their success—Luxembourg captures Charleroi—Hostile armies go into winter-quarters.

1692.

Dec. 18
Dec. 14
Jan. 9

1693.

BOTH armies remained quietly in their quarters during the winter, with the exception of an attempt made by the French on Hüy, and the capture of Furnes, after a short investment, which led to the abandonment of Dixmuyde. It was conjectured that the enemy would take the field early in the spring, and open the campaign with the siege of Charleroi. Great exertions were made by Lewis XIV.; a larger force than he had ever before assembled was in readiness to commence operations, divided into two separate armies.

King William was no less active in his Preparations: he arrived about the end of March at the Hague, and stayed at Loo till the opening of the campaign.

The French forces were commanded by Marshals Lux- 1693.
embourg, Boufflers, Joyeuse, and Villeroy. The corps
under Luxembourg was posted at Givry, between Mons
and Binch, on the road to Beaumont. The second, under
Boufflers, was encamped between Antoing and Mount
Trinité, near Tournay.

The Allies began to assemble about Dieghem, between
Brussels and Louvain. King William arrived at the   May 12
camp on the twelfth of May, where he was met by the
Elector of Bavaria, who accompanied him to Brussels:
his Majesty established his head-quarters at Dieghem.
The rest of the Confederate force, under the Duke of
Wirtemburg and General Talmash, composing the garrisons of Ghent, Bruges, and Ostend, assembled near
Ghent, where they were enabled to observe the movements of Boufflers. Lord Athlone commanded a body of
cavalry between Tongres and Maestricht, drawn from the
garrisons on the Meuse.

Marshal Boufflers left Tournay for Leuze, and, passing
Chambron, reached Obourg on the twenty-third. The
French armies consisted of one hundred and twenty thou-   May 23
sand men.

The corps at Ghent, under the Duke of Wirtemburg   May 25
and Talmash, joined the army at Dieghem.   June 4

After the King of France had reviewed his army, Luxembourg broke up from Givry, and encamped at Falay.
Boufflers's corps, headed by Lewis XIV., arrived on
the twenty-sixth at Chapelle Herlaymont, between Mons
and Charleroi. The French armies formed a junction
near Gemblours, and exceeded the Confederates by about
one half.

King William possessed himself, on the twenty-sixth, of
the camp at Parck, near Louvain, to prevent the designs of

1693. the French King on Brabant, who detached forty-six squadrons, and twenty-seven battalions, under the Dauphin and Boufflers to Germany: Lewis returned to Versailles.

List of the Confederate army, at Parck Camp:—

RIGHT WING OF HORSE—THE ELECTOR OF BAVARIA.

In the first line were twenty-six squadrons of horse, and three battalions of foot. In the second line, twenty-three squadrons of horse and three battalions of foot, composed of Spaniards, Bavarians, and Hanoverians.

BODY OF FOOT—HIS MAJESTY THE KING OF
GREAT BRITAIN.

| FIRST LINE. | Batt⁸ | SECOND LINE. | Batt⁸ |
|---|---|---|---|
| English Guards, 1ˢᵗ Regᵗ | I | English Guards, 1ˢᵗ Regᵗ | 1 |
| „ „ 2ᵈ Regᵗ | | Dutch Guards . . | 1 |
| (Coldstream) | 1 | Scots Guards . . | 1 |
| Dutch Guards . . | 1 | Royal Regiment . . | 1 |
| Scots Guards . . | l | Selwyn . . . | 1 |
| Royal Regiment . . | 1 | The Queen's or Trelawney | 1 |
| Prince George or Churchil | 1 | Bath . . . . | 1 |
| Fuziliers or Fitzpatrick | 1 | Tidcomb . . . | 1 |
| Collingwood . . | 1 | Graham . . . | 1 |
| Stanley . . . | 1 | Lauder . . . . | 1 |
| Earle . . . . | 1 | Leven . . . . | 1 |
| Scotch Fuzil. or Offerrel | 1 | Argyle . . . . | 1 |
| Mackay . . . . | 1 | Queen of Denmark . | 1 |
| Monroe . . . . | 1 | Danish Infantry . . | 13 |
| Dutch Infantry . . | 13 | | |
| Total | 26 | Total | 26 |

LEFT WING OF HORSE—PRINCE OF
NASSAU SARBRUCK.

| FIRST LINE. | Squadrons. |
|---|---|
| German Cavalry . . | 10 |
| British. Athlone . . | 2 |
| Queen's or Lumley . | 3 |
| Langston . . . | 2 |
| Wyndham . . | 2 |
| Leinster . . . | 2 |
| Galloway . . | 3 |
| Berkley . . . | 2 |
| Life Gu. Colchester | 1 |
| Life Gu. Scarborough | 1 |
| Life Gu. Auverquerque | 1 |
| Dutch Dragoons . . | 6 |
| Fitzharding's Dragoons | 3 |
| Eppinger's Dragoons . | 3 |
| Total | 41 |

| SECOND LINE. | Squadrons. |
|---|---|
| German Cavalry . . | 9 |
| Dutch Cavalry | 16 |
| Danish Cavalry | 6 |
| Total | 31 |

RESERVE OF HORSE AT PARCK CAMP, UNDER THE
EARL OF ATHLONE.

| FIRST LINE. | SECOND LINE. |
|---|---|
| German Cavalry 14 squadrons. | German Cavalry 16 squadrons. |

Likewise six Brandenburg battalions in the King of Spain's service, encamped about a league from Louvain, under Major-General Baron de Heyde.[1]

The total amount of the Allied army, at this time, was sixty thousand eight hundred and fifty.

Luxembourg besieged Hüy. July ⁶⁄₁₆

William advanced nearer to Liege : at Tongres he July ¹⁸⁄₂₈ found the Castle of Hüy had capitulated, and that Lux- July ¹⁴⁄₂₄

---

[1] History of Campaign in the Spanish Netherlands, 1693. By Edward D'Auvergne, M.A. Chaplain to the Scots Guards.

1693.    embourg was approaching Liege; his Majesty, therefore, detached ten battalions, which with difficulty entered the place: all offers of neutrality made by Luxembourg to the British in Liege were, after this, rejected.  The King

July ⅟₁    returned to his position at Neerhespen, and Luxembourg encamped at Hellick.  The French then made a feint on Liege, their real intention being to attack the Confederates encamped at Neerhespen, who were much weakened by the re-inforcements William had sent to Liege and Maestricht.[1]

July ⅟₂    The enemy quitted the camp at Hellick: their advance met at Warem one of the parties which William was in the habit of sending daily to gain intelligence.  The King resolved to fight: he might have avoided an action by crossing the Geete, which he has been censured for not doing, considering the great disparity in numbers of the two armies. The enemy's left wing of horse advanced at six o'clock P.M., under Marshal Joyeuse, and the infantry, with the greater part of the artillery, arrived about eight; but, as it was too late to engage, Luxembourg made his arrangements to attack early next morning.

When the enemy were drawn out, the King ordered Ramsey, with his brigade, consisting of five battalions, to the extreme right, to guard some hedges and ravines that covered his wing on the village of Laér.  The Brandenburg regiments were stationed in the village under Prince Charles of Brandenburg, and the Hanoverian infantry on their left under Lieutenant-General Du Mont, who was to defend the village of Neerwinden, which covered the camp between the right wing of the cavalry,

---

[1] The French were supposed to be at least thirty-five thousand stronger.—See Harris's History of the Life and Reign of William Henry.  Dublin, 1749.

and the main body of the army. They were afterwards reinforced by the first battalion of the First Guards, the second battalion of Dutch Guards, and second battalion of Scots Guards. On the left, at Neerwinden, were the first battalion of the Royal Regiment, Churchill's, Selwyn's, and Trelawney's, with Prince Frederick's battalion of Danes, and Pagel's. This village protected the left of the infantry, who extended on the right to the rivulet of Beck. Between Neerwinden and Neerlanden there was an open space; during the night a breast-work was made by the King's order from one end to the other, to cover the line of infantry. The dragoons on the left guarded the pass at the village of Dormal on the brook of Beck, whence the cavalry on the left reached to Neerlanden, where they were covered by the rivulet that inclined to the right behind the infantry.

Soon after sun-rise, the enemy formed within gun-shot. A cannonade commenced from several batteries at the extremities and along the intrenchments. At six they advanced, but in consequence of the fire of the Confederate artillery, they filed off to both flanks; Luxembourg found it necessary to make himself master of the villages of Laér and Neerwinden, and at eight o'clock advanced on the left of the latter village. The attack was commenced by General Rubantel on the right, the Duke of Berwick in the centre, and Mountchevreüil on the left. Orders to take possession of Laér were also given. The conflict at Neerwinden was for some time doubtful, and the French were about to retire, when the Duke de Bourbon arrived with the brigade of Guiche, and renewed the struggle so vigorously, that the troops which occupied the place were eventually obliged to retreat. Brigadier Ramsay was then attacked at Laér by the whole of the reserve, which had been reinforced. The Brandenburgers who lined the hedges were also assailed.    At Laér the contest was equally obstinate; but the great superiority of the enemy finally enabled them to succeed.

The Duke of Berwick, who distinguished himself in this affair, was taken prisoner, with his aid-de-camp Captain Achmuty.   Having failed at Neerwinden on the right, an attempt was made by the enemy on the left at Neerlanden, at which place only four battalions were posted, the rest having been sent away in the morning to re-inforce Brigadier Ramsay.   Four French regiments of dragoons passed the Beck, and attacked the King's flank at this village.   The Marquis de Crequi, who commanded the brigades posted at Landen, ordered them to charge at the same moment in front.

After two hours sharp fighting the enemy was repulsed and pursued into the plain.   The King being present part of the time with Selwyn's regiment, witnessed the flight of the enemy.

A fresh attempt at Neerwinden commenced, when his Majesty left Neerlanden and led the English battalions twice to the charge, who fought with the spirit they had shown throughout the day.[1]   The Allies until this period had successfully repulsed the attacks of the enemy, and but a faint fire continued at Neerwinden.

The Prince of Conti, being joined by the French and Swiss Guards with three other brigades, succeeded in carrying the village of Neerwinden and broke the Hanoverian cavalry, whilst their second line of horse and the reserve advanced on the left along the hedges of Laér. The Marquis d'Harcourt, who had been sent for from Hüy, arrived at this moment with twenty-two squadrons.

---

[1] Relation of the Battel of Landen.   Published by authority.
London.   Printed by Edward Jones in the Savoy, 1693.

Villeroy pushed in on the right of the intrenchment, which was disputed with undaunted courage by the English, who, however, were overpowered, when the intrenchment was levelled to give entrance to a large body of cavalry. "However, they did not come in upon easy " terms; the first troop of Life Guards, of which Luxem- " burg was colonel, lost their standard, which was taken " by a soldier of the Coldstream Guards (Talmash's). " The fusiliers suffered very much in this action."[1]

The Elector of Bavaria, who attempted to resist the charge, was obliged to retire to the river Geete, and succeeded in gaining a bridge, at the other end of which he rallied some horse and foot with difficulty, to protect those ready to cross. William[2] finding that his right wing was overthrown, and had passed the river in great disorder, ordered the infantry to retreat towards Dormal, which was occupied by the dragoons of the left wing, who had not been engaged.

Flight and confusion now ensued; many that were unable to gain the passes threw themselves into the river. Such was the fate of the right wing of horse and of part of

---

[1] D'Auvergne.

[2] " The King of England in the day of battle shewed him- " self, as he had already done, a brave and gallant man ; and it " was only the wonderful providence of God that preserved one " who exposed himself so much."—*Life of King William*. London. Printed at the Black Boy in Fleet Street : and F. Coggan in the Middle Temple Lane, 1702.

" The King narrowly missed three musquet shots, one through " his periwig, which made him deaf for a while ; another through " the sleeve of his coat, which did no harm; the third carried off " the knot of his scarf, and left a small contusion on his side."— *D'Auvergne's Campaigns in Flanders*, 1693, page 79.

the left, as well as of the infantry engaged at Neerwinden and Laér.   The cannon and artillery-waggons got wedged in the passes leading to the bridges, and many were captured.

General Talmash was entrusted with the care of the main body of infantry that retreated by Dormal to Lewe, which he conducted with a degree of prudence as signal as the bravery he had displayed when engaged in an unequal contest along the breast-work.

When King William passed the river at Neerhespen, he united part of his Foot Guards, and all that had crossed of Ramsay's brigade, to the horse of the left wing.   With these and the troops he had brought with him he joined the Elector of Bavaria, and retired to Boutechem, near Tirlemont.   The rest of the Allies, after their retreat by Dormal to Lewe, marched from that place and encamped at Diest.

The  French retired to Warem, near Liege.

The battle of Landen, or of Neerwinden and Neerhespen, was decidedly in their favour.   " This was occasioned " by a vast superiority of numbers ; yet their loss was so " great, that they were disabled from pursuing their " success ; which circumstance afforded a subject for " several medals, on one of which is the bust of King " William."[1]

The Allies lost ten thousand men ; the French, upwards of fifteen thousand.

No officer of the Coldstream was killed in the battle of Landen ; but these occur in a list of those that were wounded :—Colonel William Seymour, son to Sir Edward Seymour, and Lieutenant-Colonel of the regiment; Lieu-

---

[1] See engraved medal F.

tenants and Captains Wakelin, Bisset, Markham, and O'Brian;[1] Ensigns Hill and La Ferrelle.[2]

After this battle the King moved to Louvain, and encamped on the following day at Eppeghem, where his infantry, which had retreated by Lewe to Diest under General Talmash, joined him.

An order was sent to the Duke of Wirtemburg, who had been encamped two miles from Lisle, to unite with the King; but he afterwards received instructions not to press his march, as the Allied army was in much better condition than could have been expected.

William crossed the canal at Vilvorde, and the combined forces formed a junction at VVemmel, where the King established his head-quarters. The Allies were now stronger than at any former period during the campaign.

After being reviewed by the King, the troops left VVemmel for Halle, and took up the ground occupied by the army in the preceding year before the battle of Steenkirk; from Halle they moved to St. Quintin Linneck, where they encamped. Marshal Luxembourg marched to Soignies on the nineteenth, in order to join some troops sent to reinforce his army preparatory to the siege of Charleroi, which was invested on the second of September.

The Elector of Bavaria was detached from St. Quintin Linneck with thirty battalions and fifty squadrons, including the second battalion of the First Guards, the first battalion of the Coldstream, and two battalions of the Scots Guards. "These mounted the guard upon his Electoral Highness whilst he commanded this body,"[3]

---

[1] O'Brian died of his wounds, and left a widow Josyna, to whom a pension of twenty pounds a year was granted.—War-Office Records.

[2] D'Auvergne's Campaigns in Flanders, 1693, page 91.

[3] D'Auvergne's Campaigns, 1693, page 113.

## CHAPTER XIV.

William returns to Holland — Head-quarters at Bethlehem —
Luxembourg and Villeroy join the French near the Sambre—
The hostile armies concentrate — The Dauphin reviews the
French at Gemblours—Strength of Confederates in Flanders—
William returns to England — Straw huts of the Coldstream destroyed by fire — The two armies go into winter-quarters—Talmash dies of his wounds at Portsmouth—Cutts succeeds in command of the Coldstream—Expedition against Brest, in which
were thirteen companies of the Guards.

EARLY in May the King landed from England. The
French were still in their quarters and made no preparations for their departure.

1694.

An encampment was formed near Ghent, under the
Duke of Wirtemburg, and at Bethlehem and Terbank
near Louvain, under the Duke of Holstein. In May, two
battalions of the First, and the first battalion of the Coldstream Guards, left Ghent to join the camp. The English
under Count Nassau, Sir Henry Bellasis, and Major-
General Ramsay, were joined by two regiments from Dendermond, when they moved to the general rendezvous.

May 15

May 31

May 26
June 5

May 28
June 7

William reviewed the infantry, accompanied by the
Electors of Bavaria and Cologne.

May 31
June 10

Marshals Luxembourg and Villeroy headed the French
army on the twentieth, cantoned near the Sambre, and

were followed by the Dauphin, the Dukes of Chartres, Bourbon, and other Princes of the Blood.

The troops on both sides were concentrated for opening the campaign.

In June, the Allies broke up, and occupied the ground within a short distance of Tirlemont. The brigade of Guards encamped at Valeduc, to cover his Majesty's quarters. The whole army, both cavalry and infantry, were so placed that every brigade of infantry was supported by a brigade of cavalry in the rear.

The French moved to Gemblours, where the Dauphin reviewed the army, which consisted of "Sixty-and-nine " squadrons of horse in the first and second line of his " right wing of horse, and sixty-and-six in the left, and " twenty-and-nine squadrons of dragons, hussars, and " mousquetairs in the reserve, which makes in all 164 " squadrons. And because the French had reformed " their troups of horse last winter to forties, we must com- " pute each of their squadrons to be, at their coming in " the field, of 120 horsemen; which makes a total of " the horse and dragons of this army to be 19,680. The " foot consisteth of forty battalions in the first line, and " thirty-nine in the second, and three in the reserve, " which makes in all 82 battalions; which at 600 men " each battalion, at the first coming into the field, amounts " to 49,100 men. So that the total of this army, com- " manded by the Dauphin, and under him Marshals " Luxembourgh and Villeroy, came to 68,880 men, be- " sides what belonged to the artillery, as gunners and " matrosses, miners," &c. [1]

As the armies were within a day's march of each other,

---

[1] D'Auvergne's Campaign in the Spanish Netherlands, 1694, page 15.

the King caused some intrenchments to be thrown up. On the right were the villages of Tourine and Bavechein. The brigade of Guards was posted on a hill, and covered his Majesty's quarters. Part of them, and a regiment of dragoons, removed to the other side of the King's quarters, to check any parties that might be concealed in the wood of Merdal. Sixty guns and six mortars arrived; some cavalry also joined and encamped in the intervals of the brigades.

The French had in Flanders, under the Dauphin, Boufflers, and La Valette, one hundred and seven battalions, or about sixty-four thousand two hundred infantry, besides twenty-seven thousand one hundred and twenty horse, in their three armies.

The Allies moved in six columns; the first was composed of the brigade of Guards, and seven other regiments, led by the Duke of Wirtemburg. The Elector of Bavaria marched at the same time from his camp at Neer Iche, to unite with the main army at Judoigne. All the cavalry joined at this place. The King took up his quarters at Mont St. André. The Allied army now consisted of eighty-eight thousand eight hundred, besides seven thousand which were with Count Thian encamped near Ghent. There was also a considerable force in Liege, then useless, as the enemy separated the Confederates from the Mense.

The French moved on Hüy, and encamped between the villages of Vignamont and Walef; on forming their camp they intrenched themselves. The Dauphin declared he had received orders from his father not to leave his camp near Hüy as long as the Confederates remained in theirs at Mont St. André.

The Allies marched to Escanaffe, where the opposing forces were in presence of each other. From Escanaffe they moved along the Scheld to Oudenarde; here the left of the army was exposed to the enemy's cannon, which opened in the evening, but without effect. The King's head-quarters, at Berghem, were on the banks of the Scheld, and much exposed to the French guns. The rear-guard consisted of a battalion of the First, a battalion of the Coldstream, and a battalion of Dutch Guards, who had taken their position at Cordes, near the King's quarters, some distance from the rest of the army, and could not be brought up till next morning.

Aug. 14    The French guns again opened their fire on the left; batteries had been erected near the King's quarters, which answered them, without producing much effect on either side.

After four brigades and both battalions of the Scots Guards had joined the Duke of Wirtemburg, the French proceeded for Courtrai, and encamped between that place and Harleber. The rest of the army crossed the Scheld at Oudenarde, below the town, on a bridge of boats. The enemy, not thinking it convenient to remain on the same side of the Lys, passed, on the eighteenth, at Courtrai.

Aug.  25
Sept.  7    The right wing of the Confederate horse, and a large force of infantry, marched towards the Lys; the brigade of Guards, however, continued encamped near the King's

Aug.  26
Sept.  5    quarters. The Allies crossed the river on two bridges at Maichelen, and encamped at Rousselaér, on the twenty-ninth. This movement was undertaken to draw the French from the neighbourhood of Hüy, which it was resolved to besiege. The town was invested on the seventh by the Duke of Holstein, with the Dutch and Brandenburg forces, and the Prince of Tilly, with the Liege forces.[1]

---

[1] Hüy surrendered the seventeenth of September. (O. S.)

The tents were struck, and orders issued to make huts of straw. The Duke of Wirtemburg reviewed the infantry of the army, and began with the brigade of Guards. 1694.<br>Sept. $\frac{1}{12}$

The Dauphin left the French camp on the eighth of September, and returned to Versailles.

On the twentieth the King quitted the army, and arrived in England on the second of November.

About the end of September the straw huts of the Coldstream " regiment of English Guards (whereof my " Lord Cutts is now Colonel, in the room of the late " Lientenant-General Talmash) took fire; the wind drove " the flame to the left, where it chanced to be advanced " forward to the front of the Dutch Guards, or else the " fire might have done more mischief in our straw-camp, " which is very dangerous when the army is thus butted " all along in straw." [1] Sept. $\frac{19}{29}$<br>Oct. 8

In October the whole of the heavy artillery was forwarded to Ghent in charge of the Coldstream Guards,[2] whose huts having been burnt, were sent into winter-quarters.[3] The army broke up and proceeded to the different stations assigned them for the winter. Oct. $\frac{1}{11}$ Oct. $\frac{2}{12}$ & $\frac{7}{17}$

The French left the neighbourhood of Courtrai, and also went into quarters for the winter. Marshals Luxembourg[4] and Villeroy returned to Court, and Marshal

---

[1] D'Auvergne's Campaigns in Flanders, 1694, page 97.

[2] The two battalions of the First Guards and Coldstream, with a regiment of Danish Guards and other troops, were quartered at Ghent during the winter. The Scots Guards and several other English battalions were quartered at Bruges.

[3] The following officers of the Coldstream returned home on leave in October: Lieut.-Colonels Edwards, Edgeworth, and Braddock; Lieutenants and Captains Wentworth and Morrison, and Ensign Morrison.—War-Office Records.

[4] The Duke of Luxembourg died of pleurisy at Versailles the end of December this year.

Boufflers took the command at Lille, where he had been appointed Governor.

Lieutenant-General Talmash had died [1] on the twelfth of June, 1694, at Plymouth, of the wounds he received at Camaret Bay. Lord Cutts became Colonel of the Coldstream.

General Talmash was the son of Sir Lionel Talmash, third Earl of Dysart, who succeeded to the title in right of his mother, Elizabeth, daughter of William, second Earl of Dysart. He obtained a company in the Coldstream at the augmentation on the sixteenth of January, 167$\frac{1}{2}$, and soon distinguished himself. His company was one of the eight which were reduced at the termination of the French war. In 1688 he was appointed Colonel of the Fifth Foot in Holland; in December, the same year, he was made Governor of Portsmouth; and was promoted to the rank of Lieutenant-General on the twenty-third of January, 169$\frac{1}{2}$. The King gave him the command of the expedition against Brest, which sailed from England the latter end of May, to make a descent on the coast of France. At a council of war held on board the Britannia, composed of the officers of the navy and army, it was determined to proceed and land at Camaret Bay.

The forces employed on this occasion consisted of a body of troops, including thirteen companies formed out of the Guards in London, under Colonel John Hope of the Coldstream, who marched to Portsmouth on the fifteenth of May. [2] The Colonel of the regiment, Lieutenant-

---

[1] London Gazette, No. 2984.

[2] Extract from a contingent account by Colonel John Hope and Lieutenant-Colonel Francis Edwards of the Coldstream Guards.

" 15 May, 1694.   Paid thirteen carts for thirteen com-

    " panies formed out of the Guards, sixty in each com-

General Talmash, commanded in chief. Lord Cutts 1694. volunteered to head six hundred grenadiers, who took the lead on landing. The enemy having intelligence of the approach of the squadron, took the necessary precautions, directed by the celebrated engineer Vauban. The troops prepared to land, covered by a cannonade from the fleet, but they were exposed to a heavy fire from the French batteries, and on reaching the shore were received by a strong body of cavalry and infantry. Many were killed in the boats, and great confusion prevailed during the landing, without any regard to the order for conducting the disembarkation, " which my Lord Cutts proposed, and was before agreed on."[1] The killed, wounded, and taken amounted to seven hundred men, independent of a severe loss on board the fleet; among the wounded was General Talmash.

At a council of war it was agreed that the squadron should return to England. On arriving at St. Helen's, orders were received for assembling a council of war to consider in what way the forces might be most advantageously employed, when an attack on the coast of Normandy was determined on. The fleet put to sea on the

" pany besides officers; they marched to Portsmouth,
" being sixty-five miles, at 8d per mile . . . £29 12 4
" Paid two carts for carrying down Lieut Genl Talmash's
" baggage to Portsmouth . . . . . . 4 6 8
" 2d August, 1694. Paid 3 carts for carrying sick and
" wounded men at our landing at Portsmouth up to
" the hospitall at London, 8d per mile . . . 6 10 0
" 10th August, 1694. Paid 8 carts that marched with
" the battalion to Whitehall, 8d per mile, 65 miles . 17 6 8
—War-Office Records.
[1] A Journal of the Brest Expedition, by the Marquis of Caermarthen. London. Printed by Randal Taylor, near Amen Corner, 1694. Page 25.

1694. fifth of July, and having thrown a number of shells into Dieppe, and greatly damaged it, sailed for **Havre-de-Grace**, which was also bombarded and set on fire. The fleet again returned to St. Helen's, and then steered for Dunkirk with the intention of destroying that town, but the design miscarried. An attempt to cannonade Calais also failed. The thirteen companies of the Guards were then disembarked, and marched early in August to their quarters in London. The detachment of the Coldstream consisted of Lieutenant-Colonel John Hope, Captains John Wilson and Harry Lawrence, Ensign John Miller, four serjeants, six corporals, three drummers, and one hundred and thirty-eight privates.

## CHAPTER XV.

William embarks for Holland—Two armies in the Netherlands, one commanded by the Elector of Bavaria and Duke of Holstein, the other to act in Flanders under William and Prince Vaudemont—French concentrate between the Scheld and Dunkirk—Namur invested—William's head-quarters at the Chateau de la Falize—Lord Cutts reaches Templeux—Dutch break ground near Bouge—The Guards suffer severely in an assault—Siege of Namur—Town capitulates—Boufflers retires to the Castle—Cutts wounded—Citadel surrenders—Allies encamp near Nivelle—William reviews his army previous to his departure—Winter quarters of the Allies—English Guards at Ghent.

EARLY in the spring of this year William embarked at Gravesend for the Hague. The Confederates took the field, and two armies were formed in the Netherlands; one under the Elector of Bavaria and the Duke of Holstein Ploen; the other, intended to act in Flanders, commanded by his Majesty and the Prince de Vaudemont. On the twenty-seventh the whole of the forces assembled at Arseele, where the King arrived. The Allied army amounted to one hundred and twenty-four thousand seven hundred men. They moved in four columns from Arseele to Becelar.

Villeroy crossed the Scheld and Lys, to encamp within the French lines. Marshal Boufflers, who was at Gosse-

1695.
May ⅓

June ⅔

1695. lies, near the Sambre, marched with his troops to watch the Elector of Bavaria, encamped near Ninove. Although the King had no intention to force the enemy's lines between the Lys and Scheld, yet, being desirous to con-

June 4 centrate his forces, he ordered the Elector of Bavaria to
June 5 move from Ninove and approach them.

Boufflers marched a large body of cavalry to Tournay, crossed the river, and joined the reinforcement of foot sent him by Villeroy. The French, with the exception of Harcourt's corps, had concentrated for the defence of their lines, which extended from the Scheld to the neighbourhood of Dunkirk. Boufflers commanded between the Lys and the Scheld. Villeroy, with the main body, observed the Allies between the Lys and Ipres.

June 14 The King's army returned to its former position at Rousselaér. His Majesty left the camp next day under a strong escort, and proceeded towards Namur.

June 18 Prince Vaudemont, after the departure of King William for Namur, marched on the left bank of the Mandel to Wouterghem, where his troops halted. The French occupied a rising ground on the other side of the Lys, near Harlebeck, three leagues from the Allied position. Marshal Villeroy left his camp immediately after the Confederates had put themselves in motion, and on the nine-

June 29 / July 9 teenth encamped near Courtrai. Marshal Boufflers threw himself, with a considerable force of cavalry, into Namur, which place the Elector of Bavaria and the Duke of Holstein Ploen invested a few days after. The King also

June 29 / July 9 arrived, and fixed his quarters at the Chateau de la Falize, within four miles of the place. Fourteen battalions from

June 29 / July 8 Prince Vaudemont's army at Wouterghem reached Templeux, a league and a half from Namur; several other

July 11 battalions shortly after followed. Lord Cutts arrived at the camp at Templeux with six battalions, consisting of

the second battalion of the First Guards, the first of the  1695.
Coldstream, with the regiments of Trelawney, Ingoldesby,
Nassau, and Heyden; which had been detached from
Prince Vaudemont's army on the twenty-fourth of June.

The Dutch broke ground near the village of Bouge, and  July ᴕ
in the evening of the eighth an assault was ordered on the
covered-way in possession of the enemy, near the hill of
Bonge; two attacks were to be made, one on the right of
the tower of Cocklé, the other on the left.  Major-General
Ramsay advanced with two battalions of the First Guards,
the first battalion of the Coldstream, the first battalion of
the Dutch Guards, and the first of the Scots Guards, besides
detachments of the grenadiers from the other regiments.
The Guards marched under a heavy fire without making
any return till they put their pieces through the palisades,
and after a short contest took possession of them.  The
troops, flushed with success, rushed furiously forward,
attacked the second covered-way, which they also gained,
and followed the enemy among the batteries on the brow
of the hill; many of the French sought refuge in the stone-
pits, and concealed themselves from the fury of the soldiers.  The Guards returned about midnight, and arrived
early next morning at the camp of Templeux.

The Dutch attacked on the left; the enemy's fire occasioned them great loss, notwithstanding which they
carried the works.

The brigade of Guards lost one hundred and seventy-
seven killed, three hundred and sixty-six wounded, and
forty-one prisoners.[1]  The total loss of the British and

---

[1] " WILLIAM R.

" Our will and pleasure is, That out of such moneys as are or
" shall come to your hands for contingent uses, you pay unto our
" right trusty and right welbeloved cousin and councillor, Henry
" Earl of Romney, Lieu' Gen" of our forces, the summ of four hun-

Dutch amounted to five hundred killed, and twelve hundred wounded. The casualties in the Coldstream were, Captain Weston, and Ensigns Holmes and Whiterong,[1] killed; Colonel Matthews,[2] Lieutenant-Colonels Edgworth, Jones, and Pierce, Captain Markham, Ensigns Hill and Miller, and Adjutant Wyvill, wounded; Lientenant-Colonels Pierce and Morrison, and Ensign Atkins, prisoners. The following extract of a letter from King William to the Duke of Shrewsbury evinces his satisfaction with the conduct of his Guards.

" Two days ago I was obliged to attack the lines which
" the enemy had constructed to cover their works ; and
" we forced them with vigour.  All the troops displayed
" considerable courage, and particularly the five battalions
" of Guards, the English, the Scotch, and one Dutch,
" who attacked on the right.[3]

---

" dred and ninety-four pounds, which we are pleased to allow
" for levy money for one hundred and five men of our First Regi-
" ment of Foot Guards killed at Namur, at the rate of three
" pounds a man, and for one hundred and seventy-nine men
" wounded at the same time, at twenty shillings a man ; And That
" you also pay unto our right trusty and welbeloved John Lord
" Cutts, the summ of two hundred and seventy-one pounds, for
" fifty-three men of our Coldstream Regiment of Foot Guards
" killed, and one hundred and twelve wounded at the same time, at
" the like rates.  And for so doing, &c. Given, &c. 6ᵗʰ February,
" 1695-6.
         " By his Maᵗⁱᵉ command,
" To the Earl of Ranelagh."       " WILLᵐ BLATHWAYT."

[1] Probably an error, as Ensign Whiterong's name appears among the killed in the First Guards.—War-Office Records.

[2] Lieutenant-Colonel of the Coldstream.

[3] Private correspondence of the King with the Duke of Shrewsbury.  Camp before Namur, July eleventh (twenty-first), 1695.—*Coxe*, page 92, part I. chap. v.

The troops in the trenches were relieved by the brigade of Guards, commanded by Lord Cutts, appointed Brigadier of the Guards, " an honour no brigadier had enjoyed before." [1]

The Coldstream remained on duty to guard the King, the other regiments mounted the trenches, which during the night of the fourteenth were extended down the hill to the detached bastion before the gate of St. Nicholas. This gate was given up on the sixteenth. Next night the trenches were advanced far enough for an attack on the counterscarp, and having already gained the detached bastion, the men worked at the battery at the foot of the hill, which was intended to fire on the half-moon of St. Nicholas. All preparations being made, an assault on the counterscarp was ordered at the time the trenches were relieved in the evening. Five hundred grenadiers, and several regiments, were in readiness to support the attack. It commenced about five o'clock : the glacis was defended by the enemy with great·obstinacy ; every inch of ground was disputed. The counterscarp was carried. The loss of the Allies in this attack amounted to between seven and eight hundred killed and wounded.

Mr. Godfrey,[2] Deputy Governor of the Bank of England, who had visited head-quarters to make arrangements relative to an advance of money for the payment of the army, was killed by a shot in the trenches, standing near the King.[3]

Next day the battery was opened against the half-moon of St. Nicholas. The Brandenburgers also finished their parallel lines along the Meuse, and the same night Lord

---

[1] D'Auvergne's Campaigns, 1695, page 70.

[2] He was nearly related to Sir Edmondbury Godfrey, whose death or murder excited so much public interest in the reign of Charles II.

[3] D'Auvergne's Campaigns in Flanders, 1695, page 87.

1695.    Cutts mounted the trenches with the brigade of Guards;
"the battalion of Scots Guards did duty at the King's
"quarter." [1]

On the twentieth, the King heard of the surrender of
Dixmuyde, the defence of which was entrusted to Major-
General Ellemberg.  In the evening of the twenty-second,
Lord Cutts with the brigade of Guards was again in the
trenches, the Dutch Guards being on duty over the King.
July  22
Aug.  2    A battery of eighteen pieces of English artillery, which had
newly arrived, opened on the bastion of St. Roch, and
battered the stone-work; but the enemy being in possession of the covered-way on the right, towards the Porte
de Fer, it was necessary to extend the lodgement in that
direction.  The attack commenced in the evening at the
relieving of the troops, and was disputed till a late hour,
when the object was ultimately gained.  Lord Cutts commanded the brigade of Guards in the trenches this day.
Captain Wentworth of the Coldstream was killed; he
"waited on his Lordship to carry his orders to the bri-
"gade," [2] as Lieutenant-Colonel Skelton, the Major of
brigade, could not perform the duty, being at the time in
command of the Coldstream.

The Dutch advanced through a narrow defile, where
they maintained themselves for an hour, but were forced
to retire.  The loss of the brigade of Guards [3] was nine
men killed, and thirteen wounded.  His Majesty was
present from the commencement of the attack, and did
not return to his quarters till after midnight.
July  23
Aug.  3    Next day the English batteries kept up a continual fire
on the bastion of St. Roch, to make a practicable breach,

---

[1] D'Auvergne's Campaigns in Flanders, 1695, page 91.

[2] Ibidem, page 96.

[3] Captain Crespigny and Ensign Shute of the First Guards were
wounded.

as the lodgement in the counterscarp was now of sufficient extent for an assault; the fire from all the other batteries was also incessant. Count de Guiscard mounted the breach of the demi-bastion, and ordered a white flag to be hoisted, when the batteries ceased their fire : he requested to speak to Major-General Ramsay, to whom Guiscard proposed to give up the town to preserve it from further injury. The Major-General went to the Duke of Holstein, then to the King, who authorised him to make an exchange of hostages.[1] Terms of capitulation were signed, and the July $\frac{25}{4}$ Aug. following evening Colonel Lander took possession of the Porte de Fer, in presence of his Majesty. Marshal Boufflers with seven thousand men withdrew into the castle, having lost five thousand in defence of the town, including a numerous body of deserters. Twenty-two July $\frac{27}{8}$ Aug. squadrons of horse, thirteen English, and seventeen Dutch battalions under Count Nassau, were sent towards Brussels to reinforce Prince Vaudemont. The Coldstream and five English battalions remained to carry on the siege of the citadel.

The French under Villeroy advanced to Brussels, and Aug. $\frac{1}{1}$ troops daily joined him.

---

[1] British regiments before the town, "in the line of circumvallation at the siege of Namur."

| | |
|---|---|
| English Cavalry, 3 squadrons. | Columbine. |
| 1st Regiment of Foot Guards, two batts. | Royal Fusiliers. |
| | Tidcomb. |
| Coldstream Guards. | Stanley. |
| Scots Guards. | Collingwood. |
| Royals. | Lauder. |
| Selwyn. | Ingoldesby. |
| Trelawney. | Saunderson. |
| Seymour. | Maitland. |

*D'Auvergne's Campaigns*, 1695.

1695.    During Villeroy's march, ten battalions were detached from Lord Athlone's corps, then encamped at Waterloo, to reinforce the army of Prince Vaudemont. King William visited the camp at Waterloo, and then returned to the siege. After bombarding Brussels, Marshal Villeroy re-

Aug. ⁷⁄₁.  tired to Halle and Enghien, between which places he encamped : the same day Lord Athlone also changed his position and posted his right before Braine La Leud, and his left towards Bois-Seigneur-Isaac, to enable him to defend the passage from Halle to Namur, at Braine le Chateau.

Aug. ⁸⁄₁.  Prince Vaudemont, Lord Athlone, and the cavalry from Scarbeck joined in position, having their left at Genappe, and their right at Waterloo, with the road to Brussels in front. Prince Vaudemont's army at this time consisted of one hundred and eighty-two squadrons and seventy battalions, including Colonel Buchan's regiment, which had been sent to garrison Mechlin during the bombardment of Brussels. The Elector of Bavaria returned from Brussels to the siege of Namur.

Marshal Villeroy was between Enghien and Steenkirk waiting for the Rhine detachment, the remainder of the King's household, and some battalions from the coast, to march to the relief of Namur.

Aug. ⁹⁄₁.  Prince Vaudemont broke up from Waterloo, and approached Namur with one hundred and eighty-two squadrons of cavalry, and seventy battalions of infantry, and encamped near the King's quarters at Masy.[1]

On the eleventh, one hundred and thirty-six pieces of cannon, and fifty mortars and " haubitz" opened on the castle, and continued their fire without intermission.

---

[1] Masy, a gentleman's house on the little river of that name (called Orne by the maps of those times) ; the house commanded a stone bridge over the river, distant about two leagues from Namur.

The second battalion of the Scots Guards, and the *1695.* second battalion of the Dutch Guards, which arrived with Vaudemont's army, and had not been employed in the siege, were ordered to the King's quarter at Malogne, to relieve the Coldstream Guards and first battalion of Dutch Guards. Other regiments were also relieved; the same number of troops being always kept on duty.

Villeroy encamped between Senoff and Arkiennes; at *Aug.* ¹³ this place he was reinforced by the Rhine detachment, which increased his numbers to one hundred and nineteen battalions, and two hundred and thirty-five squadrons. It was resolved to attempt raising the siege of Namur; to effect this, the army took post in the plains of Fleury. *Aug.* ¹⁴ When Villeroy approached, King William left the Elector *Aug.* ¹⁵ of Bavaria and the Duke of Holstein Ploen to conduct the siege of the castle, having directed that intrenchments should be made where necessary, and every precaution taken for the security of the camp. He then proceeded to the head-quarters of Prince Vaudemont.

The battalions of Scots and Dutch Guards that had relieved the Coldstream and the first battalion of Dutch Guards, were ordered back to the camp, with some battalions of Brandenburg and Dutch, besides a body of horse; completing the army of Prince Vaudemont to ninety-seven battalions, and two hundred and thirty-seven squadrons,[1] to oppose the march of Villeroy. Thirty battalions were left to carry on the siege of the castle, and six to garrison the town.

To avoid Villeroy, Major-General Ramsay's division changed their position, and encamped with their right at

---

[1] At this time each battalion may be calculated at five hundred men each, the Guards at something more: the squadrons at one hundred and ten each squadron.

1695.
Golzenne, their left towards the small river running by
Gemblours and Masy to the Sambre, having Boissiers in
the rear. An intrenchment was made to prevent an attack
from the plain; trees were cut down to form barricades
near Corroy, and detachments ordered to maintain that
post at all hazards, and to give notice of the enemy's
appearance. St. Denis, a village which lay on the skirt
of a wood, was also strongly fortified. The Hessians,
more to the right, defended with an intrenchment a plain
between St. Denis and Meaux. The Bavarian cuirassiers,
Lumley's brigade of cavalry, and the Brandenburg horse,
were on the extreme right, between the village of Dhuy
and the wood of Meaux.

Aug. 14
The French remained in camp between Fleury and
Sombref. Next day, they moved by their left towards
Gemblours, for the purpose of approaching the right of
the Allies stationed on the most open part of the country.
The French were posted with their right on Gemblours,
and the left on Grand Lez. Their head-quarters were at
Saunier.

Aug. 15
It was believed the enemy would attack on the following day. The assault on Namur was therefore deferred,
but the artillery continued to widen the breach.

Prince Vaudemont, though much indisposed,[1] at three
o'clock A.M. descended from his coach, and placed himself at the head of the English Guards. The King also
arrived to see that every thing was in readiness, and held
a conference with the Prince. In the morning, the brigade of Guards, under Major-General Churchill, was
ordered to the right at St. Denis, to form a reserve, and
support the eight regiments, already posted there under

---

[1] Having been obliged by fever to keep his bed for several previous days.

Brigadier Fitzpatrick; these regiments were fresh troops, not having been concerned in the siege of Namur. At this spot it was expected the most vigorous exertions of the enemy would be made. The brigade of Guards occupied the enclosure from the village, and communicated with the Hessians, who had erected batteries to command the plain. The left of St. Denis was also intrenched and fortified. The French army was under arms the greater part of the night. At noon, the weather, which had been wet and foggy, began to clear. Villeroy, in order to reconnoitre, advanced to St. Denis, the road to which through the wood had been barricaded with felled trees and thick boughs; on finding he was discovered, he retired. The expected attack not being made, the King determined at once to assault the breaches of the Terra Nova and Cohorne. Detachments, consisting of thirty-six grenadiers from every company not concerned in the siege, were collected, and eighteen from those already employed. The grenadiers of the brigade of Guards were commanded by Lieutenant-Colonel Evans, Captain in the first battalion of the First Guards. Three thousand English, under Lord Cutts, were to attack the counterscarp and breach of Terra Nova. The Count de Rivera was to march on the breach of Cohorne, and part of the line of communication next the Cohorne, with three thousand Bavarians. Major-General la Cave was to attack the upper point of the Cohorne, on the right of Count Rivera, with two thousand Brandenburgers. Major-General Swerin was to force the Casotte with two thousand Dutch, and at the same time the Lower Town was to be attacked with six hundred men. A quantity of powder was to be blown up on the old battery, near the Brussels gate, as the signal to attack. The word of battle was, " God with us!"

1695.·

Aug. 18

Aug. 30

Lord Cutts ordered four serjeants, each with fifteen
men, to go on the forlorn-hope; to be followed by the
grenadiers of the brigade of Guards under Lieutenant-
Colonel Evans; and these, by the rest of the grenadiers
designed for the attack of the breach, amounting altogether to seven hundred, under a colonel.   Three hundred
grenadiers were to attack the line of communication.
Two regiments were to support those that attacked the
breach, and two regiments were to remain in reserve.
Aug. 31   About noon, the English advanced under the enemy's
fire to within nine hundred paces from the breach, exposed in front and flank to the guns of the castle.   They
resolutely pushed on in spite of the galling fire : after the
grenadiers, Colonel Courthorpe's regiment followed, with
drums beating and colours flying.   Owing to some mistake, the support being delayed, the troops first engaged
were overpowered by numbers.   Count de Rivera, Captain Mitchel,[1] of the Guards, and Colonel Courthorpe,
were killed; Lord Cutts received a contusion in the head;
Lieutenant-Colonel Evans and Sir Matthew Bridges
were desperately wounded ; Count de Mercy, Colonel
Windsor, Colonel Stanhope, and several others, more
slightly.   Count Rivera's attack did not commence with
the signal; consequently, the fire from that part of the
Cohorne next the Serra Nova fell on the English.   A
reinforcement of three regiments arrived ; but, instead of
carrying on the old attack, a fresh conflict was begun, as
Count Nogent and Monsieur l'Abadie had come down with
twelve hundred fresh men, two hundred of whom were
dragoons of the King of France's household : these troops
charged in flank and rear, and did great mischief.

Lord Cutts finding, after his wound was dressed, that

---

[1] Second battalion First Foot Guards.

the assault on the Terra Nova could not be resumed, and observing that the Bavarians, although they suffered great loss, had fixed themselves on the extreme point of the cohorn next the Sambre, which post they continued obstinately to maintain, decided to make good their attack with his whole force. A detachment was ordered to support the Bavarians, and to advance without firing a shot. These troops were directed to pass the palisades, and enter the covered way; if they could not maintain the post, they were to retire, but to make a lodgement if possible. The detachment succeeded in driving the French from the covered way, and took possession of one of their batteries, having first turned their own guns on them. Mac Kay's regiment was ordered to plant their colours on the palisades; at the same time the Bavarians renewed their assault. They gained the covered way before the breach of the cohorn, but nothing further was attempted. The other attacks were completely successful, and a lodgement of a mile in extent was made along the covered-way and intrenchments. On this day the English lost one thousand four hundred killed and wounded.

Villeroy found the position of the Allies too strong to hazard a battle, yet he was most anxious to relieve Namur. On the morning of the twentieth, he moved on the left towards Perwys, the country in that direction being more open.

The King expecting this, ordered the cavalry under Marshal Fleming and Count d'Arco, with Lumley's brigade and the Hessians, to march towards the Mehaigne; a detachment was also sent under Lieutenant-General La Forest to Taviers and Bonef on the Mehaigne, to observe the enemy. His Majesty being informed of the enemy's movement towards Perwys, ordered the army to march on the right at the same time that the besiegers were en-

1695.

gaged in the assault on the castle and outworks. The brigade of Guards was in the reserve, and encamped near the village of Dhuy, on the right of the King's quarter in a third line. The infantry encamped within the intrenchments at Dhuy, the cavalry in their rear. The intrenchment at Bossire, between Masy and Gemblours, was abandoned. Detachments were left to protect the post of Masy and the intrenchment of Golsines. Brigadier Fitz Patrick also remained, with eight battalions, at St. Denis.

Aug. 31
Aug. 22
Sept. 1

The fire against the castle continued, and preparations were made for another assault. On the following morning the besieged beat a parley, and proposed to bury those killed on the twentieth. A cessation of hostilities was agreed on. The Count de Guiscard mounted the breach before they recommenced, and called for the Major-General of the trenches, and told him he wished to speak with the Elector, who went to the breach. Count Guiscard, at first, offered to surrender the cohorn; but this was refused, unless the whole was given up. Marshal Boufflers afterwards consented to it, on honourable terms. The white flag was hoisted. The terms of capitulation were agreed on and signed the same night;[1] being the first ever signed by a Marshal of France.

The loss of the Allies, from the commencement of the siege, amounted to twelve thousand men.

Aug. 23
Sept. 2

After the surrender of the castle, Marshal Villeroy retreated in the afternoon from Perwys and Grand Rosiers, and fell back to Sombref and the plains of Fleury; next day, he continued his march to Montigny near Charleroi.

---

[1] Signed first of September (N.S.) 1695. See engraved medal o.

King William removed from Ostin[1] to the Chateau of Boucquet near Templeux. The Coldstream, with the first battalion of Dutch Guards, took its station at the King's quarter.

1695.
Aug. 24
Sept. 3

This day the garrison, with Marshal Boufflers at their head, marched out through the breach, and had not proceeded far, when a detachment of the Life Guards arrested him in the King's name, as a hostage, and carried him back a prisoner to Namur; from thence he was conducted to Maestricht, till satisfaction was obtained for the infraction of the capitulations of Dixmuyde and Deynse by still detaining the garrisons prisoners, which, during the siege, had surrendered to the army under Villeroy.

Aug. 26
Sept. 5

The Allies left Boucquet, marched to Perwys and Sombref, and next day to Bois-Seigneur-Isaac. They passed the Dyle above Genappe, and encamped between Braine le Chateau and Witersey near Nivelle.

Aug. 29
Sept. 8

Villeroy moved the same day to the plains of Chambron; but with Ath in rear of his right, he was considerably incommoded. At first it was supposed the French would besiege that place; but Namur having capitulated, and King William's army being in the field, rendered it advisable for them not to undertake it.

Aug. 30
Sept. 9

The army of the Confederates continued their march from their last station by Braine le Chateau, and encamped beyond Halle, where his Majesty reviewed them previous to his departure for Loo.

Aug. 31
Sept. 10

Sept. 5

Marshal Boufflers was set at liberty on the King of France giving his word that the garrisons of Dixmuyde

---

[1] A gentleman's house called Ostin, near the village of Dhuy, where the King took up his quarters the day of the assault.

## CHAPTER XVI.

Lewis XIV. prepares an expedition at Dunkirk — Brigade of
Guards recalled from Ghent—Fleet fitted out in the Thames—
Coldstream returns to Flanders — Athlone bombards Givet—
Enemy advance—Allies unable to make a forward movement—
William arrives in Holland—Boufflers encamps at Parck—Wil-
liam reviews the troops — Army encamps at Wavre — Boufflers
retires—Villeroy encamps between Oudenarde and the Allies—
Prince de Conti, Dukes of Chartres and Bourbon join Villeroy—
Duke du Maine and Count de Toulouse join Boufflers—Amount
of the French armies—William moves towards Gemblours—
Strength of the Confederates—Allies move to the plain of Fleury
—Boufflers advances to oppose the passage of the Sambre—Con-
federates on the plain of Chambron—Enemy encamp near Condé
— William leaves the camp — Both armies separate for the
winter.

THE French King seems to have deemed it his policy to    1695-6.
harass the English government by petty expeditions in
favour of the exiled House of Stuart, but not to make any
powerful exertion on its behalf. He was willing to encou-
rage by intrigue the disaffected in England, and to flatter
the hopes of James in France; but although profuse in
promises, his efforts to assist that King were inconsiderable. In conformity with this system, a small expedition
was prepared at Dunkirk to excite the malcontents in
England, and induce them to conspire in support of

1695-6.    James.  To oppose these machinations, the brigade of
Guards with thirteen English battalions were suddenly
March 6  recalled, and arrived at Gravesend from Ghent.  A fleet
was fitted out in the Thames, and sent to blockade the
French ports.  By these measures Lewis was forced
to relinquish his intention.  The second battalions of
the First and Scots Guards with eight other battalions
disembarked; the Coldstream and the remaining battalions were ordered back to Flanders,[1] and reached Ghent
early in April.

March 7     To divert the enemy's attention, it was decided at a
council of war, held at Brussels, that an attempt should
be made to destroy " the great magazines " prepared at
Givet for the approaching campaign.  Eight or nine
thousand troops under Lord Athlone marched from
March 9  Namur for this purpose, and bombarded the town of
Givet.  All the stores of hay and straw were burnt, and
the Allies returned to Namur on the following day.

1696.      The enemy began to move early in the spring, and
advanced towards the frontier in Flanders, where two
strong bodies were formed, commanded by Marshals
Boufflers and Villeroy.  The corps under the first-named
marshal was styled the Army of the Meuse; the latter,
April  29  that of Flanders.  Villeroy arrived at Valenciennes, and
May   9  was met by Boufflers; after an interview Villeroy proceeded to Courtrai, Boufflers to the Sambre.

At the opening of the campaign the Allies had ten
battalions less than in the preceding year.[2]  The Brandenburgers and the regiments under the Landgrave of

---

[1] " Hague, 17 April, (N.S.)  The Duke of Wirtemberg is
" arrived with the forces from England at Vere in Zealand."—
*London Gazette*, No. 3174, from 9th to 13th of April, 1696.

[2] The ten English regiments left in England.

Hesse were still in Germany; it was therefore impossible to make a forward movement without considerable risk. The Prince of Nassau Saarbruck, who did not think himself safe at Tirlemont, as long as Marshal Boufflers remained in the plain of Fleury, retreated to Louvain, and took up the strong camp of Parck to await the arrival of the troops of Brandenburg, Cologne, and Liege. Prince Vaudemont repaired to Ghent on receiving information that Villeroy's army was on the Lys between Deynse and Cruys-Houtem. He directed General Ramsay with the garrison of Bruges and some other regiments to encamp at Bellem, where the Duke of Wirtemburg took the command. This corps, reinforced by some cavalry and several battalions, received orders to continue stationary, while the enemy remained in the position they then occupied.

The King, who arrived from England, reached the camp <sub>May 27</sub> on the twenty-seventh, and took up his quarters at Mary- <sub>June 6</sub> Kirk, where the greater part of the army was assembled. His Majesty reviewed the troops during the three first days after his arrival. On the thirty-first a promotion took place among the general officers, and Lord Cutts was made a Major-General. King William left the camp June ₁₁ on the first of June, and took with him, besides his Life and Horse Grenadier Guards, both battalions of the First and Coldstream Guards, and a battalion of Dutch Guards. Next day he reached Wavre,[1] to which place the army under the Prince of Nassau Saarbruck had moved from the camp of Parck; the Dutch, Brandenburg, Liege,

---

[1] The army encamped at Wavre consisted of fifty-two battalions of infantry, and one hundred and fifty squadrons of horse and dragoons.

Cologne, Bavarian and Spanish contingents were drawn up in one line of battle.

Boufflers retired on Charleroi, and afterwards encamped between the Sambre and Gosselies. The King, to strengthen the Brabant army, sent for a strong detachment from Flanders, commanded by Prince Vaudemont, which marched under the Duke of Wirtemburg towards Dendermond.

Marshal Villeroy remained encamped from the ninth of May between Oudenarde and the Allies. On the fourteenth the Prince of Conti and the Dukes of Chartres and Bourbon reached his camp. The Duke du Maine and the Count de Toulouse joined the troops under Boufflers.

The day after the arrival of the Princes, Villeroy reviewed his forces, consisting of forty-six thousand seven hundred and fifty infantry, and of thirteen thousand two hundred horse. The army of Marshal Boufflers amounted to forty-five thousand one hundred infantry, and twelve thousand eight hundred and forty horse. The Marquis d'Harcourt commanded four thousand troops, who were directed to observe the Landgrave of Hesse, and, if required, to unite with Marshal Boufflers. The Count de Montal had also under him a body of about four thousand men behind the canal of Dunkirk and Furnes, making the grand total of the enemy's force in this campaign not less than one hundred and twenty-five thousand eight hundred and ninety men.

King William, on leaving Wavre, crossed the Dyle, and approached Marshal Boufflers. His Majesty encamped between Mount St. Guibert and the village of Corroy.

Boufflers determined to repass the Sambre and dispute the river, in preference to risking a battle on the plain. When he had crossed, he divided his army to cover the

passages between Charleroi and Namur. Marshal Ville- 1695.
roy foraged the country between the Lys and Scheld,
formed his camp at Deynse and Cruys-Houtem, and sent
strong parties to watch the Duke of Wirtemburg, who had
been detached from the Prince's army to Appels on the
Scheld.

The King waited at Corbais for the Landgrave of Hesse,
before he advanced towards the Sambre. The Landgrave, June 26
on arriving at Robermont and Jupille near Liege, sent his July 8
Lieutenant-General the Count de Lippe, and the Baron de
Gorz, to the King for orders.[1] The Duke of Wirtemburg,
who had moved from Appels to Vilvorde, was directed to
join. William decamped, and moved towards Gemblours. June 27
The advanced guard was at Sombref, and the main body July 7
fronted Charleroi. The army of Brabant now amounted to
sixty-eight thousand five hundred and fifty men, besides
several battalions forming part of the garrison of Namur,
which, should the Allies cross the Sambre, were ready to
join. The Confederates moved to the plain of Fleury: on July 14
their approach towards the Sambre, Boufflers advanced to
Biesme to oppose the passage if they made the attempt;
but this was thought too hazardous whilst the French were
so strongly intrenched on the opposite side. The Allies July 14
left Fleury for Nivelle; two days after they reached
Soignies; and the following day the plain of Chambron.
The enemy passed the Sambre at Boussiere, and encamped July 15
near Condé, where they were enabled to keep up the communication with Marshal Villeroy, who still remained at
Deynsc and Cruys-Houtem: by this operation the Scheld
was secured. The army moved to Grammont. The Cold- Aug. 11
stream and two other battalions of Guards covered the

---

[1] Joined the King's army 11 July, near the plains of Fleury, and
then returned to Germany 6 August.

1696.    King's quarter at Gamerage against any parties from the

Aug. ⅓⅓   wood of Lessines.   King William left the army under the
command of the Elector of Bavaria, and went to pursue
his usual diversion of stag-hunting about Loo and Dieren.

Sept. ⅙   On the seventeenth of September the Elector detached the
First and Coldstream Guards, and two regiments of English horse, to their winter-quarters at Ghent.   The army

Sept. ⅘   under the Elector marched from Grammont by Bois-
Seigneur-Isaac, and in eight days separated for the winter ;
the force under Prince Vaudemont followed their example.

Oct. ⅓⅓   Marshals Villeroy and Boufflers also went to the cantonments assigned them.

The only advantage gained in this campaign was, that
Villeroy subsisted his troops entirely in the country be-
longing to the Allies, between the Scheld and canals of
Bruges, Ostend, and Nieuport.

# CHAPTER XVII.

English Guards leave Ghent for the villages between Brussels and
Halle—Army of Flanders takes the field—Infantry encamp between Deynse and Nivelle—Brabant army encamps at Waterloo
and Ixelles—French assemble about Tournay, banks of the Sambre and Lys—Brabant army between the Abbey of Bois-Seigneur-Isaac and the rivulet of Leu—Catinat invests Ath—Amount
of French armies—Strength of army under William and the
Elector of Bavaria—Situation of the French—William retreats to
the plain of Bois-Seigneur-Isaac—Boufflers encamps at Steenkirk—Reinforcements arrive from England—William marches
through Brussels, and takes up a position for the defence of the
town—Peace of Ryswick—French leave the Netherlands—British quartered in Ghent, Bruges, Nieuport, and Ostend—Guards
embark for England.

THE King having signified his desire to have the British    1697.
troops under his immediate command in Brabant, an exchange of quarters took place. The first battalions of the
First and Coldstream Guards, with three regiments, under
Count Nassau, marched from Ghent to canton in the
villages between Brussels and Halle; several other regiments from Bruges and the places adjacent followed, and
were quartered near Brussels and Mechlin. The Elector
of Bavaria was at the head of the army for the protection
of Flanders. Early in April his Majesty took the field.    April 14
The infantry encamped between Deynse and Nivelle; the
cavalry were cantoned in the rear for the convenience of
forage. The Brabant army was at Waterloo and Ixelles.    April 18

1697.

The enemy's forces, destined to be commanded by Marshals Villeroy, Boufflers, and Catinat, assembled at three points; the first about Tournay, that under Boufflers on the banks 'of the Sambre, the third under Catinat on the Lys in the vicinity of Courtrai.

These dispositions obliged the Elector to countermand the English cavalry, which had been ordered to march on Brussels, the Dutch horse not having yet joined him.

Preparations were made to extend the camp from Bachtem on the Lys, to Ansbeck on the canal of Bruges, between which places troops were stationed.

Marshal Boufflers' army began to assemble about Boussiere on the Sambre.

April 28
May 8

All the Brabant army had assembled in the camp formed in a direct line from the Abbey of Bois-Seigneur-Isaac to the rivulet of Leu; it amounted to seventy-five squadrons of horse, twenty-six of dragoons, and sixty-four battalions.

May.

Ath was invested by the French on the sixth of May; at the same time Marshal Villeroy marched towards Leuse from Tournay, within two leagues of Ath. The Marquis of Crequi, with a flying camp at Celles on the river Laye, was to prevent the garrison in Oudenarde from molesting the convoys between the French army and the Scheld.

May ⁷⁄₁₇

Marshal Catinat likewise marched from Fresnes and Brussenal, and encamped in the neighbourhood of Ath, to form the siege. Marshal Boufflers crossed the Sambre on the fourth, and advanced nearer Ath in conjunction with Villeroy and Catinat. Count Tallard, Lieutenant-General under Boufflers, was between Mons and Soignies. The three French armies in Flanders amounted to one hundred and forty-four thousand seven hundred and ninety men, without including a flying camp under the Marquis d'Harcourt.

The Confederates moved and formed a junction near Ternath, where they were met by the Brandenburgers under General Heyden, and the Cologne and Liege contingents under Prince Cerclas of Tilly. The brigade of Guards encamped as usual before his Majesty's quarter at Iseringhen. William's army consisted of twenty thousand four hundred horse, and thirty-eight thousand five hundred foot. That of the Elector of Bavaria, besides ten battalions under Major-General Fagel, amounted to forty-six thousand two hundred and fifty-six effective men.

1697.
May 18

The French, perceiving from the concentration of the two armies that the Allies intended to relieve Ath, collected their troops to prevent them. Marshal Villeroy was posted at Ostiche, near Lessines, to check any attempt at raising the siege on that side of the Dender. The Marquis de Crequi was encamped at Celles, on the Scheld, in order if necessary to reinforce Montreval at Courtrai; but he passed the Scheld, and the Marquis joined Villeroy. Marshal Boufflers, with Count Tallard, left the camp of Thieux and Thieusies to secure that of Silly and Ghislenghien; King William having posted himself on the height of Silly, where his left extended towards Villeroy's army. Marshal Catinat was engaged in carrying on the siege of Ath.

William at length despaired of forcing the enemy to raise the siege; he found it impossible to attack Boufflers separately; and as a treaty of peace was under consideration at Ryswick, any failure on the part of the Allies might have been very prejudicial to their cause. He therefore determined on a retreat: the Elector returned to his former camp at Deynse and Nivelle, detaching Lord Jedborough's dragoons to join the King, whose army moved to the plain of Bois-Seigneur-Isaac. His Majesty's quarters were at Promelles, facing Nivelle and the wood

May 22

May 24

1697.  of Maltha, which was covered by the Life Guards, the English Foot Guards, and Royals. Genappe was in front of the infantry on the left.

The Count de Montreval and the Marquis de Crequi resumed their former stations to observe the Elector of Bavaria. Boufflers had marched from Silly and Ghislenghien, when the King retired towards Bois-Seigneur-Isaac. On finding that William continued at Promelles and Genappe, he encamped on the same ground which his army had before occupied at Thieux and Thieusies. Villeroy continued in camp between Papigny and Hamedé, to cover Ath. After the surrender of that town on the twenty-sixth, Marshal Catinat, desirous to repair the damage done during the siege, was detained some days; but Villeroy crossed the Dender between Ath and Lessines, and formed his camp. Marshal Catinat left Ath on the ninth of June, and posted himself at Lignes on the Scheld.

June ⅚      Early in June five battalions arrived from England; three other regiments followed soon after, when they all proceeded to join King William at Brussels.

June ⅔      Marshal Boufflers, with his army, left Thieusies and encamped at Steenkirk, his left extending to Enghien. The same day Villeroy, reinforced by the Marquis of Crequi, also marched and encamped between Enghien and Grammont.

On receiving intelligence of these movements, King William without delay assembled a council of war, when it was resolved that he should march the same evening on Brussels. The troops began to move at ten P. M., in dark and tempestuous weather; the King got into his coach at midnight. The brigade of Guards left the King's quarter at day-break, and went in rear of the column that had advanced to Waterloo. All the infantry had passed through Brussels by five o'clock on the evening of the thirteenth.

The right of the position chosen for the defence of Brussels rested on the village of Lacken, the left was between the Flanders and Anderlecht gates, facing Dilbeck. When the encampment commenced, fifty men from each battalion, amounting to three thousand four hundred, were ordered to form an intrenchment during the night on the left of the village of Berchom. Here there was an open space of four hundred yards, which joined to the height of Dilbeck, and commanded that part of the Allied camp which was the weakest part of the position.

On the same day that the army under King William arrived in the camp, Boufflers was on his way from Steenkirk towards Halle.

Villeroy marched through the wood of Lessines, and encamped beyond Goick towards St. Quintin Linneck, about three leagues on the left of Boufflers, extending his own left towards the Dender beyond Strithem. The two armies of the enemy being unable to form a junction till the fifteenth, they were not prepared to make an attack before the succeeding day, by which time William's position was sufficiently fortified.

Thirty additional men from each battalion were now ordered to work in the intrenchment; the whole number constantly employed on that service was six thousand. They continued their labours until the conclusion of the campaign. In the mean time the Confederates received a reinforcement of twenty-nine battalions and three hundred cavalry.

The forage becoming scarce, the armies of Boufflers and Villeroy fell back on the pays d'Alost.

King William left the army, and went to the Hague.

1697.    On the tenth of September (O.S.) at midnight, peace was signed in the palace at Ryswick.

Sept. 2⅛    The French armies quitted the Spanish territories in the Netherlands; and the Confederates likewise separated on Oct. 1⅟  the ratification of the treaty of peace.

The British were placed in the towns of Ghent, Bruges, Nieuport, and Ostend.

Oct. 4⅟  The brigade of Guards and Dutch Guards were forwarded in boats by the canal from Ghent to Bruges, and embarked for England.[1]

---

[1] " Deale, November 4th. Yesterday in the afternoon came into " the Downes his Majesty's ships the Woolwich, Experiment, and " Sorlinges, with the transport ships from Ostend, having on " board four battalions of his Majesty's Guards, and this morning " they sailed again for the river."

" Whitehall, Novʳ 5. The four battalions of his Majesty's " Guards are arrived in the river." — *London Gazette*, No. 3338, 4th to 8th of November, 1697.

# CHAPTER XVIII.

Coldstream disembark at Harwich—William's triumphant entry
into London—Chamberlayne's account of the Foot Guards—
First notice of the Third Guards on the establishment—Death of
Charles II. King of Spain—Duke of Anjou declared King of
Spain—Army augmented with great difficulty—James II. dies at
St. Germain's—Death of King William—A battalion formed from
the First and Coldstream sent to Cadiz—Gallant conduct of
Colonel Pierce of the Coldstream—Attack on fort Matagorda—
Troops re-embark after blowing up Fort St. Catherine's—Confederates under Sir George Rooke attack Chateaurenard in the
harbour of Vigo—Duke of Ormond lands his troops—Rondella
carried by assault—Enemy destroy their galleons and twelve
ships—Fourteen ships taken—Army embark at Rondella—Gib-
raltar surrenders—A battalion from the First and Coldstream sail
from Portsmouth with Lord Galway—Expedition lands at Lisbon
—Re-embark—Sail for the relief of Gibraltar—Prince of Hesse
Darmstadt makes a sortie—Enemy retire after seven months'
siege — Peterborough sails from England with Sir Cloudesly
Shovel—Dutch fleet join in the Tagus—Prince of Hesse and
Guards embark — Land near Barcelona—Attack on Montjuich—
Barcelona taken—Prince Charles received with great enthusiasm
—Guards remain with Prince Charles at Barcelona — Peterbo-
rough marches with a small force to Valencia.

THE Coldstream, after disembarking at Harwich, marched    *1697.*
from thence, and were first quartered about Deptford, and
afterwards in the Tower Hamlets district.[1]

---

[1] See Appendix, Nos. 131, 132, 133.

The particulars of the charges of the waggons and other contin-

1698.      King William landed on the fourteenth at Margate,
and made his triumphal entry from Greenwich into
London on Tuesday the sixteenth of October following.

Chamberlayne,[1] in his " New State of England," published during the reign of King William the IIId., says,
there were three regiments of Foot Guards, two English,
and one Dutch ; the first, of twenty-eight companies,
seventy men each, except one of eighty, in all one thou
sand nine hundred and seventy.  " The second, called the
" Coldstream regiment, is but fourteen companies, seventy
" men each, in all 980 men.   The third Guards, called
" the regiment of Blue Guards, consists of twelve com-
" panies, seventy men each, except two companies of
" eighty each, total to both 860.   The Colonel's pay, as
" colonel, is 12s. a day ; the Lieutenant-Colonel, as such,
" 7s. ; the Major 5s. ; the Adjutant 5s. ; a Captain 8s. ; a
" Lieutenant 4s. ; an Ensign 3s. ; a Serjeant 1s. 6d. ; a
" Corporal's and Drummer's 1s. ; a common soldier's
" 10d. ; and out of London 8d."

---

gent charges for the Coldstream battalion of Foot Guards on their
march from Harwich, in November 1697.

|  | £. | s. | d. |
|---|---|---|---|
| For 8 waggons to the Isle of Dogs for Greenwich quarters, being 70 miles    .    .    .    . | 14 | 0 | 0 |
| For 8 waggons from Greenwich to London, 5 miles   . | 1 | 0 | 0 |
| Payd for setting the men on shore at Harwich, and ferrying over from the Isle of Dogs to Greenwich  . | 2 | 4 | 0 |
| Charges for an express from Harwich to London and back again to give an account of the battalions landing, and for a rout to march by    .    .    . | 9 | 14 | 0 |
| Signed, | | | |
| Wᵐ MATHEWS. | £26 | 18 | 0 |

Usual warrant to pay the amount.   Dated 27th November,
1699.

    [1] Part II. page 126.

Grose,[1] also, in his " Military Antiquities," states, that   1698.
" Under William the IIId. the Guards frequently took the
" field, and often distinguished themselves in Flanders.
" He added a regiment to those before employed in the
" household ; this, however, gave umbrage, and his Ma-
" jesty, in order to remove all jealousy, very prudently
" sent them back to Holland, and entrusted himself
" wholly to his subjects." The reference in the " New
State of England " to the Blue Guards refers to the Dutch
Guards, which King William brought with him from
Holland. These troops re-embarked for their native
country on the twentieth of March, 169⅜.

The earliest notice of the Third, or Scots Guards, being
on the British establishment, occurs in March, 1686.

The following extracts from the King's warrants afford
the first information of their coming to England.

" THIRD FOOT GUARDS.

" The battalion of our Scotch Guards, upon their arri-
" val from Scotland, are to be quartered at Greenwich and
" Deptford. Dated 27th March, 1686. To march on
" Tuesday, 4th May, 1686, to Paddington, Kensington,
" &c.; and on the 26th to encamp at Hounslow Heath.
" From Hounslow Heath, Rochester, and Chatham, &c.,
" in August, 1686. From Rochester, &c., to Gravesend,
" to Canterbury, and Deal, and embark for Scotland on
" Monday, 21st March, 168⅘. Again from Scotland in
" May, 1688, and quartered in the Borough of South-
" wark. To encamp in June, 1688, on Hounslow Heath.
" From Hounslow to Hull, Wednesday, 8th August,
" 1688." Another battalion of the regiment quitted
Scotland, October, 1688, and quartered in London. The

---

[1] Vol. II. page 206.

1698.    battalion from Hull marched to Northampton and Salisbury in November, and thence to London.  In 1689 a battalion embarked for Flanders, and in February, 16$\frac{90}{91}$, the second also went abroad ; but at that time they only received the pay of the line.   One of these battalions returned from Flanders in March, 169$\frac{3}{4}$, and did duty at Windsor from 28th of September, 1696, to the 27th of May, 1697 ; and on the 1st of June was " shipped in small boats at Brentford for the transport ships in the river," which conveyed them back to Flanders.   After the peace of Ryswick, both battalions returned, landed at Hull in November, 1697, and marched through Berwick to Edinburgh.   They remained on the Scotch establishment till December, 1707, the period of the Union ; from which time they were put on the same footing as the First and Coldstream Guards.   In February, 17$\frac{11}{12}$, the battalion at home was ordered from Edinburgh and Berwick to London ; on reaching St. Alban's in May, they received orders to proceed to Dover, Deal, and Sandwich, and embark for Dunkirk, where they remained till the middle of September following.   In January, 17$\frac{12}{13}$, the Scots Guards divided the London duty, for the first time, with the English Guards.   The other[1] battalion, which had embarked at Berwick for Spain in 1709, and surrendered prisoners at Briheuga in December, 1710, landed at Deal about the same time.

1699.    From the twenty-sixth of March the establishment of the regiment was only forty-eight commissioned officers, including the solicitor, eighty non-commissioned officers, and five hundred and sixty privates, not including servants.

Dec. 12th.    In the latter end of the year, Charles II., King of

---

[1] War-Office Records.

Spain, died; he named as his successor Philip, Duke of     1700.
Anjou, second son of the Dauphin, who was declared by
Lewis XIV. King of Spain, under the title of Philip
the Fifth. On his arrival at Madrid, he was proclaimed
king.

Thirty thousand seamen were voted by Parliament, and     May.
it was also determined to send ten thousand troops to
Holland, in pursuance of the treaty of 1697 with the
States-General.

The Commons, after the peace, [1] had voted that all
troops raised since 1680 should be disbanded, and the
army reduced to seven thousand men; it was now, with
great difficulty, augmented to ten thousand.[c]

On the sixteenth of September, James the IId-died at
St. Germain's en Laye, near Paris, aged eighty-eight; and
Lewis XIV. immediately acknowledged his son as King of
England by the name of James the IIId. Lord Manchester, the British ambassador at Paris, was recalled,
and an alliance concluded with the Emperor of Germany
and the States-General. The death of James the IId was     1701-2.
soon followed by that of King William, who expired on
the eighth of March, in the fifty-second year of his age.

Previous to the demise of King William the reduction
of Cadiz had been projected; after which, it was intended
to send an expedition against the Spanish colonies in the
West Indies. Queen Anne determined to follow up the
plans of her predecessor for opposing the power of Lewis
the XIVth.

The British force under the Duke of Marlborough, sent

---

[1] Peace signed twentieth of September, 1697, between England,
Spain, Holland, and France; and on the thirtieth of October, between France, the Emperor, and empire.

[c] Journals, eleventh of December, 1697.—*Parliamentary History.*

1702. to Holland in June, 1701, was increased.[1]  The Duke of

[1] List of the forces in Holland (1702) :—

| | Commiss<sup>d</sup> Officers. | Non-comm<sup>d</sup> Officers. | Private Men. | Servants. |
|---|---|---|---|---|
| **HORSE.** | | | | |
| Major-Gen<sup>l</sup> Lumley's . . . | 39 | 46 | 475 | 38 |
| Brigadier Wood's . . . | 27 | 31 | 316 | 26 |
| Earl of Arran's 3 troops . . | 12 | 15 | 157 | 14 |
| Major-Gen<sup>l</sup> Wyndham's . . | 27 | 31 | 316 | 26 |
| Duke of Shomberg's . . . | 27 | 31 | 316 | 26 |
| | 132 | 154 | 1580 | 130 |
| **DRAGOONS.** | | | | |
| Royal regiment . . . . | 36 | 72 | 398 | 34 |
| Lord Tiviott's . . . | 28 | 54 | 298 | 26 |
| Brigadier Ross's . . . . | 28 | 54 | 298 | 26 |
| | 92 | 180 | 994 | 86 |
| **FOOT.** | | | | |
| Battalion of Guards (1<sup>st</sup> reg<sup>t</sup>) . | 45 | 89 | 645 | 55 |
| The Royal regiment . . . | 86 | 210 | 1474 | 106 |
| Colonel Webb's . . . | 44 | 104 | 736 | 54 |
| Major-General Steuart's . | 44 | 104 | 736 | 54 |
| Lord North's, late Granville's . | 44 | 104 | 736 | 54 |
| Earl of Barrymore's . . | 44 | 104 | 736 | 54 |
| Colonel Howe's . . . | 44 | 104 | 736 | 54 |
| Earl of Derby's . . . | 44 | 104 | 736 | 54 |
| Sir M. Bridges's . . . | 44 | 104 | 736 | 54 |
| Royal reg<sup>t</sup> of Ireland, command-ed by Brig<sup>r</sup> F. Hamilton . } | 44 | 104 | 736 | 54 |
| Major-Gen<sup>l</sup> Ingoldsby's . . | 44 | 104 | 736 | 54 |
| Duke of Marlborough's . . | 44 | 104 | 736 | 54 |
| Colonel Row's . . . | 44 | 104 | 736 | 54 |
| Colonel Ferguson's . . | 44 | 104 | 736 | 54 |
| Earl of Huntingdon's . . | 44 | 104 | 736 | 54 |
| | 703 | 1651 | 11,687 | 863 |
| Totall . | 927 | 1985 | 14,261 | 1079 |

= 18,252

MS. Harl. No. 7025. Brit. Mus.

Ormond was likewise appointed to command the troops destined for Spain, which were to be convoyed by the combined squadrons under Sir George Rooke.[1] Eleven regiments, and a battalion of Guards, embarked for this service. Of these, six companies belonged to the Coldstream,[2] and two to the First Guards; one company of Grenadiers was also formed from both regiments. This battalion amounted to seven hundred and sixty men, including the detachment from the First Foot Guards, and was under Brigadier William Matthew, of the Coldstream. Colonel Braddock, also of the Coldstream, being next in rank, the command of the battalion devolved on him. One hundred and eighty-five men, of Colonel Lloyd's dragoons, made the total amount of the British force nine thousand six hundred and sixty-three. The Dutch were three thousand nine hundred and twenty-four, exclusive of officers.

---

[1] " An Impartial Account of all the Material Transactions of the " Grand Fleet and Land Forces at Cadiz and Vigo, by an Officer " present in those actions." London, 1703. Pages 29, 30.

[2] See Appendix, Nos. 141, 142, 143.

1702.

DISPOSITION OF THE GUARDS, JULY 1st, 1702.

| Ships. | Officers. | Serjeants. | Corporals. | Drummers. | Servants. | Privates. | | In all, officers included. |
|---|---|---|---|---|---|---|---|---|
| Ranelagh | Col. Pierce<br>„ Bisset<br>Capt. Winn * } | 5 | 4 | 4 | 4 | 90 | | 110 |
| Prince George | Brigadier Col. Wm Matthew<br>Capt. Wakelane (Wakelyn)<br>Capt. Camperfield (Kempenfelt)<br>Ensign Bearce<br>Chirurgeon } | 5 | 5 | 5 | 10 | 100 | { 50 Brigadier's<br>50 Col. Braddock's<br>30 with officers<br>in all | 130 |
| Cambridge | Col. Newton *<br>Capt. Bodmon (Bodenham)<br>Ensign Allen<br>Ensign Dockery * (Dockwra) } | 5 | 5 | 3 | 7 | 100 | { 74 First regiment<br>26 Col. Bisset's<br>24 with officers<br>in all | 124 |
| Barfleur | Col. Seymour *<br>Col. Primrose *<br>Capt. Smith *<br>Ensign Colston *<br>Ensign Denney * (St. Dennis) } | 5 | 5 | 3 | 6 | 100 | { Of the First regt. | 124 |
| Triumph | Capt. Edgeworth<br>Col. Moore<br>Capt. Ramsden<br>Capt. Scawen<br>Capt. Wyvell<br>Ensign Gore<br>Ensign Miller } | 5 | 5 | 3 | 9 | 100 | { 50 Edgeworth<br>50 Moore<br>29<br>in all | 129 |
| Lenox | Col. Hubbard (Hobart)<br>Capt. Wilson<br>Capt. Woollet<br>Capt. Swan<br>Ensign Windross (Windress)<br>Ensign Duncom (Duncombe) } | 5 | 5 | 3 | 6 | 100 | { 56 Hubbard's<br>6 Brigadier's<br>6 Bradock's<br>6 Edgeworth<br>6 Moors<br>20 Bisset's<br>in all | 125 |
| Terrible } Fire-ship { | 31 | 30<br>1 | 29<br>1 | 21<br>.. | 42<br>.. | 590<br>24 | { 10 Col. Bisset<br>14 Grenadiers<br>in all | 748<br>26 |
| | Total 31 | 31 | 30 | 21 | 42 | 614 | | 748 |

* Those names marked with an Asterisk were in the 1st Guards, the remainder in the Coldstream.

1 MS. Harl. No. 7025. Folio 17.

Abstract of the number of the Forces intended to be put on board the Fleets.    1702.

| Present Regiments. | Officers. | Serjeants. | Corporals. | Drummers & Hautboys. | Servants. | Effective Men. | Total. |
|---|---|---|---|---|---|---|---|
| Queen's Dragoons .. (3d Light Dragoons) | 25 | 5 | 15 | 22 | 23 | 185 | 275 |
| Guards . . . . . (1st and Coldstream) | 35 | 30 | 30 | 20 | 40 | 600 | 755 |
| Bellasys's . . . . . . . . (2d Foot) | 41 | 25 | 36 | 24 | 50 | 658 | 834 |
| Churchill's . . . . . . . . | 41 | 25 | 36 | 24 | 50 | 658 | 834 |
| Seymour's . . . . . . . (4th Foot) | 41 | 25 | 36 | 24 | 50 | 658 | 834 |
| Colenbine's . . . . . . (6th Foot) | 40 | 24 | 36 | 24 | 50 | 550 | 724 |
| Fuziliers (3 Companies with 5) (7th Foot Companies of Villiers's) . (and 31st) | 50 | 31 | 36 | 21 | 62 | 633 | 833 |
| Erle's . . . . . . . (19th Foot) | 40 | 24 | 36 | 24 | 50 | 550 | 724 |
| Gustavus Hamilton's . . . . . | 40 | 24 | 36 | 24 | 50 | 550 | 724 |
| Donegall's . . . . . (35th Foot) | 40 | 24 | 36 | 24 | 50 | 550 | 724 |
| Charlemont's . . . . . (36th Foot) | 40 | 24 | 36 | 24 | 50 | 550 | 724 |
| Fox's . . . . . . . . (32d Foot) | 41 | 25 | 36 | 24 | 50 | 658 | 834 |
| Shannon's . . . . . . . . . | 41 | 25 | 36 | 24 | 50 | 658 | 834 |
| | 515 | 311 | 441 | 303 | 625 | 7458 | 9653 |

Add the Corporals . .   441

Total Rank and file . .   7899

Rank and file Dutch, besides Officers, &c. . . . . .   3924

MS. Harl. No. 7025.

Of the above-named British corps, the following only landed at Vigo :

FIRST BRIGADE.
Battalion of Guards,
Churchill,
Collumbine,
Fox.
}Duke of Ormond, Brigadier Hamilton.

SECOND BRIGADE.
Bellasis,
Seymour,
Fuziliers,
Shannon.
}Lord Portmore, Brigadier Lloyd.

The Dutch, commanded by Baron Sparr, Brigadier Pallandt.

*An Impartial Account of the Material Transactions of the Grand Fleet and Land Forces: by an Officer that was present in those actions. London: Printed for R. Gibson, in Middle Holborn, 1703. P. 31.*

1702.
June 19th. The expedition assembled at St. Helen's. Admiral Fairburn sailed with part of the fleet and a squadron of the Dutch men of war for Portugal. The remainder fol-
July 1st. lowed, and were joined off Plymouth by five sail with two regiments and five companies of Colonel Villars's on board. Rooke and Fairburn[1] joined on the eighth of August; after which they proceeded to Cadiz, and anchored in the
Aug. 13th. Bay of Bulls, about two leagues from that town. On Saturday the fifteenth the Duke of Ormond landed the troops between Rota and Fort St. Catherine.

" No sooner were about eight of our grenadiers " (commanded by Collonel Pierce of the Coldstream,) " landed,
" but they were briskly charged with sword in hand by a
" General Officer at the head of a troop of Spanish horse,
" who were so warmly entertained by our men, that they
" soon retreated, leaving their General with five troopers
" dead on the place, with several horses, besides a Captain
" and a Cornet, which were wounded and taken prisoners,
" with their horses ; and on our side we had only one man
" wounded."[2]

Aug. 22nd. Colonel Pierce summoned St. Catherine's Fort, which surrendered.

September. In the beginning of September an attack was made on the Fort of Matagorda ; but the batteries of the Allied forces sank so deep in the sands and marshy ground, from the firing, that further attempts on it were abandoned, after a loss of thirty-two men killed and thirty-three wounded.

During their stay in Port St. Mary's many excesses were committed, "notwithstanding the strict orders the

[1] The two squadrons consisted of two hundred and three sail.—
An Impartial Account, by an Officer. London, 1703. Page 7.
[2] An Impartial Account, &c. page 12.

" Duke" (Ormond) " gave against plundering ;"[1] the 1702.<br>September. churches were rifled, and the soldiers forcibly entered a convent of nuns.

The troops marched to Rota for re-embarkation, the brass guns being removed from Fort St. Catherine; it was then blown up and entirely demolished. The English grenadiers covered the embarkation. The grenadier company of the Guards, who had set fire to whatever was combustible, with a view to secure their retreat, were attacked by the Spaniards, but succeeded in getting to the ships without much loss. No officer was killed or wounded during the operations on shore.[2]

---

[1] Conjunct Expeditions. By Thomas More Molyneux, Esq. —London, 8vo. 1759. Page 112.

" A landing on the Continent was resolved on, and though the " sea was high and the danger great, yet the hope of spoil made " them venture on it. They landed at Rota ; a party of Spanish " horse seemed to threaten some resistance, but they retired, and " so our men came to St. Maries, which they found deserted, but " full of riches. He" (Duke of Ormond) " had published a mani- " festo according to his instructions, by which the Spaniards were " invited to submit to the Emperor ; and he offered his protection " to all that came in to him; but the spoil of St. Maries was " thought an ill commentary on that text. Some of the ships' " crews were so employed in bringing and bestowing the plunder, " that they took not the necessary care to furnish themselves with " fresh water."—*Bishop Burnet's History of His Own Times*, 8vo. Oxford, 1823. vol. v. page 41.

[2] London Gazette, No. 3858.

" Rooke spoke so coldly of the design he went upon before he " sailed, that those who conversed with him were apt to infer " that he intended to do the enemy as little harm as possible.

" Rooke had laid no dispositions before hand how to proceed " upon his coming thither; some days were lost on pretence of " seeking for intelligence : it is certain our Court had false accounts

The expedition was returning to England, when intelligence arrived by Captain Hardy of the Pembroke, that the galleons, under a French convoy, had put into Vigo.    Sir George Rooke called a council of war, and it was resolved to make all sail for that port.    He arrived there on the October. eleventh of October.    The entrance to the harbour was three-quarters of a mile across, secured by batteries on each side, besides a strong boom, formed of ships' yards and topmasts fastened together and moored at each end to a seventy-gun ship.    Within the harbour were five ships of the same force, under Chateaurenard, with their broadsides fronting its mouth.    The Duke of Ormond, to facilitate the entrance, landed two thousand five hundred men Oct. 12th. near Vigo, headed by five hundred English and Dutch grenadiers under Lord Shannon, Colonel Pierce of the Coldstream, and a Dutch Major.    The first brigade consisted of a battalion of Guards and three regiments under the Duke of Ormond and Brigadier Hamilton; the second was under Lord Portmore and Brigadier Lloyd; the Dutch were commanded by Baron Sparr and Brigadier Pallandt. The grenadiers gallantly carried the fort and platform of Rodendella, mounting forty pieces of cannon, at the entrance of the harbour, although the enemy had a force of ten thousand men in and near the place under the

---

" of the state the place was in, both with relation to the garrison
" and the fortifications; the garrison was much stronger, and the
" fortifications were in a better case, than was represented.

    " The Duke of Ormond told me he had not half the ammunition
" that was necessary for the taking Cadiz, if they had defended
" themselves well; though he believed they would not have made
" any great resistance, if he had landed on his first arrival, and
" not given them time to recover from the disorder into which the
" first surprize had put them." — *Bishop Burnet*, vol. v. pages 38,
39. 44.

Prince Brabançon. When the British ensign was hoisted on the fort, the squadron advanced with a press of sail directly against the boom, which was broken by the Torbay, bearing Vice-Admiral Hopson's flag, who led the van. After a vigorous opposition, the French, finding themselves unable to make further resistance, destroyed the galleons and their own ships. Eight large vessels being burnt and four sunk, not more than six French ships, three Spanish, and five galleons were taken; the remainder were either consumed by the flames or run on shore. But a quantity of silver and valuable colonial produce fell into the hands of the victors.[1] The English land-forces on this occasion lost two lieutenants and thirty men killed. Four superior officers and about forty men were wounded. In the battalion of Guards, Captain Butler Ramsden (Lieutenant of the Coldstream Grenadiers) was killed. Colonels Pierce, Newton, and Seymour, were wounded.[2] The officers of the Coldstream on the staff were, Colonel Pierce, aid-de-

---

[1] Bullion 861 lb. troy; vinnello, cochineal, &c. produced, after deducting all expenses, £5302 12s. 1d.; which was divided in the following manner: one-ninth part to the General officers, eight-ninths to the eight regiments employed.

"October ye 18th, 1702. Received for the use of the battalion of "Guards, the ninth part of the silver and vinnello within men-"tioned.

"HENRY EDGEWORTH, (Lt.-Col. and Captain
Coldstream Guards.)"
—MS. Harl. 7025, fol. 80.

[2] Colonel Pierce of the Coldstream was wounded by a cannon-shot in the thigh.—From an account published by authority, (*Appendix to the London Gazette*). Printed by Edward Jones, Savoy, 1702.

Colonel Pierce was subsequently appointed colonel of a newly-raised regiment in Ireland, and afterwards to the Fifth Foot.—War-Office Records.

1702.  camp to the Duke of Ormond, Captain William Bisset, aid-de-camp to Brigadier Seymour, and Lieutenant Camperfield (Kempenfelt), aid-de-camp to Brigadier Matthew.

Oct. 17th.  The troops marched from Rodendella to embark; two days after, they sailed for England, and arrived at Deal on the seventh of November.[1]

Sir Cloudesly Shovel was left with a fleet to intercept the other galleons, then expected to arrive at Vigo.

1704.  On the twenty-fourth of July Gibraltar surrendered to Sir George Rooke and the Prince of Hesse Darmstadt, who had landed three days before with eighteen hundred English and Dutch marines.

In the same month Lord Galway embarked at Portsmouth to take the command in Portugal, and a battalion of Guards was ordered to proceed to that country, composed of two hundred men from the First Guards, and four hundred from the Coldstream.[2] This battalion marched to Portsmouth,[3] whence they sailed on the twenty-ninth of September[4] with the fleet under Rear-Admiral Whet-

Oct. 30th.  stone, and disembarked at Lisbon.[5]

Dec. 3rd.  An express from the Prince of Hesse Darmstadt arrived at Lisbon from Gibraltar, requesting that reinforcements might be immediately sent to him, in consequence of an attack on that fortress by the Spaniards and French with a powerful force.  The battalion of English Guards, Barrymore's and Donegall's regiments, five hundred Portugnese from Lagos, and a Dutch battalion, were ordered to embark.[6]  Intelligence at the same time was despatched

---

[1] See engraved medal H.

[2] See Appendix, Nos. 148, 149, 150.

[3] London Gazette, No. 4049.

[4] Ibid. 4058.          [5] Ibid. 4068.          [6] Ibid. 4077.

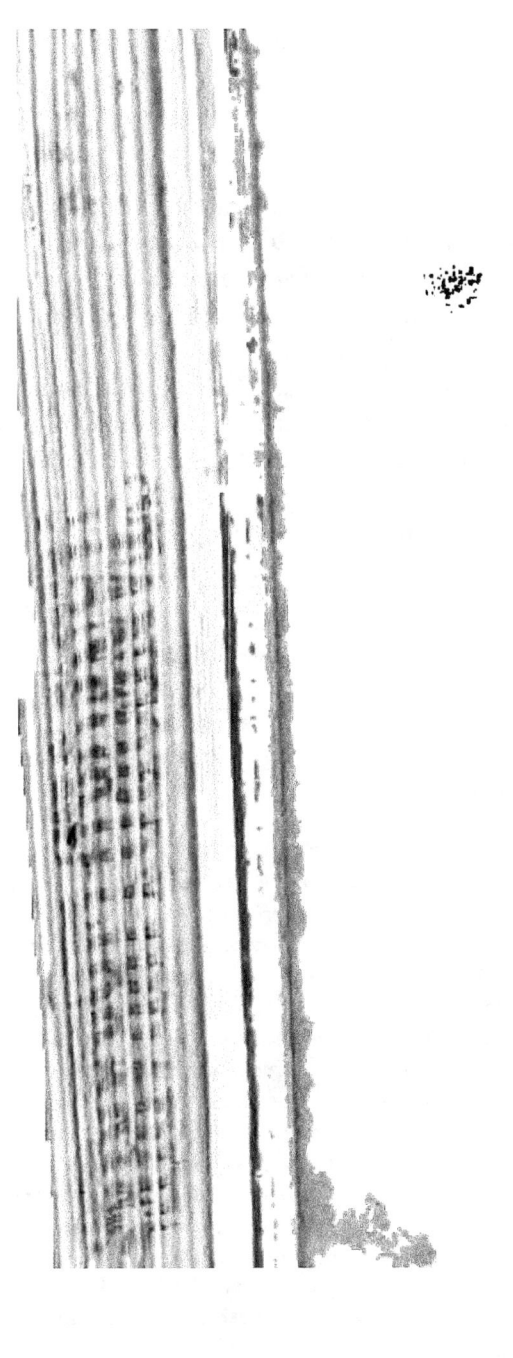

to Gibraltar, announcing the measures that had been taken for its relief.[1]

The Guards and other troops, amounting to upwards of three thousand men, sailed from Lisbon on the tenth of December[2] (N. S.) On their passage they fell in with the enemy's squadron under Monsieur de Pointi, but succeeded in arriving at their destination,[3] although some of the transports had separated.

The battalion of English Guards was safely landed on the eighteenth ;[4] strengthened by this reinforcement, the Prince of Darmstadt made a sortie on the twenty-third, and destroyed the lines that had been erected within a hundred and sixty paces of the palisade.[5]

| | | Serjˢ. | Corpˢ. | Drumˢ. | Effective Men. |
|---|---|---|---|---|---|
| [1] British Force | Battalion of Guards | 30 | 30 | 20 | 600 |
| | Barrymore's regᵗ | 39 | 39 | 26 | 650 |
| | Donnegall's regᵗ | 39 | 39 | 26 | 650 |

Military Papers, State-Paper Office.

[2] London Gazette, No. 4082.

[3] Ibid. 4084.          [4] Ibid. 4084.

[5] " Gibraltar, Decʳ 27ᵗʰ (N.S.) 1704.—On the 9ᵗʰ inst. the trans-
" port ships, having on board the battalion of English Foot
" Guards, the Earl of Barrymore's, and the Earl of Donnegal's re-
" giments of Foot, and a battalion of Dutch Foot, sailed out of the
" river of Lisbon under convoy of the Antelope, Greenwich, New-
" castle, and Roebuck, men of war. On the 17ᵗʰ, they discovered
" the French fleet, commanded by the Sieur Ponty, consisting of
" twenty-three sail. The English ships, being favoured by the
" calm, got into Gibraltar. The fleet under Vice-Admiral Leake
" endeavoured to go out of the Streight's mouth to protect them
" into the bay, but was forced, by contrary winds and the current,
" on the coast of Barbary. Seven of the transports that had got
" safe through the Enemy's fleet came to anchor in the Bay
" on the 19ᵗʰ in the morning, and the Newcastle man-of-war with
" eight more arrived on the next day. All the Guards are
" come entirely, and most of the other succours, so that here are

The enemy, encouraged by an addition of two thousand
French troops, evinced a disposition to storm the place.[1]
On the second of February an attempt was made against
the Round Tower, to ascertain what might be effected by
a larger force.

On the seventh the enemy attacked with five hundred
chosen grenadiers, French and Walloons, commanded by
Lientenant-General Thouy, and supported by one thousand
Spanish troops.   They mounted the hill in perfect silence
by break of day, and again attempted to storm the Round
Tower, which was defended by Colonel Borr.   The assailants, by throwing from above great stones and grenados
on his men, at last obliged him to retire into that part of
the works where the battalion of English Guards was
posted.   Flushed with success, they advanced too far,
when they were gallantly charged by Colonel Moncall[2] of
Barrymore's regiment, and driven from the Round Tower.
" Colonel Rivett of the Coldstream having got up the
" rock on the right of the covered way with twenty grena-
" diers, favoured very much Colonel Moncall's success."
The garrison by this time had assembled and kept up so
destructive a fire, that the enemy were obliged to make a
precipitate retreat, losing seventy men killed on the spot,
upwards of two hundred wounded, with one captain, four
lieutenants, and forty men taken.   The loss on the part of

---

" landed fifteen hundred effective private men besides officers ; and
" the Marines in garrison are about 1000.   The 22d, at night, a
" sally was made with 200 men, who burnt and destroyed the
" gabions and fascines of their nearest works : we had about 20
" men killed and wounded in this action."—*London Gazette*, No.
4093.

[1] London Gazette, No. 4095.

[2] He lost his leg at Gibraltar.—Military Correspondence, State-
Paper Office.

the garrison was twenty-seven men killed, and one
hundred and twenty wounded; among the latter was
Lieutenant-Colonel Roger James[1] of the Coldstream.

Marshal de Tessé arrived with additional troops to carry
on the siege; the garrison also received fresh reinforcements from Portugal, besides supplies of every description.[2] Sir John Leake sailed from the Tagus on the sixth
of March (O. S.); on the tenth, he attacked and captured
the French squadron under De Pointi, as it was sailing out
of the bay.[3]

After a siege of seven months the enemy retired in
April, giving up all hopes of being able to make any impression on the fortress. Their efforts were then confined
to "a very feeble blockade."[4]

A small force of the enemy was posted at a place called
the Sand Hills, whence they were in the habit of firing on
the garrison when employed in levelling the works which
had been raised during the blockade. On the thirteenth
of May (N. S.), Colonel Rivett of the Coldstream was sent
with a detachment of grenadiers to attack them; but on
his approach they retired, and the works were completely
demolished.[5]

The Earl of Peterborough sailed from St. Helen's with
Sir Cloudesly Shovel and a large convoy for Lisbon,
where he arrived in the Ranelagh on the twentieth of June

1704-5.

Feb. 12th.

May.

May 24th.

June.

---

[1] Lieutenant-Colonel Roger James, in a memorial to the Treasury, states, he served twelve years in the Coldstream Guards, was
sent to Spain with the battalion of Guards, was wounded at
Gibraltar and Barcelona; and in the year 1706 that he was again
wounded and taken prisoner. — Report on Colonel James' Memorial, dated August 4th, 1711. War-Office Records.

[2] London Gazette, No. 4104. [3] Ibid. No. 4116.

[4] London Gazette, No. 4125.—*Bishop Burnet*, vol. v. page 199.

[5] Ibid. No. 4130.

(N. S.).[1]    Prince Charles went on board the Earl of Peterborough's ship on the twenty-third of July (N. S.),[2] to proceed on the projected expedition to Barcelona.    The Dutch fleet having joined in the Tagus, the Confederate squadron sailed on the twenty-eighth (N. S.) and anchored

at Gibraltar on the eleventh of the ensuing month.    The Austrian Prince[3] went on shore for a few days.    The Prince of Hesse Darmstadt and the battalion of Guards embarked, and the fleet then sailed for Altea Bay.[4]   From thence it again proceeded on its voyage, and anchored before Barcelona on the eleventh of August (O. S.).    Next day the troops landed, without opposition,[5] near the

---

[1] London Gazette, No. 4126—4136.

[2] Ibid. 4146.                    [3] Ibid. 4152.

" The fleet of the Allies came to Lisbon with an army on board of " above 5000 men, commanded by the Earl of Peterborough.  King " Charles of Spain resolved to go on board.   Our fleet sailed from " Lisbon with King Charles ; they stopped at Gibraltar, and car- " ried along with them the Prince of Hesse, who had been so long " Governor of Barcelona that he knew both the tempers, the " strength, and importance of the place." — *Bishop Burnet,* vol. v. page 207.

[4] London Gazette, No. 4162.

" We sailed from Lisbon in order to join the squadron under Sir " Cloudesley Shovel ; meeting with which at the appointed station " off Tangier, the men of war and transports, then united, made " the best of their way for Gibraltar ; there we stay'd no longer " than to take aboard two regiments out of that garrison, in lieu " of two out of our fleet.  Here we found the Prince of Hesse, who " immediately took a resolution to follow the Arch-Duke in this " expedition.   He was a person of great gallantry ; and, having " been Viceroy of Catalonia, was received on board the fleet with " the greatest satisfaction, as being a person capable of doing great " service in a country where he was well known ,and as well be- " loved."—*Captain Carleton,* page 78,

[5] London Gazette, No. 4164.

town, when they were joined by many Miquelets and other Spaniards. Five thousand men[1] garrisoned Barce-lona : Charles being inclined to besiege the place, councils of war were held almost daily, composed of the officers holding the highest commands, who were unanimous, with the exception of Peterborough, against so wild a scheme.[2] It was, however, at last determined to make the attempt.[3] The Earl of Peterborough commenced operations by an attack on the strong fortress of Montjuich, situated on the opposite part of the town from that where the disembarkation took place. The Prince of Hesse led a body of one thousand men, followed by about six hundred under Brigadier Stanhope. Montjuich was supposed to be impregnable ; but the outworks were instantly carried, sword in hand, with inconsiderable loss. " The Governor of the " Fort with his garrison retired into the dungeon, which " is a small fort within the great one, and there made a

---

[1] Bishop Burnet, vol. v. page 209.

[2] The Earl of Peterborough's Conduct in Spain. By John Freind. 8vo. London, 1707.

[3] " Barcelona is one of the largest and most populous cities in " all Spain, fortified with bastions ; one side thereof is secured by " the sea, and the other by a strong fortification, called Mont-"juich."

" In six several councils of war the siege of Barcelona, under " the circumstances we then lay, was rejected as a madness and " impossibility. And though the General and Brigadier Stanhope " (afterwards Earl Stanhope) consented to some effort, yet it was " rather that some effort should be made to satisfy the expectation " of the world, than any hopes of success. However, no consent at " all could be obtained from any council of war, and the Dutch Ge-" neral in particular declared that he would not obey even the " commands of the Earl of Peterborow, if he should order the sa-" crifice of the troops under him in so unjustifiable a manner, " without the consent of a council of war."—*Captain Carleton*, pages 81. 87.

" resolute defence." [1]    Reinforcements were sent from Barcelona, and some of the troops succeeded in entering the fort ; but cries of " Viva" were heard, which induced the Prince of Hesse to advance, under the impression that the enemy meant to surrender.  A heavy fire was opened on him ; two hundred of his men were taken, and the remainder driven back.  Notwithstanding the failure of this attack, the result was most fortunate, as Don Velasco, on being told by the prisoners that the Earl of Peterborough and Prince of Hesse were both present, imagined that the whole Confederate force was then engaged, and withdrew the reinforcements intended for the relief of Montjuich. The Prince of Hesse was unfortunately shot while in conversation with the Earl of Peterborough, who had just returned from reconnoitring the reinforcements on their way from the city.  At the same moment the Earl was informed that a panic had seized the storming party under Lord Charlemont, and that they were flying in every direction.  Peterborough hastened to the spot, seized the half-pike out of Lord Charlemont's hands, and having rallied and addressed the troops, regained possession of the fortress before the Spaniards had any suspicion of the disaster.[2]  The Governor continued to shut himself up in the dungeon till the sixth, during which interval an incessant fire of shells had been maintained.  On that day the magazine blew up and destroyed the Governor, several officers, and fifty men; the remainder, amounting to three hundred and fifty, surrendered.

September.    Preparations were made for an attack on the city ; the ground was broken on the ninth, batteries were erected with great difficulty, and the town was bombarded and

---

[1] London Gazette, No. 4164.
[2] Carleton's Memoirs.

partially set on fire.[1] Fifty-eight pieces of cannon played constantly on the place, and at the expiration of five days a breach was made. The enemy, under the apprehension of a general assault, beat a parley; hostages were soon after exchanged, and articles of capitulation drawn up.[2]

The thirteenth of October was the day fixed for the garrison to march out. The citizens, long exasperated by the severities of their Viceroy Don Velasco, and apprehensive that he might take some of the "prisoners away " with him, contrary to the capitulation, they rose up in " arms against the garrison. Thereupon the Earl of " Peterborough marched in with the army at the breach, " and composing this disorder, saved both the town and " the garrison."[3]

Charles was received with the greatest possible enthusiasm,[4] nearly the whole garrison joined his standard, and of five thousand not one-fifth remained under the banners of the Duke of Anjou (Philip the Fifth). Catalonia, with the exception of Roses, declared for the Austrian prince.

---

[1] "The Admirals forgot their element and acted as General " Officers at land; they came every day from their ships with a " body of men formed into companies, and regularly marshalled " and commanded by captains and lieutenants of their own. Cap- " tain Littleton in particular, one of the most advanced captains in " the whole fleet, offered of himself to take care of the landing and " conveyance of the artillery to the camp. And answerable to that " his first zeal, was his vigour all along; for, finding it next to an " impossibility to draw the cannon and mortars up such vast preci- " pices by horses, if the country had afforded them, he caused har- " nesses to be made for two hundred men, and by that means, " after a prodigious fatigue and labour, brought the cannon and " mortars necessary for the siege up to the very batteries."— *Captain Carleton*, page 111.

[2] London Gazette, No. 4177.     [3] Ibid. No. 4178.

[4] Bishop Burnet, vol. v. page 213.

1705.     When the French besieged Barcelona, in the year 1697, with thirty·thousand men, they lost twelve thousand.[1] The army of Peterborough was inferior in numbers to the garrison by which it was defended; the siege terminated in three weeks.

The battalion·of Guards was left with Charles in Barcelona.[2]

Lord Peterborough with a small force proceeded·to Valencia: during his route he frequently encountered the enemy, took many prisoners,·and succeeded in reducing the province completely under the subjection of Charles.

---

[1] Captain Carleton's Memoirs.

[2] 1st December, 1705. Officers of the Guards, belonging to the battalion in Catalonia, not present.

| | |
|---|---|
| 1st Foot Guards. | Lieut.-Col. Talbor: succeeded Col. Dobbyns 25th March, 1705, and never went over. |
| | Captain Filks: Quarter-Master to the 17 Companies in England. |
| | Ensign Poultney: came sick from Gibraltar. |
| | Ensign Shrimpton: a child. |
| 2d Ditto. | Lieut.-Col. Rivet: had the Queen's leave to come home. |
| | Lieut.-Col. Churchill: served the last campaign in Holland. |
| | Lieut.-Col. Scawen: succeeded Colonel Hales, 5th Feb. 1704-5, and never went. |

—Military Correspondence, State-Paper Office.

# CHAPTER XIX.

Detachments from the two regiments of Guards embark and sail
from Portsmouth to join the battalion in Spain—Philip attempts
to recover Barcelona—Misunderstanding between Prince Charles
and Peterborough — Large sums advanced by the citizens —
Troops die in great numbers — Marshal Tessé threatens Tortosa
—Allies march for that town — Guards remain to do duty over
Prince Charles—Barcelona invested—Lord Donnegal arrives with
four regiments from Gerona—Philip joins the French army—
Peterborough returns from Valencia—Enemy repulsed in a night
attack — Conflict at Montjuich — Donnegal killed—Anecdote of
an officer's dog—French raise the siege—Troops sail for Valencia
—Galway takes Ciudad Roderigo, masks Badajoz, and arrives
at Madrid—Cruelty to a party of the Coldstream—Peterborough
leaves Spain for Savoy—Galway crosses the Tagus at Fuentes
d'Uenna—Joined at Veles by the troops under Lieut.-General
Wyndham, with whom was the battalion of Guards—Allies in
quarters along the frontier of Valencia and Murcia during the
winter.

A DETACHMENT of three hundred and thirty-eight men
in equal proportions from the two regiments of Guards,
under Lieutenant-Colonel Bissett of the Coldstream, embarked and sailed in March from Portsmouth, to join the
battalion in Spain: the other officers of the Coldstream
ordered with this detachment were Lieutenant-Colonels

1706.<br>March.

---

¹ See Appendix, Nos. 153, 154, 155, 156, 157.

Scawen, Wakelyn and Swan, and Ensign Bradbury. Lieutenant-Colonels Moryson and Stevenage received leave to return to England.

Philip resolved to attempt the recovery of Barcelona, and two armies under the Duke de Noailles and Marshal de Tessé, amounting to twenty thousand men, were put in motion towards Gerona and Lerida, to deceive the Allies. The Count de Toulouse with twelve ships sailed from Toulon, and was afterwards joined in the Bay of Barcelona by twelve more.

The English fleet after the capitulation of Barcelona sailed for Gibraltar and Lisbon.

Charles and his Court interfered with the authority of Lord Peterborough soon after the place was captured: that Prince already acted as if he were King of Spain, and Philip the Fifth had returned to Paris.[1] This naturally produced misunderstandings ; the result was, that the fortifications, which had been greatly injured by the siege, remained neglected. Ladies and balls occupied the attention of the new Court, and large sums advanced by the citizens to Charles for their defence, were squandered away, while the troops, who were ill supplied, died in great numbers.[2] Three men-of-war were expected with money, which was much wanted, the "soldiers for several weeks "having subsisted upon eighteen-pence a week, and " the officers obliged to pawn their scarfs, &c., for want of " it too."[3]

The French were so cautious in their march towards Barcelona that they deceived the Allies, who supposed they would attack Lerida or Gerona. Marshal de Tessé's

---

[1] Journal of the Siege of Barcelona, by an officer who was present. London, 1706.
[2] Ibid. page 5.        [3] Ibid.

corps moved from Lerida and threatened Tortosa; the
Allied troops were all sent to that town, with the exception
of the battalion of Guards, now reduced to three hundred
men:[1] these were entrusted with the duty of protecting
the person of the Prince.

Instead of immediately marching on Barcelona, the
French lost several days, thereby enabling a detachment
of about two hundred English to get into the town. This
delay also afforded time to repair the bastions and
breaches; to effect which, the people were excited by the
priests, many of whom worked with indefatigable zeal.
Charles positively refused to leave the city,[2] although
much pressed to do so.

On the second of April (N. S.) the French corps united
and encamped on the north side of the town; their right
wing extending to the foot of Montjuich. Next day
they attempted the weakest point of the out-works, where
one hundred of Hans Hamilton's regiment were stationed,
who had that morning been put on duty, after having
travelled seventy leagues during the two foregoing days
on mules. These men repulsed the enemy with great intrepidity.

On the first alarm, the battalion of Guards had been
ordered up, leaving only twelve men to protect Charles
and his Court.[3]

April 3rd.

Two days after this the enemy took a fort that commanded the shore on the same side with Montjuich; they
immediately began to land their cannon, ammunition, and
provisions.

Lord Donnegal arrived with four regiments from Gerona; April 5th.

---

[1] See Appendix, No. 155.
[2] Journal of the Siege of Barcelona, page 6.
[3] Ibid. page 7.

1706.  two of them had been newly raised in Spain.  The French then marched eastward, and the castle and city were nearly surrounded.[1]

April 6th.  Philip on joining the French army was saluted from their
(N. S.)  fleet, and afterwards went on board, as was supposed, for safety, the Miquelets having attacked his quarters on the preceding evening at Leriah, when he escaped by a back door, leaving his hat behind him : they seized his plate and other valuables.

Fresh reinforcements arrived from Lerida and Gerona for the garrison.  Three thousand regular troops, besides the City Militia, occupied Barcelona.

Early on the morning of the eighth, the French batteries opened on Montjuich : a sortie was made, and the enemy driven from their trenches ; but being reinforced by four thousand fresh troops, they quickly recovered them.  The Earl of Peterborough on receiving the news returned from Valencia, and posted himself on the heights near the town.[2]

April 15th.  On the evening of the fifteenth the French attacked the western out-work, where Charles's new Spanish Foot Guards were posted, who on the first advance of their assailants precipitately retreated.  At midnight the enemy reached the post occupied by the battalion of English Guards.  The grenadiers particularly distinguished themselves ; " in fine " never any soldiers behav'd better; some of them, nay, " and my Lord Donegall himself too, throwing back the " enemy's grenades upon them."[3]  To alarm the inhabitants, red-hot cannon-shot and shells were constantly thrown into the town.[4]

---

[1] Journal of the Siege of Barcelona, page 8.
[2] Carleton's Memoirs, and Journal of the Siege.
[3] Journal of the Siege of Barcelona, page 14.
[4] Ibid. page 14.

A severe conflict took place on the twenty-first at Montjuich, in which Lord Donnegal lost his life; " he " would hear of no quarter, which the enemy that knew " him offered him. He had cut to pieces half a dozen " grenadiers and an officer that had personally engaged " him, and was attacking a Captain when an unhappy " bullet shot him through the heart, and he fell."[1] In this affair four hundred prisoners were taken by the enemy with twenty English officers. The fort of Montjuich being supposed untenable, was relinquished, all the combustible matter having been burnt. The enemy then proceeded with the operations against fort Antonia. On the night of the fifth, as the English officers on guard were sitting together in a circle, with a large dog asleep in the centre, one of the enemy's shells falling upon the animal, his blood extinguished the fusee and saved them all from destruction.[2]

*1706. April.*

*April 25th.*

*May. (N. S.)*

Two days after, the French squadron stood out for sea, having received intimation that the Allied fleet, composed of thirty-seven English and thirteen Dutch men-of-war, with eight frigates, was approaching.

At noon, on the eighth (N.S.), the Allied squadron anchored, having the day before taken on board the Earl of Peterborough with fourteen hundred soldiers at Taragona: these men landed, and marched directly to the breach, on the supposition that the enemy would make a desperate effort to gain the town before the succours could be landed.[3] On the ninth, however, it became apparent that the French intended to raise the siege: most of their batteries had ceased firing, and the troops were concentrating into a smaller compass. The enemy broke up,

---

[1] Journal of the Siege of Barcelona, page 18.   [2] Ibid. p. 22.
[3] Ibid. page 23.   London Gazette, No. 4232.

and left their encampment; having lost five thousand men in their attacks on Montjuich, by the different sallies made and the fire of the garrison.[1]  It will be remembered that at the commencement of this memorable siege, there were in the place only the mutilated battalion of Guards, and the two hundred men that stole in previous to the regular investment.  At its termination the garrison consisted of eleven British battalions, besides other troops.  The hostile feeling of the Miquelets towards the French rendered it impracticable for them to carry away either their artillery or heavy baggage.  They left behind two hundred brass cannon, thirty mortars, with vast quantities of shot, shells, and other warlike stores; ten thousand sacks of corn, above three thousand barrels of powder, and the sick and wounded of their army, whom Marshal de Tessé recommended to the humanity of the British commander.[2]  The same day on which the siege was raised, (first of May, O. S.) there was a total eclipse of the sun.  Bishop Burnet, in the " History of His Own Times," relates that the superstitious looked upon it as a bad omen, and censured De Tessé, the French General, for not having raised the siege one day sooner.[3]

---

[1] London Gazette, No. 4232.     [2] Ibid. No. 4232.

[3] " Accordingly the next morning, the first of May, 1706, while " the sun was under a total eclipse, in a suitable hurry and confu-" sion, they broke up, leaving behind them most of their cannon " and mortars, together with vast quantities of all sorts of ammu-" nition and provisions, scarce stopping to look back till they had " left all, but the very verge, of the disputed dominion behind " them.

" He forthwith gave orders for a medal to be struck suitable to " the occasion, one of which, set round with diamonds, he pre-" sented to Sir John Leake, the English admiral.  The next orders " were for re-casting all the damaged brass cannon which the ene-" my had left; upon every one of which was, by order, a sun

Charles ordered medals to be struck for the com- 1706.
memoration of this extraordinary siege, with a correspond-
ing device.

Ten transports sailed with troops from Barcelona for May 22nd.
Valencia; all the infantry that could be spared followed (N. S.
shortly after, including the battalion of Guards. Charles
remained at Barcelona, preparing for his journey to the
capital.

The Earl of Galway, who had taken Ciudad Roderigo, June 27th.
and masked Badajos, arrived at Madrid.

A large force, intended to make a descent in France,
under the Earl of Rivers, had assembled at Portsmouth
and in the Isle of Wight. Lord Rivers embarked at the
end of July. The fleet sailed with nine thousand men on
the tenth of August,[2] but being impeded by contrary winds
till October, was then directed to go to Lisbon, as it was
too late in the season to commence operations; and on their
arrival, the troops were ordered to proceed and reinforce
the army in Valencia. These troops landed at Alicant on
the eighth and eleventh of February, 170$\frac{6}{7}$, (N.S.)

The battalion of Guards was placed under the command
of Lieutenant-General Wyndham, who captured Requena
and Cuenza,[3] on the line of march from Valencia to
Madrid. Captain Carleton, page 171, speaks of these
operations as follows:—" From Huette" (not far from
Cuença) " the Earl of Peterborough marched forwards
" for Valencia, with only those four-score dragoons
" which came with him from Chuicon, leaving General
" Wyndham pursuing his own orders to join his forces to

" eclyps'd, with this motto under it, ' Magna parvis obscurantur.' "
—Captain Carleton's Memoirs, page 150.

[1] See engraved medal 1.
[2] London Gazette, No. 4249.
[3] London Gazette, No. 4254, and Carleton's Memoirs.

1706.

" the Spaniards of the place at the same time fell upon
" the poor weak soldiers, killing several, not even sparing
" their wives. This was but a prelude to their barbarity;
" their savage cruelty was only whetted, not glutted.
" They took the surviving few, hurried, and dragged them
" up a bill a little without the villa. On the top of this
" hill there was a hole or opening, somewhat like the
" mouth of one of our coal-pits; down this they cast
" several, who, with hideous shrieks and cries, made
" more hideous by the echoes of the chasm, there lost
" their lives. This relation was thus made to the Earl of
" Peterborough at his quarters at Campilio; who imme-
" diately gave orders for to sound to horse. At first we
" were all surprised; but were soon satisfied that it was to
" revenge, or rather to do justice on this barbarous action.
" As soon as we entered the villa, we found that most of
" the inhabitants, but especially the most guilty, had with-
" drawn themselves on our approach. We found, how-
" ever, many of the dead soldiers' clothes, which had
" been conveyed into the church, and there hid; and a
" strong accusation being laid against a person belonging
" to the church, and full proof made that he had been
" singularly industrious in the execution of that horrid
" piece of barbarity on the hill, his Lordship commanded
" him to be banged up at the knocker of the door. After
" this piece of military justice, we were led up to the
" fatal pit or hole, down which many had been cast head-
" long. There we found one poor soldier alive, who,
" upon being thrown in, had catched fast hold of some
" impending bushes, and saved himself on a little jutty
" within the concavity. On hearing us talk English, he
" cried out; and ropes being let down, in a little time he
" was drawn up; when he gave us an ample detail of the
" whole villany. Among other particulars, I remember

1706.   " he told me of a very narrow escape he had in that ou-
" scure recess ; a poor woman, one of the wives of the
" soldiers, who were thrown down after him, struggled
" and roared so much, that they could not, with all their
" force, throw her cleverly in the middle, by which means
" falling near the side, in her fall she almost beat him
" from his place of security.   Upon the conclusion of this
" tragical relation of the soldier thus saved, his Lordship
" gave immediate orders for the firing of the villa, which
" was executed with due severity : after which, his Lord-
" ship marched back to his quarters at Campilio, from
" whence, two days after, we arrived at Valencia."

August.      Charles arrived at the camp at Guadalaxara on the
eighth of August (O. S.); but the Earl of Peterborough,
who accompanied him, soon after left Spain for Savoy,
where he was to take the command.

            The Allied army moved to Chuicon and Colmenar, and
Sept. 9th.  remained in camp one month.[1]   Lord Galway passed the
(N.S.)    Tagus with his troops at Fuenta d'Uenna : the enemy
attempted to fall on his rear, but were intimidated by the
batteries placed along the banks of the river.   From this
Sept. 12th. place the Allies marched to Barajas, and reached Veles.
There they were joined by Lieutenant-General Wyndham [2]
with three thousand English from Huette, amongst whom
were the battalion of English Guards, and the Earl of
Peterborough's regiment of horse.   The troops continued
their route towards the frontiers of Valencia, crossing the
river Xucar on the fifteenth of September at Olivares.
Sept. 27th. The Allied army soon after occupied their destined quar-
(O.S.)    ters along the frontiers of Valencia and Murcia, where
they remained during the winter.

---

[1] London Gazette, No. 4276.      [2] Ibid. No. 4269.

# CHAPTER XX.

Death of Cutts—Churchill appointed Colonel of the Coldstream—
An account of Cutts — Prince Charles deserts Galway—Allies
suffer great privations — Lewis XIV. sends reinforcements to
Spain—Battle of Almanza—Guards suffer severely—Lerida sur-
renders — Allies go into winter-quarters — Galway embarks at
Lisbon for England—A battalion of English Guards from the
First and Coldstream ordered to Scotland — Countermanded at
York—Sent to Colchester—The battalion embarks for Flanders
—Battle of Oudenarde—Siege of Lisle—Capitulation—Guards
quartered during the winter at Brussels.

On the death of Lord Cutts in this year, General    1707.
Charles Churchill was appointed Colonel of the Coldstream.

John Lord Cutts was born at Matching in Essex; and
in early life attached himself to Monmouth's service.   He
fought in Hungary under the Duke of Lorraine; was
created a Baron of the Kingdom of Ireland, and in 1690
appointed Governor of the Isle of Wight.   At the accession of Queen Anne, he was sent to Holland, with the
rank of Lieutenant-General.   In 1705, on becoming Com-

mander-in-Chief in Ireland, he was made one of the
Lord Justices of that kingdom, under the Duke of Ormond, in which situation he died at Dublin, the twenty-
sixth of January, 170$\frac{4}{5}$.

Lord Cutts signalized himself on many occasions, particularly at the taking of Buda [1] by the Imperialists, as
aid-de-camp to the Duke of Lorraine. Addison [2] speaks
of his conduct at Buda, and he also distinguished himself
at the battle of Blenheim. The motto he selected was,
" With labour and with blood." He obtained the appellation of the Salamander, from being always found in the
thickest of the fire. Swift refers to him in the Epigram
on a Salamander; and he is said, in one of the State
Poems of those days, to be " As brave and brainless as
the sword he wears." This alludes to an occurrence
which took place near Venlo, and is thus mentioned by
Burnet. [3] " There was a fort on the other side of that
" river, that commanded Venlo, which was taken by Lord
" Cutts in so gallant a manner, that it deserved to be
" much commended by every body but himself; but he
" lost the honour that was due to many brave actions of
" his by talking too much of them."

He was also " something of a poet ;" there is a small
volume by him in print, dated 1687, entitled " Poetical
Exercises, written on Several Occasions," dedicated to
Mary, Princess of Orange. In one of the volumes of the
State Poems, there are also verses by him on the death
of Queen Mary.

After the Union with Scotland, new colours were given

---

[1] 1686.                              [2] His " Musæ Anglicanæ."
[3] Burnet's History of His Own Times.

to the Coldstream, designated the " Union Colours;"[1] and
at the commencement of this year, pikes were no longer
used in the Guards, as is shown by the following
letter :—[2]

" Whitehall, 23ᵈ May, 1707.

" GENTLEMEN,

" The officers of the Foot Guards having applied to me
" in relation to the allowance of powder from the Ord-
" nance, which they alledge is abated on account of the
" detachment of six hundred men that were sent to Spain
" in the year 1704, I am therefore to acquaint you, that
" since the said detachment was made, they have raised
" ten additional men to each company, and have lately
" thrown aside all their pikes, amounting to twelve in each
" company more, for fire-arms, which they have provided
" in lieu thereof: So that it is rather necessary they
" should have a larger allowance of powder, than that any

---

[1] See Appendix, No. 159.

The Contingent Bill of Wᵐ Swan, Quarter-Master of her Majesty's Coldstream regiment of Foot Guards, from the 25ᵗʰ Decʳ, 1706, to the 24ᵗʰ June, 1707.

|  | £. s. d. |
|---|---|
| For fetching ammunition for half a year . . . . | 3 10 0 |
| For labourers to load and unload, &c. . . . . | 0 6 0 |
| For warrants for the UNION COLOURS . . . . | 2 3 6 |
| For books, paper, standishes, penns, ink, &c. . . | 1 8 0 |
| For fetching arms from the Tower, &c. . . . . | 1 10 0 |
| For mending the windows of the several Guard-roomes, and mending the locks, &c. . . . . . | 1 16 0 |
| For mending the fire hearths, grates, tongs, shovells, &c. | 3 0 0 |
| In all | 13 13 0 |

This is a reasonable bill, which<br>it is necessary to be paid.

RICHᵈ HOLMES, Major.

[2] Also see Appendix, No. 158.

1707.   " deduction should be made from them on account of the
" said detachment of six hundred men sent to Spain.

"  I am, Gentlemen,

"  Your most humble servant,

"  H. St. John.

" To the Principal Officers of the Ordnance."

The opening of the campaign this year in Spain was
most unpropitious: Charles marched away with part of
the forces into Catalonia, leaving the Earl of Galway with
the remainder of the army.[1]   The English, Austrians,
and Portuguese, suffered dreadful privations; they were
constantly harassed by the enemy, and found considerable
difficulty in procuring supplies, and even necessaries, from
the exhausted state to which the greater part of Spain was
reduced.

On the return of Philip V. to his capital, Lewis XIV.
redoubled his efforts, and sent strong reinforcements to
Marshal Berwick.

April 6th.   In April, the Allies took the field, and destroyed the
(N.S.)
magazines at Claudete, Yela, and Montalegre.   Their
army amounted to about sixteen thousand men, under the
command of the Marquis das Minas, the Earl of Galway
being then second in command.   Afterwards, the troops
besieged the Castle of Villena, and having overcome every
April 14th.   obstacle, they suddenly broke up, and advanced in four
columns towards Almanza.

Voltaire, in his " Age of Lewis XIV.," speaking of the
English and their Allies, and of the hardships they un-
derwent during the campaign, before they came in contact
with the enemy, says " they were beaten piecemeal."

At the battle of Almanza their force was inferior [2] to that

---

[1] Bishop Burnet, vol. v, page 305.

[2] Return of the English forces in Spain, dated Jan[r] 8, 1707-8,

of the Duke of Berwick.  The two armies were formed   1707.
April 25th
(N.S.)

presented to the House of Commons by M$^r$. Secretary S$^t$ John in
the months of January and February, 1707-8.

### ENGLISH FORCES AT THE BATTLE OF ALMANZA.

| HORSE. | Squad$^s$. | FOOT. | Batt$^s$. |
|---|---|---|---|
| Harvey's Horse . . | 2 | Battalion of Guards . | 1 |
| Carpenter's Dragoons | 1 | Portmore's . . | 1 |
| Essex's do. . . | 1 | Southwell's . . | 1 |
| Killegrew's do. . . | 1 | Stuart's . . . | 1 |
| Pearce's do. . . | 1 | Hill's . . . | 1 |
| Peterborow's do. . | 2 | Blood's . . . | 1 |
| The French reg$^t$ . | 1 | Mountjoy's . . | 1 |
|  | * 10 | Allnut's . . . | 1 |
|  |  | George's . . . | 1 |
|  |  | Mordaunt's . . | 1 |
|  |  | Wade's . . . | 1 |
|  |  | Bowles's . . . | 1 |
|  |  | Macartney's . . | 1 |
|  |  | Breton's . . . | 1 |
|  |  | Mark Kerr's . . | 1 |
|  |  | Nassau . . . | 1 |
|  |  |  | 16 |

* There appears to
be some error, as the
squadrons above only
amount to 9.

### IN CATALONIA, AND OTHER PARTS OF SPAIN.

| | Squads. |
|---|---|
| Royal Dragoons . | 2 |

| | Batt$^s$. | |
|---|---|---|
| Royal reg$^t$ of Fuziliers | 1 | Not reckoning Montandre's, |
| Hotham's . . . | 1 | made prisoners before the bat- |
| Sibourg's . . . | 1 | tle, besides three detachments |
| Blosset's . . . | 1 | of Marines at Girone, Alicant, |
| Elliot's . . . | 1 | and Tortosa. |
| Watkins's . . . | 1 | |
| | 6 | |

Number at the battle.     Men.
10 squadrons, at 80 men each . . 800
16 battalions, at 300 men each . . 4800
Total 5600

Besides fifty men of each of these regiments which were on

in line, and the battle commenced about three o'clock
P.M.    The left of the Confederates was, after a most
gallant resistance, overpowered.    The centre, consisting of
the chosen troops from England and Holland, drove the
enemy's first line on their second, and threw them into
disorder.    The Portuguese cavalry were seized with a
panic, and their infantry took to flight.    In consequence
of this disaster, the English and Dutch, being left without support, were out-flanked and surrounded.    These
brave men then formed into square, and retired from the
field.[1]    But being destitute of provisions, abandoned by

---

party, and at the blockade of the Castle of Montesa, not including
the sick in hospitalls.

The whole 12 squadrons above mentioned, according
   to the establishment, would make 160 men in each,
   but computed at 80 effective men each, of which
   they were reckoned to consist, amount to   .   .  960 Horse.
The whole 22 battalions above-mentioned, according
   to the establishment, would make 550 men each,
   one with another, but computed only at 350 each, of
   which they were reckoned to consist, amount to .   7700 Foot.
                                                             ⎯⎯⎯
                                             Total 8660

   At the battle.    Four Dutch squadrons at 80 effective men each.
and 7 battalions not exceeding 250 effective men each. — Extracted
from the Military Correspondence, State-Paper Office.

   [1] " To bring the Lord Gallway to a battle in a place most com-
" modious for his purpose, the Duke" (of Berwick) " made use of
" this stratagem : he ordered two Irishmen, both officers, to make
" their way over to the enemy as deserters ; putting this story in
" their mouths — that the Duke of Orleans was in a full march to
" join the Duke of Berwick with twelve thousand men ; that
" this would be done in two days, and that then they would find
" out the Lord Galway, and force him to fight wherever they found
" him.    Lord Galway, who at this time lay before Villena, receiv-
" ing this intelligence from those well-instructed deserters, im-

the cavalry, and cut off from all hope of supplies, thirteen    1707.<br>April 25th.<br>(N.S.) battalions soon after surrendered themselves prisoners of war.[1]

---

" mediately raised the siege, with a resolution, by a hasty march,
" to force the enemy to battle before the Duke of Orleans
" should be able to join the Duke of Berwick.   To effect this,
" after a hard march of three long Spanish leagues, in the
" heat of the day, he appears, a little after noon, in the face of the
" enemy with his fatigued forces.   Glad and rejoyced at the sight,
" for he found his plot had taken; Berwick, the better to deceive
" him, draws up his army in a half moon, placing at a pretty good
" advance three regiments to make up the centre, with express or-
" ders, nevertheless, to retreat at the very first charge.   All which
" was punctually observed, and had its desired effect ; for the three
" regiments at the first attack gave way, and seemingly fled
" towards their camp ; the English, after their customary manner,
" pursuing them with shouts and hallowings!   As soon as the
" Duke of Berwick perceived his trap had taken, he ordered his
" right and left wings to close ; by which means he at once cut
" off from the rest of their army all those who had so eagerly
" pursued the imaginary runaways.   In short, the rout was total,
" and the most fatal blow that ever the English received during the
" whole war with Spain.   Nor, as it is thought, with a great proba-
" bility of reason, had those troops that made their retreat to
" the top of the hills, under M. Gen¹ Shrimpton, met with any bet-
" ter fate than those on the plain, had the Spaniards had any other
" general in the command than the D. of Berwick, whose native
" sympathy gave a check to the ardour of a victorious enemy.
    " The day after this fatal battle, (which gave occasion to a Spa-
" nish piece of wit, that the English General had routed the French,)
" the Duke of Orleans did arrive indeed in the camp, but with an
" army of only fourteen attendants."—*Carleton's Memoirs*, page 208.
    [1] " M. Gen¹ Shrimpton, Brig^r Mackartney, Col. Britton, Col.
" Hill, and several other officers, assembled the broken remains
" of the English regiments, and joined some of the Dutch and Por-
" tuguese Infantry ; and this body, to the number of about 4000
" men, retreated about two leagues, to the hills of Claudete.   The
" next morning the Comm^r Officers agreed to the same capit^n as was

The Portuguese, and part of the English horse, with the infantry that guarded the baggage, retreated to Meira, where they were joined by the Earl of Galway, with about two thousand five hundred dragoons, which he had brought from the field of battle.    Three thousand men of the Allied army were killed; among them was Brigadier-General Killigrew, with many officers of distinction. The Earl of Galway and the Marquis das Minas were wounded.    The Allies were totally defeated; they lost ten thousand men, with their artillery and colours.    This was principally owing to the cowardice of the Portuguese troops, who fled on the first onset.[1]    Lord Tyrawley, Lord Mark Ker, and Colonel Clayton, were wounded:    The

---

" granted to the French at Blenheim, and surrendered themselves
" prisoners to the Count d'Asfelt.

  " Brigʳ Killegrew was wounded and afterᵈˢ killed in a second
" charge; Lt.-Col. Roper (of Major-General Harvey's), Lt.-Col.
" Lawrence (of Brigʳ Carpenter's), Lt.-Col. Dormer (of the Earl
" of Essex's), Lt.-Col. Deloches (of Col. Pierce's), and Lt.-Col.
" Green (of the Lord Peterborough's), were killed at the head of
" their respective squadrons; and Col. Pierce and Mʳ Hara (son
' to the Lord Tyrawley) were wounded.  Of the Foot, Lt.-Col.
" Austin (of the First Gᵈˢ), Lt.-Col. Mᶜ Neal (of Southwell's), Lt.-
" Col. Woollet and Lt.-Col. Withers (of Blood's), Lt.-Col. Ram-
" sey (of Mackartney's), Lt.-Col. Arskin (of Mark Kerr's), were
" among the slain.  Lord Mark Kerr and Col. Clayton were
" wounded." Battle of Almanza (25 April, N.S. 1707.)—*History of the Late War in the Netherlands*, by Thomas Brodrick, 8vo. London, 1713, page 194.

  [1] The House of Commons, early in the year 1711, passed a vote of censure on the late administration for the negligent manner in which the war in Spain had been conducted.  The House also strongly censured the Earl of Galway for yielding the right of the line to the Portuguese at the battle of Almanza; it was asserted, that in so doing he had acted in a manner derogatory to the ho-nour of the Crown of England.

Guards, under the command of Colonel Andrew Bissett   1707. of the Coldstream, suffered severely.[1] Lieutenant-Colonel Edward Austin and Captain Peachy of the First Guards, were killed. Major-General Shrimpton, Lieutenant-Colonel Philip Talhor, Captains Henry Poulteney, — Saubergue, Ensigns Thomas Poulteney and Fogg, of the First: Lieutenant-Colonels Cornelius Swan, Francis Scawen, and Captain William Bradbury, of the Coldstream; and Ensign Hamilton[2] and Adjutant Mullins, surrendered themselves prisoners.

After the battle of Almanza, the companies at home, September. from which the battalion of Guards had been formed, were newly recruited. This defeat was followed by the fall of Lerida; and the Earl of Galway embarked for Lisbon.

Colonel Hook, an adherent of the Chevalier St. George, was sent from France to ascertain whether the Pretender's

---

[1] Lieutenant-Colonel Andrew Bissett, in a memorial to the Treasury, in the year 1709, states, he was Commander-in-Chief of the battalion of Guards at the battle of Almanza, and by his post obliged to take under his care the deceased Lieut.-Colonel Austin's and Lieut.-Colonel Wakelyn's companies, and make up their accounts, &c. That he put 400 guineas on board one of his Majesty's ships to enable him to recruit these companies at his arrival in England, and afterwards on board the Admiral's Sir Cloudesley Shovell's ship " Association," which was lost on the rocks called the " Bishop and Clark's," off Scilly, on the 22nd of October, 1707. —War-Office Report Book, 1709.

Extract of a Letter, dated 22nd of July, 1712, from Sir William Wyndham, Bart. Secretary at War.

" The next vacant colours in the Coldstream Guards to be dis- " posed of towards relieving Brigadier Bissett, on account of the " loss of four hundred guineas on board the Association when she " was cast away, coming home from Spain."

[2] It is doubtful to which regiment these two officers belonged.

friends in Scotland were sufficiently numerous and willing
to receive him.   On his return, he made so favourable a
report, that Lewis the Fourteenth was induced to attempt
the restoration of the Pretender.   The French armament,
after some delay, appeared off the coast; but, not finding
the preconcerted signals answered, returned again to
Dunkirk.

1708.<br>March.    A battalion of English Guards, drawn from the First
and Coldstream, was ordered to Scotland in consequence
of the threatened invasion, the Pretender having entered
the Frith of Forth.   After his departure, the Guards, who
had reached York, were countermanded, and sent to
Colchester.[1]   This battalion, including the four com-

---

[1] The Contingent Bill for the march of the battalion of Foot
Guards, according to the several routes, commencing March the
15th, 1707-8.

|  | £. | s. | d. |
|---|---|---|---|
| For 12 carriages from London to Barnett, 10 miles; to St Albans, 10; to Dunstable, 10; to Stony Stratford, 14; to Northampton, 10; to Harborough, 12; to Leicester, 12; to Loughborough, 8; to Nottingham, 9; to Mansfield, 12; to Bautree, 16; to Doncaster, 6; to Pontefract, 10; to Tadcaster, 10; to York, 8; in all 157 miles    .    .    .    .    .    .    .    . | 62 | 16 | 0 |
| For ditto, from York to Tadcaster, 8; to Pontefract, 10; Doncaster, 10; to Bautree, 6; to Worksop, 8; to Mansfield, 8; to Nottingham, 12; in all 62 miles    . | 24 | 16 | 0 |
| For ditto, from Nottingham to Loughborough, 9; to Leicester, 8; to Harborough, 12; to Northampton, 12; to Bedford, 15; to Bigleswade, 7; to Royston, 9; to Walden, 10; to Bradfield, 10; to Coggeshall, 12; to Colchester, 8; in all 112 miles    .    .    .    . | 44 | 16 | 0 |
| For fire, and candle, and straw for the Guards, 52 days | 15 | 12 | 0 |

£.  148   0  0

W<sup>m</sup> Stevenage,
Capt<sup>n</sup> and L<sup>t</sup>-Col. Colds<sup>m</sup>.

panies of the Coldstream which had marched to York,
and Lieutenant-Colonels Rivett's and Bethell's companies, which were added, embarked and sailed on the
twenty-first of May for Flanders.[1]　Brigadier Brad-

| FIRST FOOT GUARDS. | | COLDSTREAM. | |
|---|---|---|---|
| 5 Captains | | 4 Captains | |
| 5 Lieutenants | | 4 Lieutenants | |
| 5 Ensigns | Marched to York. | 4 Ensigns | Marched to York. |
| 13 Serjeants | | 13 Serjeants | |
| 16 Corporals | | 13 Corporals | |
| 10 Drummers | | 9 Drummers | |
| 364 Private Soldiers | | 300 Private Men | |

—Official Records, War-Office.

Contingent Disbursmᵗˢ made for the Detachmᵗ of 124 men and
officers proportionable of the Foot Guards from London to Colchester.—May, 1708.

|  | £. | s. | d. |
|---|---|---|---|
| For three carriages for the private men and officers' baggage from London to Colchester, at 8ᵈ p. mile, 44 miles | 4 | 8 | 0 |
| For the march of the whole battalion from Colchester to Harwich, 12 waggons, 18 miles . . . . . | 7 | 4 | 0 |
| For five waggons for carrying the cloaths, ammunition, and tents of this detachment from London to Colchester, 44 miles . . . . . . | 7 | 5 | 8 |
| For fire and candle for the battalion for 16 days, and straw, at 3s. a day . . . . . . | 2 | 8 | 0 |
| For the poundage of the last Bill . . . . . | 7 | 8 | 0 |
|  | 28 | 13 | 8 |

To the truth of the above particulars I hereby subscribe my hand,
and do desire the money may be paid to my serjeant, Alexander
Clealand,

A. WHELER,
(Capt. and Lᵗ-Col. 1ˢᵗ Foot Guards.)
—Official Records, War-Office.

[1]　SIR,　　　　　　　Whitehall, 4ᵗʰ June, 1708.
The number of men sent over, drafted out of the Guards,
with their commission and non-commission officers, are as follows:

dock,[1] of the Coldstream, ought to have commanded, but was ordered by the Duke of Marlborough to remain in England, being senior in rank to Colonel Gorsuch,[2]

---

9 captains, 11 lieutenants, 8 ensigns, adjutant, chyrurgeon, 30 serjeants, 30 corporals, 20 drummers, and 620 private men.

This is the account Brigadier Holmes has given me.

I am, Sir,

To Mr. Sloper.            Your most humble servant,
(Deputy Paymaster-General.)        JAMES TAYLOR,
                (Chief Clerk to the Secretary at War.)

" The convoy and transports from Harwich, having on board a " battalion of her Majesty's Guards and two regiments of foot, ar" rived the 1st inst" (June N.S.) "at Ostend ; the men landed the " next day and marched to Bruges, where boats were ready to trans" port them to Ghent, from whence, after a few days rest, they are " to march to the army.

" Major Gen' Murray continues " (June 21 N.S.) "with the " detachment near Ghent, from whence the battalion of British " Guards is, by the Duke of Marlborough's orders, now on the " march to join the army."—*London Gazettes*, Nos. 4440 and 4445, May and June, 1708.

[1]    SIR,            Whitehall, 17th May, 1708.

I am sorry to be the author of such unwelcome news to you, because of the respect I have to you: I am to acquaint you, in the absence of the Secretary at War, with his Grace the Duke of Marlborough's pleasure, signified by Mr Cardonnel, that no officer of the Guards older in commission than Colonel Gorsuch is to embark for Ostend with the battalion of Guards. Your service therefore is not expected on the other side the water, where they have already more brigadiers than brigades of foot.

I am ever, with great sincerity, Sir,
                Yours, &c.
                JAMES TAYLOR.

To Brigadier Braddock,
    (Coldstream Guards.)

[2] Colonel Gorsuch was wounded at Ghent, 24th Dec. N.S. 1708, and died soon after.

of the First Guards, " who had been at the head of the battalion of Guards in Flanders for four years together."

The French King was not more successful in Flanders than he had been in his projected invasion of Scotland. On the Continent his generals no longer triumphed;— they had to contend with Marlborough.

At Oudenarde the Duke de Vendome was attacked by Marlborough and Prince Eugene. Cadogan advanced with sixteen battalions and eight squadrons. Four battalions of English infantry first forded the rivulet near Eyne,[1] broke the enemy's line, and made three battalions prisoners : the cavalry, unable to pass the marshy rivulet, turned the village. The Hanoverians then moved forward, supported by several squadrons, on the plain of Heurne. The enemy's cavalry, endeavouring to retire, were overtaken, routed, and driven across the Norken. Here "the Prince Electorate[2] of Hanover," with the characteristic courage of the House of Brunswick, having placed himself at the head of a squadron of Bulow's cavalry, charged the enemy, and had his horse killed under him. Colonel Laschky was shot by his side. More than a hundred general officers were in the field. Two hundred and fifty colonels led their respective battalions into action.[3] The French in numbers greatly exceeded the Allies, but from the commencement of the battle, even before their right began to waver, confusion and trepidation were visible in their ranks. Notwithstanding the efforts of the Duke de Vendome, they continued to lose ground ; some regiments were entirely broken, and whole

---

[1] At which place it runs into the Scheld. Eyne is about half a league from Oudenarde.

[2] Afterwards George II., who was in the habit of calling on all great occasions for his " Oudenarde sword."

[3] Voltaire.

ranks threw down their arms.   Darkness alone saved the French army from destruction; they retreated towards Ghent during the night, and finally encamped at Lovendegen.

The Princes of Orange and Oxenstiern, who advanced at the head of the Dutch infantry, on finding the enemy had abandoned the hill, changed position to the right, and formed in a semicircle; on which the French retired in the greatest confusion.   " If the night had not inter-
" vened, the French must inevitably have been destroyed;
" dismay succeeded error, and the army retreated in dis-
" order to Ghent, Tournay, and Ypres." [1]   Sir John Mathew and Captain Dean, of the First Guards, were killed.[2]

To the astonishment of Europe, Lisle was besieged.[3] This place contained the Duke of Burgundy's army, which having been reinforced with Count La Motte's corps, equalled in numbers the joint forces of Marlborough and Eugene.   Marshal Boufflers at length capi-
Oct. 25th. tulated, and the town was given up, after a siege of sixty-two days.

The route to Paris, by the capture of Lisle, was left nearly open; and it is said that a party of Dutch troops advanced from Courtray, and carried off the King's first equerry from under the windows of the palace of Versailles.

Dec. 24th. The battalion of Guards were engaged at the attack on
(N.S.) opening the trenches before Ghent.   Colonel Gorsuch, of the First, who commanded, died shortly after of his wounds.   The town surrendered, and the garrison marched

---

[1]  Voltaire.

[2]  See engraved medal κ.

[3]  Invested August 13th.   The trenches opened on the night of the 22nd (N.S.), 1708.

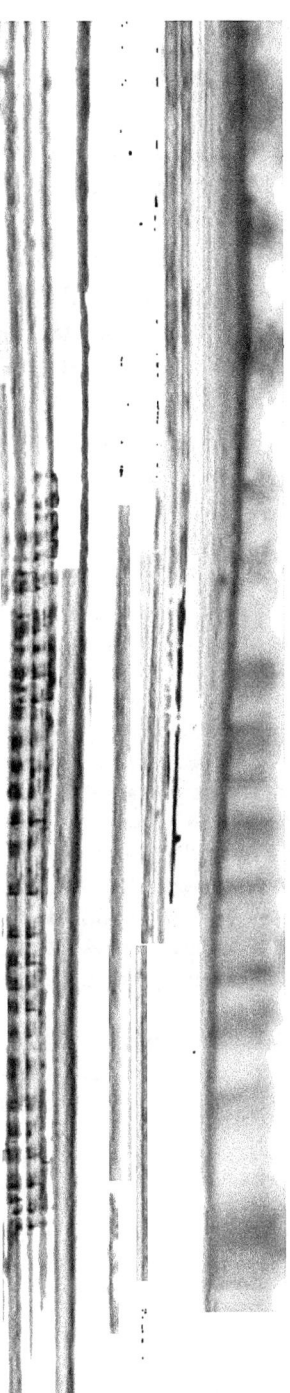

out on the second of January, when the British occupied 1708.
the place as their winter-quarters.

The Duke of Marlborough, on entering Brussels, was
received with the greatest enthusiasm. In this city the
Guards were stationed during the winter.

France was humbled; her soldiers were disheartened
by the heavy losses they had sustained in the last campaign, and the unusual severity of the winter increased
their misery.[1] Lewis the Fourteenth, reduced to extremities, made fresh advances to obtain peace. The scarcity
of provisions in France was so great, that forty-five millions of livres were laid out on supplies for the French
army. This was a heavy expenditure, as the revenue of
Lewis the Fourteenth scarcely ever exceeded two hundred
and twenty millions.

---

[1] Hague, 15th Jan. 1708-9.
"Sir, I was heartily glad to receive yours of the 22d
"past, in hopes you may soon be abroad again, but I hope you
"have been better advised than to stirr abroad this extreme cold
"weather, the most severe that has been known in this country for
"many years; the poor soldiers and other poor people freese to
"death like rotten sheep; every four words, tho' I burn by a great
"fire, I am obliged to unthaw my pen. The beginning of the next
"week my Lord Duke proposes to return to Brussells for a month
"or six weeks longer, so that I have a long campagne still before I
"see my friends in England.
"I am ever, Sir,
"Your most faithful and most obedient servant,
"Ad Cardonnel." •

"To Mr Tilson." †

—Military Correspondence, State-Paper Office.

• Cardonnel was the confidential secretary to the Duke of Marlborough, and the ancestor of the Lord Dynevor.

† Tilson was secretary to Mr. Secretary Boyle.

1708.    The Guards were brigaded with four regiments of the line, under General Primrose.

A board of general officers assembled to determine on the different counties in which regiments were to recruit. The household infantry were restricted to Middlesex, including London.

# CHAPTER XXI.

Tournay surrenders — Villars and Boufflers oppose the investment of Mons—Strength of hostile armies—Battle of Malplaquet—Cardonnel's letter—Capitulation of Mons—Both armies go into winter-quarters—First and Coldstream at the Hague—Strength of the Allies—Eugene and Marlborough move from the vicinity of Tournay—Enemy's line forced at Pont-à-Vendin—Villars reconnoitres the allied position—Aire and St. Venant taken—Marlborough returns to England.

THE citadel[1] of Tournay having surrendered at discretion, Marlborough and Eugene resolved on the conquest of Mons. Marshal Villars advanced with Marshal Boufflers to oppose the investment. The Allies met and attacked them near the road to Blangiers and the village of Malplaquet.

1709.

The hostile armies amounted to about ninety thousand men each:[2] the Confederates had the superiority in artil-

---

[1] Tournay capitulated on the 28th of July; the citadel on the 3rd of September.

[2] Voltaire says eighty thousand each; Smollett, one hundred and twenty thousand each. Coxe makes the Confederates amount " on " the day of battle to 129 battalions and 252 squadrons, with 101 " pieces of cannon and four mortars, being a numerical force of " about 93,300 men. From every rational estimate the numbers on " both sides appear to have been nearly equal."

1709.    lery. Marlborough commanded the centre and left[1] of
the army, consisting of English and German troops in the
pay of England. Prince Eugene commanded the right.
Marshal Villars led the left wing, and Boufflers[2] the
right of the French army. The ground occupied by the
French, naturally strong, had been made still more so by
triple intrenchments; trees were cut down and laid across
each other, abbatis were constructed, and palisades formed,
so as to render the position almost impregnable. Their
right was posted in the wood of Laniere, in front of Malplaquet; their left behind the wood of Taisniere and
Sart.[3]

Sept. 11th.   At three o'clock in the morning divine service was
(N.8.)    performed in the Allied camp; perfect order and tranquillity prevailed, as if merely a review had been anticipated. The French soldiers exhibited a feeling of great
excitement, very unlike the steadiness of the English.
When Villars that morning appeared before his troops, he
was received with shouts of " Vive le Maréchal Villars !"
" Vive le Roi !" and similar cries. The French, though
they had been scantily supplied with rations, threw away
part of their bread, so eager were they to begin the action.

In consequence of a fog, the battle did not commence
till about eight o'clock; this circumstance enabled the
Allies to throw up batteries on their centre and flanks.
The Prince of Orange and Count Lottum first advanced
with two strong columns. When they had reached their
stations, Schulemberg, with forty battalions, moved forward in three lines along the road to Sart, directly
on the enemy's left. Count Lottum supported the at-

---

[1] Voltaire says Marlborough commanded the right wing.

[2] Boufflers was senior to Villars, but requested to serve under
him.—*Voltaire.*

[3] Life of Marlborough, by Thomas Lediard, 8vo. London, 1736.
Vol. II. page 490.

K.

tack with vigour; and in two hours, notwithstanding the numerous obstacles that presented themselves, the enemy were driven from their intrenchments into the woods of Sart and Taisniere. The Prince of Orange again attacked the enemy's right, covered with three intrenchments, in the wood of Laniere; at this point there was great carnage, and extraordinary bravery was displayed on both sides. Count Lottum's troops were conducted steadily by Marlborough, through a swampy ground, under heavy volleys from the Brigade du Roi. The French, particularly the brigades of Picardie and la Marine, evinced great courage. Marshal Boufflers charged at the head of the Gens-d'armes; he also led on the Garde-du-Corps, the Mousquetaires, and Horse Grenadiers: these troops broke through the two first lines of the Allies, and threw the third into disorder, when this small force found itself between a cross fire from the infantry, at the same time that it was charged by a large body of cavalry brought up under Prince Eugene.[1] At length the French left and centre gave way, and Marshal Villars being wounded and taken off the field, they commenced their retreat. It has been said that Legal,[2] without the knowledge of Boufflers, withdrew with his cavalry and fifty battalions under Puysegur.

The enemy retired in good order towards Bavay,[3] Quenoy, Maubeuge, Valenciennes, and Condé, leaving the Allies in possession of the field, sixteen of their cannon, twenty colours, and twenty-six standards.[4] " Four

---

[1] About four in the afternoon Schulemberg broke in on their left. —*Parker's Memoirs*, page 162.

[2] Afterwards known as Marshal Montesquiou.—*Dict. de la Noblesse Française*.

[3] The right to Bavay, the left to Quievrain.

[4] London Gazette, No. 4595.

hundred officers, eighty of whom were of the household of France, were taken prisoners."

Marshal Boufflers wrote the following dispatch to Lewis the Fourteenth after the loss of the battle.

"It is with the greatest grief, Sire, that I am unfor-
"tunately obliged to send you the account of the loss of
"another battle; but I can assure your Majesty no mis-
"fortune was ever attended with greater glory. Your
"Majesty's troops have all acquired the greatest reputa-
"tion, as well for their valour as for their firmness and
"obstinacy, and only yielded at last to the superiority
"of the enemy, having performed wonders. The arrange-
"ments of Marshal Villars were excellent, the best that
"could be made by the most able, accomplished, and
"experienced general. He conducted himself throughout
"the action with the most intrepid bravery, besides setting
"a noble example; his great valour and want of precau-
"tion occasioned his wound, which was most prejudicial
"to the affair of this unfortunate day. He honored me
"with the command of the right wing, taking charge
"himself of the left, where he was much wanted. The
"enemy marched a large force of horse and foot against
"the centre, at which point there was only horse to
"oppose them; so that we were compelled to yield to the
"infinitely superior number and prodigious efforts of the
"enemy: after having charged them, at least six times,
"with the greatest vigour, we pushed and broke two or
"three of the enemy's lines. I can assure your Majesty
"the enemy's loss is three times greater than ours, and
"that they can make no other advantage of this unfor-
"tunate action, than to occupy the field of battle, and
"this reverse will not cost you an inch of ground. M.
"D'Artagnan, who commanded the right wing of the

" infantry, greatly distinguished himself; the Duke de
" Guiche also behaved with great skill and bravery.  M.
" Gaison performed prodigies at the head of your Ma-
" jesty's household.  The Prince de Rohan and M. de
" Vidame did all that valour could effect.  The gendar-
" merie performed wonders, the cavalry behaved ex-
" tremely well, and greatly distinguished themselves.  No
" retreat was ever conducted, after so long, bloody, and
" obstinate a fight, with more firmness and order.  The
" enemy followed in battalia and good order as far as the
" defile of Givri, but it was with respect; they dared
" not attack us."

The Allies lost twenty thousand men; the loss of the
French was estimated at five hundred and forty officers
killed, one thousand and sixty-eight officers wounded, and
three hundred and one officers taken : fifteen thousand of
their men were killed, wounded, and made prisoners.[1]  In
this action the First and Coldstream Guards were posted
on the right of the centre of the first line.  Lieutenant-
Colonels Edmond Rivett, Robert Bethell, John Arundel,
and Captain John Phillips of the Coldstream, also Captain James Gould of the First Guards, were killed.[2]

---

[1] History of the Late War in the Netherlands, by Thomas Brodrick, 8vo. London, 1713, page 312.

[2] See Appendix, No. 167, and London Gazettes, Nos. 4594,
4595, containing the names of many other officers of the army.

The following letter is from Serjeant Hall, of the battalion serving under the Duke of Marlborough, to his comrade, Serjeant
Gabe, of the Coldstream Guards.

" From the Camp before Mons, Sept[r] 26[th].
" COMRADE,

" I received yours, and am glad yourself and wife are in good
" health, with all the rest of my friends.

" Our battalion suffered more than I could wish in the action.

Among the wounded was Ensign Chudleigh: there were, however, two officers of the same name and rank in the First and Coldstream.

---

" But who can withstand fate? Poor Richard Stevenson had his
" fate, with a great many more. He was killed dead before we
" entered the trenches. We had above two hundred of our batta-
" lion killed and wounded. We lost ten serjeants, six are as
" followeth: Jennings, Castles, Roach, Sherring, Meyrick, and my
" son Smith; the rest are not of your acquaintance. I have re-
" ceived a very bad shot in my head myself, but am in hopes,
" an't please God, I shall recover. I continue in the field, and lie
" in my colonel's quarters. Arthur is very well, but I can give
" you no account of Elms; he was in the hospital before I came
" into the field. I will not pretend to give you an account of
" the battle, knowing you have a better in the prints. Pray give
" my service to M$^n$ Cook and her daughter, to M$^r$ Stoffet and his
" wife, and to M$^r$ Lyver, and Thomas Hodsdon, and to M$^r$
" Rogdell, and to all my friends and acquaintance in general
" who do ask after me. My love to M$^n$ Stevenson. I am sorry
" for the sending such ill news. Her husband was gathering a
" little money together to send to his wife, and put it into my
" hands. I have seven shillings and three-pence, which I shall take
" care to send her. Wishing your wife a safe delivery, and
" both of you all happiness, rest
" Your assured friend and comrade,
" JOHN HALL."
" We had but an indifferent breakfast, but the Mounseers never
" had such a dinner in their lives.
" My kind love to my Cousin Hinton, and M$^n$ Morgan, and to
" John Brown and his wife. I sent two shillings, and Stevenson six-
" pence, to drink with you at M$^r$ Cook's; but I have heard no-
" thing from him: it was by M$^r$ Edgar. Corporal Hartwell desires
" to be remembered to you, and desires you to enquire of Edgar
" what is become of his wife Pegg, and, when you write, to send
" word in your letter what trade she drives. We have here very
" bad weather, which I doubt not will be a hindrance to the siege;
" but I am in hopes we shall be masters of the town in a little time,
" and then I believe we shall go to garrison."—See Tatler, No. 87.
Oct. 29, 1709.

A letter from Mr. Cardonnel, written at this period, cor-
roborates the loss before alluded to.

                    " Camp at Havre, Sept<sup>r</sup> 26, 1709."

   " Sir,

   " We have no letters from yo<sup>r</sup> side to acknowledge;
" but we expect with impatience an acc<sup>t</sup> of Mr. Graham's
" reception, with the confirmation of our victory.  Yon
" have enclos'd a computation of what it cost us among
" our foot only, you will find it a very large one; but I
" hope it will lessen when the officers come to give in their
" lists upon oath; that of the horse is not yet perfected.
" 'Tis generally allow'd there was more men killed and
" wounded in this battle on both sides, then in those of
" Blenheim, Ramelies, and Audenarde, put together.

   " I send you likewise a relation of the action by a
" French officer of note, 'tis approv'd of here as a just and
" reasonable acc<sup>t</sup>.[1]  You will please to lay both these
" papers before Mr. Secr̄y.  I hope we shall be wiser
" then to make our loss publick, as they have done theirs
" in Holland.

                 " I am truly, S<sup>r</sup>,
                      " Your most faithfull and most
                        " humble Servant,
        (Signed)          " Ad. Cardonnel."[2]
   " M<sup>r</sup> Tilson,"
(Secretary to M<sup>r</sup> Secretary Boyle).


   Marlborough determined to besiege Mons, and entrusted
the direction of the operations to the young Prince of
Orange, who had greatly distinguished himself at the

---

[1] See Appendix, No. 167.
[2] Military Correspondence, State-Paper Office.

1709.

head of the Dutch infantry in the battle of Malplaquet. During the progress of the siege the right of the army was on the Haisne, and the left on the Sambre. After the capitulation[1] the hostile armies retired to their respective cantonments for the winter. Two squadrons of Dutch Horse Guards were sent to the Hague; the First and Coldstream with other English regiments were stationed at Brussels, Ghent, Tiel, and other places.

1710.
April.

Early in April the British auxiliaries under General Lumley left their quarters to prepare for the campaign.

On the seventeenth of April Marlborough, on his return from England, resumed the command at Ovrey, near Tournay. The right wing, under Prince Eugene, was composed of forty-five battalions and one hundred and one squadrons of horse; the left, under Marlborough's command, consisted of one hundred and ten battalions, with one hundred and sixty-one squadrons, and one hundred and two pieces of cannon.

At five o'clock in the afternoon of the twentieth, the army moved in two columns from the neighbourhood of Tournay, provided with three days' bread and forage. This movement was conducted with such order and rapidity that, notwithstanding the great preparations the enemy had made, their lines were forced at Pont-à-Vendin.

---

[1] " Camp at Havre, Oct. 10[th], 1709. — The disposition being " made for attacking the counterscarp of the hornwork at the port " de Havre, the same was put in execution the 8[th] inst., about 9 in " the morning, by 300 grenadiers and 400 fuziliers. We had " about threescore killed and wounded in this service ; among the " latter are Lieut.-Colonel Hara of the English, and Capt[n] Petit of " the Guards, who was shot through the arm, acting as engi- " neers."—Extract of a Letter from Mr. Cardonnel. Military Correspondence, State-Paper Office.

Villars afterwards crossed the little river Juncket, and passed Lens, where he encamped at midnight in a strong position between Douai and Bethune, with his right near Vitry, his left extending about three leagues to Gouage. Thus he was enabled completely to cover the siege of Douai.[1]

1710.
April.

The French commander had assembled two hundred and four battalions of infantry, three hundred and eight squadrons of cavalry, with ninety-six pieces of cannon, and sixteen mortars, besides howitzers. With this force he moved on Arras, crossed the Scarpe, and advanced towards Donai, intending to attack the Allies; but after reconnoitring their position, he retreated between Arras and Courtrai, with his right at Marquion.

Marlborough advanced towards Aubigny on the Scarpe, above Arras; and on the twenty-third of July laid siege to Bethune, 'which surrendered on the thirty-first of August.

June 10th.

The Allies manœuvred between Aire and St. Venant, both of which places were invested and taken.

Marlborough quitted the army for the Hague, and returned to England.

The Allies dispersed into quarters for the winter. General Lumley and part of the British troops were stationed at Ghent.

The French also retired to winter-quarters.

---

[1] John Millner's Journal, 8vo. London, 1733, page 289. Lediard's Life of Marlborough, 8vo. London, 1736. Vol. iii. page 30.

# CHAPTER XXII.

Two additional companies of the Coldstream sent to Harwich—
Detachment countermanded, from the difficulty of providing for
the Tower duty—Second-Major first appointed to the Coldstream—Allies concentrate—French lines, styled the " Ne plus
Ultra of Marlborough," forced—Ormond succeeds Marlborough
in command of the army—British encamp at Besieux—Ormond
publishes a suspension of hostilities—British retire—Winter-
quarters at Ghent — Ormond returns to England — Lumley left
in command—Treaty of Utrecht—British take possession of Dunkirk—Death of Queen Anne—Elector of Hanover ascends the
throne—Death of Churchill—Cadogan appointed Colonel of the
Coldstream—Guards encamp in Hyde Park—The Chevalier St.
George lands in Scotland—Flight of the Pretender—King George
embarks at Gravesend—Hostilities recommence with Spain—
Pretender received as King at Madrid—Ormond sails from Cadiz—Fleet dispersed—Two frigates only reach Scotland—Spanish troops lay down their arms—Seven companies of the Coldstream embark for Corunna — Expedition attacks and takes Vigo
—Rates paid for commissions—Duke of Grafton purchases Colonel John Russell's commission—Scarborough appointed Colonel
of the Coldstream—Services of Cadogan—Coldstream encamp
in Hyde Park — Death of George I. — Coldstream attend the
coronation of George II.—Roaster of the brigade of Guards—
Duke of Cumberland appointed Colonel of the Coldstream,
removed to the First Guards, and succeeded by the Duke of
Marlborough.

1711.   Mr. Granville, Secretary at War, in a letter to Mr.
February. Secretary St. John, dated sixteenth of February, says,
" Lieut.-General Withers has represented that it has been

" proposed for the good of the service, that two companies
" more of the Coldstream Guards should be sent to Flan-
" ders, in addition to the six companies already there, and
" in proportion to the number of companies furnished by
" the First Foot Guards, whereby the Guards in Flanders
" should be able to form three entire battalions."[1]   An
order was issued for "two complete companies of the
" Coldstream" to march to Harwich.[2]   The detachment,

---

[1] Military Correspondence, State-Paper Office.

At this time two battalions of the First Guards, consisting
of sixteen companies, served in Flanders, and the addition of the
Coldstream companies was proposed, that " three equal battalions
" might be formed, and the duty between them more regularly
" performed."—Military Correspondence, State-Paper Office.

[2]          SIR,                         Whitehall, 25 April, 1711.
I am commanded to acquaint you that it is her Majesty's pleasure, the two companies of the Coldstream Guards should proceed to Flanders according to her Majesty's former orders.
                         I am,

Inclosed is a Route, in              Sir,
    case the companies         Your most humble servant,
    march by land.                     G. GRANVILLE.
To Major Gen¹ Braddock.

     " ANNE R.
     " Our will and pleasure is, that you cause two compleat compa-
" nies of our Coldstream regiment of Foot Guards, under your
" command, to march from hence (according to the route annexed)
" to Harwich, where they are to embark on board the pacquet
" boats in order to joyn the other companies of the Guards, and to
" serve therewith, this ensuing campaigne, in Flanders; and upon
" their landing on the other side, the commanding officer is to give
" immediate notice thereof to our right trusty and right entire-
" ly beloved cousin and councillor, John Duke of Marlborough,
" our captain-general of our forces, for his further orders.   And

1711.  however, went by water, and remained there a few days,
but was recalled in consequence of the difficulties ex-

---

" the officers, &c.  Given at our Court at S<sup>t</sup> James's, this 25<sup>th</sup> day
" of April, 1711.  In the tenth year of our reign.
   " By her Majesty's command,

                                        " G. GRANVILLE."

   " To our trusty and well-beloved
" Charles Churchill, Esq<sup>r</sup>, Gen<sup>l</sup> of
" our Foot forces, and Colonel of
" our Coldstream regiment of Foot Guards,
" or to the Officer in Chief with the said
" regiment."

          " Route for two companies of the Coldstream regiment of
             " Guards from London to Harwich :
          " Romford, Chelmsford.        " To rest the Sunday and
          " Witham, and Kelvedon.       " one day more on their
          " Colchester, Manningtree,    " march, as the officer in
          " and Harwich.                " chief shall see cause.
                                        " G. GRANVILLE."


          SIR,                    Whitehall, 3<sup>rd</sup> May, 1711.
   By M<sup>r</sup> Granville's direction I send this to acquaint you, that the
two companies of the Coldstream Guards are not to embark
for Flanders till further order from her Majesty.
                         I am, Sir,
                   Your most humble servant,
Major-Gen<sup>l</sup> Braddock.                    SAM. LYNN,
                                   (Chief Clerk, War-Office.)


          SIR,                    Whitehall, 10<sup>th</sup> May, 1711.
   I am directed by M<sup>r</sup> Granville to acquaint you, that it is her Ma-
jesty's pleasure the two companies of the Coldstream Guards do
return forthwith from Harwich to their former quarters in London.
                         I am, Sir,
                   Your most humble servant,
   To Col. Swan,                              SAM. LYNN.
   (Coldstream Guards.)

perienced in providing a sufficient number of men for the 1711.
Tower duty, there being at this period only twelve companies of the First and six of the Coldstream left in London. Brigadier Moryson, who commanded the companies
of the Coldstream in Flanders, and who was in England
on leave of absence, had intended to take charge of the
two companies, but returned to resume his command without them.

A Second-Major was appointed to the Coldstream at April 25th.
this period. Brigadier Henry Moryson was the first; his (O.S.)
commission was dated the twenty-fifth of April.[1]

Expended on account of the Detachm[t] of the Coldstream regiment
of Foot Guards that was ordered for Flanders :—

|  | £. s. d. |
|---|---|
| For the lighter that carried the men on board the hoy | 2 10 0 |
| For the passage of 125 men to Harwich, at 3s. p. man | 18 15 0 |
| For straw for the men to lye on | 0 12 0 |
| For small boats that landed the men at the fort | 0 10 0 |
| For boats that landed the cloathing | 0 15 0 |
| For 2 carts to carry the cloathing to the colonel's quarters | 0 8 0 |
| For carrying the cloathing to Harwich | 2 0 0 |
| For the hoy that brought us from Harwich | 18 15 0 |
| For 2 carts to carry the cloathing on board | 0 8 0 |
| For bringing home the cloathing | 2 0 0 |
| For 2 boats to carry the cloathing on board | 0 15 0 |
| For small boats to put the men on board | 0 10 0 |
| For straw for the men to lye on | 0 12 0 |
|  | £48 10 0 |

> This is a reasonable bill, and what hath been justly
> disbursed by Capt. Parsons, Quar. Mast[r] of the
> Coldstream regiment of Guards.
>
> RICH. HOLMES, Major.

—War-Office Records.

[1] In a memorial to the Treasury, dated 16th of February,

The Duke of Marlborough returned to the Hague, and remained there some time to prepare for the ensuing campaign.

Marshal Villars intended to arrive on the twenty-fifth of April at Cambrai or Arras, where his army assembled.

The Allies concentrated between Douai and Valenciennes, to form a junction with the rest of their troops. Prince Eugene, who had been detained at Vienna by the Emperor Joseph's death, was also expected. On the twenty-third Eugene arrived, and the troops being assembled, were placed as follows :—Prince Eugene commanded the left, consisting of sixty-five battalions of infantry, and one hundred and twenty squadrons. The right, under Marlborough's command, included one hundred and nineteen battalions, and two hundred and twenty-six squadrons of horse, with one hundred and nineteen guns and eight howitzers.

A party of the enemy's grenadiers, supported by four hundred horse, attempted to surprise the Allies in a position they occupied at the Convent of Vermy; but they were repulsed, with considerable loss, by three hundred men under the command of Lieutenant-Colonel Cholmley of the First Guards.

The enemy, strongly intrenched between Bouchain and Monchi le Preux, extended their lines along the Saussel and Scarpe to Arras, which continued by the Upper Scarpe

---

1711, it was represented " that at present there is no pay al-" lowed on the establishment for the Second-Major of the Cold-" stream Guards, and praying that Brigadier Henry Moryson, " whose commission as Second-Major is dated 25th of April, 1711, " may be allowed pay, as in the First Foot Guards and the Royal " regiment of Foot, viz. 8s. a day."—War-Office Report-Book.

to the Cânche; these were fortified by deep ditches, redoubts, and other works.

Marlborough threatened Villars's left, causing him to move within his lines in that direction. The English General was then confident that the passage of the Saussel by Arleux had been left unprotected, and ordered Generals Cadogan and Hompesch to cross on the night of the fourth of August, whilst he passed the Scarpe, and at day-break next morning hastened towards Arleux and Bac-a-bancheuil.

Marshal Villars, when acquainted with the manœuvre of the Confederates, decamped at two o'clock A. M., and moved with such rapidity that he came in sight of the Allies about eleven next day. The Duke, joined by Count Hompesch, passed the defile of Marquion. Villars, on perceiving Marlborough's horse drawn up to attack him, retreated behind a morass.

The French Marshal on this occasion was completely out-generalled: he had sent repeated assurances to Lewis XIV. that his lines were impregnable, and that such precautions had been taken that insult was out of the question. In one of his letters to the King he styles his defences the "Ne plus ultra of Marlborough."

Thus the French lines, of which so much boast had been made, were entered and passed without opposition. Marlborough is entitled to the greatest praise for this enterprise. The departure of Prince Eugene, who received orders from Vienna to move towards the Upper Rhine, had much weakened the Allies. The two armies only saw each other; neither the valour of the soldiers, nor the skill of the subordinate generals, nor the art of the engineers, was called into action: the credit of the achievement belonged alone to Marlborough.

On the evening of the sixth, the enemy passed the

Scheld at Crevecœur, and took post between Cambrai and Bouchain, to protect the siege of the latter town. Marlborough resolved to capture Bouchain, the garrison of which had been reinforced with six thousand men. He crossed the Scheld without opposition, and encamped on that river. General Fagel, at the same time, was detached to cover the siege on the left bank. The investment was completed on the tenth, and the trenches were opened on the night of the twenty-third. The river and the fortress divided the Confederates. The French army, consisting of one hundred thousand men, being " within gun-shot," great precaution was necessary to prevent the enemy from attacking the Confederates separately.

Marlborough's lines extended nearly seven miles, and those of General Fagel about five. Intrenchments were formed, forts erected, and a causeway made through a deep morass for about ten miles, that the convoys might avoid the light troops of the French army on the one side, and the garrisons of Valenciennes and Condé on the other.

Bouchain surrendered on the fourteenth of September.

When the fortifications injured in the siege were repaired, the Confederates retired to winter-quarters.[1]

---

[1] The French army separated on the 25th of October, and the Allies marched to their respective quarters on the 27th.—*London Gazette*, from Oct. 23rd to 25th.  No. 4917.

It appears Brussels was the winter-quarters of the Guards, as is shown by the following extract from two letters from Mr. T. Laws to Mr. Tilson.

" Brussels, 4ᵗʰ April, 1712."          " On the 31ˢᵗ past, Lieut.-
" General Withers arrived here from Gand, in order to pass in re-
" view the two battalions of his Majesty's Foot Guards, which
' having done on Saturday, he returned yesterday morning towards

The military career of the Duke of Marlborough terminated with the capture of Bouchain.

The Allies were in garrison along the frontier, and in
possession of the country from the Maese to the Scheld
and Tournay, with the navigable part of the Lys.
Spanish Guelderland, Limberg, Brabant, Flanders, and
almost the whole of Hainault, were theirs; they were
masters of the Scarpe: and had Marlborough continued
at the head of the Confederates, it is not too much to
conjecture, that the next campaign would have terminated
in France.

In proportion as the influence of the Duchess of Marlborough diminished, Queen Anne more readily listened to
the advice of those who were inclined to put an end to the
war.  The Queen, who was at length entirely alienated
from Marlborough, lent a willing ear to injurious reports,[1] and addressed a letter to him, in which she made
use of very strong reproaches, dismissing him from all his
employments.  The Duke attempted to vindicate his conduct, but was not attended to: his enemies triumphed,
his party was turned out, and the opponents of the illustrious warrior and statesman, to perpetuate their power
and secure themselves in the Upper House, advised their
Sovereign to create a number of new Peers,[2] more

---

" Brussels, April 14ᵗʰ, 1712."          " The two battalions of
" Foot Guards from hence, with the regiment of Cadogan, marched
" to-day to the general rendezvous." — Military Correspondence,
State-Paper Office.

[1] The Commissioners for Public Accounts discovered the Duke
of Marlborough had annually received five or six thousand pounds
for the contract of bread.—*Smollett*, vol. v. page 223.

[2] Lord Compton, Lord Bruce, Lord Duplin,(created Lord Hay),
Viscount Windsor (made Lord Mountjoy,) Baron Burton, Baron
Mansel, Baron Middleton, Baron Trevor, Baron Lansdowne, Ba-

distinguished for devotion to themselves than to the Crown.

1712.    Marlborough being removed from the command of the army, the Duke of Ormond was appointed to succeed him, with equal powers.    The season for commencing operations drawing near, the Duke of Ormond arrived at the Hague, whence he proceeded to Tournay, and joined

May 23rd.    Prince Eugene early in May.    The British were encamped at Besieux,[1] with an additional force of sixteen squadrons of auxiliaries in the pay of England.    It was resolved, at a council of war, to besiege Quesnoy, and the

June 7th.    armies passed the Selle.    The left of the right wing extended to Cateau-Cambresis; and the right wing of Prince Eugene to Haspre, with the river Selle along its front. General Fagel invested Quesnoy on the eighth; the trenches opened on the nineteenth; and on the fourth of July, the garrison, consisting of two thousand seven hundred, surrendered.

July.    The Confederates remained stationary till the sixteenth,

---

ron Marsham, Baron Foley, and Baron Bathurst: these gentlemen, upon being first introduced into the House, when the question was put about adjourning, the Earl of Wharton asked " whether they voted by their foreman."—*Smollett*, vol. II. page 224.

[1] Extract.                    " Tournay, the 18th May, 1712."

" On Saturday, the 13th instant, his Grace the Duke of Or-
" mond reviewed the two battalions of British Guards at their
" camp at Baiseu.   Prince Eugene, the Earl of Albemarle, and the
" other general officers at this place accompany'd his Grace, and
" were all extreamly satisfy'd with the fine appearance those
" corps made, being fully compleat and newly cloath'd.   Lieut.-
" General Withers, who is Lieutenant-colonel of the First regi-
" ment of Guards, entertain'd his Grace the Prince of Savoy and
" sev¹ other generals at dinner, as General Lumley did my Lady
" Albemarle, with other ladys and persons of distinction who were
" at the Review."—Military Correspondence, State-Paper Office.

as negociations for peace had been in progress for some 1712.
time between France and England.

The Duke of Ormond having received the Queen's com- July 24th.
mands to suspend hostilities for two months, in order to
facilitate a treaty for a general peace, requested Prince
Eugene and the Field Deputies of the States to proclaim
a similar suspension in the Confederate army. He informed them that ten battalions would be sent to take
possession of Dunkirk, which fortress the French were to
give up, as a pledge of their sincerity. Prince Eugene
and the Deputies declined acquiescing, until they heard
from their respective governments. The Duke of Ormond
replied, that he must obey his instructions, and that if
they persisted in the siege of Quesnoy, he should no
longer cover it, but leave them in three days : he also
told the Generals of the contingents in the pay of England, that unless his orders were complied with, their
troops should be deprived of the arrears due to them, as
well as their pay and rations. He, however, postponed
his march beyond the time first fixed, to enable the Confederates to take part in the cessation of hostilities.

Prince Eugene marched from Quesnoy on the sixteenth
to Hartre, where he was joined by all the auxiliaries :
the commanders of these contingents in British pay declared they had received directions from their several
courts to act in concert with the Emperor's forces. The
English, therefore, were left with only some battalions of
Holstein Gottorp, and the dragoons of Waleff. On the
seventeenth an armistice between the British and French
forces was published by the Duke of Ormond and Marshal Villars for two months. The British [1] troops retired

---

[1] The British force that marched with the Duke of Ormond was
composed of the following regiments : five regiments of horse,

Tuesday the twenty-fourth; a few days after they marched through the City to the Savoy, where they were quartered till the end of April.[1]

The Scotch Guards, although placed on the British establishment at the Union, continued to be quartered for some time in Scotland. The second Lieutenant-Colonel of the regiment was reduced, and " one year's recompense allowed to him, ending the 22nd of December, 1708." An additional company was added in March, 170$\frac{7}{8}$, making the regiment to consist of seventeen companies. The battalion under Colonel Scott, after disembarking in September, 1712, from Dunkirk, was quartered in Kent, and received orders in January to relieve the Invalid companies then in garrison at the Tower. At the same time the prisoners taken at Briheuga, in Spain, landed at Deal; and the whole regiment was ordered from the Tower " to attend the garrisons of Portsmouth and Plymouth."

After the death of Queen Anne, the cause of the Pretender became hopeless,[2] and the Elector of Hanover ascended the throne with the title of George the First.

A grenadier battalion, formed from the brigade of Guards, including the two companies of the Coldstream, were ordered to Greenwich[3] to receive, and do duty over the King, who landed on the eighteenth, and took up his

---

[1] See Appendix, Nos. 170, 171, 172, 173.

[2] It was a fortunate event for the Protestant religion that the Queen died, as it is said she proscribed her brother much against her inclination, " par une politique poussée un peu trop loin."— *Lettres à la Princesse des Ursinis*, vol. ii. page 428.

[3] See Appendix, No. 176. Extract of a Letter, dated 16th of Sept., 1714, from Francis Gwyn, Secretary at War:

" The Grenadiers of the three regiments of Guards, during their " stay at Greenwich, pursuant to an order from his Majesty, are to " beat the English march and Scots Reveillez."

1714.   residence in the Park.   Two days after, his Majesty made
his public entry through the City, and proceeded to the
palace at St. James's.[1]

---

Contingent bill for the eight companies of Granadiers that went
to Greenwich to receive his Majesty the 16th Sept', 1714.

### FOOT GUARDS.

|  | £. |
|---|---|
| 12 cart loads of straw for the Granadiers' tents, at 20s. p. load . . . . . . . . . . | 12 0 0 |
| 8 carriages for officers' and private men's tents and baggage, at 10s. each . . . . . . . . | 4 0 0 |
| 8 carriages from Greenwich to London . . . . | 4 0 0 |
|  | £20 0 0 |

Sir,

The above money being disbursed upon extraordinary occasion, I
desire you will please to move his Majesty for his royal sign
manual for allowing thereof.

> I am, Sir,
> Your most humble Serv',
> GEO. STEUART,

To the Secretary at Warr.                    (3d Foot Guards.)

---

[1] London, September 20th.

The King having appointed this day for his Royal entry from
Greenwich, through the city of London, to his palace at St
James, public notice was given by the lord marshal for all the
nobility and others who were to attend his Majesty, to repair to
Greenwich Park by ten of the clock in the morning, and officers at
arms were appointed to rank their coaches in order.   About twelve
his Majesty, accompanied by his Royal Highness the Prince, set
out from Greenwich, being preceded by a numerous train of
coaches of the nobility and gentry, the juniors marching first.
When his Majesty arrived at St Margaret's Hill, in Southwark, he
was met by the lord mayor, aldermen, recorder, sheriffs, and
officers of this city.   After which his Majesty proceeded to St
James's, in the following manner.   A detachment of the Artillery

On the resignation of General Churchill, the command of the Coldstream was given to William Earl of Cadogan.[1]

1714

Charles Churchill, born February the second, 1656,

---

Company; the two city marshals on horseback, with their men on foot to make way; two of the city trumpets on horseback; the sheriffs' officers on foot, with javelins in their hands; the lord-mayor's officers in black gowns, on foot, two and two; two more of the city trumpets on horseback; the city banner, borne by the water-baliff on horseback; the city officers on horseback in their proper gowns; the four attorneys, two and two; the solicitor and the remembrancer; the two secondaries; the comptroller; the four common pleaders; the two judges; the town-clerk; the common serjeant and the chamberlain; two more of the city trumpets on horseback; the common cryer, and the city sword-bearer, on horseback; those who had fined for sheriff or alderman, or served the office of sheriff or alderman, in scarlet gowns, on horseback, according to their seniority, two and two, the juniors first; the two sheriffs in scarlet gowns, on horseback, with their gold chains and their white staves in their hands; the aldermen below the chair on horseback in scarlet gowns, two and two; the aldermen above the chair in scarlet gowns on horseback, wearing their gold chains, attended by their beadles; then the coaches of the nobility, great officers, &c. in the order they came from Greenwich; the knights-marshals men on horseback, two and two; the knight-marshal on horseback; the King's kettle-drums; the drum-major; the King's trumpets, two and two; the serjeant-trumpet with his men; pursuivants of arms uncovered, two and two; heralds of arms; kings of arms; the recorder in a scarlet gown, on horseback, uncovered; the lord-mayor of London in his crimson velvet gown, on horseback, uncovered, bearing the city sword, by his Majesty's permission. Then came the King in his coach, and his Majesty's Horse Guards closed the procession. The great guns at the Tower were fired when his Majesty took coach, as also when he passed over London Bridge; and at his Majesty's arrival at his palace, the cannon in Hyde Park were three times discharged.— *London Gazette*, September 18th to 21st, 1714. No. 5261.

[1] Commission as Colonel dated October 11, 1714.

1714.   became Colonel of the Third regiment of Foot at the Revolution.   He was present at the battle of Landen, July 29th, 1693, where he took his nephew the Duke of Berwick prisoner, and was allowed twenty thousand guilders for his ransom.[1]   King William made him a Major-General, and afterwards promoted him to the rank of Lieutenant-General.   He was also at the battle of Blenheim, and in 1707 obtained the Colonelcy of the Coldstream Guards.   At the accession of George the First, he was given to understand that his services were no longer required.

1715.
July 20th.       In July, King George informed Parliament that a rebellion had broken out, and that the country was threatened with invasion.   The Habeas Corpus Act was suspended, and a reward of one hundred thousand pounds offered for the capture of the Pretender.

Both battalions of the Coldstream [2] encamped with the other regiments of Guards in Hyde Park.

---

[1] Warrant dated 2nd March, 169?.—War-Office Records.

[2] An Account of the Contingent Expences on the Encampment of his Majesty's Coldstream regiment of Foot Guards in Hyde Park, 23d July, 1715 :—

|  |  | £. | s. | d. |
|---|---|---|---|---|
| 1715. July 23rd. | For three carts to carry tents, tent poles, mallatts, pickaxes, shovels, &c. to Hyde Park   .   .   .   . | 0 | 12 | 0 |
|  | For 140 kettles at 2s. 6d. each, being a kettle a tent, for 14 companies, and ten tents to each company   . | 17 | 10 | 0 |
|  | For 120 loads of straw for 140 tents, at £1 10 0 p. load, from 23d July to 10th December, the day of decamping   .   .   .   .   .   .   . | 180 | 0 | 0 |
|  | For 29,400 faggotts, being 3 for each tent every two days, same period, at 13s. p. hund⁴   .   .   . | 191 | 16 | 0 |
|  | For picketts and lines   .   .   .   .   .   . | 2 | 16 | 0 |
|  | For making camp colours and staves   .   .   . | 1 | 10 | 0 |
|  |  | £394 | 3 | 0 |

A. Oughton, Major.

A levy of thirteen regiments of cavalry and eight of 1715. infantry was made.  The Trained-bands were kept in readiness to act if required.  Four additional companies were raised for the Coldstream, and the following officers appointed Captains and Lieutenant-Colonels:  Henry Poultney, William Leigh, John Cope, and John Huske.

The Chevalier St. George landed in Scotland, and assumed the title of King.

In April following, George the First apprised both Houses of the discomfiture and flight of the Pretender. Soon after the rebellion was suppressed, the King em- 1716.<br>July 7th. barked at Gravesend for the Continent.  During the summer, the regiment was again encamped, and reviewed by the Prince of Wales in Hyde Park.[1]

Hostilities recommenced with Spain.  The Pretender 1718.<br>Dec. 16th. was received at Madrid, and acknowledged King of Great Britain.  In consequence of the preparations made at Cadiz, troops were assembled in the West of England. A battalion of the Coldstream, under the command of Colonel John Robinson, was quartered at Chippenham.[2]

Ten ships, with transports, having on board six thousand men, under the command of the Duke of Ormond, sailed from Cadiz to assist the cause of the Pretender;

---

[1] An Account of the Contingent Expences on the Encampment of his Majesty's Coldstream regiment of Foot Guards in Hyde Park, 1716:—

£. s. d.

Charges the same as in the preceding year.

For 18 companies, 14 tents to each company, from 14
    June to 12 October, 1716 .   .   .   .   .   631 19 10¼

A. OUGHTON, Major.
JOHN PARSONS, Quarter-Master.

—War-Office Records.

[2] See Appendix, No. 184.

six thousand pounds; the Coldstream and Third Guards 1719.-20. five thousand.

| | |
|---|---|
| First Major and Captain . ⎫ | Each three thousand six hundred. |
| Second Major and ditto . ⎭ | |
| Captain . . . . | Two thousand four hundred. |
| Captain-Lieutenant . . | One thousand five hundred. |
| Lieutenant . . . . | Nine hundred. |
| Ensign . . . . | Four hundred and fifty. |
| Adjutant . . . . | Two hundred. |
| Quarter-Master . . . | One hundred and fifty. |

The practice of selling commissions existed as early as the year 1679, although no formal regulation on that head can be found of a date prior to the twenty-seventh of February,. 17$\frac{18}{20}$.  " Upon his Majesty's disposal of the " Captainship of his Guards of Horse to the Duke of " Albemarle, in December, 1679, Sir Thomas Armstrong, " for a valuable consideration, assigned his commission to " Mr. Griffin, the Cornet ; and the Cornet's commission " was delivered to the Lord Berkley, son to the Lord

| | |
|---|---|
| Lieutenant with the rank of Captain . . . . . | 1500 |
| Ensign . . . . . . . . . | 900 |

These prices were in force till the first of August, 1821, at which period the following were fixed by a board of general officers, consisting of Field-Marshal the Duke of Wellington ; Generals Lord Howden, the Earl of Rosslyn ; Lieutenant-Generals Sir Frederick Maitland, Sir Hildebrand Oakes, Viscount Beresford ; Quarter-Master-General Sir J. Willoughby Gordon, and Adjutant-General Sir Henry Torrens.

| | |
|---|---|
| Lieutenant-Colonel . . . . . | £9000 |
| Major . . . . . . . | 8300 |
| Captain with the rank of Lieutenant-Colonel | 4800 |
| Lieutenant with the rank of Captain . . . | 2050 |
| Ensign with the rank of Lieutenant . . . | 1200 |

—Return to an order of the House of Commons, ordered to be printed 4th July, 1822.

1719-20.    " Berkley who was formerly Lord-Lieutenant of Ire-
" land."[1]

Charles the Second paid five thousand one hundred
pounds to Colonel John Russell for his commission as
Colonel of the First Guards, and gave it the Duke of
Grafton[2] in December, 1681.

1722.    This year, General the Earl of Cadogan was appointed
to the command of the First regiment of Guards, and the
Earl of Scarborough became Colonel of the Coldstream.[3]

---

[1] The True Domestick Intelligencer, No. 46.    Friday, December
12th, 1679.

[2] " The turns of Court are such, that after all this hustle and
" composition between us about this regiment of Guards, a third
" person, not then thought of for such a command, nor so much as
" in the army, luckily got it from us both by the Duke of York's
" being absent in Scotland, and Russel's quitting his interest on
" account of the Popish plot, and so renewing his desire to sell.
" The Duke of Monmouth at that time was in such disfavour as to
" have his government of Hull and lord-lieutenancy of Yorkshire
" given to me ; which, with the old Holland regiment I had before,
" was already more than, being so young, I could reasonably pre-
" tend to.    The King therefore at last bought that command of
" Colonel Russel for his other son the Duke of Grafton.    What ap-
" pears in this story most remarkable, is the probability that in
" those early days the Duke of Monmouth had some thoughts of
" what he attempted afterward ; and the suspicion of him thus ac-
" cidentally infused into the Duke of York was not without some
" ground, since that regiment consisted of two thousand four hun-
" dred men, a great part of our little army, always kept together,
" and quartered in London, when the other few regiments were se-
" parated into all the garrisons of England.    This appeared suffi-
" ciently at King Charles's death, when it had not been impossible
" for the Duke of Monmouth to succeed him, if he had then flou-
" rished in Court, at the head of so considerable a regiment."—The
Works of Sheffield Duke of Buckingham, 4to. London, 1723. Vol. II.
page 20.

[3] Commission dated June 18th, 1722.

William, first Earl of Cadogan, entered the army early in life, and gradually rose to be Commander-in-Chief. He distinguished himself under King William at the battle of the Boyne, and in Flanders. He behaved with great gallantry at the attack of Schellenburg, at Blenheim, and at the forcing of the French lines near Tirlemont. At Ramelies, Brigadier Cadogan was taken prisoner whilst serving under the Duke of Marlborough, and carried into Tournay. After his release he came home; and on the first of January, 170⅘, was promoted to the rank of Major-General. On the death of Mr. Stepney he became Minister Plenipotentiary to the Spanish Netherlands. In January, 170⅞, he was made Lieutenant-General. At the accession of George I., the Colonelcy of the Coldstream was given him; and in the following year he was appointed Governor of the Isle of Wight. Afterwards he was created a peer, by the title of Lord Cadogan, and subsequently raised to the dignity of Earl. On the death [1] of the Duke of Marlborough, he became Commander-in-Chief, and Colonel of the First Guards.

The Coldstream regiment was encamped in Hyde Park, with the other regiments of Guards.

A conspiracy being discovered for placing the Pretender on the throne and seizing the Tower, additional troops were raised, and a suspension of the Habeas Corpus Act took place.

In September the camp in Hyde Park was broken up.

On the eleventh of June George the First died at Osnaburg. The Coldstream attended at the coronation

---

[1] At the Duke of Marlborough's funeral the detachment from the Coldstream was commanded by the Earl of Scarborough. August 9th, 1722.

1727.   of George the Second, on the eleventh of October following.

1731.   At the end of June, a battalion of the Coldstream was sent to Rochester, Chatham, and Stroud.

1738.   Nothing of moment appears to have occurred from this time up to the year 1738.

The following is an extract from the Coldstream orderly-book :—

" 1738.   We the Colonels of his Majesty's three regi-
" ments of Foot Guards agree, that the expedition in the
" year 1719, being seven companies of each regiment sent
" to Vigo, and in the year 1727, ten companies of the
" First regiment being sent to Gibralter, leaves, in each
" of the three corps, eleven companies which have not
" been on any foreign service since the year 1712: there-
" fore it is agreed by us, that to complete and finish the
" Roaster for that service, that the first duty of that kind
" shall begin with the First regiment, and so on the
" Coldstream and Third, which finishing the Roaster, it
" shall then for the future begin according to the Roaster
" settled by us June the 24ᵗʰ, 1737 ; viz'.

" 1ˢᵗ regiment.   Coldstream.   1ˢᵗ regiment.   3ᵈ regiment.
" 1ˢᵗ regiment.   Coldstream.   3ᵈ regiment.

" The First regiment having formerly sent one battalion
" to Rochester, and in the year 1719 each of the three
" regiments one battalion to the West, and in the year
" 1731 the Coldstream sent one battalion to Rochester: [1]

---

[1] " Wednesday, June 30th, 1731.—The same day orders were
" issued by the Right Honorable the Earl of Scarborough, for the
" first battalion of the second regiment of Foot Guards to rendez-
" vous on the parade in Sᵗ James Park, on Friday morning, in
" order to march to Rochester, and thence to proceed to Spithead,
" to assist in conveying Don Carlos into Italy."   " July 3ᵈ.—Yes-

" therefore, for parties of the like kind that may happen,
" it is agreed, that the 1ˢᵗ regiment is the first on com-
" mand for such duty, and the 3ᵈ regiment the second,
" after which the tour of duty is to begin as the Roaster
" settled as above.

" CHARˢ WILLS.
" DUNMORE.
" SCARBOROUGH."

His Royal Highness William Duke of Cumberland,
after the death of the Earl of Scarborough, succeeded him
in the command of the Coldstream.[1]

Richard, second Earl of Scarborough, was one of the
gentlemen of the bed-chamber to the Prince of Wales,
and Colonel of the first troop of Grenadier Guards. He
died on the twenty-ninth of January, 17¾, and was
buried on the fourth of February, in St. George's Chapel,
Andley Street.

The Duke of Cumberland, on being removed to the
First regiment of Guards, was succeeded by the Duke of
Marlborough as Colonel of the Coldstream.[2]

---

" terday morning the first battalion, nine companies, of the Second
" regiment of Foot Guards crossed the water at the Horse Ferry,
" Westminster, and proceeded for Dartford, in their way to Ro-
" chester, where they are to remain till further orders." The battalion of the Coldstream, at Rochester, were ordered to return to
London, and arrived Wednesday, the ninth of August following.—
*Daily Press.*

[1] Commission dated April 30, 1740.
[2] Commission dated February 18, 1742.

## CHAPTER XXIII.

George II. supports the Allies—Earl Stair sent ambassador to Holland—First battalions of the Foot Guards embark at Deptford and Woolwich—British winter in Flanders—War declared against France—George II. and Duke of Cumberland sail for Holland — Confederates assemble in Germany — British quit Flanders and move, under Lord Stair, towards the Rhine—Confederates encamp between Mentz and Frankfort — Duke de Noailles remains in the Palatinate, on the banks of the Rhine — George II. and Duke of Cumberland join the army — Battle of Dettingen — Allies arrive at Hanau — Reinforced by twelve thousand Hanoverians and Hessians—Confederates go to Mentz, and separate for the winter—Coldstream in quarters at Brussels —Treaty of Worms — George II. goes to Hanover, and returns to England—France declares war against Great Britain — Lewis XV. heads his army — French overrun Flanders— Charles of Lorraine enters France — Allies posted behind the Scheld — Reinforced by the Dutch — Duke of Cumberland appointed Commander-in-Chief — Allies in quarters near Ghent — Allies separate for the winter — Coldstream at Ghent — Death of Charles Duke of Marlborough.

1742. April.   THE King of England determined to support the cause of the Allies in the Netherlands; and the Earl of Stair, whom he intended to place at the head of the forces, was sent ambassador to Holland.

April 27th.   Several regiments were embarked for the purpose of making a powerful diversion for the relief of the Queen of Hungary. A force amounting to sixteen thousand three hundred and ninety-nine men,[1] after being reviewed 1742. by the King, embarked on the Thames for Flanders.

On Wednesday the twenty-sixth of May, the first May. battalion of the First Guards, the first battalion of the Coldstream, and the first battalion of the Third, embarked at Woolwich. The brigade, including officers, amounted to two thousand two hundred and forty-two men. The troops landed, and were joined at their camp in the vicinity of Brussels, early in October, by twenty-two thousand Hanoverian and Hessian auxiliaries in the pay of England: detachments from the Austrian troops in the garrisons of Mons, Charleroi, Ath, Dendermond, and Luxembourg, also joined them. From the tardiness of the Dutch, nothing was undertaken. The British troops received orders to winter in Flanders, when on the eve of setting out for Germany.

About the middle of February the British quitted their 1743.<br>February. quarters in Flanders, and moved towards the Rhine. The Earl of Stair, who was commander-in-chief, appointed Hochst on the Maine as the point of concentration for the Confederates; but the roads being impassable on account of the snow, the troops remained in Aix-la-Chapelle.

George the Second, accompanied by the Duke of Cum- April 27th. berland, embarked at Gravesend for Holland, landed at May 2nd.

---

[1] The following regiments: Third and Fourth of Horse Guards, with the Second troop of Horse Grenadier Guards, the King's regiment of Horse, and Major-Gen¹ Ligonier's; the six regiments of Dragoons, commanded by Generals Honeywood, Campbell, Hawley, Cadogan, Rich, and Cope; the three regiments of Foot Guards, with the twelve regiments of Howard, Cornwallis, Durowre, Pultney, Campbell, Peers, Handasyde, Huske, Bragg, Ponsonby, Johnson, and Bligh.— *Historical Memoirs of William Augustus Duke of Cumberland.* 8vo. London, 1747.

Helvoetsluys, and arrived at Hanover four days after.    In
the mean time, the Confederates assembled their forces in
Germany.

The British left their cantonments on the twentieth of
April, passed through the duchy of Juliers and the electorate of Cologne, crossed the Rhine at Newidt, and, proceeding along its banks, reached Hochst early in May.
Marshal Neuperg and the Duke d'Aremberg, with the
Austrians, arrived about the same time.    The Hanc-
verians, under General Ilton, did not get to the rendezvous till the end of the month.    The Confederates, under
Lord Stair, were encamped in one line, between Mentz
and Frankfort: their numbers amounted to about thirty-
eight thousand.

The French, commanded by the Duke de Noailles,
remained in the Palatinate, on the banks of the Rhine ;
and consisted of fifty-eight thousand.

Lord Stair determined not to decline a battle ; he
therefore proceeded up the Rhine to Aschaffenburg : the
enemy followed on the opposite side.    As the Allies pursued the course of the river, and the French took the
direct line, the latter gained the wood near the bridge
about the same time that the Allies reached the town.

The King of England and Duke of Cumberland joined
on the ninth of June, and found the contending armies encamped on the plains near the banks of the Maine, opposite each other, under a ridge of wooded hills ; the Confederates on the north, the enemy on the south side.

Aschaffenburg lies four miles east of Dettingen, where
the Maine is about sixty yards broad.    The country
through which the river flows is low and level for about
a league, and becomes afterwards mountainous and
woody.    A mile below Aschaffenburg, the small river
Aschaff runs from the hills and falls into the Maine ;

another rivulet, called the Beck, falls into the same river just above Dettingen, between which and the Aschaff is the village of Klein Ostein. On the south of the Maine, Hochstadt is situated. Facing Dettingen is the village of Mainfling. The south bank of the Maine is generally much higher than the opposite side, and the lower part of the ground, to within a mile and a half of the river, consists of wood and morass.

The position of the Allies extended about two miles from Aschaffenburg to Klein Ostein, and inclined towards the mountains a few hundred paces from the river. The right wing, composed of Austrians, was at Klein Ostein; the Hanoverians, posted in two lines, formed the centre. The British, on the left, occupied the town and vicinity of Aschaffenburg. The enemy reached, on the south, from the bridge of Aschaffenburg to the river Selingenstadt.

The Confederates suffered great privations from want of provisions,[1] and were nearly surrounded by the enemy.

At this time intelligence of the success of Prince Charles of Lorraine in Bavaria, and of the speedy junction of twelve thousand Hanoverians and Hessians, who were within two days' march of Hanan, arrived at the camp.

As the enemy commanded the lower part of the river, it was apprehended that any troops attempting to advance beyond Hanan would be intercepted. But George the Second had resolved that the junction should be accomplished, and determined on marching for that town to join Prince George of Hesse Cassel, who was expected there.

Marshal Noailles, on the night of the thirteenth, moved

---

[1] Voltaire says it was proposed to hamstring the horses, so much were they in want of forage.

1743.    his camp further up in the woods, to prevent the King's purpose: the same evening the enemy set fire to great quantities of wood and straw, which at first led the Allies to suppose they intended to retreat; but, notwithstanding the smoke, it was discovered that they were hard at work intrenching themselves.

June 15th.    George the Second, observing certain movements made by the French to the left, ordered the tents to be struck " at gun-fire," [1] and the troops to remain under arms till day-break, when they were to move from the right in two columns.   As the King felt confident that any attempt of the French would be on his rear, three battalions of English Guards, [2] four of Lunenburg, which protected the head-quarters, and twenty-six squadrons of the Hanoverian cavalry, with artillery, were ordered to cover this operation.

The French Marshal, suspecting the Allies would commence their march during the night, gave orders that the Duke de Grammont should cross the Maine at Selingenstadt, to prevent his Majesty from uniting with the Prince of Hesse.   The French General also marched twelve thousand men on Aschaffenburg, to get possession of the bridge on its being quitted by the Allies, which he calculated would leave them no retreat on that side.   The

June 16th. enemy were in motion, early in the morning, towards the bridge of Selingenstadt.   To conceal this movement, they left the banks of the Maine, and in profound silence took a circuit through the woods; it was, however, soon dis-

---

[1] Historical Memoirs of William Augustus Duke of Cumberland, page 57.

[2] With whom " his Majesty chose to be in person at the place of action."— Published by authority, *A complete Collection of Accounts relating to the late Glorious Action of Dettingen*. London, 1743, page 64.

covered that they had " passed over a great body of   1743.
" troops during the night. Their horse, the Household
" at the head, passed at fords, or swam over: the foot,
" which we saw marching without baggage along the
" river, passed over the bridge." " During the whole
" disposition, which lasted from eight to twelve, the
" French batteries, posted on the rising grounds on the
" other side of the Mayn, did us a great deal of harm,
" flanking us from left to right within 200 paces."[1]

The French were drawn up in order of battle in a plain
behind the wood where the right wing of the Allies was
posted. The enemy formed in two lines. Their right was
covered by the Maine, and protected by a battery on the  June 16th.
other side of the river; the household troops were in
the centre, supported by the infantry; the left wing extended towards the hills. In the morning the French
infantry crossed two bridges at Selingenstadt, and their
cavalry forded the river at the same place. About twelve
o'clock, on the approach of the French, the King ordered
his first line of infantry to advance, headed by the Duke
of Cumberland, Lieutenant-Generals Clayton and Sommer-
feldt; half way they halted, a hearty huzza was given, and
they continued to move forwards on the enemy. The
French household troops from their right advanced on the
left of the Confederates, and commenced an irregular fire,
which became general along the front of both armies: the
Allies, however, still proceeded, notwithstanding a tremendous front and flank fire from the enemy which galled
them very severely.[2] On the left the French cavalry
gained some advantage, when Lord Stair ordered Lord

---

[1] London Gazette, from Tuesday, July 12th, to Saturday, July
16th, 1743. No. 8240.
[2] London Gazette, from July 12th to July 16th, 1743. No. 8240.

Ligonier to oppose them with the King's and his own regiment of horse: these were, however, obliged to retreat, from the great superiority of their adversaries. Five regiments of the Confederate horse were then ordered to pass through the intervals of infantry; but General Honeywood at the head of the Horse Guards was repulsed by the Gensd'armes, who, flushed with success, rushed on the British foot. They opened their ranks to admit them, which exposed the French cavalry to a flank fire, and they were totally destroyed. The Allied cavalry were afterwards twice repulsed and rallied, but on the third charge they drove back the French horse. Lord Stair then rode up to the infantry, and told them they might yet have the glory of beating the French, whose third line was to be seen drawn up in beautiful order. This information was received with three cheers, and the troops again advanced. The attack was conducted with such gallantry that the enemy gave way and retired in disorder; their confusion was completed by some Hanoverian artillery that was brought up at this juncture from the wood.

Marshal Noailles remained at Hochstadt till he was informed that his nephew had passed the defile, on which he exclaimed, "Grammont has ruined all my plans."

As the French had quitted the field,[1] and were drawn up in position on a height that commanded the plain, he crossed it to superintend their movements.

King George by his bravery added greatly to the natural confidence of the British. On this occasion his Majesty rode between the lines, fearless of the fire of artillery and

---

[1] It was in vain the Marquis of Puysegur, son of the Marshal of that name, called the soldiers of his regiment, and tried to rally them; he even killed some that were running away, crying out—" Sauve qui peut."—*Voltaire's Age of Louis XIV.*

musketry, gave his orders with calmness, and placed 1743.
June 16th.
himself at the head of the infantry.[1]

Generals Clayton and Murray were killed; the Duke of
Cumberland, the Earl of Albemarle, General Huske, and
several officers of rank were wounded.

Voltaire observes that the French suffered greatly, and
the excellent dispositions of their General were rendered
abortive by that precipitate ardour and want of discipline
which occasioned the loss of the battles of Poictiers,
Crecy, and Agincourt.[2]

The day after the battle the Allies continued their June 17th.
march, and arrived at Hanau the same evening; where
twelve thousand Hanoverians and Hessians joined them.
Prince Charles of Lorraine forced Marshal Broglio to retire through Swabia, into Alsace. The Austrians then
moved to Heidelberg, with the intention of surrounding
Marshal Noailles; but the French General, aware of their
purpose, quitted his encampment on the night of the July.
second, having set fire to his magazines. After a rapid
march of forty miles he passed the Rhine between Worms
and Oppenheim, entered Alsace, and reached the celebrated lines of Lauterburg near Landau, which had been
constructed by the Germans for the defence of their frontier against France previous to the fall of that place.

During the stay of George II. at Hanau, arrangements
for carrying on the operations of the campaign were con-

---

[1] Lord Carteret gives the following account:—His Majesty rode
down the line, flourished his sword, and thus addressed the British
Infantry: " Now, my brave boys! Now, for the glory of England,
advance boldly and fire."

[2] In this battle Lord Stair said the French were guilty of one
great fault, in not having patience to wait for us; and we of two,
first in getting into the scrape, and then in not taking the advantage we ought to have done. See engraved medal L.

certed.   His Majesty and the Duke of Cumberland, at the head of the Confederate army, left Hanau, crossed the Rhine above Mentz, on their route to Worms, at which place the King took up his quarters.   The army encamped, to wait the arrival of twenty thousand Dutch auxiliaries under Count Maurice of Nassau : when they entered the Palatinate of the Rhine, the Allies moved on Spire, and Sept. 25th. the Dutch joined.

Marshal Noailles remained in the strong intrenchments at Lauterburg.

On the Allies leaving Hanau, Prince Charles of Lorraine also quitted Heidelberg with sixty-four thousand men for the Brisgaw.

The arrangement made at Hanau was, that the combined army should enter Alsace and attack the French garrisons ; but, as Marshal Boufflers had made preparations for the defence of Landau, and Prince Charles was unable to cross the Rhine, it was impossible to carry into effect the operations planned at Hanau.   The Confederates therefore returned to their former camp at Spire on the eleventh of October ; thence they proceeded to Mentz, and soon afterwards separated for the winter.

The Coldstream was quartered in Brussels.

A treaty of peace had been concluded at Worms on the second of September by England, Hungary, and Sardinia, called " a definitive treaty of peace, union, friendship, and mutual defence" between the three Monarchs.

The English, Austrians, and Hanoverians, in the pay of England, returned to Flanders, the Dutch to Brabant and Guelderland, the Hanoverians and Hessians to their respective countries.

The King of England, accompanied by the Duke of Cumberland, went to Hanover, from thence to Holland, and arrived in London about the middle of November.

War was declared by France against Great Britain. The French made arrangements for the invasion of Flanders, and assembled in force about Lisle. Lewis the Fifteenth placed himself at the head of his army, which consisted of one hundred and twenty thousand men.[1]

Two days after his arrival at Lisle the Allies encamped in the vicinity of Brussels: their army consisted of twenty-two thousand English, sixteen thousand Hanoverians, and twenty thousand Dutch. Marshal Wade commanded the English and Hanoverians, Count Maurice of Nassau the Dutch, and the Austrians were under the Duke d'Aremberg.

From the disparity of the two armies the French were enabled at once to overrun the country.

The States-General, instead of acting offensively in the field, and defending their towns, thought only of negotiating for peace.

Whilst Lewis the Fifteenth was at Dunkirk, elated with the success of his arms, he received intelligence that Prince Charles of Lorraine had crossed the Rhine and entered the French provinces.

On the second of June the Allies left their encampment in the vicinity of Brussels, and took post near Oudenarde, with the Scheld in their front, where they were joined by six thousand Dutch, and by another reinforcement of double that amount, commanded by General Ginckel. Had the contingents been furnished according to their stipulated quotas, the Confederate troops would

---

[1] Voltaire makes it only eighty thousand men.

The army was furnished with " 160 pieces of battering cannon " from 12 to 48-pounders, with 100 field pieces, and several mortars, forty of which threw bombs, called cominges, of 500 pounds " weight, managed by a large body of skilful engineers."—*Historical Memoirs of the Duke of Cumberland*, page 154.

have exceeded ninety thousand men; but they were deficient, and did not, with the casualties, amount to more than seventy thousand: a sufficient number, however, to oppose the enemy, as great part of the French army had been sent to prevent the entry of the Austrians under Prince Charles into Alsace.

No advantage was taken of this circumstance by the Allies, and the result was an inglorious campaign, which was principally owing to the dissensions among the Confederate Generals and the obstinacy of the Dutch. In consequence of these disagreements it was proposed that the Duke of Cumberland should be invested with the supreme command in the ensuing campaign, which, it was expected, would have the beneficial effect of making all the inferior generals act together.

The army of Prince Charles of Lorraine amounted to seventy thousand men, at the head of which he accomplished the passage of the Rhine.

The French had fifty thousand under Marshal Coigni to defend the river: thirty thousand more were concentrating on the Moselle under Marshal Belleisle; while twelve thousand Bavarians, commanded by Seckendorf, possessed themselves of the imperial fortress of Philipsburg; an occupation in direct violation of a late treaty.

The Allies closed the campaign and returned to occupy their quarters near Ghent, till the sixteenth of October, when they separated for the winter. The British troops were quartered at Brussels, Bruges, Oudenarde, and Ghent, in which place the Coldstream was stationed.

Count Saxe destroyed the fortifications at Courtrai, and then retired to quarters.

Charles, Duke of Marlborough, was appointed Colonel of the thirty-eighth regiment in 1738, and afterwards removed to the command of the first regiment of dragoons.

In 1740 he became Captain and Colonel of the second troop of Horse Guards. In 1742 he obtained the Colonelcy of the Coldstream Guards, and in the following year was promoted to the rank of Brigadier-General. He accompanied George the Second to the battle of Dettingen, where he commanded the brigade of Guards. On the fifth of October, 1744, he resigned his regiment, which was given to the Earl of Albemarle, and the same year succeeded, on the death of Sarah Duchess of Marlborough, to the estates of her husband the first Duke. In 1745 he became Major-General, and in 1747 Lieutenant-General. His Majesty, on leaving the kingdom for a short time, appointed the Duke one of his Lords Justices of the Government. He was placed also in command of the British forces serving in Germany under Prince Ferdinand of Brunswick, and died of a fever at Munster on the twentieth of October, 1758.

1744.

## CHAPTER XXIV.

Duke of Cumberland arrives at Brussels — Saxe takes the field—
Investment of Tournay—Duke of Cumberland and Konigseck,
the Austrian General, reach Halle on their march to Chambron—
Lewis XV. and Dauphin arrive at the camp before Tournay—
Battle of Fontenoy—Tournay surrenders to the French—Allies
retire—Ghent taken by surprise—Bruges, Oudenarde, Ostend,
and nearly all Flanders, submit to the French—Charles Edward
lands in Great Britain—Arrival of the Guards in England—List
of rebel army at Dalkeith—First battalion of the Coldstream
march to join the Duke of Cumberland—Duke of Cumberland
appointed Commander-in-Chief — Troops assemble at Litchfield
—Arrival of the Coldstream at Litchfield—Camp at Finchley
—Charles abandons Derby—Battle of Culloden.

1745.    THE Duke of Cumberland, with the concurrence of the
March.   States-General, was appointed Commander-in-Chief of the
Confederate forces.   At a council of war held at Brussels,
it was agreed that the army should be ready to take the
field on a fixed day, if approved by the Duke, who arrived
April 7th. at the Hague on the seventh of April.   He reached
Brussels on the tenth, when he commenced his inspection
of the troops.

It was computed that to garrison the towns nearly
eighteen thousand men would be required.   However,
fifteen thousand and fifty-eight only could be spared: the
detachment on the canal, which ought to have been seven
thousand four hundred and ninety-five, amounted to only
six thousand one hundred and fifty; and the army, when

completed, instead of fifty-one thousand six hundred and 1745. sixty men, did not muster more than forty-three thousand four hundred and fifty.

Marshal Saxe, who commanded the French, had obtained great celebrity by the able manner in which he had conducted his retreats in Germany. He not only displayed considerable military talents, coolness and intrepidity, but evinced the practical knowledge of a skilful commander. The French [1] brought into the field thirty-five thousand men more than the Confederates.

The campaign opened with the investment of Tournay. April 15th. The Duke of Cumberland and Marshal Count Konigseck, the Austrian General, left their encampment at Ander- April 19th. lecht for Halle, where they received reinforcements from Namur. On the twenty-second they were at Soignies, and two days after at Cambron; from which place a April 24th. detachment was sent to drive the enemy from Leuse, who retired. Lewis the Fifteenth, accompanied by the Dauphin, reached the camp before Tournay. Marshal Saxe told the King he suspected the Confederates were bold enough to fight a battle; " and as he was conscious " that the French were unable to stand before the British " fairly in the field, he was determined to depend upon " stratagem more than open strength: " [2] the most advantageous disposition of his troops was made. Eighteen thousand men were left before Tournay; six thousand were placed to defend the bridges on the Scheld, and keep the communications open. The French had on their right a river and the village of Antoine, where a commanding

---

[1] The French had 106 battalions, including the militia, and 172 squadrons; whereas the Allies had only 46 battalions and 90 squadrons.—*Voltaire*.

[2] Historical Memoirs of the Duke of Cumberland, page 195.

battery was erected; another defended their centre; and in front was the village of Fontenoy, strongly intrenched and fortified. The wood of Barri, on the left, was filled with artillery, and a fourth redoubt constructed at the point of it. The French camp rose with a gentle ascent from the plain. Numerous lines behind each other intersected all the level ground, which would expose the Allies to a galling fire if they attempted to pass. The French, independent of the security of their position, were greatly superior in numbers, and had besides two hundred and sixty-six pieces of cannon.

On the twenty-sixth of April the Confederates re-
April 28th. ceived orders to be ready at a moment's warning. At six A. M. the Allies moved in two columns; but were impeded by the badness of the roads, and did not reach their ground till six in the evening.

April 29th. Early next morning, the Prince of Waldeck and Marshal Konigseck held a conference with the Duke of Cumberland, when the necessary preparations were made for the approaching attack.

The Dutch, being placed opposite Antoine, extended themselves till they fronted Fontenoy. The English occupied the space to Veson, and the valley from the village leading through the wood of Barri. Some hussars were thrown out to skirmish on the plain between Fontenoy and the woods occupied by the English.

April 30
May 11 At two o'clock A. M. the Confederates advanced in four columns, and drew up on the plain. The right wing was composed of English and Hanoverians; the latter were in the centre, under Major-General Zastrow, and formed in four lines in front of Veson. The left wing, composed of Dutch and Austrians, were in two lines, reaching to the wood of Peronne. In front of Veson was a fort mounted with cannon, and sufficiently large to con-

tain six hundred men.  The Duke of Cumberland ordered
Brigadier Ingoldsby, with four battalions, to carry it by
assault.  Prince Waldeck at the same time was to attack
the village of Fontenoy.  Whilst the first line was forming " an inconceivable number of bullets plunged in
among the British," but they stood undaunted.  The cannonade commenced at a quarter after four A. M., and
continued without intermission.  Sir John Ligonier was
ordered to advance with the brigade of Guards and seven
guns to check a destructive fire from the enemy's field
artillery, which was quickly silenced.  At nine o'clock
the Allies had completed their formation, when Sir John
Ligonier sent his aid-de-camp to acquaint the Duke of
Cumberland that he was ready, and only waiting for the
signal of Prince Waldeck's attack on Fontenoy.

The troops then moved forward with astonishing intrepidity to their respective points of attack.  The Duke
of Cumberland passed between Fontenoy and the wood of
Barri, notwithstanding the " fire of cannon making whole
" lanes through the ranks of the Confederates, particularly
" the English." [1]  The Dutch infantry, which covered the
left flank of the British, were broken, and could not be
rallied during any part of the day: the cavalry were also
thrown into great confusion.  Lord Cranford remarks that
" this deroute of the Dutch had an extremely bad effect
" on the mind of the troops in general, though not so
" much on ours, who were the first ranged, and still
" marched towards the enemy, the noblest sight (says
" his Lordship) I ever beheld, and never stopped till
" they got through a shower of bullets and musquetry."

Ingoldsby, who had been ordered to carry the redoubts
of the wood of Barri, imagined the difficulty to be

[1] Historical Memoirs of the Duke of Cumberland.

greater than it really was; and, instead of at once attacking the work and clearing the wood, he returned to the
Duke for artillery. This afforded the enemy time to
strengthen the redoubt, and the opportunity was lost.[1]
The first line, headed by the Duke of Cumberland, succeeded in passing Fontenoy and the redoubts, and got
within thirty yards of the enemy. At this distance, the
British having received the fire of their opponents, doubled
up in a column and advanced between the batteries, all of
them playing on a spot not half a mile broad. Entire
ranks fell, but the intervals were immediately closed.
They broke the brigade of French Guards at the second
charge, and forced them back on the Irish brigade; the
enemy's cavalry then advanced, but went about, unable to
face the fire.[2]

---

[1] Ingoldsby was tried by a court-martial: he afterwards published his vindication, and denied ever having received orders on
this occasion, and stated, his orders were so contradictory he knew
not which to obey.

[2] The officers of the English Guards, when in presence of the
enemy, saluted the French by taking off their hats. The Count de
Chambanne and Duke de Biron, who were in advance, returned
the salute, as did all the officers of the French Guards. Lord
Charles Hay, Captain of the English Guards, cried, " Gentlemen
of the French Guards, fire." The Count d'Anteroche, Lieutenant of Grenadiers, replied, in a loud voice, " Gentlemen, we
never fire first; fire yourselves." The English then commenced a
running fire in divisions, so that one battalion made a discharge,
afterwards another, during which the first reloaded. Nineteen
officers of the Guards fell by the first discharge. Messieurs de
Clisson, de Ligney, de la Peyre, and ninety-five soldiers, were
killed, and two hundred and eighty-five were wounded ; also
eleven Swiss officers, and two hundred and nine of their soldiers, out
of which sixty-four died on the spot. Colonel Courten, his
Lieutenant-Colonel, four officers, and seventy-five soldiers, were
killed ; and fourteen officers, and two hundred soldiers, dangerously

At this period the British had decidedly the advantage over the left wing ; for, notwithstanding several of their squadrons rallied, they were again forced back by the fire of the British infantry. This body, unsupported by the cavalry, bore down all before them ; drove the left three hundred paces beyond Fontenoy, and made themselves masters of the field from the ground on which they stood to their own camp. The left wing of the enemy having retired, to avoid fighting at close quarters, opened and uncovered two batteries of heavy guns, which poured on the British such a shower of " musket balls" in front and flank, that it was impossible to face them. The column however rallied, and, returning to the charge, threw the French into complete disorder. They were fairly beaten ; and had some fresh battalions from the reserve been ordered to replace those that suffered from the grape-shot, or had the second line advanced to enable the cavalry to get past the redoubt, the enemy could not have recovered the day. According to the first plan drawn out, the French would have been taken in flank by Lord Cranford, who was to advance along the edge of the wood leading to the road of Leuse, where Prince Waldeck's regiment, with some hussars, had endeavoured to penetrate in the morning ; and if the troops under Lord Crauford had been reinforced, instead of being withdrawn on the failure of

---

wounded. The first rank being swept away, the three others, finding themselves unsupported except by a regiment of cavalry at some distance, dispersed. The Duke of Grammont, their Colonel and First Lieutenant-General, who might have rallied them, was killed. Mons' Luttaux, next in rank to De Grammont, did not reach the spot till they had abandoned the ground. The English advanced as if performing part of their exercise ; the Majors levelling the soldiers' muskets with their canes to make their discharge more sure.—*Voltaire*.

the Dutch, the results of the battle would probably have
been different.    Lord Cranford himself gives it as his
" real opinion," that orders were at one time issued for the
retreat of the French.    The left, although supported by
the fire from the English artillery, did not succeed ; and
Fort Vezon not being carried, the British were placed between a cross-fire of cannon and musketry, which obliged
them to retire on the height of Fontenoy.

At twelve o'clock a second attack was made.    The
Duke of .Cumberland determined to carry the redoubt in
the road, and Prince Waldeck was to attack Fontenoy.
The troops, still in the finest spirit, renewed their efforts,
and drove the French back on their 'intrenchments with
prodigious slaughter, breaking their infantry and routing
their cavalry.    The British infantry gradually advanced,
under a constant and regular fire.    The French Marshal,
perceiving the dismay of his men, ordered the household
troops forward, supported by his infantry : their efforts,
however, produced no effect.[1]    Guns were brought to bear
on the English artillery, which in some degree slackened
its fire, and gave time for the Irish brigade to form.
This corps was the last resource left to Marshal Saxe, and
consisted of the regiments of Clare, Lally, Dillon, Berwick, Ruth, and Buckley, with the horse of Fitz-James,
supported by the regiments of Normandy and Vaisseaux.
They advanced on the British, whose ranks were already
thinned, and the men wearied by the exertion of fighting
over the dead and wounded of both armies.    The British
troops remained unshaken, although unsupported ; line
after line of the enemy presented themselves, threw in

---

[1] The French Marines, commanded by Mons^r de Guerchi, were
thrown into disorder, on which Marshal Saxe observed, " How can
it possibly happen that such troops should not be victorious ? "—
*Voltaire.*

their fire, and fled. But no additional corps were sent to
the relief of the British, whose compact formation had
hitherto enabled them to repair the repeated losses occasioned by these incessant attacks. No fresh orders were
issued. No cavalry was within reach to follow up the
panic which had seized the enemy; the Dutch did not appear in any quarter, nor was there any probability of a
sortie from Tournay to aid this isolated body. As no
favourable circumstance seemed likely to occur, it became
evidently impossible for the British, who had lost their
generals, their officers, and more than one-third of their
numbers, to sustain without reinforcements the repeated
efforts of fresh troops, united with those rallied under the
eye of their monarch.[1] The encounter between the British and Irish brigade was fierce, the fire constant, and the
slaughter great; but the loss on the side of the British
was such, that they were at length compelled to retire.
During this retrograde movement the French cavalry attempted to break them, but were received by the brigade
of Guards and some Hanoverians under Major-General
Zastrow. These troops sustained the attack with such
persevering coolness, that the carabineers and the regiment of Noailles were nearly annihilated. Nothing being
effected on the left, it was decided that the army should
retreat. General Howard's regiment was posted in the
church-yard of Vezon, and the Highlanders behind some
hedges which they had occupied from the preceding day.
The cavalry were drawn up in good order, and some battalions faced about every hundred paces; but no attempt
was made to molest the retreating army, which passed
Bruffoel, then moved and encamped at Lessines, near
Ath.

---

[1] The King of France and his son were separated in the confusion.—*Voltaire.*

1745.
April 30
May 11

In the list of killed and wounded of the Coldstream Guards were, Ensigns the Honourable Shaw Cathcart and Robert Molesworth, two serjeants, one hundred and ten privates killed. The Earl of Albemarle, Colonel of the Coldstream regiment, Colonels Samuel Needham, Thomas Corbet, William Kellett, John Mostyn, Lord Robert Bertie; Captains Francis Townshend and Julius Cæsar; Ensigns Thomas Burton and Vanbrugh; four serjeants, and one hundred and twelve privates wounded. Of the officers, Needham, Kellett, Townshend, and Vanbrugh, died of their wounds.[1]

---

[1] The French lost about eight thousand men in this battle, whilst the Allies had about twenty-one thousand killed or wounded.—*Voltaire's Age of Lewis XIV.*

The following account of the battle of Fontenoy was published in Paris, May 26th, 1745:—

" Our victory may be said to be complete; but it cannot be " denied the Allies behaved extremely well, more especially the " English, who made a soldierlike retreat, which was much " favoured by an adjacent wood. The British behaved well, and " none could exceed them in advance, none but our officers when " the Highland furies rushed in upon us with more violence than " ever did a sea driven by a tempest. I cannot say much for " the other auxiliaries; some looked as if they had no concern in " the matter. We gained the victory, but may I never see such " another."

Lord Crauford conducted the retreat in excellent order till his troops came to the pass. He then pulled off his hat, and returning thanks, said, they had acquired as much honour in covering so great a retreat as if they had gained the battle.—*Earl of Crauford.*

Marshal Saxe said, in his account of Fontenoy, " he could not " suppose any General was bold enough to venture to make his " way through that place."

At Fontenoy the Guards behaved with great heroism. — *Grose's Military Antiquities*, vol. II. page 208.

After the surrender of Tournay, the French advanced on **1745.** the Confederates at Lessines, where they had encamped since the battle of Fontenoy. On the approach of the enemy, the army, after exchanging a few shots with the out-posts, moved to Grammont. The Allies retired towards June 27th. Brussels, and encamped at Anderlecht.

Ghent was surprised and taken by sixteen hundred men: Bruges submitted without resistance on the first summons, the Scotch Fusiliers having previously retired to Ostend.

The enemy invested Oudenarde, which was defended July 6th. by three English battalions, some Austrians and Dutch; the Governor, however, surrendered on the fourth day. After the capture, reinforcements arrived from the Moselle to the French, when they moved to Alost, where Lewis XV. and the Dauphin arrived on the twenty-fourth. July 24th.

A battalion of Guards, drafted from companies of the three regiments at home, was sent from England to keep up the communication, and strengthen the garrison of Ostend,[1] which consisted of four thousand men under

[1] On Wednesday morning, (10th of July,) 500 men were drafted " out of the Foot Guards, on the Parade in St James's Park, in " order to be sent to Ostend."

" Colonel Braddock, of 2d regiment of Foot Guards, was " expected in town last Monday night from Ostend, where he " has been to know the state of that place, in order to acquaint the " Lords of the Regency thereof."

" July 27th. The draft of the Foot Guards, which were lately put " on board the transports for Ostend, still lie in Margate Roads, " waiting there for further orders."—*Westminster Journal*, Nos. 189. 191.

" Hague, August 10th, N.S.—By letters from Zealand there is " advice that the transports and convoy with the troops and stores " for Ostend arrived happily in that road last Saturday evening." (27th July, O.S.)—*London Gazette*, No. 8454.

Lieutenant-General Count Chaneles, of the Austrian service.   After a siege of thirteen days, the General capitulated, the troops being allowed to march out with military honours, and conducted to the Austrian territories: the Guards proceeded to Mons.[1]  Nieuport surrendered immediately; but Ath was maintained for twenty-

one days, notwithstanding an incessant fire of bombs and red-hot shot.

The French were now masters of Flanders, with the exception of Sluys and a few insignificant places in the possession of the Dutch.   The Allies intrenched themselves beyond the Antwerp Canal, with the right on that city, and their left on Brussels.

Lewis XV. encouraged Charles Edward, the eldest son of the Pretender, and grandson of James II., to make an attempt on Great Britain, and proposed to assist him with about twenty-five thousand troops.   This armament set sail; but, either from tempestuous weather, or the dread of meeting the English fleet, the enterprise was abandoned.

Charles Edward was then in the twenty-first year of his age, of a graceful exterior, engaging and affable in his manners, and of a brave, active, and adventurous disposition.   He had served with credit at the battle of

---

[1] "On Monday (19th of August) Colonel Hildesley, of the 2d " regiment of Foot Guards, arrived in town with dispatches from " his Royal Highness the Duke of Cumberland."

" Last Sunday morning (1st September) several subaltern officers " with 40 private men and two drums, who were taken prisoners " by the French at the siege of Ostend, arrived in town from Har- " wich, where they had landed from Helvoet Sluys, being " set at liberty by the French after the siege was over.   Next " day they were reviewed at the orderly-room in Scotland Yard, " and ordered to their respective companies in the Guards."— *Westminster Journal*, Nos. 195 and 197.

Dettingen. A powerful party was formed in his favour 1745. among the Highland Chiefs, whose influence over their clans was unlimited; a circumstance which was likely to facilitate the Young Pretender's design. It was, therefore, determined that another attempt should be made, and Prince Charles repaired to France, where he was supplied with nine hundred stand of arms, eight hundred broad-swords, and two thousand pounds in money.

He embarked at St. Nazaire in Britanny, on board a vessel of eighteen guns, accompanied by seven exiled adherents, and sailed on the fourteenth of July. The Eliza- July. beth French man-of-war, of sixty guns, which had been expressly fitted out for the expedition, joined off Belleisle with several volunteers on board. The plan was to sail round to Scotland by the coast of Ireland; but on their passage, they were attacked by the Lion, an English ship of fifty-eight guns, when the Elizabeth was completely disabled, and obliged to put back to Brest: the smaller vessel escaped, pursued her course, and reached the coast of Lochabar, where Charles was landed between the islands of Skye and Mull. Some Chiefs of clans resorted to their favourite Prince, but were disappointed at the manner of his arrival, having expected him at the head of sixteen thousand French troops well supplied with every necessary.

Many of the principal Highland Chiefs associated themselves to support his cause, and the young Adventurer soon found himself in a condition to commence active operations. He defeated the King's troops, and made himself master of the greater part of Scotland. In con- September. sequence of this alarming state of affairs, the three battalions of Guards and seven regiments of the line were recalled from the Continent.[1]

---

[1] " On Monday" (23ᵈ September) " a battalion of the First Foot

1745.    The Duke of Cumberland also left the command of the
Confederate army, and hastened to London, where he
arrived on the eighteenth of October.

October.    The London Gazette of the twenty-fifth states, that
the battalion from the three regiments of Foot Guards
lately taken prisoners at Ostend disembarked at the
Tower, from whence they proceeded to their respective
quarters.

The Rebel army was encamped at Dalkeith. It was
composed of the following regiments :—

| HIGHLAND CLANS. | | | | LOWLANDERS. | |
|---|---|---|---|---|---|
| Locheil | Mac Kinnon | Mac Loughlan | | Athol | Edinburgh. |
| Appin | Mac Pherson | Strowan | | Ogilvie | |
| Keppock | Glengarry | Glen Morrison | | Perth | |
| Glenco | Glenbucket | | | Nairn | |

HORSE.

| | |
|---|---|
| Lord Elcho | Lord Pitsligo |
| Lord Balmerino | Earl Kilmarnock. |

The horse consisted of private gentlemen, uniformly
clothed in blue faced with red, scarlet waistcoats laced
with gold; and were styled the Prince's Life Guards.

Charles at length marched to England, and reached
Derby, where, as usual, he proclaimed his father King.

Carlisle had surrendered on the fifteenth of November,
" and, contrary to the opinion and protestation of the
Deputy Governor," Colonel Durand, of the First Guards,
who was shut up with a few men in the Castle, which he

" Guards, as likewise a battalion of the Third Foot Guards, which
" landed that day at the Tower from Flanders, came to the Parade
" in St James's Park. A battalion of the Second regiment of
" Guards landed at the same time, and marched into the Tower.
" On the 13th" (of September) " the regiments left the camp at ·
" Vilvorde, and embarked at Williamstadt the 19th."—Westminster
rnal, No. 200.

was compelled to abandon.[1]  The Colonel was afterwards
tried by a court-martial, when it appeared that the Mayor
and Corporation had made the best terms they could for
themselves and the inhabitants, without any reference to
him.  He was, therefore, honourably acquitted.

Much alarm prevailed in London, and the government
directed that the Guards who had arrived from the
Continent should immediately be put in motion.  On
the twenty-fourth of November the first battalion of the
Coldstream was ordered to parade in Hyde Park the next
morning, and to march[2] and join his Royal Highness the
Duke of Cumberland.  The Duke, to whom the chief
command was entrusted, assembled the troops near Litchfield.  By an express of the twenty-ninth of November
from that town, " it is written, that the two battalions of
" Guards which went from hence on Saturday last were
" expected there to-morrow, a great many horses having
" been sent from those parts to Coventry to forward their
" march, and the town of Birmingham having distin-
" guished itself by providing two hundred horses for that
" purpose at their own expense."[3]

" Whitehall, December the 1st.—The three battalions
" of Guards which went last from hence, notwithstanding
" the excessive badness of the roads, were expected to be
" at Litchfield upon the 30th, or this day at furthest."

" Whitehall, December the 2d.—By advices from Lan-
" cashire of the 30th past, the whole body of the Rebels
" was in and about Manchester that day, and their artil-
" lery was expected.  A report prevailed strongly there as
" if they would endeavour to slip through Derbyshire or

---

[1] London Gazette, No. 8486.
[2] See Appendix, Nos. 213, 214, 215.
[3] London Gazette, No. 8488.

after the rebels had left that place. The subsequent proceedings will be best described by the following extracts from the Gazettes and Journals of that period.

" Stafford, Monday, December the 2d, past eleven at
" night.—By the freshest advices from our advanced post,
" which is at Newcastle, a large party of the rebels were
" at Cogleton, within nine miles of that place, and their
" whole army, with all their artillery and baggage, was to
" be there this night. His Royal Highness the Duke
" had before ordered the cavalry at that post to be alert,
" and the two battalions of infantry to retire to Stone,
" which is six miles on this side of it, in case of the
" enemy's approach. The Duke marched himself from
" hence (Stafford) this night at about eleven, with three
" battalions of Guards, to the same place ; where the
" army, consisting of eleven old battalions of foot, six
" regiments of horse and dragoons, will be formed to-
" morrow morning ; if they are disposed to fight, there
" may be an action to-morrow."[1]

" His Royal Highness the Duke of Cumberland is
" returned hither, with the army under his com-
" mand, which was assembled at Stone by four in the
" morning."[2]

" Whitehall, December the 7th.—By advices from
" Litchfield, his Royal Highness the Duke of Cumber-
" land arrived there with the army on Thursday last
" (the 5th instant), and having received advice that the
" rebels had taken possession of Swarkston bridge before
" the orders for breaking it down could be put in execu-
" tion, it was resolved to encamp on the 6th on Meriden

---

[1] London Gazette, No. 8480.          [2] Ibid. No. 8490.

1745.　" Common, between Coleshill and Coventry, and this day
" near Northampton."[1]

" Meriden, December the 9th.—Sir John Ligonier is
" this moment marching from hence with the brigade of
" Guards and Semphill's regiment to Litchfield, on intel-
" ligence received that the rebels were marched towards
" Lancashire in order for Scotland."

" Litchfield, December 11th.—We have advices here
" that the rebels left Manchester yesterday, marching
" northward, and that his Royal Highness the Duke of
" Cumberland had made two forced marches after them,
" and continued in pursuit of them."[2]

The Guards returned to their quarters in London,[3] leav-

---

[1] London Gazette, No. 8490.　[2] Westminster Journal, No. 211.
[3] Money paid for Carriages, &c. by the first Battalione of the
Coldstream regiment of Foot Guards on their march from Merriden
Camp to London, 1745:

| | | | £. s. d. |
|---|---|---|---|
| December 8th. | From Merriden to Coventry, for the sick | | 0 8 0 |
| ,, 9th. | From Merriden to Litchfield | | 4 16 0 |
| ,, 16th. | From Litchfield to Birmingham | | 3 12 0 |
| ,, 17th. | From Birmingham to Coventry | | 5 14 0 |
| ,, 18th. | From Coventry to Daventry | | 5 14 0 |
| ,, 19th. | From Daventry to Towcester | | 4 4 0 |
| ,, 21st. | From Towcester to Stoney Stratford | | 2 2 0 |
| ,, 23d. | From Stoney Stratford to Dunstable | | 5 14 0 |
| ,, 24th. | From Dunstable to St Albans | | 3 18 0 |
| ,, 25th. | From St Albans to Barnett | | 3 0 0 |
| ,, 26th. | From Barnett to London | | 3 18 0 |
| November 25th. | For 10 Waggons from London to Barnett | | 5 10 0 |
| ,, 27th. | For Carriage of the Tents, &c. sent after the regiment from London to Barnett | | 2 0 0 |
| | from Barnett to St Albans | | 2 0 0 |
| | | | £52 10 0 |

ing at Carlisle a strong detachment of volunteers from the
brigade that accompanied the army; all the horse and
the Foot Guards were cantoned round the town at a mile
or two distance.

" The night of the 29th of December was spent in rais-
" ing a new battery of three eighteen-pounders, which was
" completed by the morning; but on the first platoon of
" the old battery firing against the Castle, the rebels hung
" out the white flag. His Royal Highness ordered Lieu-
" tenant-Colonel Lord Bury of the Coldstream, and
" Colonel Conway," (his aid-de-camps), " to go and

|  |  | £. | s. | d. |
|---|---|---|---|---|
| | Brought forward | 52 | 10 | 0 |
| November 28th. | from St Albans to Dunstable . . | 2 | 2 | 0 |
| ,, 29th. | from Dunstable to Stoney Stratford | 3 | 16 | 0 |
| ,, 30th. | from Stoney Stratford to Towcester | 1 | 8 | 0 |
| December 1st, | from Towcester to Daventry . . | 2 | 16 | 0 |
| ,, 2nd. | from Daventry to Coventry . . | 3 | 16 | 0 |
| ,, 3rd. | from Coventry to Litchfield . . | 2 | 8 | 0 |
| | | £63 | 16 | 0 |
| | Poundage | 3 | 7 | 2 |
| | | 67 | 3 | 2 |

E. BRADDOCK.

These are to certify that there was expended, by order of the
Right Honble the Earl of Albemarle, the sum of £58 17 0 for carriage
of the baggage, sick, and lame, of the first battalion of the
First regiment of Foot Guards, as also the sum of £67 3 2 for
the like use of the first battalion of Second regiment of Foot
Guards; and likewise the sum of £53 6 6 for the same use of the
first battalion of the Third regiment of Foot Guards, which said
sums amount in the whole to £179 6 8, and were expended on the
said three battalions marching from Merriden Camp to London, in
December, 1745.

E. BRADDOCK.

London, Septr 8th, 1746.
—Official Records, War-Office.

1745.    " deliver two messages in writing. In about two hours
" they returned. The rebels capitulated, on which Bri-
" gadier Bligh was ordered immediately to take posses-
" sion of the town, and he will have there this night four
" hundred Foot Guards, and seven hundred marching
" foot, with one hundred and, twenty horse to patrole the
" streets. His Royal Highness the Duke will enter the
" town himself to-morrow."

The detachment of volunteers of the Guards from
Carlisle soon after this period returned to London, and
1745-6.  joined their respective regiments the latter end of January.

The Young Pretender contined his retreat through
Dumfries to Glasgow. At Perth he was reinforced with
about two thousand men.

1746.    General Hawley, with some dragoons and other troops
which he had collected, attempted to intercept the rebels
at Falkirk, and was defeated.

The Duke of Cumberland was then in Edinburgh with
fourteen battalions, two regiments of cavalry, and a body
of twelve hundred loyal Highlanders under Colonel Campbell; he moved from that city, and secured the posts of
Stirling and Perth, which he garrisoned with Hessians.
The Royal army next advanced on Aberdeen, where it was
joined by the Duke of Gordon, the Earls of Aberdeen and
April 12th. Findlater, the Laird of Grant, and others.    The Duke
left Aberdeen, and crossed the river Spey without opposition, although the rebels might successfully have disputed the passage, the river being deep and rapid. He
then marched to Nairn, at which place information was
received that the enemy were at nine miles' distance, having advanced from Inverness to Culloden, intending to
make a stand and offer him battle.

Great indecision appears to have prevailed in the rebel
councils. It was the Young Pretender's intention to make

a night march, surround the King's forces, and attack
them on all sides at the same moment: for this purpose
he set out, expecting to reach the English quarters at day-
break; but in consequence of several halts, made without
necessity, his columns became entangled, and many of the
men, worn with hunger and fatigue from being under arms
all the preceding night, laid down to sleep; and others,
unperceived, left the ranks. The arrangements in every
respect were badly planned, and a total want of discipline
rendered the forces of Charles inefficient. Finding it
impossible to execute his design, he retraced his steps to
Culloden.

The Duke of Cumberland lost no time in following him.
A few hours after quitting Nairn, he perceived the Highlanders drawn up in line. The enemy's front was formed
by the clans in thirteen divisions, under their respective
chiefs. On the right were forty of the principal gentlemen
dismounted. Next stood five hundred of the Athol men.
The rest of the clans were stationed in the following order:
—One hundred and fifty Mac Laughlans; six hundred
Camerons of Lochiel; two hundred Steuarts of Appin;
three hundred Steuarts of Gardentilly; five hundred
Frasers of Lovat; four hundred Mac Intoshes; one hundred and fifty Chisholms; three hundred and thirty
Farquharsons; three hundred Gordons of Glenbucket;
three hundred Mac Kinnons; three hundred Mac Leods
of Rasy; one hundred Mac Leans; two hundred and
fifty Mac Donalds of Clanronald; three hundred Mac
Donalds of Keppock; four hundred Mac Donnells of
Glengarry: making a total of four thousand nine hundred and ninety, with four pieces of cannon, which were
planted in the centre in front of the Mac Kinnons and
Farquharsons.

On the right of the second line were posted two battalions of the regiment under Lord Lewis Gordon, of five hundred men each, who were supported by two battalions, of similar force, under Lord Ogilvie. In line with them was the regiment under Lord John Drummond, of five hundred men, headed by his cousin Lord Lewis Drummond; the remainder on the left were headed by the Earl of Kilmarnock and Colonel Creighton: being in all two thousand.

The Royal army was in excellent order. At one o'clock, all the preparations being made, the attack commenced with a cannonade, which did great execution among the rebels. About five hundred Highlanders rushed headlong on the Duke's left wing, and shook one of the regiments; but two battalions immediately advancing from the second line, restored order, and poured in a steady and well-directed fire. Hawley then brought up his cavalry, and the Argyleshire militia, pulling down a park wall on their right flank, completed the disorder of the enemy. A piquet on the left covered their retreat by keeping up a brisk fire; after which they retired to Inverness, and surrendered themselves prisoners of war.

In less than thirty minutes the rebels were entirely defeated, and the field was covered with slain. Notwithstanding the general rout, a body of the Highlanders marched off with their pipes playing, and the Pretender's standard unfurled. The young Adventurer, whose eagerness to regain a crown for his family did not allow him to perceive that by involving England in a civil war he was merely operating a diversion in favour of Lewis, after enduring many privations, reached France in safety. His dangers and escapes while wandering a fugitive among the mountains, raised him to the dignity of a hero of romance; and the tale of his sufferings has caused many tears to flow, which would have been better bestowed on the unfortunate beings who were the victims of his folly, and of the ambition of their leaders. It is related of this Prince, that when he had worn out his shoes in his flight, a Highland woman gave him others, and taking possession of the pair he had thrown off, said, in a familiar tone, " If you forget me when you have recovered your right, I will walk up to St. James's and shake these old shoes at you." In this anecdote may perhaps be found the secret of those, who, reckless of the bloodshed and misery they may create, are ready to join in any attack on established governments or settled institutions, from which it does not happen to be their fortune to expect preferment. The Highland chiefs who compelled their followers to support the claim of a family for which they had been accustomed to evince but little respect or affection when the Stuarts reigned in Scotland, can scarcely deserve credit for any higher inducement than the desire to establish a King, at whose hands they might calculate on favour and promotion in return for the aid he received from them. Human nature is always the same. The adherents of the Houses of York and Lancaster fought for their own private interests, in maintaining the cause they publicly avowed : the Highland chiefs who raised the standard of Prince Charles, and the warriors that flew to join Napoleon on his return from Elba, hoped to benefit themselves amidst the troubles of their country, and were probably unconscious of any more elevated sentiment of devotion and attachment than the Highland dame who, when she relieved the Prince in his necessity, thought of future reward, and kept his worn-out shoes to witness against him. Wherever disinterestedness and true patriotism exist, they will be found to reside with those who value the general tranquillity, and abhor agitation and bloodshed, whether it be to change a dynasty, or to divide a people. The

1746.   selfish motive for disturbing the public repose, and deso-
lating a country, remains unchanged, although the form
in which the guilty purpose exhibits itself may sometimes
vary.   At the present moment Ireland can boast of
patriots who would hazard the peace of a mighty empire
to dissolve a union which, however little it may suit their
own secret purposes, has married a poor country to a rich
one, and placed the sister Isle on the same footing as
Wales and Scotland.   To be identified with England in
her prosperity, was all that Ireland had to ask; but neither the advantages arising from that which is established,
nor the calamities of civil war attendant on its overthrow,
enter into the calculations of men whose object is their
own aggrandisement.   A few months terminated the enterprise of Charles Stuart; but it has required more than
half a century to repair the mischiefs it occasioned.

# CHAPTER XXV.

Intended expedition under Lestock and Sinclair—Duke of Cumberland lands at the Hague — Second battalion of the Coldstream embarks for Flushing—Second battalion employed at the
siege of Bergen-op-Zoom — In quarters at Bois-le-Duc — Confederates leave Maestricht, encamp at Terheyde — Go into winter-
quarters—Serjeants of the Foot Guards to leave off ruffles—
Duke of Cumberland returns from England—Reinforcements
arrive—Army assemble near Ruremonde—Brigade of Guards at
Eyudhoven—Treaty of Aix-la-Chapelle—British return to England—Coldstream dispersed in a gale, seven companies land at
Harwich, rest reach the Downs—Albemarle dies in Paris — Tyrawley succeeds in command of the Coldstream — Second battalion of the Coldstream occupy " the new buildings at Whitehall"—First battalion of Coldstream joins the expedition for St.
Maloes—Marlborough's marches to St. Servan and Solidone—
Coldstream marches for Dol—Troops embark and land in the
Isle of Wight—Marlborough sent to command the British on the
Continent—Marine expedition under Bligh sails—Guards commanded by Drury—Fleet anchor in Cherbourg Roads—Army
disembark—Troops enter Cherbourg—Troops re-embark—Land
to the westward of St. Maloes—Shepherd's dog—Bligh marches
for the interior—Rear-guard defeated at St. Cas.

A SECRET expedition being fitted out for the coast of
France under Admiral Lestock and General Sinclair, the
Guards, under General Fuller, composed of the third
battalion of the First, and second battalion of the Cold-

1746.
September.

stream,[1] commanded by Colonel Edward Braddock,[2] were ordered to join the convoy at Plymouth, but it had sailed before their arrival. The Westminster Journal gives the following account of their proceedings. " Early last " Wednesday morning (tenth of September), two bat- " talions of the Second and Third[3] regiments of Guards, " consisting of 2000 men, met on Great Tower Hill, from " whence they marched to the King's Stairs on Tower " Wharf, where they embarked. His Royal Highness the " Duke of Cumberland was present at their going abroad, " and spoke to every man as they passed him with the " greatest freedom."[4]

" By an express arrived last Tuesday from Plymouth, " of the 21st of September, there is advice that six or " seven companies of the Fusiliers came into that place " by land on that day, and that some of the transports " with the Guards were arrived, and the rest are every " moment expected."[5]

" Letters from Plymouth of the 12th of October assure " us that the men-of-war and transports, with two bat- " talions of the Foot Guards and General Huske's regi- " ment of Welch Fusiliers, sailed from thence on the tenth " instant, in order to join Admiral Lestock."[6]

" On the 19th of October, in the morning, General

---

[1] See Appendix, No. 219.

[2] The other captains of companies were Lieutenant-Colonels Russell, Parsons, Lord Bury, A'Court, John Lambton, in the room of Legge, Lethieullier, Noel. Lord John Sackville was ordered, but neglected to embark, and was in consequence ob_ liged to quit the service.

[3] See quarters showing the embarkation. It should be Third battalion of the First Guards.

[4] Westminster Journal, No. 250.

[5] Ibid. No. 252.     [6] Ibid. No. 255.

" Fuller, with the transports having on board the Guards     1746.
" and Fusiliers, returned to Plymouth, from whence the
" transports returned to the Downs on the 24th."[1]     October.

The Guards disembarked at Deptford and the Tower
on the twenty-seventh, and marched to their quarters in
London. " Admiral Lestock and the troops composing
" the expedition to Quiberon and L'Orient returned to
" Spithead on the 26th of October."[2]

The Duke of Cumberland landed at the Hague on the
thirtieth of November, and took the field in February, with     1747.
the English, Hanoverians, and Hessians.

On the ninth of May the second battalion of the Coldstream, under Colonel Braddock,[3] proceeded in barges
from the Tower to Gravesend, where they embarked for
Flushing, and arrived on the thirteenth. The battalion
was subsequently employed with the army under the
Prince of Orange in an attempt to raise the siege of Bergen-
op-Zoom, which had been vigorously pushed on since the
battle of Val;[4] but, notwithstanding the united efforts of
the Allies, the place was carried by storm on the sixth of

---

[1] Westminster Journal, Nos. 256 and 7.     [2] No. 257.

[3] Appointed, twenty-first of November 1745, Lieutenant-Colonel of the Coldstream. The remaining captains of companies
were Lieutenant-Colonels Russell, Barrington in the room of
Legge, Lord Bury, Noel, Parsons, Lethieullier, Cæsar, and
A'Court.

[4] " His Royal Highness the Duke of Cumberland has been
" pleased to appoint Thom⁵ D'Avenant, Ensign in General Wolf's
" regiment, and nephew to Thom⁵ Boothby Skrymsher, Esq', to be
" an Ensign in the Coldstream regiment of Guards. This young
" gentleman had the good fortune to take one of the standards be-
" longing to the Irish brigade in the late battle of Val," (fought
July 2ᵈ, 1747, N.S.).—Dublin Journal, No. 2138.

1747.　September.[1]　The Coldstream was afterwards quartered in Bois-le-Duc.[2]

October.　In October the army under the Duke of Cumberland left the neighbourhood of Maestricht, and in November encamped at Terheyde, from whence they separated, and cantoned in the adjacent towns. The British, Hanoverians, and Dutch retired into winter-quarters in the vicinity of Breda. The Imperialists were stationed between the Maese and Rhine.

December.　At this period the serjeants of the Foot Guards were ordered to leave off wearing ruffles, the Duke of Cumberland having said it was impossible to distinguish the non-commissioned from the commissioned officers.

1748.　His Royal Highness passed the winter in England, and returned in the spring. He was followed in March by twenty sail of transports with additional troops, and in April a detachment of one hundred and twenty-eight men arrived to reinforce the brigade of Guards. The army assembled near Ruremonde, and on the eleventh of May marched from that place and encamped at Grave. In July they removed into cantonments ; the brigade of Guards to Eyndhoven, the Duke of Cumberland's head-quarters.

The definitive treaty of peace was signed at Aix-la-Chapelle on the eighth of October, and in November the

---

[1] " We hear that Lieutenant-Colonel John Parsons of the " (Coldstream) " Foot Guards was dangerously ill at Bergen-op-" Zoom when the place was taken."—*Dublin Journal*, No. 2141.

[2] " Head-Quarters at Argentan, September 28th, N. S.

" The Prince of Orange has put the battalion of British Guards, " and Brag's, into Bois-le-Duc ; and the two battalions of the " Royals into Heusden."—*London Gazette*, No. 8678.

British embarked at Williamstadt, on their return home. The Guards sailed from Williamstadt on the sixteenth of December; the transports were dispersed in a gale of wind; part of the Coldstream landed at Yarmouth on the twentieth, the remainder arrived in the Downs on the twenty-ninth of January following.

At this period the Coldstream received new colours, as appears from a charge in the regimental contingent account for the year ending the twenty-fourth of June: " Paid in fees at the several offices, for receiving new " colours for the regiment,[1] £8 14s." The companies subsequently raised obtained the colours described among others in the annexed account of The Colours and Badges of the Coldstream Regiment of Foot Guards, given by his Grace the Duke of Marlborough, as Master of the Great Wardrobe. [2]

---

[1] Both the other regiments of Guards received new colours at the same time, a similar charge for fees having been made in their contingent accounts.

[2] The colours now used by the Coldstream (1832) are the same as here described.

1751.

| | | |
|---|---|---|
| Colonel's Ensign | A Star and Garter, and St. George's Cross, as worn by the Knights of the Order of St. George . . | |
| Lt.-Colonel's | A Star within a Garter, and in the dexter corner of the Ensign the Union . . . . . | |
| Major's | A Star and Garter as the Colonel, with the Union in the corner; from that a Pyle wavy, or . . | |
| 1st Captain's | The Ensign the Union on the centre, on a Mount Vert, a Lion Passant, Argent, over it an Imperial Crown . . . . . . | |
| 2d Captain's | The Prince of Wales's Three Feathers, Argent, Quilled; or, a Prince's Coronet; or . . . | Union |
| 3d Captain's | On a Mount Vert a Panther, Argent, spotted with various colours, and issuing flames of fire from his mouth and ears, proper . | Union |
| 4th Captain's | Two Swords in Saltier, Argent, Hilt and Pomel; or . . . . | Union |
| 5th Captain's | St. George slaying the Dragon, all proper . . . . . . | |
| 6th Captain's | A Red Rose, seeded, or, Barbed Vert within the Garter . . | |
| 7th Captain's | A Centaur, proper, on a Mount Vert . . . . . . | Union |
| 8th Captain's | Two Sceptres in Saltier, or . . | |
| 9th Captain's | The Knot of the Collar of the Order, or, within the Garter . . | |
| 10th Captain's | An Escarbuncle, or . . . | |
| 11th Captain's | On a Mount Vert, a Boar Passant, Argent, bristled, &c.; or . . | Union |
| 12th Captain's | On a Mount Vert, a Dun Cow, proper . . . . . | |
| 13th Captain's | A red and white Rose, empaled with a Pomegranate, or, stalked and leaved, Vert . . . . | |
| 14th Captain's | On a Mount Vert, a Horse Current, Argent . . . . . | Union |
| 15th Captain's | The Charlemain Crown, or . . | |
| 16th Captain's | White Horse (crest of the House of Brunswick) . . . . . | Union |

July 1st.　　A royal warrant, regulating the colours, clothing and numbering of regiments, made its appearance on first of July; shortly after instructions were given to the commissaries of musters to annex the number as well as name of the colonel to the respective returns. Thenceforth regiments were distinguished by numbers, although the practice of designating them by the Colonel's name continued till the year 1753; when all official records adopted the numbers.[1]

It appears by the following extract of a letter from the Secretary at War, that wooden ramrods continued to be used by the Guards up to this period.

Extract of a letter from Henry Fox, Secretary at War, dated 28th of January, 1752:—

" To be delivered from the Ordnance stores to the 1st " and 3rd battalions of the 1st Foot Guards, 969 iron ram- " rods in lieu of their present wooded ones."

" For the 1st battalion of the Coldstream, 459 iron " ramrods in lieu of their present wooded ones."

The same order was issued for the first battalion of the Third Guards.

On the twenty-second of December the Earl of Albemarle, Colonel of the Coldstream, died at Paris.

William Anne, second Earl of Albemarle, was educated in Holland, and returned to England in the sixteenth year of his age. On the twenty-fifth of August, 1717, he was appointed Captain of a company, with the rank of Lieutenant-Colonel, in the Coldstream regiment of Foot Guards. At the beginning of 1722 he went back to Holland. The Order of the Bath was conferred on him, and he was appointed aid-de-camp to the King. In the next reign he retained his situation as Lord of the Bedchamber, and was also made Colonel of the 29th regiment of Foot, then stationed at Gibraltar. Afterwards,

[1] See Appendix, No. 229.

1754.   he was constituted Captain and Colonel of the third troop of Horse Guards; Governor of Virginia;[1] and a Briga-dier-General of his Majesty's forces, and was Ambassador

1755.   at Paris at the time of his death. The Earl of Albemarle was succeeded in the command of the Coldstream by James Lord Tyrawley, whose commission as Colonel bears date April 8th, 1755.

1756.  
May 14th.   "The new buildings at Whitehall" were now first occupied by the nine companies of the second battalion of Coldstream, who were " cantoned in the New Horse Guards."[2]

1758.   Vigorous preparations for war were commenced, and Government determined to make a descent on the coast of France: two squadrons were fitted out, and placed under the command of Lord Anson and Sir Edward Hawke.

May 9th.   A battalion from each regiment of Guards, including the first battalion of the Coldstream,[3] and the four gre-nadier companies, formed into a battalion, joined the army destined for the expedition, which consisted of six-teen battalions, and nine troops of Light Horse, under Lientenant-General the Duke of Marlborough. The two squadrons sailed on the first of June; that under Lord Anson for the Bay of Biscay; the other, with the troops, steered for St. Maloes, and arrived at Cancalle Bay,[4]

---

[1] 1737.

[2] The brigade of Guards gave up the occupation of the Horse Guards on the tenth of December, 1758.—War-Office Records.

" 9th December, 1758.—It is his Majesty's pleasure that the 2nd " battalion of the Third regiment do move out of the lodgement at " the Horse Guards, on Monday morning next, the 11th instant, " into quarters in the Borough of Southwark." — Coldstream Or-derly Room.

[3] See Appendix, Nos. 231, 232.

[4] " The inhabitants of Cancalle fled, and left their village to the " mercy of the invaders; and it was plundered by the soldiers and " sailors; for which one soldier was hanged, and seven seamen

about two leagues to the eastward of that town, which was strongly fortified. At this place the Grenadiers of the army, with the brigade of Guards, were put on shore in flat-bottomed boats, carrying seventy men each, under cover of the frigates. A battery erected on the beach by the enemy was silenced, and the remainder of the troops were landed in perfect order.

The Duke of Marlborough[1] commenced his march to St. Servan and Solidone, and succeeded in destroying whatever ships or stores fell in his way.[2]

The first battalion of the Coldstream, under the command of Colonel Cæsar, marched to Dol, about twelve miles from St. Maloes; they paid for every thing they required, and were well received by the country people: the next day they returned, not having seen any troops of the enemy, or gained the least information.

---

" flogged and sent on board the ships."—*Entick's Late War*, vol. iii. p. 85.

[1] The following is a translation of the concluding part of a manifesto published in Britanny the day after the troops landed at Cancalle:

" If, notwithstanding this declaration, which we have been " pleased to make, the inhabitants of the towns or villages carry " away their furniture, effects, or provisions, and abandon their " houses or dwellings, we shall treat such delinquents as enemies, " and destroy by fire and sword, or such other methods as shall " be in our power, their towns, villages, dwellings, or houses. " Given at our head-quarters at Parome, June 7, 1758.

" MARLBOROUGH.
" By his Grace's command,
" BRYANT."

[2] The following ships were totally destroyed: one of fifty guns, one of thirty-six, one of thirty, one of twenty-two, one of twenty, one of eighteen, two of sixteen, one of twelve; besides sixty eight merchant ships, six sloops, and many small craft, and the whole of the naval stores. The damage done was estimated at £800,000.

1753.     The Duke of Marlborough, finding St. Maloes c
not be carried by a coup-de-main, and receiving ir
mation that the enemy had assembled in great fo
deemed it more prudent to return to Cancalle, where
June 11th. troops were re-embarked.

On the twenty-sixth, when off Havre-de-Grace, e
preparation was made for another descent; but on re
noitring, the enemy were too well prepared, and
fleet bore away for Cherbourg, near which place the s
June 28th. cast anchor.    Several transports received consider
injury from the different batteries of the enemy, and
French troops were seen in readiness to oppose any
tempt at landing.    At length it was determined
the three forts should be attacked during the night by
grenadiers of the Guards and the battalion of the I
regiment of Guards : the men were distributed in·the
bottomed boats, waiting the order to push off; but
tempestuous state of the weather rendered every atte
to effect a landing unavailing.    It was then thought e
dient to stand in for the land, that the fleet might c
a general disembarkation: this plan, however, could
be put in execution, as they were on a lee-shore,
the storm continued to increase.    These circumstan
combined with a scarcity of provisions and of hay for
horses, caused the enterprise to be abandoned.    '
fleet made sail, and arrived at St. Helen's on Saturday
thirtieth.

As the designs on the coast of France had b
checked by the tempestuous weather, the troops w
July 5th. landed in the Isle of Wight, but received orders to
prepared for re-embarking on the shortest notice.

The Duke of Marlborough having been placed at
head of the British troops serving on the Continent,
command of the marine expedition was entrusted to Li
tenant-General Bligh, an experienced officer.

The troops, on being again embarked, sailed on their second expedition. The Guards were commanded by Major-General Dury. The fleet in seven days anchored in Cherbourg Roads. The French had intrenched themselves with batteries, placed at certain intervals, extending the distance of four miles along the coast. The attention of the enemy was distracted by bomb-vessels, which kept up an incessant fire, and caused considerable mischief: under cover of this fire the Guards and Grenadiers were conveyed in the flat-bottomed boats with great regularity to the shore : on landing, they immediately formed. The enemy soon showed themselves from behind some sand-hills, but they were seized with a panic, and fled before the Guards and Grenadiers which composed the first division. In the course of the day all the infantry, with the exception of the light troops, disembarked, and during the ensuing night the French retreated. Several detached parties occupied the village of Querqueville, but the main body encamped for the night at the village of Erville. On the morning of the eighth the lines and batteries along the shore were found to be deserted. The army was formed into two columns, and began its march to Cherbourg, the gates of which being thrown open, they entered.

A manifesto had been published, containing a promise of strict discipline if no resistance was made ; this quieted the inhabitants, prevented them from deserting their habitations, and contributed much to the civility with which they received their guests. Notwithstanding, the soldiers committed great outrages, and the general discipline of the army was relaxed. " The soldiers," says Entick, " lived at large, and indulged themselves like " brutes in riot, licentiousness, and plunder; a breach " of faith very unbecoming the English, and which had

" well-nigh proved fatal to themselves: had it not
" been through the strict discipline with which the Foot
" Guards set a laudable example of sobriety, the whole
" army were in danger of being cut off, in that dissolute
" scene of drunkenness that ensued a discovery of the
" wine magazines; though there was a body of the ene-
" my's troops superior to them, under a Marshal of
" France, and within a few hours march."

The bason of Cherbourg, with the piers at the entrance, were blown up, and the harbour rendered useless,
together with all the forts, which were destroyed.

The enemy's force in the mean while grew formida-
ble, and, from the reports of the peasants and deserters, was every day increasing. The Commander-in-Chief
thought it advisable to retire; the troops therefore
quitted the town at three o'clock in the morning of the
sixteenth of August, and got on board the fleet without
molestation from the enemy. The next day they sailed,
Aug. 19th. and arrived off Weymouth.

On the twenty-second at midnight the fleet again
stood out to sea, but returned to their anchorage, being
unable to proceed from contrary winds. Soon after
they were more fortunate: the squadron with some
September. difficulty again steered its course, and on the third of
September anchored in the Bay of St. Lunaire, westward
Sept. 4th. of St. Maloes, where the army disembarked and encamped at a short distance from the shore.

Sept. 6th. A council of war was held, when the Admiral
stated the impossibility of co-operating in any attack on
St. Maloes, as the forts and the armed vessels in the harbour could reach any batteries raised by the troops on
landing, or the ships that might endeavour to enter the
usual channel.

All attempts on St. Maloes were therefore abandoned;

and as there was no safe anchorage in Lunaire Bay, the 1758. ships removed to the Bay of St. Cas, a few leagues to the westward: it was determined without delay to march the troops into the interior, taking care to proceed in such a manner as to keep up the communication with the fleet. On this occasion a French shepherd was compelled to act as a guide to the Coldstream Guards, by whom they were purposely misled. The late General, then Colonel Vernon, ordered him to be hanged. That officer used to say that he never witnessed a more affecting sight than the efforts made by the shepherd's dog to interrupt the men when they proceeded to put the rope round his master's neck. The executioner had no small difficulty in managing to keep the affectionate animal off, though assisted by two drummers, who enjoyed the reputation of having been practised dog-stealers in Westminster. " But," added the General, " John Bull is a poor crea- " ture when it comes to the pinch : I could not find it in " my heart to put the stubborn fellow to death for his " patriotism, and after well frightening him, and almost " breaking his heart by threatening to have his dog de- " stroyed, I let him go, and the faithful creature with him."[1]

General Bligh marched for Guildo : the next day, in Sept. 8th. crossing a rivulet at low water, some armed peasantry, Sept. 9th. collected behind the hedges and houses, annoyed the troops by their fire. On reaching the village of Matignon, after a little skirmishing, two battalions in line were discovered : these, on the approach of the British, after exchanging shots, and receiving a few discharges from the artillery, dispersed. General Bligh, who was encamped about three miles from St. Cas Bay, was informed that the

---

[1] Related by the late General Vernon to my much-valued friend Thomas Edwards, L.L.D.

1758.    Duke d'Aguillon's forces, composed of twelve battalions, and six squadrons of horse, two regiments of militia, eight mortars, and ten pieces of cannon, were within five miles, and intended to attack him the next day.  At a council of war, held the same evening, it was determined that the English should embark early in the morning :[1] however, the men did not reach the beach till past nine o'clock. During the retreat, and until the embarkation commenced, only skirmishing had taken place ; but the French, who were in possession of an eminence that commanded the beach, then opened ten guns and eight mortars with great effect ; this fire sank several boats on their passage to the ships.  As the embarkation proceeded, the enemy descended the hill, though they suffered severely in their approach to the shore from their exposure to the shot from our vessels.  The greater part of the British troops, including the Coldstream, who had reached St. Cas the previous day, got on board, but the grenadiers of the Guards and half of the First regiment of Guards, amounting altogether to fifteen hundred men, remained under Major-General Dury to cover the embarkation.  When the French advanced on these brave men, " who had fired away all their ammunition,"[2] they formed into grand divisions, and prepared to charge ; but it was too late ; they were overpowered, and officers and men dropped on all sides.[3]  General Dury was severely wounded, and after-

---

[1] The Coldstream had been ordered to return to the bay for provisons, and to escort them back to the camp, which of course became unnecessary.

[2] An Authentic Account of our Last Attempt on the Coast of France.  By an Officer.  London, 1758.

[3] Prince Edward, afterwards Duke of York, (brother to George III.) then a youth serving on board Lord Howe's ship, attempted to go on shore to assist in bringing off the troops.

wards drowned in attempting to reach the ships; many
officers and men shared the same fate.[1]   In the grenadier company of the Coldstream[2] Volunteer Johnson was
killed, and Captains Mathew, Caswell, and Volunteer
Steel, were made prisoners.   The slaughter was increased
by a battery which from an eminence commanded the
beach.   No sooner had the fire from the shipping ceased,
than quarter and protection were instantly granted to the
English who remained.   Upwards of a thousand picked
men of the British troops were killed or taken on this
occasion.   The humanity of the victors deserves every
praise; for it cannot be denied that the British had during
their stay in the country been guilty of many excesses.

These descents on the coast of France seem to have been
injudicious, and badly planned.   It is strange that it
should have been deemed advisable to employ so large a

---

His Royal Highness, who was maddened at the sight, clandestinely
got out of the port-hole into a boat alongside, but was stopped
by the Commodore from proceeding on the desperate service.

[1] See Appendix, No. 235.

[2] The following is an account of the affair at St. Cas, published
at Paris, September 22nd, 1758. (By authority.)

"The enemy first advanced in column from the centre; but
"from the fire of some cannon, commanded by M. de Villepa-
"tour, which had been sent to the right, the enemy were thrown
"into confusion, and obliged to retire.   The conflict was general,
"and lasted nearly two hours.   The English then gave way, and
"great numbers were killed in endeavouring to re-embark.
"Three boats full of their soldiers were sunk, many more
"killed, in boats on their way to the fleet.   About 1900 were left
"on shore; amongst them were several officers of distinction, and
"in particular a Colonel and Lieutenant-Colonel of the English
"Guards.   General Dury was among the number of drowned.
"We have taken upwards of 600 men, and 39 officers, some of
"whom are of the first families in England.   This body of troops is
"totally destroyed."

1758.   force for so insignificant a purpose. To explain why such fruitless and ill-judged measures were adopted would be difficult; they were attended with great waste of human life, a vast expenditure; and, even if crowned with the most brilliant success, no advantageous results were likely to accrue from them beyond the burning of a few ships, which could not occasion a loss to the enemy at all in proportion to the cost of the enterprise. As diversions, they were on too small a scale to be of much efficacy. In these expeditions the British soldiers behaved with their accustomed intrepidity. That their valour led to no satisfactory consequences, cannot be a subject of surprise. They were sent to a part of France well supplied with troops both of the line and militia, and landed without maps, without guides, and without any object in view except that of a marauding excursion.

September.   The fleet returned to Spithead, and in September the army, having disembarked at Cowes, encamped at Newport. On the twenty-sixth the First Guards moved to London, and the Coldstream followed on the eighth of October.[1]

---

[1] See Appendix, Nos. 233, 234.

Return of the Coldstream Guards, commanded by the Right Honourable James Lord Tyrawley. Feb. 28, 1759.

FIRST BATTALION; ON EXPEDITION TO CHERBOURG, ST. MALOES, &c.

| | Captains. | Lieutenants. | Ensigns. |
|---|---|---|---|
| Gren' Comp<sup></sup>. | Lt-Colo. Clavering | { Cap<sup>a</sup> Mathew<br>{ Cap<sup>a</sup> Caswell | |
| | Ld. Tyrawley, Colo. | Lt-C¹ Burgoyne, C. L¹ | Ens. Smith |
| | Col. Cæsar, 1st Major | Cap<sup>a</sup> Martin | Ens. Lambton |
| | Lieut-Colo. Gansel, acting Maj<sup>r</sup> to the Exp<sup>n</sup>. | Cap<sup>a</sup> Thornton | Ens. Bishopp |
| | Lieut-Colo. Vernon | Cap<sup>a</sup> Rainsford | Ens. Leheup |
| | Lieut-Colo. Evelyn | Cap<sup>a</sup> Scott | Ens. Twisleton |
| | Lieut'-Colo. Sandys | Cap<sup>a</sup> Clarke | Ens. Banks |
| | Lieut'-Colo Sorell | Cap<sup>a</sup> Wright | Ens. Schutz |
| | Lieut'-Colo. Listers | Cap<sup>a</sup> Trelawney | Ens. Ch<sup>a</sup> Morgan |

Staff Officers. 1758.

| | |
|---|---|
| Mr Jefferies, Chaplain | Mr Mc Cullock, Mate |
| Capn Rainsford, Adjut | Mr Elliot, Solicitor |
| Capn Wright, Qr Master | Mr Thorp, Drum-Major |
| Mr Tricquet, Surgeon | Mr Hoddinett, Depy Marshal. |

SECOND BATTALION; AT HOME.

| | Captains. | Lieutenants. | Ensigns. |
|---|---|---|---|
| Grenr. Compy. | Lieutt-Colo. Chs Craig | Capn Craig<br>Capn Hussey | |
| | Majr-Gen. Noel, Lieutt-Col. | Capn Wyndham | Ens. Dilkes |
| | Colo. A. Court, 2d Major | Capn Wynch | Ens. Wolseley |
| | Lieutt-Colo. Thomas | Capn Gwyn | Ens. Geo. Morgan |
| | Lieutt-Colo. Blayney | Capn Sloper | Ens. Eden |
| | Lieutt-Colo. De Cosne | Capn D'Avenant | Ens. Dive |
| | Lieutt-Colo. Bodens | Capn O Hara | Ens. Bowyer |
| | Lieutt-Colo. Fs Craigs | Capn Wyvell | Ens. Edmondes |
| | Lt-Col. Sir Wm Wiseman | Ct Buckeridge | Ens. Birch. |

Staff Officers.

Ct D'Avenant, Adjut. Mr James, Surgeon mate.

# CHAPTER XXVI.

War in Germany—French under Broglio—Allies leave their cantonments—Hereditary Prince surprises Zierenberg—Cleves surrenders—Hereditary Prince repulsed in an attempt to surprise the French camp — Allies move by Genderick — Enemy attack their van-guard — Troops cross the Rhine — Hereditary Prince raises the blockade of Wesel—Broglio reinforced by Prince Xavier—Allies in cantonments about Warbourg—Troops left to defend the passages of the Dymel — Allies go into winter-quarters—Guards at Faderborn.

1760.  THE war still raged in Germany. Marshal Duke de Broglio commanded the French forces, consisting of one hundred thousand men; a separate corps was formed under Count de St. Germain.

May 5th.    In May the Allies left their cantonments near Osnaburg,
May 20th. and encamped on the heights near Fritzlar, where three regiments of English dragoons joined them.

July.    Prince Ferdinand on the eighth of July quitted his camp for the heights of Braunau, as he perceived that the enemy intended to turn his right.

The French determined to seize the heights of Corbach; for which purpose Broglio pressed forward his advance, and followed with the main body.

Ferdinand at two A.M. on the tenth of July resumed his march; the Hereditary Prince also moved from Saxenhausen towards Corbach, where the van of the Count de St. Germain's corps had preceded him, and formed on the heights close to the place. The Hereditary Prince, supposing they did not exceed ten thousand foot and seventeen squadrons, attacked. As the enemy were continually reinforced, and had besides a numerous artillery, and it was found impossible to send fresh troops in sufficient time to support the assault, Ferdinand gave orders for him to rejoin the army: the retreat was made in great confusion. Shortly after this the Allies surprised the enemy in a defile among the mountains. The English defeated a body of the French at the village of Emsdorf.

Both armies manœuvred: the French Marshal divided his troops into three corps, one of which, amounting to fifteen thousand men, he sent towards Hirchfield and Fulde by the left of the Confederates, in the hope of separating General Sporcken's corps from the main army under Ferdinand. The Confederates encamped near Halle.

The Chevalier de Muy, who had succeeded the Count de St. Germain, crossed the Dymel at Stadtberg, to cut off the Allies from Westphalia; the Duke de Broglio at the same time moved towards their camp; and Prince Xavier of Saxony, who commanded the reserve on the left, advanced on Cassel, for the protection of which place General Kilmanseg remained with a body of troops, and Ferdinand crossed the Dymel between Liebenau and Dringelburg. At five o'clock A. M. the Allies were under arms on the heights of Corbach, having made a night march. The Hereditary Prince reconnoitred the position of the Chevalier de Muy, who was strongly posted with his right at Warbourg and his left extending towards the hill of Ossendorff. Ferdinand determined to attack. The

1760.    Hereditary Prince and M. de Sporcken were ordered to
the left, whilst he advanced on the enemy's front. The
French, finding themselves assailed in flank and rear at the
same time, gave way after a sharp contest, and fell back on
Warbourg. In the mean time the army moved to attack in
front, but were too late to charge. Lord Granby advanced
with the cavalry on the right, and the English artillery
seconded "the attack in a surprising manner."[1] Many
of the French were drowned in endeavouring to ford the
Dymel. They lost ten pieces of cannon, some colours,
with fifteen hundred men left on the field; the prisoners
exceeded that number.[2] On this occasion the brigade of
English grenadiers and the Scotch Highlanders greatly
distinguished themselves.

Aug. 20th.    The enemy attempted to cross the Weser near Busch-
feldt to support Prince Xavier; but were repulsed by
General Wangenheim at Uslar. During the night of the
twenty-first of August Broglio marched by his right.

The Hereditary Prince next day passed the Dymel with
about twelve thousand men to turn the enemy's left. He
brought up with him the Greys and Inniskillen dragoons,
supported by the English grenadiers, which force drove
the enemy with great precipitation and loss to Zierenberg.

Prince Xavier of Saxony having taken Gottingen, raised
a heavy contribution on the inhabitants, and directed the
works of the town to be repaired.

Aug. 25th.    The three battalions of the British guards, under the

---

[1] London Gazette Extraordinary, Saturday, August 9th, 1760.—
Operations of the Allied Army under Prince Ferdinand, by an
Officer in the British Service, page 161.

[2] London Gazette Extraordinary, August 9th, 1760.
The loss of the British in killed, wounded, and missing, was
590.—*Ferdinand's Campaigns*, page 161.

command of Major-General Julius Cæsar, joined the
Allied army near the village of Buhne.[1]

---

[1] See Appendix, Orders for Embarkation, Nos. 237, 238.

Companies of the second battalion of the Coldstream Guards, which embarked for Germany the end of July, 1760:—

| Captains of Companies. | Lieutenants and Captains. | Ensigns. |
|---|---|---|
| 1. Major-General Bennet Noel, Lieut.-Colonel; absent in England | Wadham Wyndham | Henry Dilkes |
| 2. Major-Gen. Julius Cæsar, first Major | William Wynch | William Wolseley |
| 3. Lt.-Col. Chas. Craig | William Gwyn | William Bowyer |
| 4. „ Cadwallr Blayney | William Charles Sloper, A.D.C. to Prince Ferdinand | Robert Eden |
| 5. „ Charles Vernon (Grenadier Company) | { James Craig { Richard Hussey | |
| 6. „ Wm. Evelyn | Thomas d'Avenant (Adjutant) | Lewis George Dive |
| 7. „ George Boden | Charles O'Hara, A.D.C. to Lord Granby | George Morgan |
| 8. „ Francis Craig | George Augustus Wyvill | Richard Byron |
| 9. „ Sir Wm. Wiseman, Bart. | William Wright (Quarter-Master) | James Birch |

Chaplain, the Rev. John Loftie.
Adjutant, Thomas d'Avenant.
Quarter-master William Wright.
Surgeon's Mate, Nicholas James.
„        Samuel Billingsley.
„        . . . . Fellows.

During the service of the battalion in Germany the following officers joined from England; viz.

| Lt.-Col. Rubigny de Cosne | Lt. and Capt. Charles Cooper | Ensigns. |
|---|---|---|
| „ Thomas Clarke | „ „ John Lambton | John Twisleton |
| „ Charles Rainsford | | George Banks |
| „ Edward Mathew, A.D.C. to Major-Gen. Julius Cæsar | | Richard Clive |
| | | James Hamilton |

Quarter-master, William Hoddinett.
Surgeon's Mate, Peter Mow.

The following officers died, or returned to England:—

Lieut.-Col. Charles Craig, died March 30, 1761.

to possess themselves of the convent of Campden, half a    1760.
league in front of the army.   They afterwards advanced,
but the opposition gave M. de Castries time to prepare;
the firing commenced at five o'clock A.M., and continued   Oct. 16th.
without intermission for sixteen hours, when the Allies
were repulsed.   The infantry having expended their ammunition, and the French occupying the wood, a retreat
was ordered.   The loss on this occasion was ten officers,
sixteen non-commissioned officers, two hundred and
twenty-one rank and file, killed; sixty-eight officers,
forty-three non-commissioned officers, and eight hundred
and twelve rank and file, wounded; seven officers, six
non-commissioned officers, and four hundred and twenty-
nine rank and file, taken prisoners.   The enemy's loss was
eight hundred and forty-one killed; one thousand seven
hundred and ninety-five wounded.   Lientenant-General
de Segur, with several officers of rank, and about four
hundred men, were made prisoners.   Two pieces of cannon
and one pair of colours were also taken.[1]

The Allies moved by Genderick; their vanguard was   Oct 17th.
attacked in a wood in front of Elverick, along the Rhine.
The advance of the enemy under M. de Chabot arrived
and posted themselves among the thickets, a quarter of a
league in front of the Confederates.   Early next day the
bridge across the Rhine was completed, and the troops
crossed.   During the night the Hereditary Prince raised   Oct. 18th
the blockade of Wesel, and proceeded to Brunnen, where   and 19th.
he encamped.

The Duke de Broglio was reinforced by the corps under   Oct. 25th.
the Prince Xavier, two days after the Prince's corps
quitted Diegerode, and went into quarters.

---

[1] Operations of the Allied Army under Prince Ferdinand, by
an Officer in the British Service, 1764, page 179.

## CHAPTER XXVII.

French enter Duderstadt—Town retaken—Confederates assemble
—Brigade of Guards join the advance — Enemy defeated by
Prince Ferdinand at Kirchdenkern — Soubise raises the siege of
Munster — Brigade of Guards join the main body — Early in
December the hostile armies go into winter-quarters — British
infantry in the Bishoprick of Osnaburg.

EARLY in January the French entered Duderstadt on the left of the cantonments of the Confederate army. The town was abandoned by General Mausberg, who retired to the heights of Herbishagen, till joined by Generals Kilmanseg and Luckner. The following day they retook the place, and drove the enemy as far as Witzenhausen.

1761.
Jan. 2nd.

The Confederates were at their different rendezvous, the main body of the army on the Dymel and the Rhume. Two corps under the Hereditary Prince assembled in the Sauerland. Prince Ferdinand crossed the Dymel, and the army advanced on Cassel by West Usseln. Next day the army continued its march; the advanced guards of the columns united, and were joined by the grenadiers of ·the Guards, Elliot's dragoons, Baur's hussars, the brigade of Chasseurs of Lindinch, and Storkhoriens. These troops were placed under Granby, who took post at Ehlen.

Feb. 9th.

Feb. 11th.

The brigade of British Guards joined Lord Granby on the twenty-first of February; they then marched to Treysa, where the enemy had been posted in force; but

Feb 21st.

1761.  on the approach of the advance, withdrew to Ziegenhayn, which was immediately blockaded.

Mar. 11th.  Lord Granby crossed the river Lahn below Marpurg. The troops were quartered at Lohr, Dam, Rodgen, and other places, and four regiments were left in Marpurg.

During the months of April, May, and June, the hostile armies continued to manœuvre, and occasional skirmishes took place.

July.  On the fourteenth of July the main body of the Confederates was on the heights of Wambeln, the Prince of Anhalt between Illingen and Hohenover. The Hereditary Prince was on the right, Granby formed the left on the heights of Kirchdenkern, and Lieutenant-General Wutgenau was encamped on the heath of Untrup. In the

July 15th.  evening Soubise advanced by his right, dislodged Granby's post at Hanse Neble, and evinced an intention of moving on the camp. Granby was directed to maintain his post to the last: he had with him ten battalions, six squadrons, and ten six-pounders. Wutgenan, with his corps, was ordered to act in concert with Granby, whose right was to be supported by the Prince of Anhalt. with ten battalions and six squadrons; the Prince's right extended to the river Aast, above Kirchdenkern.     Lieutenant-General Conway with eight battalions, seven squadrons, some English artillery, and a battalion of Saxe-Gotha, occupied the ground left by the Prince of Anhalt between Illingen and Hohenover. Lieutenant-General Bose crowned the heights of Wambeln, and Count Kilmanseg remained on the side of Bureck. Great part of the artillery was in front of the left. The arrangements being completed, his Serene Highness visited Granby, who held the French at bay till General Wutgenau joined his left, took the enemy in flank, and drove them into the woods. Wutgenau kept the ground he had gained, extended his right,

and turned his left towards the road of Ham, the defence
of which was important.

Broglio marched from Erwite at day-light, in conjunction with Soubise, to attack the Allies. General Howard was ordered up with a brigade of cavalry and infantry under Lords Pembroke and Frederick Cavendish, two battalions went to Kirchdenkern to fortify and barricade that village, and, if necessary, they were to be supported by General Howard. The enemy had possession of some posts opposite the piquets, and maintained an incessant skirmish during the night with the patroles. Next morning they renewed their efforts against Wutgenau's corps, which terminated without making any impression.

The enemy were desirous to place some batteries opposite Granby's position, on an eminence which he could not enclose within his lines. As Sporcken's detachment had just arrived, Prince Ferdinand resolved to take advantage of the irresolution that appeared among the French; ten battalions were ordered to advance: this movement met with complete success; the enemy precipitately retired, leaving their wounded and several pieces of cannon. They were followed as far as Haltrup; afterwards the light troops went in pursuit. When the right of the enemy was broken, Ferdinand carried with him great part of the heavy British artillery, and an English brigade, to the side where the Hereditary Prince commanded; but before they got up, the enemy had retired. Three hundred and eleven of the Confederates were killed, one thousand and eleven wounded, and one hundred and ninety-two made prisoners.

The loss of the French in killed and wounded was between five and six thousand; nine of their guns and six colours were taken. After the battle the Allies returned to their former encampment at Hohenover.

Ferdinand, at the head of Granby's corps, and all the British, with the exception of the Guards, proceeded by rapid marches, with a view to force the enemy at Dringelbourg : after making three hundred prisoners, the troops crossed the Dymel and encamped near Cassel. Granby was at Bhune and Corbeke. Soubise raised the siege of Munster : next day he crossed the Lippe in three columns near Dorsten. The Hereditary Prince reached Dulmen, and the brigade of British Guards marched from the vicinity of Hoxter towards Brogentrick, near which they encamped, and joined the main body under the Prince on the sixteenth of September.

The Allies crossed the Rhine in four columns on the eleventh of October, above Warbourg ; but this led to no event of importance, and the troops went into cantonments on the twelfth of November, with the exception of ten battalions. These consisted of the senior regiments in each brigade, and were encamped under the command of General Conway on the Huve, near Eimbeck, with a train of sixteen guns. The army had orders to assemble on the firing of nine guns, and join the corps under General Conway.

On the twenty-eighth the British Guards and Highlanders left their stations for winter-quarters. The ten battalions encamped on the Huve broke up, and joined their respective brigades.

Early in December, Marshal Broglio's army went into cantonments. His infantry was in the vicinity of Eisenach, Gotha, and Mulhausen; his cavalry in the district of Fulda, and villages about Frankfort. Marshal Broglio's head-quarters were at Cassel.

Prince Ferdinand fixed himself at Hildesheim, and the army marched off successively to the places assigned

1761.
Aug. 24th.

Sept. 4th.

October.

November.

December.

Dec. 4th.

# CHAPTER XXVIII.

The enemy assemble near Mulhausen—Confederates in camp at Brakel—French advance—Battle of Gravenstein—French retreat—Cross the Fulda—Allies about Holtzhausen and Weimar —Guards near Hoff— French between Cassel and Munden—Castle of Waldec capitulates to Conway—Death of Lieut.-General Cæsar—Battle of Brucken Muhl—The armies move into winter-quarters—British troops march through Holland and embark at Williamstadt—General Gansell rescued by some soldiers —Brigade order.

A BODY of the Allies was placed in the vicinity of Eimbeck to check the excursions of the garrison of Gottingen, which, however, on the night of the tenth sallied from the town : the only result was, that many men were killed on both sides. *1762. Mar. 20th.*

Early in April the enemy assembled near Mulhausen. The Confederates were at the time in motion about Eimbeck. *April.*

Marshal Soubise arrived at Cassel, and, in conjunction with Marshal d'Estrées, was to command the French army on the Upper Rhine and the Maine, while the Prince de Condé placed himself at the head of that on the Lower Rhine. *April 20th. April 24th.*

The English troops who were in cantonments near Bielevelt united with the corps under General Sporcken, near Blomberg, and encamped on the heights of Belle. On the eighteenth of June the Confederates were in camp at Brakel. *June 4th.*

The main body moved on the twentieth for Burgholtz, and Granby's corps, forming the van-guard, advanced to Warbourg: next day the army was in position between Corbach and Tissel, near Buhne.

The French under d'Estrées and Soubise proceeded to Gravenstein and Meijenbracksen. At the same time, the corps under Marshal de Castries was on their right flank between Carlsdorff and Gravenstein. This latter place covered the right of their army, which was also protected by several rivulets.

Prince Ferdinand prepared for an attack, after observing the manœuvres of his opponents. Lieutenant-General Luckner at Sulbeck on the Leihne, with Eimbeck in front, was to watch Prince Xavier between the Werra and Gottingen. The Hessian hussars were to remain near Mohringen, to conceal the movement of General Luckner's corps from Hollenstadt to Gotsbuhren, and also to check the corps under Prince Xavier. The army crossed the Dymel in several columns, between Liebenau and Sielen. The left, under General Sporcken, consisting of Hanoverians, with the cavalry of the left wing, moved towards Humme and Beverbec for the purpose of forming on the enemy's right. The orders were to attack the right under Marshal de Castries, whilst General Luckner was to charge the rear: if successful, they were to continue their march, which would enable them to take the enemy encamped at Gravenstein in flank and rear. Sixteen squadrons that followed the fifth column halted near Giesmar to menace the front, whilst the attack was to be made on the right. His Serene Highness at the head of the other five columns, consisting of twelve English, eleven Brunswick, and eight Hessian regiments, with the English cavalry and part of the Germans of the left wing, moved to Langelberg, and formed before Kelts in front of

the enemy. The piquets of the army formed the left of
the advance, and the chasseurs of the English infantry,
with some Hanoverians, the right. Marshal de Castries,
finding his right turned, in order to make head against
General Sporcken, commenced a sharp cannonade, and
drew up his cavalry to oppose Luckner. The Allied
cavalry advanced, broke the enemy's infantry, took two
guns, and, after some severe fighting, Marshal de Castries
was driven back in great disorder on the enemy's right.
The main body attacked in front; Granby at the same time
advanced by Ersen and Furstenwalde to turn the left.
The French, finding their situation critical, endeavoured to
reach the heights of Wilhelmstal, by breaking into as
many columns as the ground would admit. In doing this
they abandoned all their equipages at Gravenstein, and a
general rout might have ensued if General Stainville,
seeing that by the manœuvre of Lord Granby the retreat
was cut off, and more particularly that of his own corps,
had not gained the wood of Meijenbracksen with the
Grenadiers of France, the Royal Grenadiers, the regiment
of Aquitain, and other chosen troops, the flower of the
French infantry: this step was taken to cover the retreat.
The operation cost him, however, dear; he was attacked
by Granby, and, after a most gallant defence, the whole
of his infantry, with the exception of two battalions, were
killed, taken, or dispersed. The enemy's loss exceeded
five thousand.

The casualties in the Coldstream were twenty-three
men; in addition to which, five privates of the grenadier
company, forming part of the grenadier battalion, were
killed.[1]

---

[1] The colours taken from the French at Gravenstein were presented to the King at St. James's on the 26th of July, 1762.

" Lord Granby acquitted himself upon thi*
" with remarkable valour, and had a great sh*
" victory." [1]

" The enemy's army retreated under the wal
" sel, and a great proportion rapidly crossed the

June 28th. The brigade of Guards moved from their g*
July 1st. encamped at Winter-Kasten. The enemy as*
force of cavalry and infantry near Hombour*
their communications with Frankfort. Prince
was determined to dislodge them, and sent Lord
Cavendish from Lohn to Feltzberg, and Lord G*
Hoff to Fritzlar. Lord Frederick had order*
towards Hombourg, and to cut off the corps
sungen and Fulda. Their retreat to Ziegenha
be intercepted by Lord Granby. Lord Freder*
dish was to fire three guns as the signal of 1
After the advance had reached within a mile of 1
the enemy formed at the foot of the mountain a
near the town; their cavalry drew up on the 1
the signal being fired, the French infantry
covered by their cavalry, closely followed by 1
and Elliot's dragoons, who engaged them till 1
diers and Highlanders could get up, on which
and were pursued with great ardour. The .
about eighty men; the enemy two hundred
prisoners, besides the killed and wounded.

July 6th. The two armies occupied nearly the same 1
before. The Confederates remained encampe*
Holtzhausen and Weimar, with a force on th*
well as Uslar in the Solling. The brigade of G

---

[1] London Gazette Extraordinary, Thursday, July 1st
10222.

[2] London Gazette, July 10th, 1762. No. 10225.

posted near Hoff. Great part of the French army were 1762. on the high ground between Cassel and Munden, leaving strong detachments about Dransfeldt; a corps of fifteen thousand was between Melsungen and Hombourg.

The castle of Waldec near Fritzlar capitulated, and July 11th. General Conway, after a bombardment of forty-eight hours, took possession.

Lieutenant-General Julius Cæsar, with the brigade of July 13th. Guards under his command, moved to Gudensberg, where Lord Granby's force was assembled, who then marched for the Eder.

Prince Ferdinand determined to oblige Prince Xavier to July 23rd. quit his position of Lutterberg; for which purpose eight battalions were to pass the Fulda at Spele, eight squadrons to cross at Spiegehnuhl, and an additional force at Willemshausen. Troops were posted at Bonnafort to cover the left attack and keep in check the garrison of Munden, and, in conjunction with another force sent towards Gottingen, they were also to pass the Werra at Heidemunden, and, if possible, take the enemy in the rear. The attack was well conducted, and met with complete success. The Saxons, apprehensive that their retreat might be intercepted, retired in disorder to Cassel, by which two regiments of grenadiers and one regiment of cavalry were made prisoners. Prince Frederick of Brunswick in the mean time marched for the enemy's intrenched camp on the Kratzenburg, and cannonaded their lines. General Stainville, who was posted there with ten thousand men, hearing of the defeat of the Saxons, left his intrenchments to cover the retreat of Prince Xavier. The camp was taken by Prince Frederick, who directed the redoubts to be destroyed. Granby ordered the First July 24th. Guards and a battalion of Hanoverians, with one hundred men from each of the other regiments, to attack the heights in several columns; the river, swelled by a sudden rain, rendered it dangerous for the troops to ford; part of the right wing, however, crossed and drove the enemy from one of the passes, and occupied a post in front of their centre. The French made frequent attempts to dislodge them, but were as often repulsed with loss.  Detachments from the Coldstream and Third Guards were ordered to attack Melsungen; they succeeded in cutting down the chevaux-de-frize, and endeavoured to force the gates, but failed.  The army bivouacked till the morning of the tenth, and then returned to their former ground.

was.
Aug. 8th.

The French left Hirschfeldt for Mohr.  The object of the Prince of Condé, then at Grunberg, was to form a junction with the grand army.  The Hereditary Prince, to prevent this, moved to Trillengen, attacked his advance, and obliged him to retire, with the loss of one hundred and fifty men, on the main body.

Aug. 22nd.

The French army had retired on Friedberg.  The Prince of Condé left his position on the twenty-ninth to unite with the two Marshals.  The Hereditary Prince arrived about the same time at Wolfersheim; he sent General Luckner to the other side of the Wetter to occupy the heights, whilst he went with his main body to Assenheim.  On the march he found the French assembling in force near Friedberg; instead, therefore, of continuing his route to Assenheim, he returned to support General Luckner.  The Hereditary Prince, who was not aware that Count de Stainville's corps had joined the Prince of Condé, or that the grand French army was at hand, attacked the enemy near Newheim and Friedberg, and drove them from the mountains of Johannesberg into the plains.  But the French, being reinforced by the two Marshals, resumed the offensive, when the Hereditary Prince was obliged to

Aug. 30th.

orders to enter the battery and relieve the Hanoverians,
which was effected with the greatest bravery: the men had
to march four hundred paces, exposed to a tremendous fire
of musektry and grape. Several twelve-pounders were
brought up with great effect. The struggle was maintained
with great resolution on both sides; night at length put
a stop to it. No attempt to cross the bridge was made by
either party, although within three hundred paces of the
French batteries. The troops were relieved in the redoubts
after they had expended their sixty rounds of ammunition.
This obstinate contest continued without intermission fourteen hours. Fifty pieces of cannon kept up a constant fire
within the limited area of four hundred paces. The loss
of the Allies amounted to about eight hundred men.
Captain Twisleton, Ensign Clive, and two rank and file of
the Coldstream were killed: Captain Wyvil, two serjeants, one drummer, and twenty-three rank and file
wounded.

The French acknowledged a loss of three hundred killed
and eight hundred wounded.

Their batteries continued to play on the town of Amone-
bourg all night; and a breach being made, the assault was
attempted without success.

General Conway left the heights of Wetter. A movement was also made by the main body of the army, who
encamped between Schonstadt and Straultzenbach. Lord
Granby's corps occupied the ground before Niederkleiss, to
be in readiness to defend the passage of Brucken Muhl.
General Wangenheim remained on the heights near Daurot
to oppose the Saxons, and General Luckner was on the
right of Conway.

The armies began to repair to their quarters; the English to the Bishoprick of Munster.

1762.     From the abdication of James the Second to the termination of the German war, excepting the period of Marlborough's triumphant career, the history of British continental warfare is little more than an uninteresting narrative of military manœuvres and indecisive battles of rare occurrence, which did not lead to any thing.  Those incidents that might in some degree have relieved the monotonous detail of marches and countermarches, are no longer known; neither can a soldier of the modern school derive much pleasure or instruction from tracing out the movements of hostile commanders who on both sides seem to have carried to perfection the art of keeping clear of each other.  There is an anecdote told of an officer educated under their system who is said on one occasion to have cried out, "I don't like all this moving about; I should not wonder if some day or other we were to fall in with the enemy."  This anecdote, whether genuine or not, was in the spirit of those tactics which for a long period tried the endurance and hardihood of the soldier to the uttermost, and, instead of terminating his career on the field of battle, or restoring him to his home crowned with laurels, sent him to his death-bed in a foreign hospital.  In giving an account of the services of the Coldstream, the writer cannot flatter himself that this part of his work will be perused with much interest; his only resource was to abridge it in such a manner as to preserve all that he could find connected with the regiment.  It was reserved for the present century to see the power of France crushed to atoms in a campaign of a few days, and the object of an age of timid operations accomplished in a single battle.

England and France were at length tired of this fruitless contest, and wished for peace.  George the Third, in his speech from the throne on the twenty-fifth of November, informed both Houses that preliminaries had been signed ~~~ at Fontainbleau early in that month, between England, France, Spain, and Portugal.

On the twenty-fifth of January part of the first division January. of British troops began their march through Guelderland, Nimeguen, and Breda, to Williamstadt, where transports waited to convey them to England.[1]

The second battalion of the Coldstream arrived at Yar-

---

[1] " First of January, 1763.

" Return of the effective number of officers, men, servants, wo-
" men, and horses, each regiment will consist of on their march
" through Holland to embark for England."

| Regiments. | Officers. | Men. | Servants. | Women. | Horses. | Regiments. | Officers. | Men. | Servants. | Women. | Horses. |
|---|---|---|---|---|---|---|---|---|---|---|---|
| FIRST DIVISION. | | | | | | THIRD DIVISION. | | | | | |
| Blues (Horse Guards) | 27 | 434 | 55 | 21 | 508 | Conway's — Dragoons | 14 | 329 | 24 | 35 | 423 |
| Carabineer's (Horse) | 12 | 285 | 38 | 36 | 358 | Grey's | 11 | 340 | 42 | 35 | 425 |
| Honywood's (Horse) | 9 | 291 | 32 | 44 | 394 | Inniskilling's | 13 | 551 | 22 | 44 | 360 |
| 1st Regt. of Guards | 18 | 727 | 15 | 45 | 102 | Cornwallis's | 22 | 665 | 3 | 55 | 127 |
| Coldstream Guards | 17 | 717 | 8 | 49 | 105 | Erskine's | 28 | 674 | 4 | 80 | 77 |
| 3rd Regt. of Guards | 11 | 745 | 13 | 43 | 104 | Griffin's | 20 | 706 | 1 | 71 | 84 |
| Hodson's (regiment) | 27 | 692 | 0 | 54 | 67 | Stewart's | 31 | 676 | 0 | 87 | 106 |
| Barrington's | 34 | 642 | 2 | 86 | 110 | Totals | 139 | 3721 | 96 | 407 | 1602 |
| Totals | 155 | 4533 | 163 | 378 | 1745 | | | | | | |
| SECOND DIVISION. | | | | | | FOURTH DIVISION. | | | | | |
| Bland's — Dragoons | 21 | 486 | 33 | 56 | 560 | Mostyn's — Dragoons | 19 | 326 | 33 | 42 | 410 |
| Waldegrave's | 15 | 325 | 31 | 31 | 405 | Mordaunt's | 16 | 315 | 29 | 39 | 420 |
| Howard's | 14 | 328 | 32 | 35 | 434 | Ancrum's | 13 | 330 | 27 | 29 | 397 |
| Bockland's | 28 | 728 | 0 | 60 | 94 | Elliott's | 19 | 611 | 40 | 46 | 577 |
| Napier's | 27 | 689 | 1 | 80 | 110 | Carr's | 29 | 697 | 2 | 64 | 128 |
| Kingsley's | 27 | 699 | 7 | 83 | 79 | Brudenell's | 30 | 712 | 3 | 102 | 106 |
| Boscawen's | 29 | 689 | 3 | 89 | 97 | Keith's | 27 | 626 | 6 | 81 | 126 |
| Totals | 161 | 3944 | 107 | 434 | 1779 | Campbell's | 29 | 639 | 0 | 44 | 101 |
| | | | | | | Totals | 182 | 4256 | 140 | 447 | 2265 |

| | Officers. | Men. | Servants. | Women. | Horses. |
|---|---|---|---|---|---|
| General Totals | 637 | 16454 | 505 | 1666 | 7391 |

Thos. Hay, D. A. Gen.

1763.  mouth on the twenty-sixth of February, and
through Sudbury to London.[1]

1770.      A general officer in the course of this year w&
for debt, and rescued by some soldiers of th&
which occasioned the following order from his
forbidding the interference of the military on a
occasion in future :—

"Brigade Orders.—His Majesty has signifi
"field-officer in waiting, that he has been acqua
"Serjeant Bacon of the First Guards and Serje
"of the Coldstream Guards, with four priva
"First regiment, were, more or less, concerned in
"of Major-General Gansell"[2] (late of the Coldst
"September last. The King hopes, and is wil
"lieve, they did not know the Major-General wa
"and only thought they were delivering an offi
"tress. However, his Majesty commands that tl
"be severely reprimanded for acting in this b
"they have done, and strictly orders for the f
"no commissioned officer or soldier do presum
"fere with bailiffs or arrests on any account o
"whatever, the crime being of a very atrociou
"and if any are found guilty of disobeying this o
"will be most severely punished. This order
"immediately at the head of every company of tl
"of Foot Guards, that no man plead ignoran
"future."

It is curious to see how this trifling occurrence
nified by party spirit.

[1] See Appendix, Nos. 240, 241.
[2] He died at his apartments in the Fleet Prison on
eighth of July, 1774.

Junius's Letters, p. 183.—" A Major-General[1] of the   1770.
" army is arrested by the sheriff's officers for a consider-
" able debt. He persuades them to conduct him to the
" Tilt-Yard Guard in St. James's Park, under some pre-
" tence of business, which it imported him to settle before
" he was confined. He applies to a serjeant, not imme-
" diately on duty, to assist him, with some of his com-
" panions, in favouring his escape. He attempts it; a
" bustle ensues; an officer[2] of the Guards, not then on
" duty, takes part in the affair, applies to the Lieut.[3]
" commanding the Tilt-Yard Guard, and urges him to
" turn out his guard to relieve a General Officer. The
" Lieut. declines interfering in person, but stands at a dis-
" tance, and suffers the business to be done. The Officer
" takes upon himself to order out the guard; in a moment
" they are in arms, quit their guard, march, rescue the
" General, and drive away the sheriff's officers, who in
" vain represent their right to the prisoner, and the nature
" of the arrest. The soldiers first conduct the General into
" the guard-room, then escort him to a place of safety,
" with bayonets fixed, and in all the form of military
" triumph."

---

[1] M.-Gen. Gansell.      [2] Lt. Dodd.      [3] Lt. Garth.

# CHAPTER XXIX.

Death of Tyrawley—Waldegrave succeeds in command of the
Coldstream—Preparations to reduce America—France encourages them to hold out—Government stores seized in Rhode
Island—Gage retaliates — Hostilities commence — Congress of
Massachusetts—General Congress at Philadelphia—Howe, Burgoyne, and Clinton arrive at Boston with reinforcements—Colonies of New York and North Carolina united with the other provinces — Washington appointed Commander-in-Chief—A battalion formed by draughts from the three regiments of Guards
embark for America—Battle of Long Island — British advance—
Reinforced by foreign troops in English pay—Washington retreats
—Fort Washington carried—Enemy abandon Fort Lee—Washington retreats to the Delaware—Guards in quarters at Brunswick
for the winter—British commence operations—Cornwallis obliges
Lord Stirling and General Maxwell to retreat—Howe returns
to Amboy—Army embarks—Lands at Elk Ferry—Washington
crosses the Delaware—Crowns the heights of Brandywine Creek
—Battle of Brandywine—Supineness of Howe — Washington
attacks Germantown—Fort of Mud Island abandoned—Washington quits his position at Skippack Creek—Burgoyne takes
command of the northern army.

1773.    LORD TYRAWLEY, who had commanded the Coldstream
for upwards of eighteen years, died at this period. He
served with distinction in the wars of Queen Anne.

The Earl of Waldegrave succeeded to the command of
the regiment on the fifteenth of July.

1774.    During the winter great preparations were made by
England to reduce her Transatlantic Colonies to obedience.
France secretly encouraged the malcontents in America,
and held out expectations of future aid. Each party prepared to have recourse to arms. Stores and cannon be-

longing to Government were seized in Rhode Island, and 1774.
other places. General Gage, the commander-in-chief in
America, being determined to retaliate, sent a body of grenadiers, under Colonel Smith, to destroy the magazines at 1775.<br>April 19th.
Concord, about twenty miles from Boston: the attempt
succeeded; but, in returning, a bridge was to be crossed,
for which purpose it was found necessary to dislodge a
party of provincials who were posted there; the whole
country was in arms; the grenadiers found themselves pressed on all sides; an incessant fire from the
houses and from behind the hedges and trees was kept up
on the King's troops. General Gage, having foreseen the
danger of the party under Smith, ordered Lord Percy to
march to Lexington to support that officer, where he joined
him; a fortunate occurrence for Colonel Smith, as his men
had expended all their ammunition.[1] After a fatiguing
march, they arrived at Charlestown, and crossed the har-
hour in boats under the protection of the Somerset man-of-
war. The King's troops lost three hundred men during
the day, whilst the loss of the provincials did not exceed
ninety. Thus the war with the Colonies commenced under
inauspicious circumstances.

The National Congress of Massachusetts met soon after
the disastrous retreat from Lexington, when it was unanimously resolved that a force of thirty thousand men should
be speedily raised, and that Generals[2] Ward, Putman,
Heath, and Thomas, should be entrusted with commands.

---

[1] " Lord Percy now formed his detachment into a square, in
" which he enclosed Colonel Smith's party, who were so much ex-
" hausted with fatigue that they were obliged to lie down for rest
" on the ground, their tongues hanging out of their mouths like
" those of dogs after a chase." — *Stedman's History of the American War.* 4to. vol. i. page 118.

[2] Colonels Ward, Priddle, Heath, Prescott, and Thomas."—
*Stedman*, vol. i. page 120.

whose character for honesty and probity being held in high estimation by his countrymen, was elected Commander-in-Chief of the American troops.

A battalion of one thousand men, formed of fifteen men from each of the sixty-four companies, besides commissioned and non-commissioned officers, of the three regiments of Guards, was reviewed on Wimbledon Common by his Majesty, accompanied by the Duke of Wirtemburg: this battalion shortly afterwards, under the command of Colonel Edward Mathew of the Coldstream, embarked for America,[1] and sailed from Portsmouth with the fleet under

---

" of commerce ; the net produce of the duties last mentioned to
" be carried to the account of such province, colony, or plantation·
" respectively."

[1] 13th February, 1776.                       Brigade Orders.

The Earl of Loudon orders that a detachment from the brigade of Guards, consisting of 10 captains, 11 lieutenants, 9 ensigns, 42 serjeants, 40 corporals, 14 drummers, 6 fifers, and 960 private men, do hold themselves in readiness for embarkation.

The captains are to be taken from the eldest of each regiment not having the rank of colonel, the lieutenants and ensigns from the eldest of each regiment.

The First regiment furnish four captains, five lieutenants, four ensigns, 18 serjeants, 18 corporals, 7 drummers, and 2 fifers.

The Coldstream regiment, three captains, three lieutenants, three ensigns, 12 serjeants, 11 corporals, 4 drummers, and 2 fifers.

The Third regiment, three captains, three lieutenants, two. ensigns, 12 serjeants, 11 corporals, 3 drummers, and 2 fifers.

The three regiments fifteen privates per company.

The draught from the companies is not to be made till further orders, and the officers are to continue to do duty.

15th February, 1776.   .                       Brigade Orders.

His Majesty has been pleased to appoint Colonel Mathew of the Coldstream regiment of Guards, to command the detachment from the brigade of Guards intended for foreign service.

17th February, 1776.                       Brigade Orders.

His Majesty has been pleased to order a company of Light

Commodore Hotham. On the twelfth of August the Guards arrived at Staten Island,* where an army was

---

Infantry to be formed from the detachment of the Guards intended for foreign service. The Earl of Loudon theretore orders the commanding officers of regiments to give the necessary orders for arms, accoutrements, and clothing for that company in the following proportions:

The First regiment—Two serjeants, two corporals, and 42 privates.

The Coldstream regiment—One serjeant, one corporal, and 27 privates.

The Third regiment—The same number.

18th February, 1776.                    Brigade Orders.

The Earl of Loudon orders each regiment of Guards to furnish another lieutenant for the detachment to replace the major of brigade, adjutant, and quarter-master.

8th March, 1776. Regimental Orders, (Coldstream Regiment.)

The commanding officer orders the draught for foreign service to be made to-morrow when the regiment is under arms; the draught to be made by lot from such men as are in every respect fit for service.

12th March, 1776.                    Brigade Orders.

His Majesty has been pleased to appoint the following officers on the staff of the detachment ordered to serve in North America: Captain Stevens, Brigade-Major; Captain Cox, Adjutant; and Captain Lister, Quarter-Master.

12th March, 1776.                    Brigade Orders.

His Majesty has been pleased to permit the officers of the detachment to make up an uniform with white lace, like the privates of their respective regiments; the serjeants to have their coats laced with white lace instead of gold, and the coats of the officers, non-commissioned officers, privates, and drummers of the Light Infantry company, to be cut according to the pattern to be seen in the Orderly-room of the Coldstream regiment. This order relates only to the present clothing.

The officers and serjeants, on this occasion, were ordered to lay aside their " spontoons" and " halberts," instead of which they were to be armed with " fusees."

already formed under General Howe. On the twenty-second they disembarked near Utrecht, on Long Island. The British amounted to nearly thirty thousand men.

---

23ᵈ January, 1777.        Brigade Orders.

His Majesty has been pleased to order two captains, one lieutenant, and one ensign, to be added to the detachment of Guards in America. The First regiment furnishes one captain and a lieutenant; the Third regiment one captain and the ensign.

His Majesty has also ordered that the officers of the detachment in America, when promoted, are to be replaced according to the first order for the detachment, which is to be composed of the senior officers of each rank.

Return of officers, serjeants, corporals, drummers, fifers, private men, women, and children, of a detachment from his Majesty's three regiments of Foot Guards embarked at Portsmouth.— 29ᵗʰ April, 1776.

| Ships' Names. | Colonel. | Lt.-Colonel. | Major. | Captains. | Lieutenants. | Ensigns. | Brigade Major. | Chaplain. | Adjutant. | Quart.-master. | Surgeon. | Mates. | Serjeants. | Corporals. | Drummers and Fifers. | Private Men. | Women. | Children. |
|---|---|---|---|---|---|---|---|---|---|---|---|---|---|---|---|---|---|---|
| Royal George | 1 | | | 1 | 2 | | 1 | 1 | 1 | 1 | 1 | 1 | 7 | 4 | 3 | 113 | 9 | |
| Selina . . . | | | | 1 | 1 | 1 | | | | | | 1 | 4 | 6 | 2 | 128 | 13 | |
| Æolus . . . | | | | 2 | 2 | 1 | | | | | | | 7 | 6 | 4 | 151 | 11 | |
| Johnson . . | | | | 1 | 1 | 2 | | | | | | 1 | 5 | 5 | 2 | 126 | 11 | |
| Hannah . . | | | | 1 | 2 | | | | | | | | 4 | 4 | 2 | 93 | 8 | 1 |
| Integrity . . | | | | 1 | 1 | 1 | | | | | | | 5 | 5 | 2 | 109 | 8 | |
| Kitty . . . | | | | 1 | 1 | 1 | | | | | | | 3 | 3 | 2 | 70 | 10 | |
| Fanny . . . | | | | 1 | 2 | | | | | | | 1 | 4 | 4 | 2 | 91 | 8 | 12 |
| Beverly . . | | | | 1 | 1 | 1 | | | | | | | 3 | 3 | 2 | 76 | 8 | 4 |
| Total . . | 1 | | | 10 | 13 | 7 | 1 | 1 | 1 | 1 | 1 | 3 | 42 | 40 | 21 | 959 | 86 | 17 |

| Names and Rank of Absent Officers. | By whose Leave. | One man left sick at Chichester. |
|---|---|---|
| None. | | EDW. MATHEW, Commandant. |

Official Records, War-Office.

It cannot but be matter of regret, that the reinforcement sent from England this year was delayed for so considerable a time. General Washington's army never mustered nine thousand men, of whom two thousand were unarmed; consequently, had the English taken the field a few weeks sooner, the Americans must have been crushed by superiority in numbers alone, putting discipline and the well-known valour of British soldiers out of the question.

General Clinton and his troops having joined the army, the campaign was opened.

Colonel Donop's corps of chasseurs and the Hessian grenadiers disembarked the same day at Long Island, with forty pieces of cannon; their landing was covered by three frigates and two bomb-ketches. When the first division under Lieutenant-General Clinton approached, the enemy abandoned this position, after setting fire to their granaries, and retired to the high woody ground which commanded the road from Flat Bush to their works at Brooklyn. Lord Cornwallis immediately proceeded to Flat

August. Bush with two battalions. The army extended from the ferry at the Narrows through Utrecht and Gravesend to the village of Flatland. Lieutenant-General de Heister joined the army on the twenty-fifth with two battalions of

Aug. 26th. Hessians from Staten Island: on the following day he took his post at Flat Bush. After dusk Lieutenant-General Clinton's division moved across the country for the purpose of seizing a pass on the high ground, extending from east to west in the centre of the island, about three miles from Bedford, on the road to Jamaica: this movement was for the purpose of turning the left of the enemy

Aug. 27th. posted at Flat Bush. General Clinton's division arrived two hours before day-light, and halted, when arrangements were made for an immediate attack. At the dawn of day Clinton took possession of the pass, which was found unoccupied. The main body of the army, composed of the Guards, second, third, and fifth brigades, with two guns, under Lord Percy, supported General Clinton. About half-past eight the troops reached Bedford, in rear of the enemy's left: an attack, in which four companies of the Guards joined, was made with the greatest gallantry on the Americans, who were about quitting the heights to return to their lines. The Provincials opened a fire of artillery and small arms; the British, however, still kept advancing on their rear, and approached within musket-shot of the principal redoubt of the intrenchments at Brooklyn, from which, after repeated orders, they reluctantly retired.[1] Lieutenant-General de Heister, on the advance of the British right, commenced a cannonade from his front, and ordered Colonel Donop to move forwards with his corps. Major-General Grant, with the fourth and sixth brigades and the Forty-second regiment, diverted the enemy's attention on the left. A brisk fire was at the same time kept up from the ships of war on a battery at Red Hook, behind the enemy's camp. Clinton's attack in rear of the enemy's position was completely successful. The force of the Americans detached from the lines consisted of ten thousand men; great numbers were drowned in attempting to cross the swamp. General Sulivan and ten field-officers were taken.

Five officers, fifty-six non-commissioned officers, and about three hundred of the King's troops were killed and wounded. The loss of the Americans is differently stated:

---

[1] It has been said, that had the troops not been called off, the redoubt would have been carried, " but it was apparent the lines must have been ours at a very cheap rate."—*Field of Mars*, vol. II. Long Island.

Next morning the Americans lost about three hundred
men in the attempt to maintain a wood in front of their right. After a sharp contest, they precipitately retreated to their intrenched camp.

The greater part of the British army again embarked in flat boats; and after passing the difficult passage called Hell Gate, landed on the twelfth of October at Frogs' Neck near West Chester. Afterwards the troops re-em- barked and proceeded to Pell's Point, where a sharp skirmish took place. The British then advanced to New Rochelle, where they were reinforced by foreign troops in English pay, under General Knyphausen. On the twenty-eighth of October the Royal army moved from its encampment on the banks of the Brunx. Sir William Howe commanded the left wing, Sir Henry Clinton the right. As they advanced in two columns, the troops under Clinton fell in with several parties of the Provincials, who were quickly driven back to their camp, which was placed on the brow of a ridge of hills, and defended by lines formed in great haste. Their right flank rested on the Brunx, their left was thrown back, and posted in ground difficult of access.

The Royal army on this occasion consisted of about thirteen thousand men; the Americans exceeded eighteen thousand. Part of the left wing of the Royalists crossed the river and attacked the enemy's advanced posts, which retreated on the main body, sustaining some loss. General Howe, on perceiving that their position was much strengthened, determined to wait for the reinforcements expected from York Island. On their arrival, fresh preparations were made; but owing to heavy rains, the attack was postponed. The casualties in the brigade of Guards were one rank and file killed, and two missing.

During the night, Washington retreated to a still

stronger position on some high lands covered with woods bordering on the North Castle district.

Howe made a demonstration towards Kingsbridge, and suddenly invested Fort Washington on the north side of the river: on the south side, and almost opposite, was Fort Lee. Fort Washington, on being summoned, refused to surrender. Preparations were promptly made for the attack, under the command of Brigadier-General Mathew, consisting of the Guards and the first and second light-infantry battalions. The place was carried by assault in the most vigorous and gallant manner. Upwards of two thousand men were made prisoners. Lord Cornwallis, after the capture, advanced with a strong force to invest Fort Lee; but the garrison had abandoned it, leaving their stores, provisions, baggage, and artillery. On the approach of Lord Cornwallis, Washington retreated to Brunswick.

Such was the aspect of affairs at this period in America, that the war appeared to be fast drawing to a close. Washington, who was then decidedly of opinion that the prospect of American independence was most gloomy, retreated across the Delaware, and intended to retire with his army amongst the recesses of the Allegany mountains. "There can be no doubt," he says in one of his letters, "that Philadelphia is the object of the enemy; that he "will pass the Delaware as soon as possible. Happy "should I be, if I could see the means of preventing "them; at present, I confess I do not."

On the twenty-fourth of November Lord Cornwallis was reinforced by two English brigades and a regiment of Highlanders; he proceeded to New Bridge, Hackinsac, Newark, Elizabeth Town, and Brunswick.

It must have been well known that the river Raritou is fordable every tide at Brunswick, and that the Americans were panic-struck, a feeling which, once imbibed by raw 𝑠𝑟𝑒̃. levies, is not easily overcome; therefore, the measure adopted by the British General of quartering the army in that town was a great oversight. Had the British troops pursued the enemy, instead of halting a whole week, the brow-beaten and terrified Provincials would have been made prisoners.

On the seventeenth of December the army, excepting December. the Guards who remained at Brunswick, advanced, and the same afternoon arrived at Prince Town, which place Washington had left only an hour before the entrance of the British. Here the Royalists lingered seventeen hours, and did not resume the pursuit till nine o'clock next morning; the value of hours, and even of minutes in military movements, being apparently not understood by the British commander. The consequences were to be expected ; the troops arrived at Trenton at four in the afternoon, just as the last boatful of Washington's troops was crossing the river.

The severity of the winter prevented further operations. The army occupied quarters between the Delaware and Hackinsac rivers ; the Guards were stationed at Brunswick; General Clinton and Sir Peter Parker at the same time took quiet possession of Rhode Island. Dec. 8th.

In justice to Sir Henry Clinton it ought to be stated, that he strongly remonstrated on the inutility of sending a force for such a purpose, at the same time observing that the troops might be better employed by advancing to the Delaware.[1]

The army under General Howe, which amounted to

---

[1] " Lord Howe insisted on the possession of Rhode Island for the " fleet. On the approach of Clinton, the Provincials abandoned " the island, and a large body of troops were kept unemployed " during three years."—*Stedman's American War*, vol. I. p. 220.

manded by Lieutenant-Colonel Thomas Howard, of the First.[1]

The British army, from mismanagement, was unable to commence the campaign till the thirteenth of June. Sir William Howe then endeavoured to bring Washington to action; but he had to contend with a man in every way his superior, who eluded by his coolness and steady judgment all the crude plans of his opponent for making him quit his position, and venture a general action. On

---

38, 40, 42, 43, 44, 45, 46, 49, 52, 54, 55, 57, 63, 64, and two battalions of the 71. Amounting in all to—

1233 Officers.

1766 Non-commissioned Officers.

14638 Rank and File fit for duty.

781 Sick.

---

18318

5187 Wanting to complete.

1008 Contingent men.

---

24513 Total establishment.

The British force under the command of Major-General Guy Carleton :

Infantry—8, 9, 20, 21, 24, 29, 31, 34, 47, 53, and 62, regiments.

385 Officers.

572 Non-commissioned Officers.

5358 Rank and File fit for duty.

520 Sick.

---

6835

282 Wanting to complete.

330 Contingent men.

---

7447 Total establishment.

Recruits on their passage to join both armies, 2423 men.

—War-Office Returns.

[1] The senior officer present commanded the brigade, the next in rank the first battalion, and the next the second; which arrangement continued during the American war.—Evidence on the Court-Martial held at New York on Colonel Cosmo Gordon, August, 1782.

pass this way on their route to Philadelphia. The principal fords were properly secured by the enemy, who were resolved to defend them.

The British formed in two columns, and advanced. The right was commanded by General Knyphausen; the left by Lord Cornwallis, in which was the battalion of Guards under Brigadier-General Mathew, who made a circuit of some miles, and crossed the forks of Brandywine, to get into the enemy's rear. General Knyphausen marched direct for Chad's Ford, where he attacked a body of men who had got over the river: after some resistance, they retired under cover of the batteries erected for the purpose of commanding the pass. These attacks were successful. The first column forced the passage; the other, led by Knyphausen, carried the batteries, in which were five pieces of cannon and one howitzer. Lord Cornwallis took the road to Delworth, which led to the right wing of the American army.

Washington, on being acquainted with the movements of Cornwallis, immediately detached a considerable force to oppose him. The American General placed his troops on the height above Birmingham church; his left extended towards Brandywine, a thick wood covering his flanks. Cornwallis deployed and advanced about four o'clock P. M. The attack was commenced by the light infantry and chasseurs. The Guards and grenadiers moved forward under a heavy fire of artillery and musketry; the Americans received the shock with intrepidity; but the steady advance Sept. 11th. of the English could not be resisted. The enemy were driven into the woods, where they rallied, and afterwards retreated by different roads towards Philadelphia, Lancaster, and Reading, making an obstinate resistance, though in much confusion. Washington, with all the troops, artillery, and baggage he could collect, precipitately retired to Chester, and continued his march next morning through Derby

1777.    to Philadelphia.  The Americans had three hundred men
killed, six hundred wounded, and four hundred taken
prisoners, besides losing several guns.  The loss of the
British did not exceed . one hundred killed, and four
hundred wounded.  The Guards lost one rank and file
killed, five wounded, and one missing.

Washington halted three days at Philadelphia, re-
organised his troops, and crossed Sweed's Ford on the
road to Lancaster.

Howe remained inactive on the field of battle.  He does
not seem to have been aware that the advantage already
gained by his troops might be improved.  When Washington's right flank was turned, his army was hemmed in;
General Knyphausen and the Brandywine were in his
front, Howe and Cornwallis on his right, the river Delaware in his rear, and the Christiana river on his left.  The
American General had to march twenty-three miles to
Philadelphia, whilst Howe was only eighteen miles from
that place.[1]

The British crossed the Schuylkill without opposition,
and a detachment took possession of Philadelphia on the
twenty-sixth.

Washington's army was at Skippack Creek on the river
Schuylkill, about seventeen miles from German Town,
near which the English were encamped.

October.    At six o'clock P. M. on the third of October, Washington, under cover of a thick fog, marched all night to sur-

---

[1] The Marquis de la Fayette, who had lately entered the American service as a volunteer, was in the action of Brandywine.  Before he went to America he visited London, where he was received
with all the attention due to his rank, that appears to have been
little deserving of it.  On one occasion, at a dinner, he endeavoured to sift out of the late General Vernon information respecting the character and military talents of British officers then serving
in America.  The General, a shrewd old Coldstreamer, gave him
his shoulder, and turned to a gentleman on the other side.

prise the English, and arrived before dawn at German Town, where the Fortieth was stationed. This regiment made a most gallant defence, and alone kept the Americans in check till reinforced by the third and fourth brigades, which immediately advanced to its support. Nearly at the same moment the right wing arrived from the other side of the village, and, falling on the Provincials, drove them back; they, however, effected their retreat without losing a single gun. The Royalists lost six hundred killed and wounded; the Americans about thirteen hundred; the Guards had only three rank and file wounded. On the nineteenth the Guards marched from German Town to Philadelphia. The English commander has incurred great blame for his conduct in this affair: he was informed on the preceding day that Washington intended to attack him; and had a proper disposition been made, the enemy's army would, in all probability, have been destroyed. The British, with the exception of the Fortieth regiment, were taken by surprise.

Colonel Donop with some Hessians attempted to storm Red Bank, but was repulsed with great loss.

On the fifteenth of November, the fort of Mud Island, under the apprehension of an assault, was abandoned by its garrison, and entered by the grenadiers of the Guards.

Washington having received a reinforcement of four thousand men from the Provincial Northern Army, left his strong position at Skippack Creek, marched to White Marsh and Valley Forge, and encamped within fourteen miles of Philadelphia.

Sir William Howe supposed that Washington might be induced to attack him with a view to regain the capital of Pennsylvania. In consequence, he left Philadelphia at night, and posted his army next morning on Chesnut Hill, opposite the enemy's right. The Provincials remained quietly in their encampment, with the exception of some

CPSIA information can be obtained
at www.ICGtesting.com
Printed in the USA
BVHW08s1120030818
523477BV00018B/505/P